MW01057177

Defying Empire

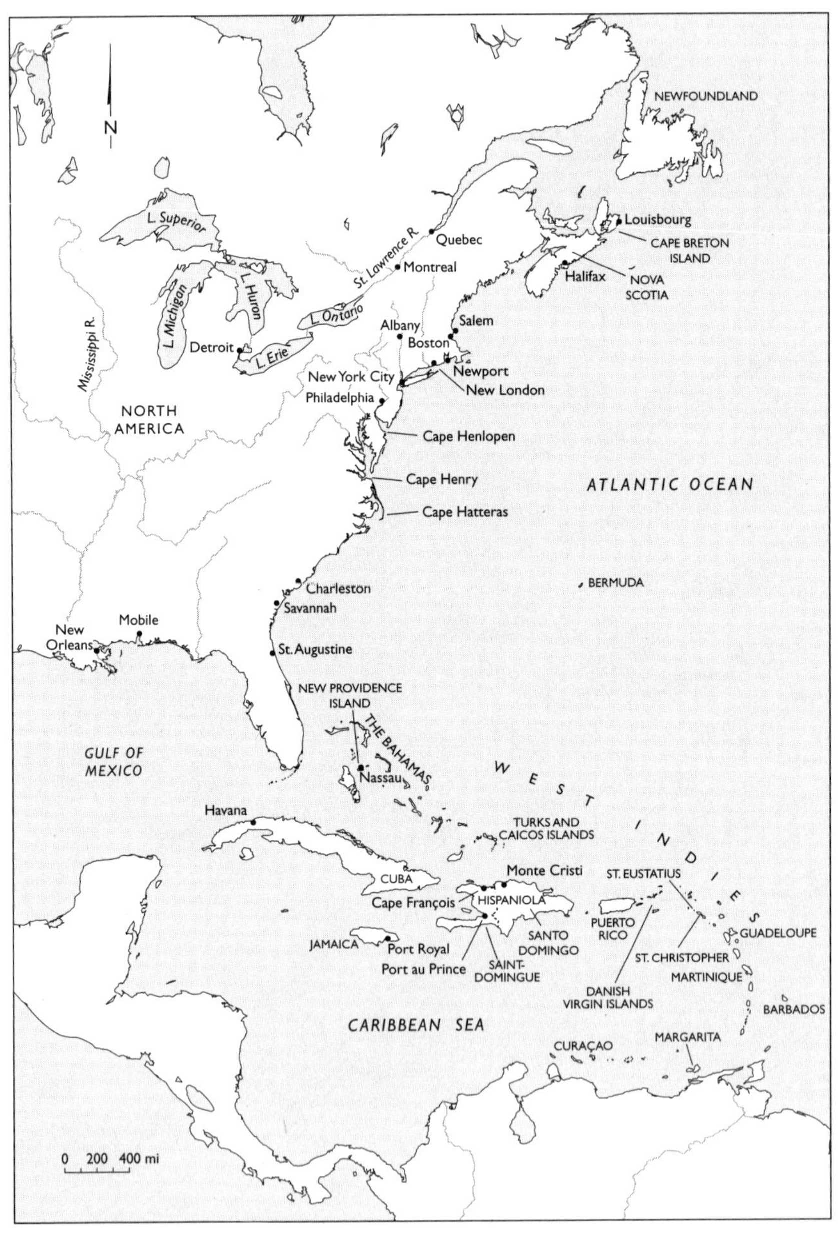

America and the West Indies, 1755–65

Defying Empire

Trading with the Enemy in Colonial New York

Thomas M. Truxes

Yale University Press New Haven & London

Published with assistance from the Annie Burr Lewis Fund and from the Kingsley Trust Association Publication Fund established by the Scroll and Key Society of Yale College.

Maps by William L. Nelson.

Set in Caslon by Keystone Typesetting, Inc. Printed in the United States of America by Courier.

Library of Congress Cataloging-in-Publication Data
Truxes, Thomas M.
Defying empire : trading with the enemy in colonial New York / Thomas M. Truxes.
p. cm.
Includes bibliographical references and index.
ISBN 978-0-300-11840-7 (alk. paper)
1. United States—History—French and Indian War, 1755–1763—Economic aspects. 2. Merchants—New York (State)—New York—History—18th century. 3. Trials (Treason)—New York (State)—New York—History—18th century. 4. New York (N.Y.)—Commerce—History—18th century. 5. West Indies, French—Commerce—History—18th century. 6. New York (N.Y.)—Commerce—France. 7. France—Commerce—New York (State)—New York. 8. New York (N.Y.)—History—Colonial period, ca. 1600–1775. 9. Great Britain. Royal Navy—History—18th century. 10. United States—History—French and Indian War, 1755–1763—Navy operations, British. I. Title.
E199.T87 2008
973.2′6—dc22 2008014511

A catalogue record for this book is available from the British Library.

This paper meets the requirements of ANSI/NISO Z39.48-1992 (Permanence of Paper).
It contains 30 percent postconsumer waste (PCW) and is certified by the Forest Stewardship Council (FSC).

10 9 8 7 6 5 4 3 2 1

For my children
Patrick, Emmet, and Yi-Mei

America. New York, . . . Several persons in trade of considerable rank in these parts, have been taken up, being charged with high crimes and misdemeanors little short of treason, and are now out upon bail, which was not taken without difficulty, and even then for very large sums. It is said there is undoubted intelligence and proof that not only provisions, but all sorts of naval and warlike stores have been sent from these parts to the enemy's islands, and that naval and warlike stores have been sold at Cape François out of English vessels to the French fleet there.

—*Belfast News-Letter,* October 1, 1762

Contents

Maps

Preface

The antecedents of this history of New York City's trade with the enemy during the Seven Years' War (better known in the United States as the French and Indian War) reside in the work of a small group of American and British scholars, none of whom focused his attention on the city per se. In 1907 George Beer, an American, laid out the broad parameters of the subject in a work congenial to the British perspective. A decade later Frank Wesley Pitman, a student of Charles McLean Andrews, discussed the trade as a feature of commercial rivalry between Britain's West Indian and North American colonies. In the mid-1930s the subject's greatest student, the British historian Richard Pares, took an expansive view of wartime commerce sympathetic to the American perspective.

In the years after World War II, the subject benefited from the contributions of four American scholars who linked it—in very different ways—to the story of the American Revolution. In the mid-1950s the first of these, Lawrence Henry Gipson, underscored the powerlessness of British authority in the face of a determined American citizenry. Thomas C. Barrow, in 1967, fit Britain's concern over trading with the enemy into the postwar reform of the British customs service. Then five years later, Neil R. Stout pointed out the relation between the wartime trade and the law-enforcement role of the Royal Navy in American waters in the 1760s and 1770s. Douglas Edward Leach, in *Roots of Conflict: British Armed Forces and Colonial Americans, 1677–1763* (1986), stated explicitly what his forebears had only suggested about the colonial American merchants and mariners who are the subject of this book: "Their almost constant economic dealing with the French during the Great War for the Empire was, from the perspective of the British professional armed forces, a shameful stain. Using the Royal Navy as a principal tool of repression, the government persisted in its determination to bring the North American colonies into conformity with the imperial system as defined by Parliament." Strong language. But the story behind them is far more nuanced.

This book had its genesis in a documentary editing project that I undertook for the British Academy in the 1990s, published in 2001 as *Letterbook of Greg & Cunningham, 1756–1757: Merchants of New York and Belfast* by Oxford University Press. Piecing together the affairs of the New York branch of this Irish-American transatlantic partnership, I realized that the firm was deeply involved in a vast citywide enterprise to supply the French enemy during the Seven Years' War. About the time the letterbook was published, I was asked to contribute an essay to a festschrift honoring my mentor, Professor Louis M. Cullen of Trinity College, Dublin. I took that opportunity to explore aspects of the story I had seen only as shadow detail while editing the *Letterbook*. Court records and naval documents in the British National Archives led to the Colden, Duane, and Kempe Papers at the New-York Historical Society and the Chalmers Collection of New York documents at the New York Public Library. When I began examining court records related to trading with the enemy in the office of the New York County Clerk on Chamber Street in New York City, the hidden world of mid-eighteenth-century New York City opened before me.

The following portrayal of colonial New York City's wartime trade would not have been possible without the generous support of individuals and institutions on both sides of the Atlantic. In the United Kingdom, for access to their collections and permission to quote from documents, I would like to express my gratitude to the National Archives of the United Kingdom (Kew, Richmond), the British Library Board and the Trustees of Lambeth Palace Library (London), and the Deputy Keeper of the Records, Public Record Office of Northern Ireland (Belfast). I was also the beneficiary of much kindness from librarians and staff at the Guildhall Library (London), the Institute of Historical Research (London), the Rhodes House Library (Oxford), and the Cambridge University Library.

For permission to quote from manuscripts in New York City, I would like to thank the New-York Historical Society; the Division of Old Records at the New York County Clerk's Office; the Manuscripts and Archives Division of the New York Public Library, Astor, Lenox and Tilden Foundations; and the

Rare Book and Manuscript Library, Columbia University. I would, in addition, like to extend my gratitude to librarians and staff at the U.S. National Archives and Records Administration, Northeast Region (New York City); the Chancellor Robert R. Livingston Masonic Library of Grand Lodge of New York; and the New York Genealogical and Biographical Society.

Elsewhere in the United States, the American Antiquarian Society (Worcester, Massachusetts); the Historical Society of Pennsylvania (Philadelphia); the Huntington Library (San Marino, California); the Newport Historical Society (Rhode Island); the Phillips Library, Peabody Essex Museum (Salem, Massachusetts); and the William L. Clements Library at the University of Michigan (Ann Arbor) generously granted me access to their collections and permission to quote from documents. I am grateful, as well, for kindnesses shown by the staffs of the Connecticut Historical Society (Hartford); the Library of Congress (Washington, D.C.); the Massachusetts Historical Society (Boston); the New England Historic Genealogical Society (Boston); the New London County Historical Society (Connecticut); the New York State Archives, New York State Education Department (Albany); the Pennsylvania State Archives (Harrisburg); the Rhode Island Historical Society (Providence); the Yale University Library (Manuscripts and Archives); and the Beinecke Rare Book and Manuscript Library at Yale University.

For unwavering support and insightful criticism, I would like to thank John J. McCusker of Trinity University, San Antonio, Texas, and Fred Anderson of the University of Colorado. Along the way, I have benefited from the comments and suggestions of scholars and wish to express my gratitude to Patricia Bonomi of New York University; Nicholas Canny of the National University of Ireland, Galway; Glenn S. Gordinier of the Munson Institute of American Maritime Studies, Mystic Seaport; Patrick Griffin of the University of Virginia; David Hancock of the University of Michigan; Julian Hoppit of University College London; Daniel Hulsebosch of the New York University School of Law; Wim Klooster of Clark University; James McClellan of Stevens Institute of Technology; Kerby Miller of the University of Missouri, Columbia; Nicholas Rodger of the University of Exeter; Hamish Scott of the University of Saint Andrews; Simon Smith of the University of York; Simon Q. Spooner of the Anglo-Danish Maritime Archaeological Team, and Michael J. Thomas of the University of Strathclyde. For launching me onto the path that led to the study of the mid-eighteenth-century Atlantic world, I am indebted to Louis M. Cullen of Trinity College, Dublin, and the late George Cooper and Glenn Weaver of Trinity College (Hartford).

I have received much encouragement and support at Trinity College, Hartford, and wish to thank Borden W. Painter, Jr., my colleague in the history department, for commenting on the manuscript. Thanks, as well, to Alice Angelo, Pat Bunker, and Mary Curry at the Trinity College Library for their many kindnesses. Jeffrey Kaimowitz, Peter Knapp, and the staff of Trinity's Watkinson Library were always eager to share the treasures of their collection. Each of my lay readers represented a particular perspective or body of knowledge. Bill Cosgrove, Mary Alice Dennehy, Katherine Hart, Tom Hazuka, Lee Kuckro, Donna Sicuranza, and Bob Traut commented on the manuscript in its entirety, and Doug Conroy, Glenn Falk, Edward Gutiérrez, Seth Howard, and Dick Mahoney commented on chapters. I am grateful to all of them for their contributions and the good fun we shared along the way.

For their not-so-random acts of kindness, thanks to Bruce Abrams of the Division of Old Records at the New York County Clerk's Office; Susan Anderson at the American Antiquarian Society; Janet Bloom of the William L. Clements Library in Ann Arbor, Michigan; Jim Eastland of Eastland Yachts in Essex, Connecticut; Jeffrey M. Flannery and Patrick Kerwin of the Manuscript Division at the Library of Congress; M. Clair French of the Monmouth County (N.J.) Archives; Marcia Grodsky at the Darlington Library, University of Pittsburgh; Steve Jones and his staff at the Beinecke Rare Book and Manuscript Library; Ted O'Reilly of the Manuscript Department at the New-York Historical Society; Tim Padfield and Martin Willis at the National Archives of the United Kingdom, and my cartographer, Bill Nelson of Accomac, Virginia. I was fortunate to be in contact with descendants of two of the book's characters: the New York ship captain William Heysham (Steve Hissem of San Diego, California) and a member of the Irish merchant community in New York City, John Torrans (Charlotte Hutson Wrenn of Charlotte, North Carolina, and Anne Torrans of Shreveport, Louisiana). The project was the beneficiary of financial support from the Gilder Lehrman Institute of American History and the Faculty Research Committee at Trinity College, as well as, at an early stage, the National Endowment for the Humanities in the form of a Fellowship for College Teachers and Independent Scholars.

I am indebted to Lara Heimert for bringing this project to Yale University Press in October 2004. Chris Rogers, my supportive and patient editor, has been with me through every stage of this unfolding story. Laura Davulis skillfully coaxed the manuscript out of the author's grip in September 2007 and set in motion its transformation into a book under the watchful and confident eye of Susan Laity, senior manuscript editor. No author could ask for a more congenial blending of professional rigor and enthusiastic support.

I reserve particular thanks for my family. To my brother, Jim, and sisters, Rosanne and Margi (R. James Truxes, Rosanne T. Livingston, and Margaret Mary Hixson—artists all), I extend my appreciation for the many, many encouragements. Our mother, Margaret Mary O'Donnell Truxes (1913–2007), is present on every page. She loved the characters in this story—Waddell Cunningham in particular. "That boy has a glint," she said. "But someone ought to settle his hash." I expect she has. If the author has a speck of a glint, it is lit by the love and unflinching confidence of his wife, An-Ming. In February 1988, in another preface, I wrote that my children, Patrick, Emmet, and Yi-Mei (then ages eight, four, and one-and-a-half) "helped me maintain a sense of humor and perspective in the face of mounting work and closing deadlines." They are now young adults and have enriched their father's work their entire lives. This book—informed by their critical judgment (Patrick), artistic vision (Emmet), and insight into human nature (Yi-Mei)—is dedicated to them.

A Note on the Text

In quotations from printed and manuscript sources, spelling and capitalization have been modernized, but the original punctuation has been retained. In quoted text, all ellipses are mine unless otherwise indicated. All references to weather are based on logbook entries of nearby British warships or other contemporary sources.

Unless otherwise stated, all monetary values in this book are expressed in British pounds sterling, the currency of Great Britain in the eighteenth century. One pound contained 20 shillings, each of which contained 12 pence. Adjusted for inflation, £1 sterling in the period from 1755 to 1765 was worth roughly $127 in present-day United States currency (2008).

Each British colony in North America and the West Indies had its own currency convertible into British pounds sterling. Like British pounds sterling, colonial currencies were denominated in pounds, shillings, and pence. During the Seven Years' War, £100 sterling, at par, cost £178 in New York currency. One pound in New York currency was thus equal to roughly $71 U.S. (2008).

This book includes scattered references to various coins, such as the peso de ocho reales (silver), otherwise known as pieces of eight or dollars, and pistoles (gold). These were two Spanish coins that circulated widely in the eighteenth century. At this time the peso, "the premier coin of the Atlantic world," was worth $1 (£0.225 sterling) or roughly $29 U.S. (2008). The gold pistole was worth approximately £0.825 sterling or roughly $105 in 2008 U.S. currency. There is a mention in the book of the French louis d'or (gold) that was worth £1.02 sterling at the time and thus about $130 today.

For more on historical currencies and their conversion to current U.S.

dollars and pounds sterling, readers are urged to consult John J. McCusker, *Money and Exchange in Europe and America, 1600–1775: A Handbook* (2nd ed.), and *How Much Is That in Real Money? A Historical Commodity Price Index for Use as a Deflator of Money Values in the Economy of the United States* (2nd ed.).

Introduction

In the autumn of 1762, an Irish newspaper stunned its readers with a brief but vivid account of dramatic events in New York City. A few weeks earlier, eighteen men, among them the most prominent merchants in the city, had been arrested, "charged with high crimes and misdemeanors little short of treason," and incarcerated in the New York City Jail. Their offense—trading in provisions and "all sorts of naval and warlike stores" with the enemies of Great Britain—led to a series of high-profile public trials and altered the course of history.[1]

The characters and events in the story that follows will be recognizable as distinctively New York. Huge and populous, the compact and crowded New York of the mid-eighteenth century is the same city as the metropolis of the twenty-first; its spirit remains unchanged. Founded in 1609, Dutch New Amsterdam became English New York in 1664 and flourished with the growth of the British Empire. Today, New York City is the crossroads of the world; in the late 1750s and early 1760s it was a crossroads of the Atlantic. From its Dutch beginnings to the present moment, it has been a town driven by commerce and ambition, money and power.

New York City's trade with the enemy during the Seven Years' War, also known as the French and Indian War (1754–63), did not flow from disloyalty to the Crown or indifference to the fate of the nation, at war with a determined and resourceful enemy. It was, rather, the naked manifestation of a powerful commercial impulse synonymous with the great metropolis. Among the participants were leading figures in the political, economic, and social life of the city: the mayor, several aldermen, the families of Supreme Court justices, in-laws of two lieutenant-governors, members of the provincial assembly and the Governor's Council, two provincial grand masters of the

Masons, and, of course, New York City's merchant elite. Several went on to play crucial roles in the American Revolution, divided more or less evenly between Loyalists and Patriots. Among them were four of the five New York delegates to the Stamp Act Congress (1765) and two signers of the Declaration of Independence. What they did during the Seven Years' War helped to set the stage for the American Revolution.

The New York merchants who traded with the enemy did not think of themselves as disloyal. As Fernand Braudel noted, in early-modern Europe "war did not automatically interrupt commercial relations between the belligerents." London and Bristol merchants, for example, did business at Bayona and other Iberian outports through much of the Anglo-Spanish conflict that brought the Spanish Armada into the English Channel in 1588. And in the War of the Grand Alliance, William III's epic struggle against Louis XIV a century later, English and Dutch merchants proved endlessly creative at subverting their governments' determination to deprive the common French enemy of material support. Such exchanges were a normal feature of war before the French Revolution.[2]

Trading with the enemy found fertile soil across the Atlantic. Conditions that fostered trade among belligerents in Europe—the possibility of high returns, the connivance of government officials, lax enforcement of customs regulations, and a distinction between the rights of civilians and those of combatants—likewise pertained in North America and the West Indies, supporting wartime commerce. Distance also played a role, as did a legacy of lawlessness handed down from the formative period of the Atlantic economy when there was—literally—no peace beyond the line.[3]

In the eighteenth-century Atlantic, the Dutch set the standard for free-flowing transnational trade. The islands of Saint Eustatius and Curaçao (located in the Lesser Antilles and just north of Venezuela, respectively) were centers of the Dutch *kleine vaart* (small navigation), unfettered inter-island commerce embracing the ships and goods of all nations. Whether in war or peace, the Dutch paid little heed to the mercantilist codes of the great powers, and by the War of the Spanish Succession (1701–14), the kleine vaart had become fully realized. "The Dutch from Curaçao," wrote a frustrated English official in 1702, "drive a constant trade with the Spaniards as if there was no war."[4]

The discomfiture of European mercantilists notwithstanding, the kleine vaart—and the transnational trade it encouraged—was well suited to the wartime circumstances of British North America and the French West Indies.

Without food-producing colonies and naval bases close at hand, French planters and their slaves risked starving in a sea of sugar. North Americans, on the other hand, stood to reap huge profits from the sale of cheap French sugar, rum, molasses, indigo, and cotton taken in exchange for provisions, lumber, naval stores, and manufactured articles—most of them from workshops in Great Britain.

The scale of trade among belligerents during the War of the Austrian Succession (fought in America as King George's War, 1744 to 1748) reflected the growing importance of the French West Indies and the volume of agricultural surpluses in Great Britain's North American colonies. Most cargoes passed through Saint Eustatius. But that trade was disrupted in the summer of 1747 when European politics spilled into the Caribbean: "The trade betwixt Statia and Martinique is wholly stopped," mourned a Boston newspaper in July; "the French and Dutch having mutually seized one another's vessels in port, in expectation of an immediate war. By this means a large and valuable branch of trade is lost to such as used to carry large supplies of all kinds of provisions for the enemy, without so much as 'the blind of flags of truce.'"[5]

"Flag-trucing"—trade with the enemy under the guise of seaborne prisoner-of-war exchanges licensed by the government—became widespread during King George's War. New York City, along with Boston, Newport, and Philadelphia, figured prominently in the practice, but there was strong opposition to it. "Scarce a week passes," wrote an indignant New Yorker in June 1748, "without an illicit trader's going out or coming into this port, under the specious name of flags of truce, who are continually supplying and supporting our most avowed enemies, to the great loss and damage of all honest traders and true-hearted subjects, and in direct violation of all law and good policy."[6]

"Here now we may see a great and notable advantage which God and nature have given us over our enemies," wrote another critic in the 1740s. "We are much abler to live without them than they without us," he argued. "We having the necessaries of life and the sinews of war within ourselves, are able, both to carry on the war more vigorously and feel at the same time the ill-effects of it less sensibly than they."[7]

True enough. But by the time of the Seven Years' War—the greatest of the Anglo-French colonial wars—the Atlantic economies of the belligerents had become inextricably linked. By then it was commonplace for French Canadian trappers to market their furs through Albany for consumption in the British Isles or for Massachusetts fishermen to sell their catches to Boston merchants with connections in the French Caribbean. Merchants in North America enjoyed the added benefit of usurping a piece of the sugar trade, the branch of Atlantic commerce jealously guarded by their arch-rivals, the British West Indian planters. War made such exchanges cumbersome, but it did not end them.

The Seven Years' War grew out of frontier skirmishing in 1754 between British colonial militiamen and their Indian allies, on the one hand, and a small number of French regulars, on the other. They fought over competing claims to lands beyond the Allegheny Mountains. By 1756 what had been a border dispute was an all-out struggle for control of much of North America and the West Indies. The conflict spawned fighting that reached around the globe and set the stage for another great struggle two decades later, the American Revolution.

New York figured prominently in what the historian Lawrence Henry Gipson has labeled "the great war for the empire." In addition to serving as a military headquarters, the city was the principal British communications and supply center, a rendezvous point for warships of the Royal Navy, the main staging area for amphibious operations, and the largest privateering port on the North American mainland. New York City was, as well, the strategic objective of the French forces north of Albany that were attempting to work their way into the Hudson River valley. As in earlier contests, the logistic advantage lay with the British, "it being very certain," according to one observer, that "there is no enemy harder for mankind to conflict with than hunger." But this advantage could be squandered. From the outbreak of fighting in 1754 through the spring of 1762, New York City was a source of supply for the French in North America and the West Indies.[8]

"The greatest part of the vessels belonging to the ports of Philadelphia New York and Rhode Island, are constantly employed in carrying provisions to and bringing sugars &c. from Monte Cristi; or the enemy's islands," wrote a British officer on the army headquarters staff in New York in 1760. But the trade took other forms as well. Some of these were short-lived; others predated the war and continued for years afterward. Early in the fighting, goods found their way into French Canada through Cape Breton and even Newfoundland. For the most part, this trade had been suppressed by the formal declaration of war in May 1756, whereas commerce via the Gulf of Mexico into French Mobile Bay and New Orleans—never a large-scale operation—continued through 1762. Far more important were the exchanges conducted through neutral sites in the Caribbean. A lively indirect trade with the French by way of the Dutch and Danish West Indies lasted until the end of hostilities despite the interventions of the Royal Navy.[9]

The most important of these neutral shipping points during the Seven Years' War was San Fernando de Monte Cristi, a sleepy Spanish port a few miles east of the border between Spanish Santo Domingo and French Saint-Domingue (present-day Haiti) on the north coast of Hispaniola. Between 1757 and 1762 it was one of the busiest seaports in the North Atlantic. New York was well represented among the sloops, schooners, snows, brigs, and ships (a term used for a specific type of vessel in the eighteenth century) that entered Monte Cristi Bay to offload cargoes onto local coasting vessels in exchange for disguised French West Indian produce.

A large share of the wartime commerce was conducted in French Caribbean ports. Most of it was under the cover of flags of truce, an activity that grew to huge proportions. More lucrative—and daring—were voyages without the benefit of covering documents. By the final year of the war, after the navy took over responsibility for prisoner-of-war exchanges in the West Indies, unprotected direct trade between New York and Cape François (present-day Cape Haitian), Port au Prince, and other destinations in Saint-Domingue had become commonplace.

The nature of New York's trading with the enemy makes it impossible to do more than guess at the volume of exports and imports or the earnings of participants. It was, however, a thriving, large-scale enterprise. In spite of the setbacks and losses resulting from the interdictions of British warships and privateers, trade with the French accounted for a large share of what entered and departed the port and was—along with British military spending—the source of wartime prosperity for New York City.

Although New York's wartime commerce had precedents in earlier practices, it was nonetheless illegal. Giving "aid and comfort" to the king's enemies was forbidden by English statutory law, and maintaining "correspondence or communication" with the French king or his subjects had been expressly prohibited by King George II's declaration of war in May 1756. In addition, the New York provincial legislature in 1755 had banned the "sending of provisions to Cape Breton or any other French port or settlement on the continent of North America or islands nigh or adjacent thereto."[10]

In practice, however, the relationship between the belligerents was not so clear-cut. British courts continued to uphold French property rights, for example, and London merchant bankers provided financial services for their French correspondents. Under special circumstances, open and direct trade continued as well. The best-known example is the tobacco trade. According to the historian Jacob Price, "licenses to export tobacco from Britain to France were authorized almost immediately after the declarations of war." In spite of harassment by the Royal Navy, the wartime prohibitions did not apply to indirect commerce through neutral sites when there was no contact with Frenchmen or to trade conducted under flags of truce in strict conformity with the terms of government-issued commissions.[11]

The Treason Act of 1351 (amended during the reign of Queen Anne) defined treason as adhering "to the king's enemies in his realm, giving to them aid and comfort in the realm and elsewhere." The crime of betraying one's country, according to the 1351 statute of Edward III, required intent, and there is no evidence that New Yorkers conspired with the enemy to achieve a French victory. Within the scope of the Treason Act, trading with Spanish, Dutch, and Danish neutrals was not "adhering to the king's enemies," nor was doing business in French West Indian ports under licenses that permitted trade as a means of covering the costs associated with prisoner-of-war exchanges. The legality of trade was muddled further by indecisive politicians, contradictory admiralty judges, and British naval officers taking the law into their own hands (and enriching themselves in the process).[12]

Although it threatened to, in none of the prosecutions brought by the Crown in New York—those of 1756 and 1759, and the show trials of 1762, 1763, and 1764—did the government ground its case on a charge of treason. The terms *treason* and *treasonous* occasionally appeared in the popular press, but treason was a capital offense requiring a high standard of proof that a crime had taken place and that there had been intent to commit treason. New York's attorney general had enough problems prosecuting under the terms of the declaration of war and the Flour Act of 1757, a wartime statute that prohibited North American exports of provisions to non-British destinations. This in spite of abundant circumstantial evidence that merchants and ship captains—in a city awash in French West Indian produce—were doing a lively business with the enemy. Witnesses were unwilling to come forward, however, and the code of silence held firm.

The city's commerce with the French was not the work of a few reckless disaffected souls. It strained the resources of an entire city. Dockworkers, carters, warehousemen, packers, butchers, millers: every tradesman associated with the busy life of the port struggled to keep up with the work provided by both sides in the great war for the empire. Even the city's large and aggressive privateer fleet was employed escorting ships doing business with the enemy.

None of this could have happened without friends in high places. James DeLancey, lieutenant-governor of New York, for example, was the father-in-law of William Walton, Jr., a senior partner in Walton and Company, the city's preeminent merchant house and a firm active in every stage of wartime trade with the French. Walton's uncle William Walton, Sr., was a member of the Governor's Council; his brother Jacob—even more deeply involved in the trade—was married to the niece of the mayor of New York; and his sister Catharine was married to an Irishman, James Thompson, who was one of its boldest participants. Before the end of the war, Thompson was doing business from Cape François, and Catharine was managing his firm's affairs in New York (dispatching cargoes, meeting incoming vessels, and disposing of shiploads of French sugar). Similar links within the commercial and political hierarchy—reaching even into the judiciary—pervaded the city's trade with the enemy.

One conspicuous feature of this trade is the large role played by the city's expatriate Irish merchants. Accounting for no more than 10 percent of the roughly 125 participants, they represented a disproportionately large share of the committed inner circle of about 20 merchants. Of this group, 8 were Irishmen representing all the major Irish ports and religious denominations. New York's Irish merchants—many of whom had arrived as ambitious young men on the eve of the war—benefited from a strong Irish presence in French Atlantic trade and displayed a vigorous contempt for British navigation laws. They revealed, as well, an impressive talent for making mid-eighteenth-century New York City work to their advantage.

It is striking how little of that exciting time survives in the collective memory of the modern city. Even the physical dimensions have changed. Centuries of land filling have cut into the East River and the Hudson River, giving lower Manhattan broader shoulders than its colonial forebear and an entirely different waterfront. And there are hardly any surviving buildings, the notable exceptions being the old DeLancey mansion at the intersection of Broad and Pearl Streets (today's Fraunces Tavern) and Saint Paul's Chapel on Broadway—the miraculous survivor of the World Trade Center attacks—which was consecrated just as this story ends.

There is even less awareness of the colorful characters associated with New York's wartime trade, though a surprising number have been immortalized as disembodied street names: Chambers Street, Delancey Street, Desbrosses Street, Duane Street, Harrison Street, Lispenard Street, Morris Street, Van Dam Street, White Street, Francis Lewis Boulevard. But unnoticed in the shadow of New York's financial district, some of the most energetic participants in the city's trade with the enemy rest silently in Trinity Church graveyard awaiting their final judgment.[13]

This account of trading with the enemy in colonial New York does not choose sides. That is for the reader alone. Then as now, the city's most successful businessmen were daring, resourceful, and often ruthless. By their lights they were fervent patriots, and in some cases the same men freighting cargoes to the French were outfitting British and colonial troops, as well as victualing the warships of the Royal Navy. "The loss of Oswego is a great one to us," wrote one of New York's most active traders with the enemy after a catastrophic British defeat in the summer of 1756, "and a very great help to the French to accomplish what they so long desired. We are in hopes we shall rassle them," he added, "and indeed we may easily do it if we join heartily to it and the provinces would get out of their present lethargy." But business was business.[14]

Prologue
The Informer

Manhattan sparkled in the crisp October night. Two large bonfires on the Common, thousands of candlelit windows, and a sea of ships' lanterns, like autumn fireflies, lit the tiny city and its harbor. Four weeks earlier, Major-General James Wolfe's British regulars had defeated a force under the marquis de Montcalm on the Plains of Abraham at Quebec, the key to French control of Canada and the interior of North America. When news reached New York City, Lieutenant-Governor James DeLancey declared Friday, October 12, 1759, a day of public thanksgiving.

Church bells across the city proclaimed the British victory. With colors flying, merchant ships and privateers on the East River answered the cannons of Fort George. Evening brought the illumination of the city and a flood of toasts: To His Majesty's health, To the might of British arms, To the heroes of Quebec, To final victory. The drawing rooms, coffeehouses, taverns, and streets of the city filled with joyous New Yorkers celebrating the greatest achievement of British arms in North America.[1]

With Wolfe's victory, as well as recent British successes at Fort Ticonderoga and Crown Point, the expulsion of the French now seemed inevitable. But the war was not yet won. Great Britain and France remained locked in an armed conflict that reached around the world. Armies were colliding in Europe, Africa, the Indian subcontinent, and the Philippines, and there were naval operations with an even longer reach. In the North American and Caribbean theaters, Great Britain and France struggled for control of a vast and rich colonial empire.[2]

Although weakened by its losses, France still held on at Montreal and New Orleans, as well as in the West Indian Islands, that great wealth-producing garden of the eighteenth century. The country's grip was precarious, however. The Royal Navy, though spread thin, had effectively cut off the flow of French supplies and was blocking the return of colonial sugar, indigo, and coffee to Bordeaux, Nantes, and other home markets. Securing a lifeline to French America was a pressing concern of strategists at Versailles.[3]

All of this seemed far away that October night. New Yorkers were eager to forget the defeat of British regulars and colonial militia at Forts Oswego, William Henry, and Ticonderoga earlier in the war, as well as the carnage of Indian raids along the colony's sparsely settled frontier. In spite of setbacks, the war had been good to the city, particularly to those New Yorkers who recognized opportunity and had an appetite for risk. That night the homes of the city's merchant elite glittered with wartime wealth, and in smoke-filled dockside taverns, sailors and privateersmen had money in their pockets to celebrate Wolfe's victory and compete for women of easy virtue.[4]

Nearby, in the shadow world of New York harbor and the darkened warehouses, storerooms, and cellars of the commercial district, lay the source of the city's prosperity. Hundreds of barrels of flour, salted provisions, and naval stores, together with vast quantities of lumber, cordage, and dry goods of all kinds, stood ready for shipment—either directly or along clever serpentine paths—to Cape François, Port au Prince, and New Orleans. Wartime New York was growing rich through its trade with the French enemy.[5]

For months, Major-General Jeffery Amherst, commander of British forces in North America, had been demanding an end to this trade, and in April 1759, under pressure from Amherst, Archibald Kennedy, the collector of customs for the port of New York, had appealed to the public. "Whereas there has been lately carried on a most pernicious trade with the French," he declared in the city's newspapers, "Whoever will discover to me, or any other of the officers of His Majesty's customs, the landing of any foreign rum, sugar, or molasses, within this district, before entry made, and the duties paid, shall, upon condemnation and charges deducted, receive one full third part of the whole, with the thanks, doubtless, of his country."[6]

No one had come forward, and in September, Kennedy had issued a second appeal "to prevent, as far as it is in our power, that flagitious practice of carrying provisions to the enemy; which, besides the iniquity of supplying our enemies, our own navy and troops may in all probability want." Before the end of the month, on evidence from two informants, the New York Supreme Court of Judicature had issued warrants for the arrest of two well-known merchants, James Depeyster and George Folliot. The former was the son of Abraham Depeyster, treasurer of the colony, and the latter was the son-in-law of George Harison, provincial grand master of the Masonic order in New York and a powerful figure in the city's business community. The ship captain in their employ had chosen to flee the city rather than face a charge of high treason for "giving aid and comfort to the enemy by boldly sailing into the French port of Cape François with a load of provisions." In mid-October, Depeyster and Folliot appeared in a New York courtroom to face criminal charges.[7]

The government was unprepared for the anger the arrests fomented along the docks and in the countinghouses. The city was now on alert. The merchant community knew that there was no way to predict the behavior of judges, witnesses, and juries. No fewer than two dozen New York trading vessels on the high seas faced condemnation on their return home. An informer, like those who had given evidence against Depeyster and Folliot, stood to make a fortune from a single successful prosecution.[8]

Onto this stage stepped George Spencer—calculating, tenacious, and desperate. Probably a native of London, Spencer emigrated to New York sometime in the mid-1730s. He established himself in the wine trade, working primarily as a supercargo—responsible for the sale of goods abroad—on voyages to France, Portugal, Spain, and the Wine Islands. In 1738 he married Florinda Pintard, the sister of Lewis Pintard, one of the most respected merchants in the city.[9]

Spencer presented himself as both well educated and well connected, but by the outbreak of the war he was better known for his financial embarrassments and for having squandered his wife's fortune. While abroad in 1757 he sought and received the protection of a London court in a bankruptcy proceeding. Although in compliance with arrangements worked out in London, Spencer incurred the wrath of his New York creditors when he returned home.[10]

Following the arrest of Depeyster and Folliot—and emboldened by Kennedy's announcement in the press—the failed wine merchant began snooping around the warehouses, wharves, and docks along the East River. He saw many irregularities, such as flour loaded without certificates; pitch, tar, cordage, and other naval stores taken aboard ships destined for neutral ports; and hogsheads of French sugar, coffee, and indigo that had been brought into the port disguised as "British" produce. Unlike others—"either indolent, ashamed, or afraid to discover frauds so very injurious to the community"—Spencer was prepared to act. But he needed evidence if he was to prove that New York merchants were in violation of the acts of navigation and the statutes governing wartime trade.[11]

So it was that George Spencer approached his nephew John Pintard of Norwalk, Connecticut. Pintard was a partner in a Connecticut merchant house that procured false documents from corrupt customs officials in New Haven. It was a thriving business, and in late October, Spencer offered to assist his nephew in his dealings with New Yorkers. "I induced Messrs. Cannon and Pintard, by a stratagem, to write me," Spencer later admitted, "in order that I might prove to the lieutenant-governor . . . that what I had told him . . . was true."[12]

Then, on the last day of October 1759—a Wednesday—George Spencer stepped out of his home at 19 Broadway and began the short walk to Fort George at the tip of Manhattan. Unsettled weather was closing in on the Atlantic coast as Spencer met with Lieutenant-Governor DeLancey, informing him about a trade that "greatly enriched the enemy and impoverished ourselves, except such as were concerned in it."[13]

The enemy was being supplied with great quantities of provisions and gold coin "contrary to the act of parliament" and "in contempt of the law." Spencer could prove that cargoes of sugar were being brought from Hispaniola to the port of New York under the cover of false papers. He then presented the documents obtained from his unsuspecting nephew.[14]

DeLancey's response was not what Spencer had anticipated. The lieutenant-governor listened patiently to the informer's accusations but showed little interest. "The affair would be laid before the parliament," he said, dismissing his visitor and returning to work. Spencer repeated the performance at the customhouse just a few steps away. He informed Archibald Kennedy, the collector of customs, that there were five or six vessels in the harbor "waiting for their fictitious clearances."[15]

Whereas DeLancey had listened passively as Spencer revealed the secret inner workings of the city, Kennedy grew impatient and "seemed greatly displeased that I had told him of it," Spencer recalled. Like DeLancey—the champion of the city's mercantile interest—Kennedy understood the consequences of Spencer's sweeping claims. Rooting out New York City's deeply embedded trade with the enemy would mean taking on the political, economic, and social hierarchy of the city. That, the gentlemanly Kennedy was not about to do. From the customhouse in lower Manhattan, news spread that an informer was at large in New York.[16]

On Thursday evening, November 1, 1759, perhaps a dozen men who "conceived an inveterate hatred against the discoverer" gathered in a small office on the first floor of the Merchants' Coffee House. The group—who constitute the main characters in this story of wartime New York—included William Kelly, Jonathan Lawrence, Thomas Lynch, Samuel Stilwell, James Thompson, Jacob Walton, Thomas White, and, it is likely, James Depeyster, George Folliot, and one or two others. The most outspoken were George Harison, forty years old and a former surveyor of customs for the port of New York, and his good friend Waddell Cunningham, ten years his junior and de facto leader of the city's Irish merchants.[17]

Rum and punch flowed as the group concocted an elaborate plan that would "render [Spencer] infamous and invalidate his testimony, and at the same time be a warning to others not to dare to make a farther discovery for fear of the like treatment." Each conspirator was to have a role in Spencer's punishment. If the plan succeeded, there would be no more informers, nor would witnesses dare speak out against Depeyster and Folliot at their upcoming trial. Anticipating the events of the following day, it was agreed that Spencer must be given one final chance to recant. (By coincidence, he was at that time in the upper room of the coffeehouse playing backgammon with a fellow merchant and unaware of the conspirators below.)[18]

Late in the evening, Cunningham ushered the bewildered Spencer into the small room crowded with angry men. George Harison spoke for the group. "We are told you are turned a common informer." Spencer did not deny the charge. Another of the men snapped that he "would throw him into the dock" if he caught him on the wharves near any of their vessels. Spencer held firm. Then Harison's anger overflowed. If Spencer was not out of the city in eight hours, "he would get him hanged." The others joined Harison in "loading [Spencer] with foul language and denouncing threats." Unwilling to recant, the informer was much shaken when he left the Merchants' Coffee House that night.[19]

At about nine-thirty the next morning, Harison and Cunningham paid a visit to the home of John Bogert, Jr., a New York alderman who held George Spencer's promissory note for £400 (New York currency). Because the note was overdue but not in default, they had to persuade Bogert that a suit against Spencer for the balance would be a service "to the public." When they offered to recover Bogert's money at their own expense, the reluctant alderman surrendered the document, taking cash from the conspirators, who intended to sue in Bogert's name.

Harison and Cunningham then made their way to City Hall and the office of the Supreme Court of Judicature. Bogert wanted Spencer to be sued in the Supreme Court, but without Bogert's written authorization or a power of attorney the clerk would not issue an arrest warrant. Harison and Cunningham were on a tight schedule, and there was no time to draw up a power of attorney, return to Bogert's home for his signature, and then prepare the warrant. "That this opportunity might not be slipped," the conspirators stopped at the nearby office of the mayor's court. The clerk—a man deeply involved in trade with the French—provided a warrant, which Cunningham signed "with Mr. Bogert's name without his knowledge, order, or directions."[20]

Thus armed, Harison and Cunningham, now joined by Deputy Sheriff Philip Branson, Jr., stepped out onto Wall Street and headed west. At Broadway, Cunningham and Branson turned south in the direction of the Bowling Green, and Harison headed north toward Vesey Street, site of the Drovers' Inn.[21]

Without a search warrant, the deputy sheriff could not justify "breaking open [Spencer's] house to take him," so as they neared Spencer's home, Branson disappeared into the shadows. Cunningham stepped up to the front door and knocked. When Spencer invited his visitor inside, Cunningham demurred. He wished to discuss last evening's business, he said, but would only do so outdoors. As Spencer stepped out, Branson seized him, presented the arrest warrant, and took him prisoner.

Spencer made no objection as the trio began its march up Broadway to the new jail on the New York Common. Between Wall Street and Garden Street (present-day Exchange Place), they encountered George Harison waiting outside his home opposite the Lutheran church. "So, I see you have got the rogue," he said to Branson. And to the bewildered Spencer, "You shall have your deserts presently. I hope by and by to see you go upon a cart to the gallows."[22]

Spencer and his escort continued up Broadway until they reached the Drovers' Inn, located just across from the Common (present-day City Hall Park). Branson announced that he was stopping for a bottle of wine. When Spencer objected, the deputy sheriff forced him through the doorway. Seeing the informer enter, the men inside "abused him with opprobrious Language as did also Mr. Harison who was likewise there."[23]

The plan concocted at the Merchants' Coffee House called for an angry mob, which was conveniently provided by a short-tempered sailor with appalling table manners. On the Saturday following Depeyster and Folliot's arraignment in September, Henry Cobb was arrested for the murder of a shipmate. As the two had been sharing a meal earlier that day, the victim's pestering of his testy companion had precipitated violent and instant death, Cobb stabbing his companion, according to the surgeon, between the ninth and tenth ribs and penetrating the heart. At his trial a month later, the jury had found Cobb guilty of murder, and, on the following day, October 25, Attorney General John Tabor Kempe had asked for the death penalty. Accordingly, the judge ordered Cobb taken to the place of execution on November 2, there to be hanged by the neck until dead.[24]

George Spencer's enemies intended to make stunning use of "the multitude that attended the execution" on the New York Common, "who at such times are much inclined to outrages." At the gallows Cobb "earnestly entreated the prayers of all good and Christian people for him, explaining to others the horrid consequences of a debauched life and hasty disposition." By eleven o'clock, the hanging was over, and the taunting, jeering crowd had become a violent and dangerous instrument.[25]

From inside the Drovers' Inn, Spencer saw a large body of sailors coming across the Common. Angry men surrounded the building, drinking and cursing, fresh from the excitement of the hanging. As the sailors crowded into the tavern, demanding the informer, Harison led them to the terrified victim. "Take him, put him on the cart, cart him about the town, and give three cheers at every corner," instructed one of the merchants.[26]

In an instant, the sailors became a mob. "With violence," they thrust Spencer into a horse-drawn cart and swept him across the field opposite the inn, heading down Beekman Street past Saint George's Chapel. The mob stopped at the intersections of Nassau, William, Gold, Cliff, and Queen Streets to pelt Spencer with "stones and filth" from the streets. "Any body may heave at every corner," offered Harison, urging the mob forward.[27]

At Queen Street (present-day Pearl Street), the riot turned in the direction of Hanover Square, the commercial center of the city. It lurched past the open stalls of the Fly Market at the foot of Crown Street (present-day Maiden Lane), where garbage in the street provided missiles to hurl at the terrified victim. Now in the neighborhood of the wharves, the roaring, moving mass drew the attention of sailors and dockworkers ready to abandon themselves to the madness of a riot. The man in the cart was numb with fear, convinced that his end was at hand.

The spectacle moved up Queen Street past dozens of stores and fashionable shops, as well as the countinghouses of merchants deeply enmeshed in the events of this day. It was a cold, wet morning, and the streets were muddy. "Mr. Spencer was continuously pelted with filth, dirt, &c., and received several blows and bruises on different parts of his body." Violent club-wielding rioters surrounded the cart to prevent their prisoner's escape.[28]

The fury of the riot attracted fresh participants, as well as the stares of frightened onlookers. Near Broad Street, two aldermen were pushed aside when they attempted to rescue Spencer. The excited mob became so violent that "the thigh of the horse that drew the cart, and the cart itself, was broke by the blows aimed at the unhappy man and the object of their fury." As the riot moved toward Fort George, it drew out Lieutenant-Governor DeLancey and a detachment of soldiers. DeLancey confronted the mob before it entered Whitehall Street. "Though not without great danger," he demanded that the crowd disperse. Fearing a confrontation, the mob melted into the taverns and haunts of the waterfront. As suddenly as it had begun, it was over.[29]

The victim was exhausted, numb, and filthy. For the rest of his life, Spencer believed that DeLancey had snatched him from certain death. Although he had no broken bones, Spencer sustained multiple bruises and a serious eye injury in his "carting" through the streets of New York.[30]

DeLancey ordered Spencer taken to the safety of "a gentleman's back entry out of the way of the mob." As his compassionate hosts were sending for clean clothing and Spencer prepared to bathe, an unwelcome guest arrived. Deputy Sheriff Branson entered the safe house with a pistol in his hand and the warrant for Spencer's arrest. In shock, Spencer was led outside at gunpoint and forced to mount the deputy sheriff's horse just behind Branson. The two men galloped off into the chilly afternoon. Like a madman Branson retraced the route of the riot through still-disheveled streets, crying out that he had "the devil behind him and was riding to Hell." Before the sun set, George Spencer was behind bars.[31]

The informer fought back. The following day, he summoned John Tabor Kempe, New York's twenty-four-year-old attorney general, demanding immediate action. Spencer expected Kempe to prevail against James Depeyster and George Folliot in the Supreme Court, and he wanted to move rapidly with his own prosecutions. After what he had suffered the previous day, the informer planned to use the full weight of the law to punish his tormentors. In addition to legal action related to their trade with the enemy, he intended to press charges for riot and assault against the ringleaders of the mob.[32]

At first, it appeared that Spencer would get his justice. An announcement in the *New-York Mercury* on Monday declared that George Harison "intend[ed] leaving for England in a very short time." The following day, November 6, the Governor's Council met at City Hall to examine affidavits relating to the "notorious riot" and recommended that the perpetrators be brought before the justices of the Supreme Court. Soon after, George Harison, Waddell Cunningham, and Philip Branson, along with three others, were charged with "rioting and assaulting George Spencer." All pleaded not guilty.[33]

On the Wednesday of his first week in jail—November 7—Spencer sent DeLancey a list of names, along with incriminating details relating to New York City's trade with the French. By Spencer's estimate, the Crown had been defrauded of duties in excess of £200,000. But when he asked DeLancey for a meeting, he was denied; "I did not think it proper, as you are confined for debt," wrote DeLancey, "to order you to be brought to me by the jailer. You will be pleased to set down in writing the affair you have to communicate to me, and I will send my servant for your letter." The lieutenant-governor had no interest in stirring up further trouble.[34]

So Spencer remained in jail. His enemies worked hard to make his time behind bars long and memorable, ensnaring the informer in a web of legal and financial charges. Although Alderman Bogert had resented being drawn into the affair, he was now cooperating with the conspirators. Spencer must pay his debt to regain his freedom. To raise the funds, he would have to sell his house on Broadway. On December 9, as the informer struggled with his predicament, Bogert's brig *Polly & Fanny* arrived from Saint-Domingue carrying 196 barrels of French sugar.[35]

There was also the matter of Spencer's £4,000 debt incurred in the Madeira wine trade, which he owed to creditors in Britain and North America. In 1757 a London court had approved a settlement protecting Spencer against these creditors. Though Spencer had been jailed upon his return home, the court in New York had freed him when he established proof of the London ruling. To satisfy the angry creditors, the New York court had appointed Francis Lewis, a prominent local merchant involved in trade with the French, to act as a referee and determine whether Spencer was in compliance with the London agreement.[36]

As Spencer was about to be released, having paid his debt to Alderman Bogert, he was rearrested, on December 31, 1759. A new suit brought against him by Lewis on behalf of the remaining creditors would require a vigorous and costly defense. Predictably, Spencer responded with fresh prosecutions, and his enemies countered with "everything their malice can invent in order to render [him] odious and contemptible." The informer began to believe that he was at war with the city of New York.[37]

Meanwhile, the case against James Depeyster and George Folliot fell apart. The inexperienced attorney general, John Tabor Kempe, had the misfortune of presenting before a judge with a nephew active in trade with the French. Justice John Chambers postponed the matter until the following term, when it began a long string of continuances and was dismissed without trial in October 1760.[38]

"I do not think they will be made examples of, though they were apprehended and bound over," DeLancey wrote Amherst. "Depeyster and Folliot have connections[,] the former with two of the judges and the latter in the customhouse." And he added, "They have prevailed upon the witnesses." George Spencer began his long imprisonment in the city jail as New York's men of affairs returned to the urgent business of war.[39]

CHAPTER ONE

A City at War

A British warship bound for New York City cut a striking figure during the Seven Years' War. A formidable presence, it could be trim and handsome under cloudless blue skies, white sails bright with reflected sunlight, or raw, dirty, and weather-scarred, battling gales and lashing rains in the North Atlantic.

If it were arriving from the northeast—perhaps from the Royal Navy base at Halifax, Nova Scotia—its officers would keep a keen watch for Montauk Point at the eastern end of Long Island. If coming in from the West Indies or the colonies to the south, it would have worked its way north along the Capes—Hatteras, Henry, and Henlopen.

By whatever route, the New Jersey highlands would be a welcome sight from high atop the mainmast of one of His Majesty's fighting ships, especially before the inauguration of Sandy Hook Lighthouse in 1764. Known variously as Navesink, Never Sink, Never Sunk, Navasink, and even Navysunk, those coastal hills with their distinctive shape guided thousands of ships toward Sandy Hook, New Jersey, the entry point into lower New York Bay.[1]

Approaching Sandy Hook, a warship would fire one of its great guns to call a harbor pilot to guide it through the difficult passage. The seemingly easy entrance into the broad lower bay was, in fact, obstructed by sandbars, shoals, and mudflats. Much of the twenty-one-mile journey from Sandy Hook to New York City was treacherous to both a warship and the career of its commanding officer, who was required to account for damage to his vessel.[2]

To enter the bay, the pilot would guide the ship close to Sandy Hook through a narrow and intricate channel just twenty-one feet deep. Once inside, some captains would make their anchorage in six fathoms of water and use small sailing craft to shuttle back and forth to the city. But most preferred mooring closer to New York. To achieve this, the pilot would continue west into the lower bay until the vessel reached a point directly north of Navesink. He would then guide it north-by-northeast following a channel that ran between two large and dangerous shoals. Off Coney Island, the pilot would once again alter course. Sailing north-by-northwest, the fighting ship would move through the center of the Narrows between Bluff Point on Staten Island and New Utrecht, Long Island (present-day Bay Ridge, Brooklyn).[3]

As the ship entered upper New York Bay, a breathtaking vista would open up. In the distance on a clear day a compact little city nestled comfortably between rivers of blue. Tiny spires and cupolas; slate, tile, and wooden roofs; and the stonework of the citadel caught the glint of the sun as harbor craft moved about in a forest of masts. A rolling green landscape enclosed the remaining upper bay, sweeping from the high bluffs west of the city down to Staten Island and then back around again to the city along the western shore of Long Island. New York City was a jewel in a magnificent setting.[4]

Now under light sail, the warship would work its way toward Manhattan along a familiar passage through muddy shoals that reached out from New Jersey on the west and Long Island on the east. As the journey neared its end, the captain would guide the imposing vessel past Governors Island into a busy river thoroughfare where the vital and energetic city pushed hard against the water's edge, the sights and sounds and smells tumbling aboard the ship as it lay "moored in the East River."[5]

The New York that became so deeply entangled in wartime trade with the French combined elements of an elegant city, a cosmopolitan seaport, and a raw frontier town. "I had no idea of finding a place in America consisting of near 2,000 houses, elegantly built of brick, raised on an eminence, and the streets paved and spacious; furnished with commodious quays and warehouses, and employing some hundreds of vessels in its foreign trade and fisheries," wrote a British naval officer aboard a warship in the East River. "Such is this city, that a very few in England can rival it in show, gentility, and hospitality."[6]

The population stood at about 13,000 in 1756 and rose to a wartime high of just over 20,000 by 1760—infinitesimal compared to Manhattan's peak population of 2.3 million in 1910 and its present population of about 1.6 million. (In 2008 the population of the five boroughs of modern New York City was roughly 8.4 million.)[7]

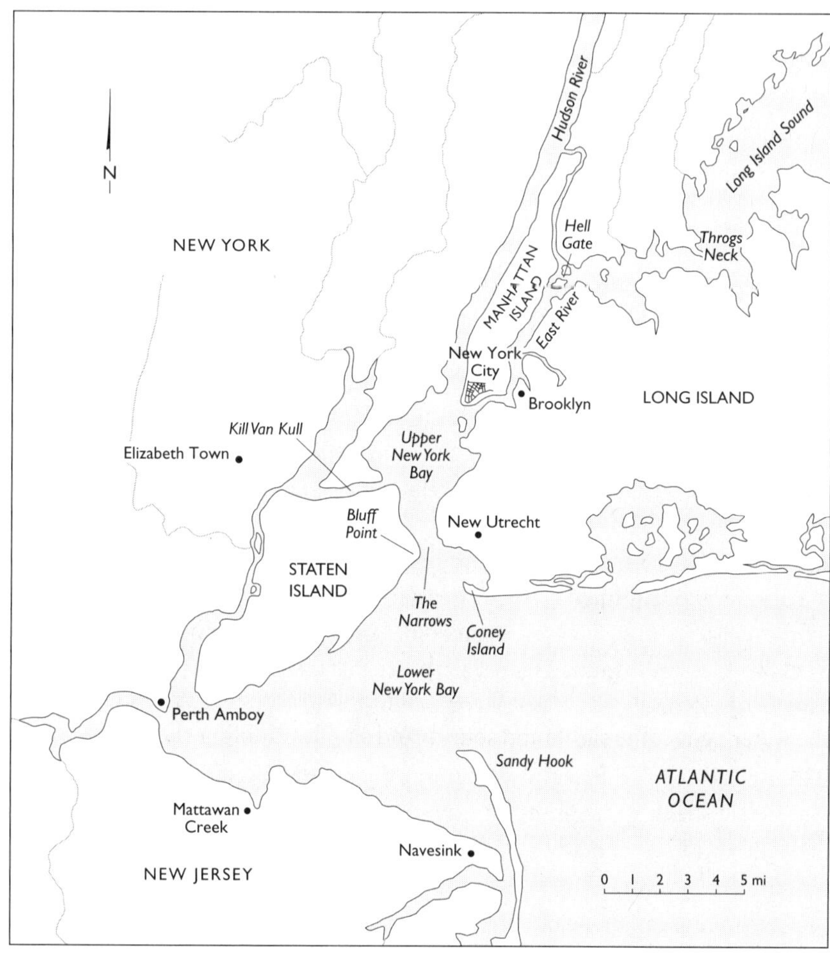

New York Waterways, 1755–65

Still, colonial New York was a crowded and diverse city, "a great mixture of manners and customs," noted an Irish visitor in 1760. In addition to the Dutch, French, Germans, and English, there were Irish and Scottish newcomers, who figured prominently in urban life, as did the small but important Jewish community. Free and enslaved black Africans, who, in the words of a naval officer, "lie under particular restraints," made up roughly 18 percent of the population.[8]

This mixing of peoples was evident in the city's non-English-speaking churches—three Dutch, one French, and one German. There were Dutch and French translators at City Hall to expedite legal business, and enough

Spanish was spoken to justify the commissioning of a Spanish interpreter in 1753. The city's large itinerant population, drawn by the lure of privateering and a wide array of wartime opportunities, represented an even broader sampling of ethnicities.[9]

For those with the means to enjoy it, New York was a charming city. There were simple pastimes like strolling under the shade trees of Broadway or through the parklike Bowling Green. Wealthy men and women in the latest London fashions flocked to European-style pleasure gardens, such as those along the Hudson at the upper edge of the city (near present-day Greenwich and Warren Streets) that offered dancing, strolls through dimly lit groves, and a romantic setting for fine dining. The Spring Garden just south of the Common was a popular getaway from the hectic pace of the commercial district. In the early 1760s, the Spring Garden House offered "breakfasting, from 7 o'clock till 9; tea in the afternoon from 3 till 6; . . . pies and tarts . . . from 7 in the evening, till 9; where gentlemen and ladies may depend on good attendance, and the best of Madeira, mead, cakes, &c." There was theater in the evenings (including Shakespearean tragedies and popular comedies right off the English stage) as well as an abundance of music, ranging from organ works by George Frideric Handel performed at City Hall to popular favorites sung by the officers' glee club at Fort George.[10]

Social gatherings of New York's elite, whether elegant balls at Cranley's Assembly Room on Broadway or sumptuous parties at the Walton mansion on Queen Street—"the proudest private dwelling in this city"—were displays of wealth and status made possible by the extraordinary vitality of commercial life.[11]

Commanding one of the world's great deep-water harbors, New York was a busy Atlantic seaport. Its compact size—a mile wide and, on average, a half a mile long—"facilitates and expedites the lading and unlading of ships and boats, saves time and labor, and is attended with innumerable conveniencies to its inhabitants," promised one booster. "Our importation of dry goods from England is so vastly great, that we are obliged to betake ourselves to all possible arts, to make remittances," wrote William Smith, Jr., New York's first historian, in 1756. The city's seaborne commerce (across the Atlantic, to the Caribbean, and along the North American coast) was smaller than that of Philadelphia or Boston, but entrepôt activities and brokerage services allowed a favorable balance of trade, in spite of an endemic imbalance in the direct two-way exchange with Great Britain. "It is for this purpose we import cotton from St. Thomas's and Surinam; lime-juice and Nicaragua wood from

Curaçao; and logwood from the Bay, &c., and yet it drains us of all the silver and gold we can collect," explained Smith.[12]

New Yorkers had become adept at warehousing, sorting, and reshipping commodities such as rice and indigo from South Carolina, wheat and flour from Maryland, flaxseed from Connecticut, Pennsylvania, and the Merrimack Valley of northern Massachusetts, and a wide variety of articles from the European continent that entered the city in violation of British customs regulations.[13]

The city's entrepôt trade—the importing of goods for redistribution abroad—was a legacy of New York's Dutch past. "Our merchants are compared to a hive of bees, who industriously gather honey for others," bragged Smith. Visitors commented on the vitality of the port and "the multitude of shipping with which it is thronged perpetually." "It is generally allowed, that there is not a colony in America, which makes a better figure than this for its trade," wrote a British commentator, "or where the people seem to have a greater spirit of industry and commerce."[14]

Not surprisingly, commercial property was expensive in a town that already understood the connection between real estate and power. Leading mercantile families like the Crugers, Marstons, and Waltons controlled their own wharves and warehouses, and received substantial income from the rental of waterfront property. Docks and wharves along the East River were often in deplorable condition, however. "A person can't walk them without being attacked with the most nauseous smells."[15]

Merchants prided themselves on the speed and efficiency with which they moved goods in and out of the port. Dockworkers, crane operators, porters, carters, and teamsters were in constant motion, and a flotilla of scows and lighters shuttled between the docks and trading vessels riding in the harbor. The clatter of handcarts bouncing over cobblestones echoed along the East Side, together with the steady rhythm of heavy-footed horses straining before wagonloads of sugar, lumber, and flaxseed moving back and forth between the docklands and warehouses tucked into adjoining streets.[16]

Hanover Square, the center of New York's business district, was just a block inland from the waterfront. Three- and four-story buildings of red and yellow brick crowded into the busy intersection where Queen Street and the upper end of Dock Street (which together make up present-day Pearl Street) met Smith Street (where the lower end of present-day William Street becomes Hanover Square). Expensive shops and the offices of wealthy merchants collided with tradesmen, street venders, and pickpockets. Here at the commercial crossroads of the city, the Times Square of eighteenth-century New York, colorful signboards—"The Golden Key," "The Dial," "The Bible and Crown"—competed with displays of fine fabrics, watches, and books for the attention of shoppers with a keen eye for quality and fashion.[17]

New York City was a flourishing British seaport, but the Dutch presence in the commercial district was unmistakable. Old Dutch trading firms, like that of David Van Horne, had roots in the New Amsterdam of the seventeenth century; others, like the one managed by Robert Crommelin, were extensions of enterprises based in Amsterdam and Rotterdam; still others, like Nicholas and Isaac Gouverneur, had partners in New York City and on the Dutch West Indian islands of Saint Eustatius and Curaçao. The Dutch preference for free-flowing Atlantic commerce lived on in New York long after the peaceful transfer of the city from Dutch to English hands in 1664, and it defined the character of wartime trade.[18]

In streets around Hanover Square, overseas traders with English, Scottish, and Irish roots rubbed shoulders with heirs to the city's Dutch past, as well as members of the French Huguenot community, men such as Lewis Pintard, and Jewish merchants like Hayman Levy with widely dispersed commercial contacts. Notable among the hundred or so New Yorkers involved in trade with the enemy, William and Jacob Walton had strong English roots; the two Livingstons, Philip and Peter V. B., had family ties to Scotland; and Waddell Cunningham was the exemplar of the dynamic Irish presence in the city.[19]

Ethnic identity was strong, but it did not constrict the flow of business. The wartime partnership of James Depeyster, the scion of a respected Old Dutch family, and George Folliot, a recently arrived Irishman and Depeyster's neighbor on Dock Street, was typical of trading arrangements in mid-eighteenth-century New York.[20]

The diversity evident in the merchant community characterized the civil administration as well. Lieutenant-Governor James DeLancey was the son of a French Huguenot merchant who had emigrated to New York in the mid-1680s and married into a prominent Dutch family. Archibald Kennedy, the Scottish civil servant who became the collector of customs for the province of New York, likewise married into an Old Dutch merchant-landowning family.[21]

From the New York customhouse on lower Broadway, Kennedy and his staff attempted to regulate the commerce of the port, and nearby, at the foot of Broad Street, the Royal Exchange was a popular gathering place for those who owned the ships and cargoes. Opened in 1755, the Exchange boasted an arcaded lower level that made an ideal setting for markets and a large hall on the second floor that, with its twenty-foot ceiling, was a favored location for diners, balls, and concerts. At the top of Broad Street, City Hall housed courts and administrative departments that brought order to the busy port city. Notable among these were the Supreme Court of Judicature, the court of vice-admiralty, the office of the common clerk, and the office of the mayor of the city of New York, John Cruger.[22]

A significant share of business was conducted in coffeehouses and taverns. The Exchange Coffee House, situated in a room on the upper floor of the Royal Exchange, and the Merchants' Coffee House, on the corner of Wall and Little Dock Streets opposite the slave market, were by far the most important. One of New York's two maritime insurance brokerages occupied a small office on the first floor of the Merchants' Coffee House; the other was located next door. Two taverns on Broadway—the City Arms (between present-day Thames and Cedar Streets) and the nearby King's Arms—were popular retreats for merchants and army officers from Fort George. The City Arms was renowned for its ballroom and public entertainments, while the dining room at the more fashionable King's Arms, at Broadway and Crown Street (present-day Liberty Street), was spacious and well furnished; it included a barroom containing private boxes screened by silk curtains.[23]

In sharp contrast to the coffeehouses and taverns frequented by men of affairs were the dives, brothels, and haunts along the East River that catered to itinerant laborers and seafarers, many of them drawn to the city by the prospect of quick wartime riches. The New York waterfront was also a magnet for runaways, criminals, and lost souls, as well as for the footloose rogues and misfits who peopled the underbelly of eighteenth-century society. Theirs was a hard-edged world made perilous by cheap alcohol, the scourge of urban life throughout the British Empire. In the slums along the docks, violence was commonplace, and death often sudden, brutal, and pointless. In 1759, to cite one of many examples, a young woman "at midnight, being in liquor, fell from Cruger's Wharf into the river and was drowned," reported the *New-York Gazette*.[24]

Early in the war, newspapers noted a sharp rise in street crime "which, till of late, was scarce heard of amongst us." According to the *Mercury*, "not a night passes, but some or other of the inhabitants of this city are . . . stopped in the streets by loose vagrant fellows." In 1756 a shopkeeper reported that "one of these villains had the impudence to run his hand thro' the glass window and carried off two watches."[25]

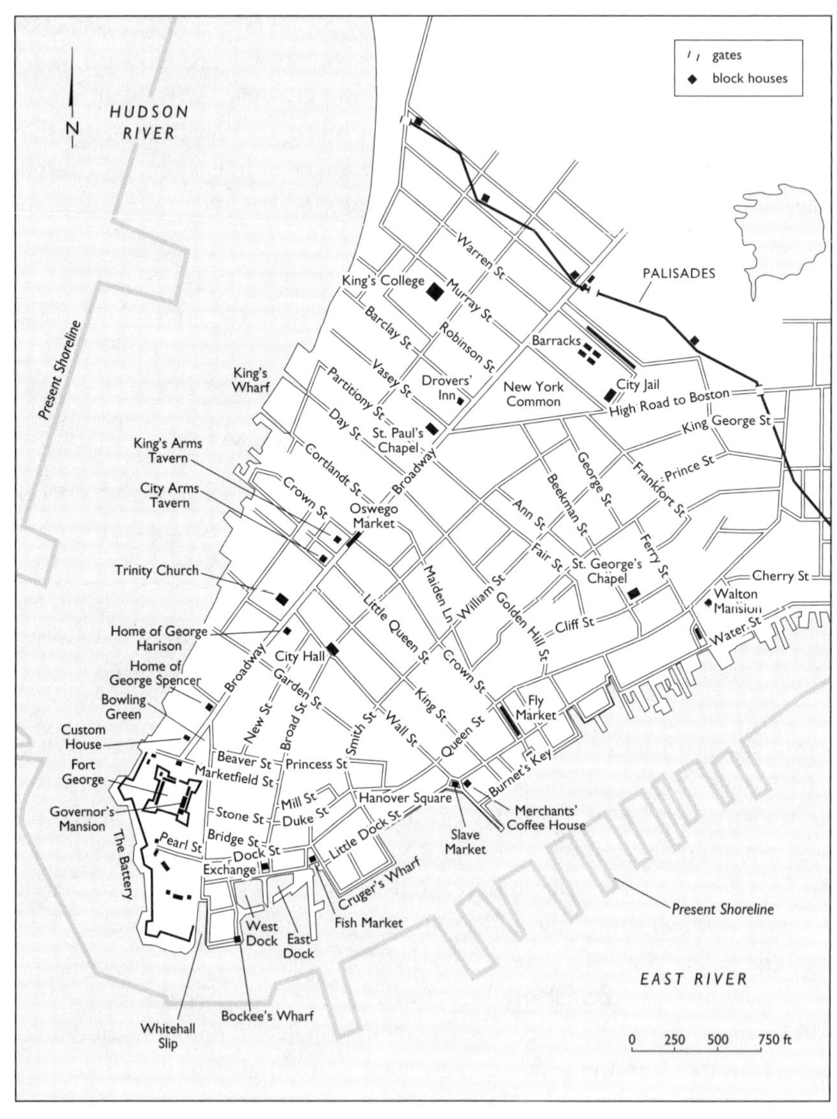

New York City, 1755–65

Crime flourished in spite of harsh consequences. Typical was the fate of James Wilson, a stonecutter, executed on the Common in February 1759 for stealing money from the home of the New York privateer captain Isaac Sears. If a thief were lucky, he would only be publicly whipped or "exalted on carts, and carted round the town," to quote the *Mercury*.[26]

From elegant drawing rooms on lower Broadway to countinghouses in Hanover Square to squalid boardinghouses on Water Street, New York was a city of opportunity. At all levels, war in the mid-eighteenth century released a bold commercial energy and competitive drive that would not be surpassed until after the Revolution. The great war for the empire, known to Americans as the French and Indian War (and to Europeans as the Seven Years' War), was a climactic struggle between Great Britain and France, and later Spain, that energized the city and lifted it out of the torpor of prewar recession. Even so, the first year of the war was a time of anxiety and foreboding.[27]

"Dark tidings of late, like Job's messengers, come in thick succession, one after another," wrote an American clergyman in 1756. God had revealed his displeasure with the world, it was thought, when he allowed the destruction of the city of Lisbon by an earthquake in November 1755, and as many as a hundred thousand people died. Aftershocks and tidal waves, felt over vast distances, continued into the spring of 1756. "The minds of many people [are] deeply affected with a prospect of public calamities," John Wesley told his London congregation.[28]

To New Yorkers, the greatest public calamity would be defeat in a ruinous war with France. Britain's North American colonies, from the Maritimes in the north to Georgia in the south, were coastal settlements, vulnerable to a determined enemy operating from the interior of the continent or from aboard a warship with the firepower to rain havoc. Many on Manhattan island feared their city could not withstand an assault if a French and Indian force broke through the Lake Champlain corridor and seized control of the Hudson River valley below Albany. Ominously, after two years of undeclared war, the enemy appeared to be gaining on every front, fulfilling a long-held fear of French domination. The colonies had suffered two years of embarrassments, reversals, and defeats.[29]

The immediate cause of the conflict lay in a dispute arising from the Treaty of Aix-la-Chapelle of 1748 over territory west of the Appalachian

Mountains. The rich Indian lands of the Ohio Valley fell within the claims of both New France and the colonies of Virginia and Pennsylvania. By the early 1750s, settlers from those places had spilled over the Appalachians to farm and trade with Indians in the Ohio Valley. In May 1754, France's determination to remove British "trespassers" led to the capture of George Washington's tiny expeditionary force at Fort Necessity, not far from the French Fort Duquesne in western Pennsylvania. Thus began the Seven Years' War.[30]

Eleven months later, Major-General Edward Braddock, recently arrived as commander-in-chief of British forces in North America, met with five colonial governors at Alexandria, Virginia. They had convened to formulate a plan to remove the French from the Ohio Valley, as well as from positions along the border of the province of New York. The plan called for a simultaneous attack on three major French forts in the summer of 1755: Fort Duquesne, located in southwestern Pennsylvania at the confluence of the Ohio, Allegheny, and Monongahela Rivers; Fort Niagara, at the meeting point of Lake Ontario and the Niagara River; and Crown Point, situated on the western shore of Lake Champlain about halfway between Albany and the Quebec border.[31]

The catastrophic defeat of Braddock's force of 1,900 on the banks of the Monongahela on July 9, 1755, left all British North America vulnerable to attack and turned the war into a struggle for control of the continent. The period following was one of frustration and political infighting—but mostly fear. Rather than regroup and move on Fort Duquesne, Colonel Thomas Dunbar, Braddock's successor, ordered the destruction of much of his equipment. He then marched the dispirited remnant of Braddock's army north to the safety of Albany, with its fort, guns, and small garrison of regular soldiers, the last physically secure place along the northern frontier.[32]

The weakness of the British position was increasingly evident as northern provincial New York became the center of the conflict. The colony was poorly prepared to defend itself against an assault by the French. There were too few men and nowhere near enough supplies. "Small arms we have none in the public magazine but six chests that belong to the four independent companies," reported Governor Charles Hardy early in the war.[33]

In the autumn, Governor William Shirley of Massachusetts, now commander of British forces in North America, returned to Albany with the bulk of his army, having abandoned his attempt on Fort Niagara in favor of a strategy of shoring up defenses at Fort Oswego, the most important British trading post on Lake Ontario. Meanwhile, General William Johnson, although failing to take Crown Point in a defensive battle at the southern tip of

Lake George on September 8, 1755, had inflicted the only serious loss the French would endure on the North American mainland until July 1758 and the British victory at Louisbourg on Cape Breton Island.[34]

As the fighting moved to the region between Albany and Ticonderoga, the province of New York lay open to attack from an adversary whose Indian alliances and control of the Great Lakes compensated for its small army and inadequate system of supply. In November 1755, Governor Hardy told his superiors in London that he feared further campaigning would leave the province's frontier "subject to the incursions of the enemy" at a time when Britain's own problems of supply and transport frustrated the gathering of materiel for a stand against the French.[35]

The defeat of Braddock's army was followed by French-coordinated Indian raids in the sparsely settled and undefended Pennsylvania backcountry. Throughout the autumn months, accounts of slaughter along the frontier terrorized the middle colonies. "'Tis not easy to conceive," wrote a pamphleteer, "what we have suffered from the barbarous natives, under the influence, and by the assistance of the French." Typical of the devastation were attacks in the neighborhood of Easton, Pennsylvania. "The country all above this town, for fifty miles, is mostly evacuated and ruined," said a witness. "The enemy made but few prisoners, murdering almost all that fell into their hands, of all ages and both sexes."[36]

The violence was concentrated in Pennsylvania and parts of New Jersey, but there was widespread fear that it would spread to New York, where anxiety was building over the loyalty of the Six Nations of the Iroquois. In an address to the governor, the New York General Assembly expressed concern for "the safety of our frontiers in general, and the protection of our unhappy fellow subjects in particular, whom a hard lot has thrown so near a cruel enemy." The New York backcountry was less disturbed than that in Pennsylvania, but sporadic Indian raids, such as the incursions into Ulster County after December 1755, unnerved settlers mindful of the declining fortunes of the British Army in North America.[37]

The forces holding the line against the French faced serious problems. For one thing, British troops were wholly unprepared for war in the North American woodlands. To bring their superior firepower to bear on the enemy, both officers and men required thorough training in the ways of backwoods Indian fighting. In addition, the condescension of British regulars—particularly their officers—toward provincial soldiers undermined the cohesiveness of the army in the northern wilderness.[38]

Worse still, there was little cooperation among colonies providing militia for service against the French. Each colonial government, jealous of its autonomy within the loose organization of the first British Empire, weighed the choice of contributing scarce manpower for service in some faraway place or keeping it close at hand for defense of home and hearth. With no colony wishing to do no more than its share, political and military leaders worked at cross purposes. "One colony will not begin to raise their men," wrote a frustrated Governor Hardy in 1756, "doubting whether their neighbors will not deceive them, in completing their levies."[39]

Within the army itself, the lack of cooperation between Shirley and Johnson in the months following Braddock's defeat contributed to the failure of the Niagara campaign and allowed the consolidation of the French position. With powerful enemies in New York's provincial government arrayed against him, Shirley's power slipped away.[40]

In the New York provincial assembly, factional rivalries further undermined the colony's defense. The DeLancey and Livingston factions, which dominated mid-eighteenth-century New York political life, were embryonic political parties centered around powerful families. Their political philosophies roughly corresponded to the English Tories and Whigs: the DeLanceys, whose core strength lay in families associated with overseas trade, embodied the Tory principal of order from above, while the Livingstons, who drew their support mostly from the great land-owning families, favored a Whig sensibility of the people as the source of political power.[41]

The Livingstons with interests allied to imperial expansion and Albany's dominance of the fur trade, insisted that the full weight of colonial resources be brought to bear against the French. The DeLanceys, on the other hand, eager to curb the Livingstons and expecting adequate aid from Britain, were reluctant to finance the war effort. The bitterness of the fractious infighting weakened royal authority in the province.[42]

Meanwhile, the military situation grew desperate. In May 1756, the New York militia began pressing men into service. "We long impatiently for the troops from England," wrote the New York surveyor of customs Alexander Colden; "we also pray heartily for the arrival of our new general." In spite of the deepening crisis, the provincial assembly resolved in July that "this colony has stretched its strength and substance to the greatest pitch, and . . . is not in a condition to enter into heavier expenses."[43]

Such were the preoccupations of New Yorkers three years before George Spencer's ordeal. Lord Loudoun, the new commander-in-chief of all British forces in North America, arrived aboard HMS *Nightingale* on July 23, 1756. A

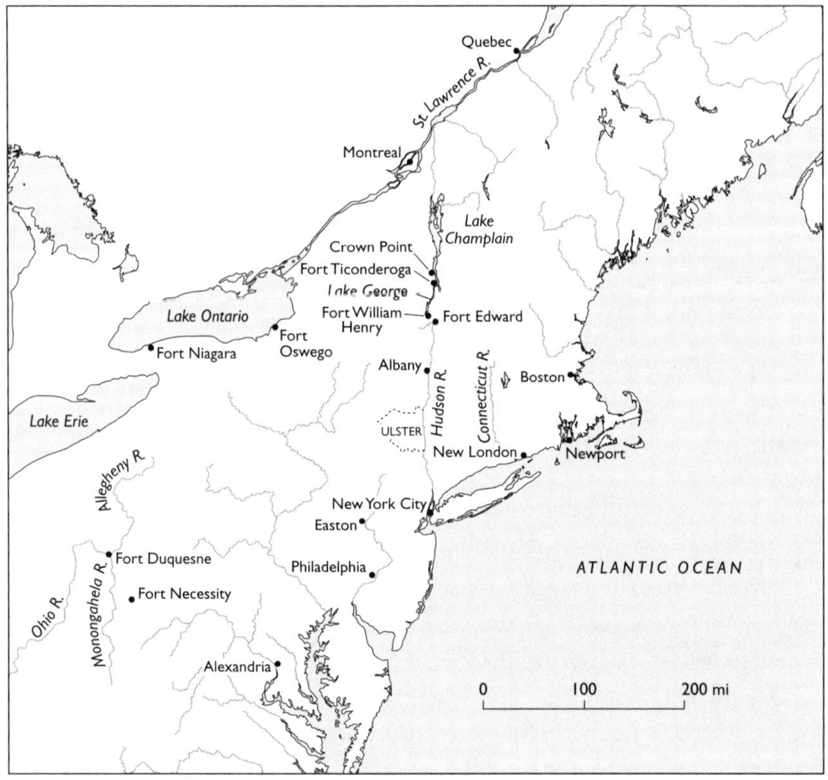

North American Theater of Military Operations, 1754–63

week later, in the courtyard at Fort George, civil and military dignitaries gathered under a clear summer sky for the formal public reading of King George's declaration of war against France.[44]

Within a year, no fewer than fourteen thousand British troops had disembarked at the port of New York. The colorful fighting men crowding the streets gave New York the feel of a wartime city. Swords hanging at their sides, with white-powdered wigs, wide-lapeled scarlet coats, and gold gorgets, the officers were resplendent versions of the brightly clad common soldiers of the British Army. The travel-weary troops disembarking at East River wharves, red-faced sergeant-majors drilling recruits on the Common, and heavy-laden soldiers boarding sloops along the Hudson for duty in the north country blended into the bustle of everyday life.[45]

Living accommodations were in short supply, and disputes over quartering were a source of contention between the army and the civil government. The most serious of these occurred in the autumn and winter of 1756. In November a thousand fatigued troops arrived in New York from the fighting front north of Albany. Lord Loudoun expected the mayor, John Cruger, and the New York Common Council to quarter his troops for the winter, providing adequate food and shelter. Although the provincial assembly had passed a quartering bill in October, the Council balked, and Loudoun threatened to march in as many as four battalions of soldiers and take quarters by force. The quartering bill that Governor Hardy signed on December 1, 1756, accommodated ordinary soldiers in public houses when possible and in private homes when necessary. "This caused at first some uneasiness and grumbling," Alexander Colden told his brother-in-law George Harison, "but the people now see the necessity of the service requires it, and the inhabitants cheerfully submit."[46]

In 1757, the Common Council authorized construction of a twenty-room, two-story barracks on New York Common accommodating just over 700 men. The city also fitted out a nearby house to serve as an officers' billet. This was in addition to the 214 soldiers housed in the barracks within Fort George and the 18 men lodged in each of six blockhouses outside its gray stone walls. Governors Island had already begun its long service as a military base in 1755 with the 51st Regiment of British colonial militia under the command of Sir William Pepperrell. A year later, the 62nd Regiment of Foot (designated the 60th Royal American Regiment of Foot in 1757) was formally organized, also at Governors Island. Large encampments on Staten Island and Long Island sprang up whenever the city served as a staging area for large-scale operations.[47]

The soldiers converging on New York contributed to the vitality of the city, but there was a dark side as well. One visitor in 1760 characterized the army as "a school of vice." Hundreds of prostitutes took up residence in the neighborhood surrounding the New Barracks in what was then the upper West Side, not far from King's College (present-day Columbia University, now relocated). This was in addition to those inhabiting brothels along New York's tough East Side waterfront.[48]

Drunkenness and public fighting among soldiers, along with the general rowdiness inevitable in an overcrowded wartime city, contributed to the insecurity of the streets. The connection between war and crime was unmistakable; in 1757, for example, the *Mercury* depicted a sailor off a trading ship "knocked down by three soldiers in the Common, who robbed him of twenty odd shillings of money, and beat him in such a manner that he remained ill for some days."[49]

A great chasm separated the social world of the private soldier from that of his officers. Along with their counterparts in the Royal Navy, officers in the British Army became ornaments of social life, and a sprinkling of red and blue uniforms graced the many balls and private parties that made New York an attractive billet. For the officers there were torrid liaisons, romantic love affairs, and, occasionally, marriages. In 1758, for example, Brigadier-General Thomas Gage married Margaret Kemble, a wealthy New Jersey woman related to the DeLanceys. And near the close of the war, Susannah Alexander—"a young lady of many amiable accomplishments, and a large fortune"—married "Col. [John] Read of the 42nd, or the Royal Highland Regiment." The whirl of social life also contributed to petty jealousies and bitter rivalries that bred dueling, endemic in the eighteenth century among military officers. Two duels were fought "near this city" in just one week in October 1761.[50]

The Royal Navy's relationship with New York City was very different from that of the army. The port lay about halfway between two larger naval stations: Halifax, Nova Scotia, and Port Royal, Jamaica. Both were in close proximity to critical points of engagement. The Halifax squadron stood ready to interdict the resupply of New France by way of the Saint Lawrence River, while vessels based at Port Royal performed the same service in the western Caribbean and the Gulf of Mexico. Even so, the British navy was essential to the defense of New York City.[51]

Before the war, with just one frigate assigned to it, New York had been unimportant as a naval station. That changed when the city became the principal supply depot and port of embarkation for British forces operating in North America. After 1755, ships of the Royal Navy regularly called at New York, sometimes rendezvousing for convoy duty or to escort troop transports and supply ships to Canada and the West Indies. Although warships occasionally arrived needing emergency repairs, the Turtle Bay careening yard on the East River (approximately present-day 43rd Street and First Avenue) was a source of complaint. Problems arose, according to Captain James Campbell of HMS *Nightingale,* "for want of a convenient wharf, it being greatly out of repair, and careening gear, as well as the extraordinary expense that will arise from the dearness of materials and labor, . . . at this place."[52]

The fighting ships riding off Manhattan were impressive, and so were His Majesty's sea officers in their tasteful blue-and-white uniforms. Like their counterparts in the British Army, naval officers became part of the wartime landscape and the New York social life. But they appeared restrained and subdued in contrast to the common sailors allowed shore leave, who, with black ribbons hanging from tarred queues and decked out in their flamboyant shore-going outfits, made a strong impression on the streets of the city. But few ever stepped onto dry land, unlike the large number of mariners from the merchant vessels, transports, supply ships, and privateers that crowded the port of New York.[53]

Discipline aboard British warships was harsh. On HMS *Trent,* moored off Fort George, for example, there was nothing exceptional about Captain John Lindsay's logbook entry for Wednesday, April 18, 1759: "Mustered the ships company and read the Articles of War and punished Edward Williams and Joseph Mary Pritty with 2 dozen lashes each for drunkenness." Such floggings were routine, whereas wartime discipline on merchant vessels and even ships in government service was relaxed because of the scarcity of sailors.[54]

This was certainly true aboard the ordnance ship *Alexander,* moored in the East River in the autumn of 1761. On Monday, October 5, a day on which half the *Alexander*'s crew returned from shore leave "much disguised in liquor," its logbook reported that "Peter Nilson was very mutinous and quarrelsome and fighting and abusing John Chapman without provocation." The following day, "Peter Nilson was demanded to do duty but positively denied; in the afternoon he again was asked but would not. . . . About 8 in the evening Peter Nilson asked pardon for what he had been guilty of and promised not to transgress again." The difference between this and the Royal Navy was not lost on the common sailor.[55]

High pay and tolerable working conditions in the merchant service, along with the prize money that could be earned privateering, led to wholesale desertions from the British men of war anchored in New York harbor. The deficit was so severe in the spring of 1757 that Lord Loudoun's expedition against Louisbourg was delayed for want of sailors, many of whom had slipped away from the warships to find berths aboard New York's large fleet of privateers. To rectify the situation, at two o'clock on the morning of May 20, 1757, with the cooperation of Governor Hardy and Lieutenant-Governor DeLancey, "about 3,000 soldiers were passed round this city," wrote Hugh Gaine, publisher of the *New-York Mercury,* "whilst many different parties, patrolled the streets, [and] searched the taverns, and other houses, where sailors usually resorted." The operation, which ended at six in the morning, netted about four hundred men.[56]

But the problem persisted. The case of HMS *Fowey* was typical. When a dozen sailors slipped away in the sleet and snow of the East River in early 1761, a press gang under the command of the ship's lieutenant drafted replacements out of trading vessels entering the harbor. According to its logbook, before the warship departed Sandy Hook in May on a routine cruise to Nantucket, *Fowey* "gave chase to a privateer of 20 guns and fired several shot to bring her to." Then he "sent the barge and 2 cutters manned and armed on board; brought her to an anchor and impressed 28 men." Faced with that prospect, sailors aboard merchant vessels and privateers became adept at eluding press gangs, and many put ashore on Long Island before their vessels entered lower New York Bay.[57]

Once in a while, the targets of impressment fought back. In mid-April 1759, when the longboat of HMS *Lizard* with a press gang aboard approached the *Martha*—a Liverpool brig moored in the Hudson River off Trinity Church —"their people fired into her and killed Thomas Elliott one of the boat's crew," according to the captain's logbook.[58]

An even more serious incident occurred on August 22, 1760, when the 22-gun privateer *Sampson* of Bristol, newly arrived in the East River, fired on the barge of HMS *Winchester* as it approached with a boarding party. Four men were killed "though not one piece was fired from the barge at any time," according to the official report. The crew of the privateer, determined to preserve their freedom, reached the safety of dry land before *Winchester* could react. In the ensuing manhunt, only one of the privateer's sailors was captured. Undoubtedly there were deserters among the fugitives, most whom slipped out of the city and found their way to nearby ports, where they disappeared into the free-flowing labor force of the Atlantic. A few were absorbed into the anonymous underworld of the New York waterfront.[59]

There was another dangerous underworld in wartime New York. From early in the conflict, French agents and spies found it easy to infiltrate the multilingual, multi-ethnic city. Their missions evolved in response to the changing fortunes of war. French agents reported troop strength, sorted out the system of supply and transport, and attempted to divine the intentions of the British military.[60]

They also played a critical role in sustaining the French war effort by coordinating shipments of provisions and supplies from New York to Cape Breton, the Mississippi, the French West Indies, and certain neutral sites in the Caribbean. Although the government periodically rounded up and imprisoned subjects of the French king—as it did in October 1756—French agents operated effectively in New York until May 1762.[61]

Long before the dramatic events of that spring—and well before New York City became a link in the French chain of supply—military planners saw security threatened from a far less ominous quarter. In the mid-eighteenth century, smuggling, especially that conducted through Dutch and Baltic ports, was a feature of the Atlantic economy embedded in the commercial culture of New York. The government's aggressive crackdown on smuggling in the spring of 1756 had far-reaching—and unintended—consequences.

CHAPTER TWO

Admiral Hardy and the Smugglers

May 1, 1756. A pilot boat carrying a lone customs officer slid past the navy's careening yard at Turtle Bay on the East River. The rain became steady and the wind picked up. "It was night before I got to the place," Alexander Colden wrote, describing the events of that—literally—"very dark and stormy" Saturday evening.[1]

Meanwhile, officers on horseback, including Tommy Kennedy, son of the head of the New York customhouse, followed Bowery Lane north out of town until it became the Boston Post Road and moved up the east side of Manhattan. Their destination, Prospect Farm (located near what is today the intersection of 85th Street and First Avenue), was the country estate of Nathaniel Marston, one of the wealthiest merchants in New York City. Earlier in the day, an informer had reported seeing sailcloth that had been smuggled in a sloop from Copenhagen on Prospect Farm's East River wharf. More would be taken off later that night. And a few days before, a Rhode Island fishing boat carrying a small quantity of Dutch tea, gunpowder, and brandy had been seized by customs officials in New York harbor.[2]

But Governor Sir Charles Hardy, a career officer in the British navy, wanted a more dramatic show of force. A successful raid on Marston's country estate would signal his intention to put an end to the smuggling from Amsterdam, Rotterdam, Hamburg, and Copenhagen known collectively as "the Dutch trade."

News of the impending raid reached Prospect Farm sometime that afternoon. Marston was outraged that Archibald Kennedy, the once-cooperative collector of customs in New York, had taken a step that not only would injure Marston's business, it would upset time-honored arrangements. The raid was an affront to a man of property and position. But all that could be dealt with later. Now it was time to act. As quickly as possible, workers at Prospect Farm hid the bales of sailcloth that were already landed. Marston then dispatched his vessel, the 20-ton sloop *Relief*, north through Hell Gate, the narrow strait between today's Astoria and Ward's Island in the East River entryway to Long Island Sound. Then he waited.[3]

The ambitious Colden—son of Cadwallader Colden, a powerful figure in provincial politics—was determined to impress his superiors in New York and London. Nathaniel Marston may have been a wealthy and respected man, but Alexander Colden had a search warrant to execute and a career to advance. At first, Marston managed to make the customs men looked foolish. "We got a candle and searched as well as we could that night but could find no goods," Colden reported, as Marston adamantly denied the presence of contraband. Frustrated but unwilling to give up, Colden, young Kennedy, and the others spent the night at Prospect Farm.[4]

But a tip early Sunday morning, perhaps from one of Marston's slaves, led Colden and his men to "a cellar under his outer kitchen," where they found a large cache of high-quality sailcloth. Spared the embarrassment of failure, they seized goods worth over £1,000. "Some attempts were made to bribe me but in vain," Colden boasted; "all his estate should not bribe me from my duty."[5]

Colden was the model of rectitude when there was a promotion in the offing: "I make no question but Sir Charles and Mr. Kennedy, will mention my diligence to the Commissioners of the Customs," he wrote to his father. And to his brother-in-law George Harison, a customs official then in London advancing his own career, he boasted, "My conduct I am sure you will approve of." "The merchants," Colden had told his father a few days after the raid, "are vastly uneasy as they find bribing will not do and vast numbers of vessels [are] expected with prodigious quantities of Holland goods. I hope to have some more slaps at them."[6]

The Marston raid "made great noise," which reached far across the Atlantic. "Our governor is resolved to stop the trade here," Waddell Cunningham wrote a correspondent in Rotterdam the following Monday. "A large value of goods that came by way of Copenhagen is seized, and indeed that trade is now on such a footing all over the continent that there is no managing it with safety."[7]

In a mercantilist frame of reference, the British Empire was like a wheel, with Great Britain at the hub and the colonies located on the rim. Commerce moved up and down the spokes, but it might move along the rim as well. The imperial trading system, governed by a complex (and sometimes contradictory) set of rules—Acts of Trade and Navigation—required that certain colonial articles, such as sugar, tobacco, and dyestuffs, be shipped exclusively from ports within the empire and that the shippers pay the various duties prescribed by law. In addition, the navigation acts required that westbound cargoes be sent from ports in Great Britain. There were exceptions, of course, such as the shipping of provisions and linen directly from Ireland or wine from the Madeira Islands.

British subjects were allowed to trade with foreign nations and their colonies as long as they were at peace with the Crown and trade conformed to the strictures of the Acts of Trade and Navigation. Shipping tea from Amsterdam to New York was perfectly legal, for example, so long as the ship called at a port in Great Britain, off-loaded then reloaded the tea, and paid the required duties, fees, and handling charges before continuing the voyage to New York.

The Acts of Trade and Navigation had multiple purposes. Most significant, they generated revenue for the Crown in the form of import and export duties. The acts also fostered economic growth by creating an interdependent imperial economy in which colonial produce (raw materials and semi-tropical goods) flowed into the metropolitan center (Great Britain) and manufactured articles flowed back to colonial markets. And the British carrying trade—benefiting from the requirement that goods be shipped aboard British vessels registered at British ports and manned largely by British crews—was a nursery for seamen who would then be available for service in the Royal Navy in time of war.[8]

Smuggling, broadly speaking, was trade that circumvented the Acts of Trade and Navigation. It thrived in British North America, and nowhere was it more pervasive than in New York City, where merchants were "accustomed to despise all laws of trade," according to Cadwallader Colden. Smuggling there took a variety of forms. In the mid-1750s, for example, Waddell Cunningham's snow *Johnson* routinely visited the Isle of Man to load contraband tea, India goods, and spirits after clearing Liverpool for home. There was, as well, a steady flow into the city of "foreign" (code for French) sugar and sugar products obtained through Dutch, Danish, and Spanish intermediaries in the West Indies or directly from the French themselves.[9]

Of all New York smuggling activities, the one known to contemporaries as "the Dutch trade" was the most sophisticated and best integrated into the city's commercial culture. The Dutch trade was, at its core, the shipping of goods from Amsterdam and other northern European ports to North America without fulfilling the Crown's requirement that the merchant vessel stop at a port in Great Britain and enter its goods. By shipping directly from Amsterdam to New York, a merchant stood to save the cost of off-loading and reloading his goods, as well as the import and export taxes. He was then able to undercut his competition by selling his smuggled goods at a lower price.

"There is no trade here that brings so much gain as this contraband trade from Holland, Hamburg, &c.," wrote a New Yorker in the 1750s. "Teas and Dutch India goods in general are now sold by our retailers cheaper" than in the British Isles. The commerce was encouraged by large Northern European trading firms like Adrian and Thomas Hope in Amsterdam, Herman Van Yzendoorn and Company in Rotterdam, and William Burroughs and Company in Hamburg, all eager to undercut London in the transatlantic dry-goods business and all involved in wartime trade with the French.[10]

New York–bound ship captains in the Dutch trade followed the "north about" route, embarking from Amsterdam, Rotterdam, Hamburg, and Copenhagen and sailing through the cold waters north of Scotland into the Grand Banks of Newfoundland and down the coast of New England. "If spoke with by any vessels you may answer [that you are] from the Isle of May," instructed the owners of the brig *Brilliant* of New York in January 1756; "If any fishermen or others comes on board of you treat them with civility." It was customary for northern European merchants doing business with New York to provide false documents, and Captain Richard Jeffery, Jr., of the *Brilliant* was told to "conceal all other letters and papers in case of being brought to by a man of war or privateer in case of a war."[11]

Most vessels in the Dutch trade entered lower New York Bay at Sandy Hook, placed their goods into temporary storage, and came up to the city in ballast. There was a long history of cooperation between merchants in New York and customs officials at Perth Amboy, New Jersey, where documents were readily available that allowed ships to enter at the New York customhouse. Small vessels, including the pilot boats that worked New York Bay, moved contraband into the city past customs officials bribed to look the other way. Occasionally, the government erected barriers to this obvious smuggling route. Merchants then sent their vessels to ports in Connecticut, "from whence it is not very difficult to introduce their goods through the Sound to New York, and even to Philadelphia."[12]

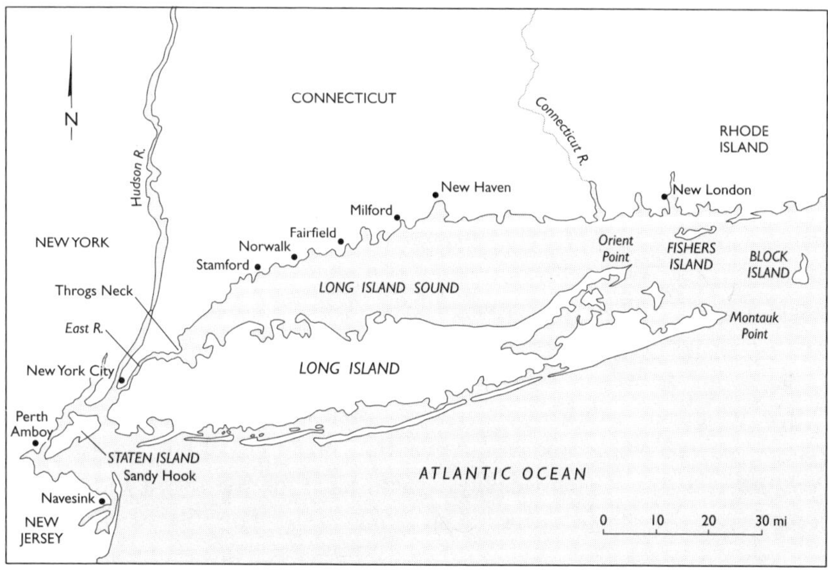

Long Island Sound and Environs

Long Island Sound offered a convenient back door. "Much of the Dutch trade is carried on to Rhode Island and Connecticut, and thence through the Sound to this city," Lieutenant-Governor DeLancey told the Board of Trade in July 1757. Neither colony had a royal charter, which meant that customhouses were not directly accountable to London and supervision was lax. In Connecticut, bribed officers in a string of ports between New London and Stamford provided documents—along with a wink and a nod—that protected vessels off-loading as they moved up the Sound. Some arrived at New York in ballast or entered goods as though they had been re-exported from Great Britain. Few merchants dared bring entire shiploads of smuggled tea, linens, gunpowder, and other articles all the way up to the city.[13]

In early 1756, for instance, Captain Jeffery and the *Brilliant* entered the eastern end of Long Island Sound through the fast-moving tidal currents leading toward Fishers Island. Other incoming ships were met by small vessels off New London that waited to escort them to safety. Still others, like the 70-ton snow *Charming Sally*—which entered the Sound in late September 1756—"steered over for New London harbor" where Joseph Chew, a merchant and customhouse officer, was the principal source of information and documents for captains sailing westward toward New York.[14]

With instructions in hand, Captain Israel Munds and *Charming Sally* "weighed and run over to Fishers Island," where he left part of his goods in storage for transfer to coasting vessels from as far away as Philadelphia. During Munds's sixteen days at Fishers Island in October 1756, five ships departed for New York, one for Boston, and another for Newport under the command of a Rhode Island shipmaster active in New York's Dutch trade. With off-loading to the coasters and warehouses complete and the wind rising, *Charming Sally* "turned out in the Sound then made all sail we could set," according to the captain. Soon, it was running "abreast of Connecticut" along a coast replete with rivers, creeks, and inlets, communicating with prefixed drop-off points by signal flags and lanterns to "unload without the inspection of any officer."[15]

Merchants in New York sometimes dispatched fast-sailing sloops to intercept their incoming vessels and take in goods. In early 1756, for example, *Brilliant*'s owners, William and John Ludlow of Queen Street, asked Captain Jeffery to rendezvous with their sloop. "You may send us directly down about twenty cases of tea and . . . as much oznabrig [coarse linen] as you can stow under the deck," they said. "And if you can spare the mate or a trusty hand, send one along."[16]

Agents in New Haven, Milford, Fairfield, Norwalk, and Stamford facilitated the Dutch trade. The most important of these was John Lloyd at Stamford, Joseph Chew's counterpart at the western end of Long Island Sound. *Brilliant*'s captain was instructed to anchor in the middle of the Sound and send a mate to confer with Lloyd, "whose direction you are desired to follow in the delivery of the cargo. . . . Mr. Lloyd will provide you a clearance from Fairfield in ballast." Fast-moving sloops, like Lloyd's 18-ton *Weymouth* and 15-ton *Stamford,* busied themselves ferrying cargoes from Stamford and Fairfield to wharves along the length of the East River.[17]

The final leg took vessels like the *Brilliant* and *Charming Sally* past Sands Point, Execution Rock, and the Stepping Stones to "Frogs Point"—the name Captain Munds's logbook gave to Throgs Neck—where, on October 20, 1756, *Charming Sally* dropped anchor while the owner, John Laurence of Queen Street, came up from the city under cover of darkness to take possession of his ship and the remaining cargo. Then began the hazardous passage into the East River and through Hell Gate, feared for its violent currents and treacherous outcroppings.[18]

From the holds of vessels like *Brilliant* and *Charming Sally,* smuggled goods passed through East Side warehouses onto shelves in Hanover Square and shops throughout the city. John Fell, a merchant on King Street, told a committee of the British House of Commons in the early 1750s that he had seen a piece of Dutch linen in a shop at New York marked cheaper at retail than he could purchase the equivalent British linen at wholesale. Although Fell was unable to estimate "what quantity of linen goods are smuggled into New York," he remarked that it was common practice for them to be "publicly landed, though not entered" at the customhouse. As long as officials in New York were cooperative, the Dutch trade thrived. "I am on such a footing with the officers here," bragged Waddell Cunningham, one of the most active participants, "that if any Person can have favors, I will."[19]

The goods that entered New York through the Dutch trade fit comfortably into the flow of North Atlantic commerce. For example, merchants in Amsterdam and Rotterdam did a large business in Bohea tea, a Chinese black tea, which undercut the equivalent product from the British East India Company. The Dutch ports and Hamburg were also convenient sources for oznabrig, a cheap German linen that was popular throughout British America. Russia duck, ideal as sailcloth, was sent from these places but could be had even more favorably through Copenhagen. The Dutch trade was likewise a source of calico, muslin, and taffeta from India, as well as more prosaic articles like paper and glazed tiles.[20]

Smuggled armaments were an important component of the trade during wartime. Early in 1756, the British government prohibited the exportation of arms of all kinds, "for which reason I could not send the sword blades without the risk of their being seized," wrote a Quaker merchant in London. Yet through the spring and summer, as the military situation deteriorated, weapons flowed into the city from northern Europe. Robert Crommelin, a merchant on Queen Street linked to the great Amsterdam banking and trading firm Crommelin and Son, carried everything necessary to outfit a privateer for duty against the French, including cutlasses, broadswords, backswords, pistols, muskets, and a variety of swivel and carriage guns.[21]

Crommelin was representative of the many New Yorkers with close family ties to Amsterdam and Rotterdam. But the Dutch trade was not confined to this group. It encompassed a broad sampling of the city's merchant community and included men of wealth and status—and a good deal of political influence—whose roots cut across ethnic boundaries. John Cruger, the mayor of New York; James Depeyster, son of the treasurer of the colony; James

Jauncey, a rising New York politician tied to the DeLancey faction; and William Kelly, an Irishman and until recently the partner of Alexander Colden in a firm that supplied forces under the command of Sir William Johnson —all were involved in the illicit trade.[22]

New York's Irish merchants were among the most active participants. They had become an important part of the city's trading community in the 1740s when flaxseed exports rose sharply to meet the demand of the expanding Irish linen industry. Between the first week in December 1755 and the end of February 1756, for example, New Yorkers shipped about 90,000 bushels of flaxseed to Ireland for the opening of the spring planting season. By the start of the Seven Years' War, the flaxseed trade had become the city's most important wintertime commercial activity. Correspondents at home regularly sent back broadcloth, lace, and other proscribed goods bundled with Irish linens. Such articles "though contraband, can be shipped here without the least risk," wrote a merchant in Cork with a large American business.[23]

Waddell Cunningham, Thomas Lynch, James Thompson, and the other Irishmen who managed this trade lost little time ingratiating themselves with the city's commercial elite and embracing New York's pragmatic smuggling culture. Cunningham alone was involved in no fewer than six vessels in the Dutch trade in the spring of 1756. One, the snow *Prince of Wales,* was the property of a consortium of New York Irish merchants dominated by his firm Greg and Cunningham that also included George Folliot and John Torrans. The Dutch trade "was carried on in so public a manner," Cunningham wrote, "that all people in trade was obliged to be concerned in it in their defense."[24]

Officials in New York were well aware of the Dutch trade. "We have great reason to believe, there has been for some time lately carried on, a clandestine illegal trade, by some of the traders of this place, to Holland and other parts," wrote Archibald Kennedy on the eve of the war. On paper, the penalties were steep. In 1753 Lieutenant-Governor DeLancey had signed tough new legislation to curb smuggling. According to the statute, persons convicted of "the clandestine running" of goods faced forfeiture of their cargoes and a fine of £20 (New York currency). A three-month jail sentence awaited those unable to pay, and there were six months in jail without bail for the second offense. Kennedy went so far as to offer protection, anonymity, and "one third of all forfeitures" to informants. According to the customs collector, "it cannot be imagined, that any information of this kind, can be thought odious, when the trade of Great Britain, the interest of the fair trader, and the general character of the merchants of this place, are so nearly concerned."[25]

But the legislation and calls for informants had little effect. They were no more than a polite nod to London by New York politicians resentful of British restrictions on colonial trade. As long as enforcement was in the hands of smugglers like George Harison, a high-ranking official at the customhouse, the Dutch trade flourished. But the understanding between merchants and customs officers was subject to change without notice.[26]

War with France—raging yet undeclared in the summer of 1755—brought a new governor. Sir Charles Hardy, a congenial but efficient British naval officer, arrived in New York aboard HMS *Sphynx* on September 2, 1755, barely nine weeks after Braddock's defeat in western Pennsylvania. The demoralized remnant of Braddock's army had taken up positions near Albany, and Governor Hardy immediately set about preparing the defense of the province.[27]

Among the concerns of Hardy's superiors in London was New York's long history of cooperation with French Canada in marketing furs and supplying provisions to Cape Breton. Written instructions to the new governor included a directive that he end all commerce between "His Majesty's subjects in the province of New York under your government and the French settlements in America." To achieve this, Hardy intended to eradicate all forms of illicit trade in New York and, by extension, the northern colonies of British America.[28]

"When I first arrived at New York I found this iniquitous trade in a very flourishing state," Hardy told the Board of Trade in 1757. Bringing it to an end was a formidable challenge. For one thing, Kennedy and other customs officials were not subject to the direct control of colonial governors. For another, the tolerant Kennedy believed that British restrictions on North American trade frustrated commercial development of the empire and served only narrow interests at home.[29]

But the "timorous gentleman," as Kennedy was called by one customhouse officer, became compliant when Hardy threatened to complain to London about irregularities in New York. As he increased the pressure on Kennedy in late 1755, the new governor busied himself with gathering information on New York's Dutch trade, and an aide recorded the "names of every vessel and master that he could suspect [of] going to or coming from Holland." In the weeks leading up to the raid on Prospect Farm, merchants in New York, Boston, Philadelphia, and other North American ports—doing no more than had been tolerated for decades under the Crown's tacit policy of "salutary neglect"—began to feel the tightening grip of enforcement as colonial governors responded to wartime instructions from London that all forms of illicit trade must be curbed.[30]

After Hardy struck in May 1756, "there was no possibility of getting

[Dutch goods] here safe, occasioned by our officers being resolved to stop all contraband trade," lamented one New Yorker. Seizures continued "almost daily," Waddell Cunningham reported. In one form or another, most of the city's merchants were affected by the government's crackdown. Worst of all, "money now won't bring them to reason."[31]

Connecticut was not immune. "I acquainted Governor Fitch with some informations I had obtained," Hardy reported, "and requested him to direct the customhouse officers of his colony to do their duty." To the consternation of New York smugglers, they did. In late June, goods valued at £2,500 (New York currency) were seized in a single raid at Norwalk, with more costly confiscations at Stamford later in the summer. Merchants in New York lamented the difficulty of moving goods from New England into the city; "our customhouse officers being so strict that no contraband goods that comes from thence hardly escape."[32]

The assault on the Dutch trade continued through the summer. In June a sloop of Cunningham's freighted at Stamford for Philadelphia was seized "either by the ignorance or villainy of the boatman." "Like a madman," wrote the Irishman, the captain attempted to run his cargo through Hell Gate and up the East River, passing directly by the city. Concerned that "they may begin to seize with you as they have done in other parts of your province," Cunningham urged Joseph Chew to send sloops into the eastern end of Long Island Sound. They were to intercept the snow *Prince of Wales* when it arrived from Amsterdam, sending the cargo to Philadelphia where it would be safe.[33]

The Pennsylvania city was a convenient distribution point for contraband. Cargoes could be landed at Marcus Hook or other hiding places downriver before being carried to Philadelphia aboard small vessels. However, like Hardy, Pennsylvania's deputy governor Robert Hunter Morris was staging a crusade against smuggling in the summer of 1756. In several late-night raids in August, Morris roamed the waterfront area, forcing open windows and doors to gain access to suspected hiding places. Merchants responded as best they could. "We have divided the [tea] . . . for fear of an information being lodged," wrote a nervous Philadelphia merchant to his supplier in New York.[34]

As in New York, there was a general tightening of the rules governing trade. "Notice is hereby given, that all captains or masters of vessels are required to enter and clear, as the law directs, . . . [or] they will answer the contrary at their peril," declared the Philadelphia customhouse in September. With a resolute governor, anonymous informers, and the possibility of three to six months in jail facing convicted smugglers, risks far outstripped rewards.

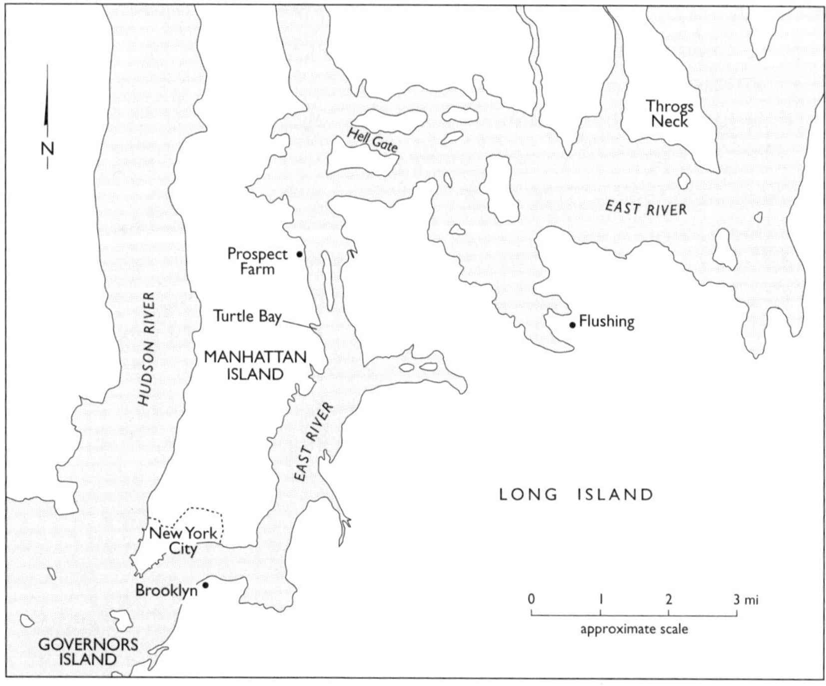

The East River

As New York's Waddell Cunningham told a London correspondent in mid-September 1756, "The trade from Holland is entirely stopped."[35]

London's determination to bring colonial trade under control even affected Massachusetts, a colony with an impressive record of disregard for commercial regulation. "It is to be hoped [that] the most reputable merchants in New-York will follow the good example given by those of Boston," editorialized the *New-York Gazette* in December 1756, "to put an end to a clandestine trade, chiefly injurious to the interest of Great Britain, and . . . beneficial to the Dutch."[36]

Merchants lost heavily, and newspapers in New York announced public auctions of confiscated goods. But like other aspects of the contest between smugglers and the government, there were ways of getting around this problem. "By giving a fee to the proper hand," Cunningham told a friend, the terms of sale could be manipulated. Opening bids were set unrealistically low, and officers were bribed not to bid against merchants recovering their goods. Cunningham even solicited favors in Philadelphia, where his goods had been seized in a warehouse raid. Meeting with the collector of customs there, he negotiated terms for the sale of seven chests of arms and nine casks of powder. Through all his difficulties, Cunningham reassured his partner in Ireland that he expected "great favors showed me in the sales of our seized goods."[37]

Waddell Cunningham and a small circle of hardened New Yorkers had no intention of permanently giving up their smuggling operations. Although he had written in October that "it would be imprudent at present to touch" the Dutch trade, a month later he placed a standing order for eight chests of tea to be loaded aboard every vessel leaving Amsterdam, Rotterdam, and Hamburg for Rhode Island. "[As] I look upon it," Cunningham told his partner, "the trade can be carried on safely there, and we can wait our time to bring it from that here or to Philadelphia." By December, the brash Irishman was smuggling once again and beginning his even more lucrative trade with the French enemy.[38]

Trading with the enemy was Governor Hardy's real concern. The culture of smuggling would have to be extirpated and commerce brought under control if the French were to be denied access to the food, supplies, and "warlike stores" readily available in New York City.[39]

In April 1755, before his departure from England, Hardy had been told to enforce a legally binding but loosely interpreted 1686 "treaty of peace and neutrality in America, concluded between England and France." According to its terms, "the subjects, inhabitants, &c. of each kingdom are prohibited to trade and fish in all parts possessed, or which shall be possessed, by [the other] . . . in America."[40]

The government in New York had already begun to curtail trade with the French. In February 1755, DeLancey had signed legislation to bring an end to "the sending of provisions to Cape Breton, or any other French port or settlement." The law was aimed at the "pernicious trade carried on from hence and some other of the northern colonies." By means of this commerce, according to the preamble to the act, the French were "supplied with great quantities of flour and other provisions" and thus able to maintain their forces in Canada, at Crown Point, and elsewhere in North America. Unless stopped, trading with the French "may prove to be of very fatal and dangerous consequence to this and all other [of] His Majesty's northern colonies."[41]

This law—An Act to Restrain Provisions Exports from New York—sought to end the trade "by laying such reasonable penalties fines and restric-

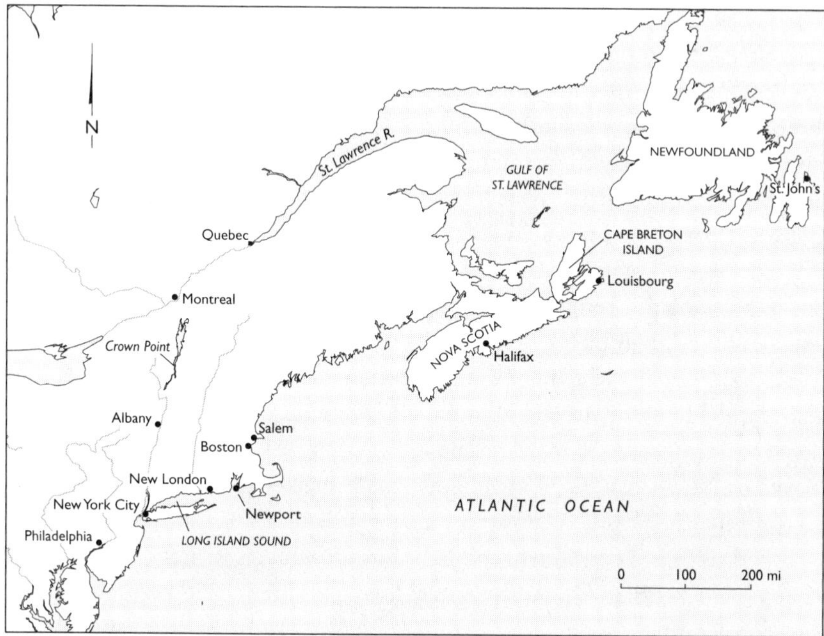

Louisbourg, Cape Breton Island, and the North American Coast

tions on the owners factors freighters and masters of vessels using such trade or otherwise offending . . . as shall be thought just reasonable and expedient." Under the February 1755 act, the authorities were empowered "to commit to prison any master or commander of any ship or vessel owner factor freighter mariner or any other person" who failed to cooperate. Although the statute articulated the problem, it failed to define the offence precisely or to provide an effective means of enforcement. Worse still, because the New York General Assembly distrusted the intentions of other colonies, the act was "to continue in force for the space of four months after the publication thereof and no longer."[42]

Soon after passage of the act, DeLancey was informed by Deputy-Governor Morris of Pennsylvania that "no less than forty English vessels" were "at one time in the harbor at Louisbourg, that had carried provisions there." Most were from New England and the middle colonies, with a strong representation from New York City. "The great supply," Morris told DeLancey, "will last them all the next summer, and enable them to maintain an army in the back of us, which they could not otherwise have done."[43]

In July 1755, on the eve of Braddock's defeat in western Pennsylvania, the

New York General Assembly replaced the weak February statute with a new law effectively prohibiting trade with France and its colonies. The Act to Prevent Exports of Provisions and Other Goods from New York to the French required merchants to post bonds in the amount of £1,000 (New York currency) as security to guarantee that shipments of flour, salted provisions, cordage, and other articles "shall not be landed and put on shore at any port or place subject to the French king."[44]

The second statute's rhetoric was matched by an enforcement mechanism, but violators, emboldened by years of illicit commerce, continued and even enlarged their business with the French. Commercial ties binding New York, the French West Indies, and merchant houses in Amsterdam, Rotterdam, and Hamburg were underpinned by the availability of cheap French sugar and tropical produce. And the French, whose war effort depended upon access to North American provisions and "warlike stores," were determined to continue their trade by whatever means possible.[45]

And so things continued, through the autumn and winter of 1755 and into the following spring. On April 12, 1756, less than three weeks before the raid at Prospect Farm, an anonymous writer in the *New-York Mercury*—styling himself "The Informer"—announced that "by my means, there was seized on board a small vessel from Rhode Island, on the 9th instant, a considerable quantity of foreign gun-powder, grape shot, canvas, tea, &c." The author linked the Dutch trade and trade with the French. Participants in New York's Dutch trade were "unworthy members of the community," he argued, bringing "the destruction of his country." Men active in clandestine commerce with Amsterdam, Copenhagen, Hamburg, and Rotterdam were supplying the enemy "with everything necessary for our destruction, either directly, or by way of the Dutch [islands]."

The Informer pointed out that goods from New York had flowed into the hands of the French during earlier colonial wars, and it was happening again. "That Louisbourg is by this time, or soon will be supplied by us, with a sufficiency, . . . is past all doubt." The French in Canada, the Mississippi, and the West Indies had been stockpiling the necessities of eighteenth-century warfare, much of it acquired through New York City. "Can any honest man, or a man that has the least regard for the trade or interest of his country, sit silent, for fear of being called an informer?"[46]

Hardy watched in dismay as colonial governors responded to the French buildup with short-term embargoes but little else. "We lose great advantage for want of the provisions colonies uniting," he told the Board of Trade.

Governor Hardy attempted to enforce the July 1755 statute, but customs officials in the neighboring colonies of Connecticut and New Jersey falsified bonds and allowed New York vessels to enter and depart without scrutiny.[47]

Meanwhile, a handful of Dutch and Danish islands in the West Indies—Saint Eustatius, Curaçao, Saint Croix, and Saint Thomas—were emerging as critical points of supply for the French in North America and the West Indies. These "neutral islands" became, for a time, the centerpiece of New York commerce.

CHAPTER THREE

Frenchified Bottoms

As midnight of Tuesday, May 18, 1756, approached, Samuel Stilwell and two slaves made their way along Dock Street in the direction of Whitehall Slip. At Bockee's Wharf, they joined laborers working by lantern light to load flour and bread aboard a waiting harbor sloop. The vessel belonged to Stilwell's partner John Burroughs, a grain dealer from Matawan Creek, New Jersey. It was taking on the last of a provisions cargo that had been assembled on Bockee's Wharf, Moore's Wharf, and Whitehall Dock.[1]

At four o'clock in the morning the workboat slipped its mooring in the shadows of the New York waterfront and entered the East River. Burroughs guided it past Governors Island into upper New York Bay, entering Kill Van Kull at the northeastern tip of Staten Island. Moving cautiously through the channel, he found Stilwell's 30-ton sloop *Catherine* riding at anchor. It was early in the afternoon of Wednesday, May 19, before the men had transferred the heavy barrels from Burroughs's boat into the hold of the ocean-going sloop.[2]

The *Catherine* had arrived in New York under the command of Obadiah Hunt, who had brought with him a large order for flour and bread from a French merchant at Saint Eustatius. After clearing customs for New Jersey, Hunt had taken his sloop into Kill Van Kull to await a clandestine lading from Stilwell's warehouse in the city and Burroughs's mill on Matawan Creek. Once the 180 barrels of flour and 50 casks of bread had been safely stowed, Captain Hunt guided the *Catherine* down Kill Van Kull into upper New York Bay and through the Narrows. Sometime after sundown, his vessel passed Sandy Hook and was soon under full sail bound for the tiny Dutch island in the eastern Caribbean.[3]

Meanwhile, far-reaching events were taking place across the Atlantic. In

London, on May 17, 1756, two days before the *Catherine* left New York, King George II had appeared at Kensington Palace before "the greatest council that has been known for many years." The seventy-three-year-old monarch then declared war on the French king, Louis XV, in an elaborate ceremony in which he placed his sword across the royal seal on the freshly signed document.[4]

At noon the following day, as Stilwell and Burroughs gathered together their cargo for Saint Eustatius, a procession of dignitaries brought the king's proclamation to the people of London. Snare drums and trumpets announced the marchers as Horse Guards cleared a path from Westminster to the City of London. "The concourse of people in the streets through which the procession passed, was the greatest ever known," reported a witness, "and several persons were thrown down and trampled." Royal heralds read the king's declaration aloud at Charing Cross and other points along the way. "The spectators, almost innumerable, expressed their great satisfaction by loud acclamations of joy."[5]

The declaration was celebrated across the nation, nowhere more than in naval towns and commercial seaports, where war with France meant commerce raiding and prize money. The Royal Navy began to seize enemy ships, and in early June privateers—privately owned but officially licensed ships of war—from London, Bristol, Liverpool, and other British ports swarmed into the Channel and the North Atlantic. Merchantmen on European routes were handy targets, but the most sought-after prizes were French ships in the West Indian commerce.[6]

France finally declared war on June 9, although for months, peace had been no more than a drawing-room illusion. In April and May, French land and sea forces had invaded the island of Minorca and captured Great Britain's principal naval base in the Mediterranean. The stunning defeat at a stronghold of British power had embarrassed the Royal Navy and shaken confidence in the London government.[7]

Now the French unleashed their privateers on British merchant shipping. The London press reported heavy losses as the most brazen enemy cruisers operated within sight of the homeland. According to a story in *The Daily Advertiser* datelined Dublin, June 19, "the purser of an East Indiaman, who came from Kinsale yesterday by land, informs us, that a French privateer had taken three homeward-bound West India merchantmen off that harbor last week, and carried them to France."[8]

The war on commerce drifted west. French trading vessels and neutral ships carrying French cargoes in the North Atlantic became easy prey for

British warships and privateers. In late June, Captain James Campbell in HMS *Nightingale,* bound from Portsmouth to New York City carrying Lord Loudoun and a copy of the declaration of war, took a 350-ton French ship, along with a Danish schooner, after a chase of fourteen hours and a brief engagement. About the same time, a fleet of French merchant ships bound from Martinique to France under the convoy of French warships, "sailed in triumph by all our islands, without any interruption from our men of war," according to a witness impatient for the formal announcement of hostilities.[9]

New Yorkers were eager to get into the fight. News that a French fleet had sailed against Minorca and that a declaration of war was imminent reached the city in the first week of July, well ahead of *Nightingale.* "The above news gains such credit here, that our merchants are beginning to fit out privateers," wrote one New Yorker. According to a newspaper account, Governor Hardy "left a number of blank commissions behind him, signed, for the use of the privateers" before departing for Albany in late July.[10]

New York City was in the grip of privateering fever when the king's proclamation was read at Fort George on July 31. "The declaration of war having put such spirits in persons here," wrote a New York merchant in September, "that no less than 12 privateers are out and fitting with the greatest dispatch; there [are] already 5 prizes sent in here." By the end of the year, there were 26 privateers in service carrying nearly 350 guns and 2,700 men. In 1756 these privateers captured 33 enemy vessels and destroyed 6; the following year they captured 103, destroying 7. New York City far exceeded any other British American port during the Seven Years' War in its totals of enemy vessels captured (381) and destroyed (20).[11]

The vitality of New York privateering is embodied in "the little diminutive, but victorious *Harlequin,*" partly owned by Waddell Cunningham, who also served as its agent. A former pilot boat, the 45-ton sloop and its crew of fifty had a share in twenty-one prizes (thirteen unassisted). The privateer brought its first capture—*L'Amérique,* a large French schooner—into the East River on September 18, 1756. In all, *Harlequin*'s prizes exceeded £50,000 (New York currency).[12]

The French gave as good as they got. "A great number of English vessels have been taken by the enemy's ships of war," wrote a frustrated American. In November 1756, the *New-York Mercury* reported nine French men of war, "chiefly frigates, continually cruising in the Windward Passage, so that no English vessel durst attempt coming through there." At least a dozen French privateers patrolled off Saint Christopher (Saint Kitts) in early 1757, stopping everything entering and leaving that island. In March a Boston ship captain saw "55 French privateers between Barbuda, and Guadeloupe, in a chain, about a mile distant from each other." " 'Tis not in the least to be wondered that nothing escapes them," noted the *Antigua Gazette* in July 1757.[13]

The brig *Brilliant* was among the dozens of New York ships lost to enemy privateers. Still active in the Dutch trade, it was returning from the Netherlands in February 1757 when it was taken and carried by a French privateer into Morlaix on the Brittany coast, where Captain Richard Jeffery, Jr., and his crew were stripped of their money and clothes "and confined in a close jail, with a great many more of their unfortunate countrymen."[14]

Although most of the New York vessels that fell into enemy hands were taken in the West Indies, a significant number were seized along the coast of North America, and a few just off Sandy Hook. In the spring of 1757, for example, a pair of Port-au-Prince privateers—one "painted very gay, as with red, yellow, black and green"—cruised "the coast of New York and thereabouts," according to the *Mercury*.[15]

In spite of aggressive French privateering, Great Britain held the advantage. Too few French warships were available for convoy duty in the western Atlantic, with the result that homeward-bound merchantmen were often left defenseless just a few miles off Saint-Domingue, Guadeloupe, and Martinique. Many set out with no protection at all. In February 1757, a New York privateer captain reported twenty-two vessels loaded and ready to sail from Cape François without convoy, "and there are 12 sail of English privateers lying at the above port," he added. "We can see every vessel that goes in or out."[16]

The French merchant fleet was being swept from the sea. In April 1757, the governor of Saint-Domingue forbid trading vessels to set out from any part of the island before the arrival of French ships of war. And few French supply ships made it safely across the Atlantic. It was the same at Guadeloupe and Martinique, as well as at Cape Breton and on the Mississippi. Only rarely did a French naval squadron relieve the pressure. "We have reason to hope," editorialized the *New-York Mercury* in May 1757, "that, unless our enemies receive a speedy supply, we shall be enabled to do as much with the sword of famine, as those of steel."[17]

Neutral trading ships moving between the Atlantic ports of France and its West Indian islands provided relief for the beleaguered merchant fleet. An even larger number worked routes connecting neutral ports in Europe with neutral islands in the West Indies, where cargoes could be conveniently collected and distributed to the French colonies. These "Frenchified bottoms," as they were described in the *New-York Mercury*, carried red wine, flour, coarse linen, and a wide variety of articles critical to the war effort. Among these were Irish salted beef, pork, and butter for use aboard the French privateers scouring the western Atlantic.[18]

Ireland and its merchant communities abroad figured prominently in the French supply chain. The Kingdom of Ireland, though it shared a monarch with Great Britain and was governed by a colonial administration appointed in London, had a long-standing commercial relationship with France. Not all trade was legal—notably the clandestine exchange of Irish wool for French wine along the southern Irish coast—but much of it was. For decades, in peacetime commerce allowed under the British navigation acts, France and the French West Indies had provided a large market for Irish salted provisions such as beef, pork, butter, herring, and a few specialty items like pickled tongue and spiced salmon.[19]

In 1700 France was the second largest customer for Irish salted beef, taking 33,000 barrels, compared to the 43,000 barrels sent to British America (out of a total of 92,000 barrels exported). The Dutch Republic and Spain imported about 6,000 barrels each. At mid-century, the French share had grown to 50 percent of Irish beef exports, while the British West Indies and North American colonies were accounting for just over a quarter of Ireland's export of 160,000 barrels.[20]

Predictably, beef exports increased during the Seven Years' War, reflecting shipboard demand in the Atlantic. But a reconfiguration of the composition of exports (notably the dramatic growth in Dutch, "Baltic," and Spanish purchases) underscores the role neutral carriers played in delivering Irish beef to French buyers (many of them in the Caribbean) at a time when commercial contacts between Ireland and France were disrupted—but not ended—by war.[21]

Such contacts had been made illegal by Great Britain's declaration of war, which forbade British subjects "to hold any correspondence or communication with the said French king, or his subjects." The proclamation also warned "all other persons, of what nation soever, not to transport or carry any soldiers, arms, powder, ammunition, or other contraband goods, to any of the territories, lands, plantations, or countries of the said French king; declaring, that whatsoever ship or vessel shall be met withal, transporting or carrying any soldiers, arms, powder, ammunition, or any other contraband goods, to any of the territories, lands, plantations, or countries of the said French king, the same, being taken, shall be condemned as good and lawful prize."[22]

The royal admonition notwithstanding, direct commercial contact between provisioners in Dublin and Cork and clients in France continued through the end of the war. In one instance, three Dublin merchant houses shipped beef and butter to "one Mr. Black, an Irish merchant, [who] since the war, has resided at Bordeaux." They brought back wine and brandy aboard the brig *Betsey* owned by "Popish merchants, resident in Dublin." To mask the true character of this trade, the Dubliners secured Spanish documents from "one Bartholomew Arthur French, an Irish merchant, resident at Saint Sebastian's" disguising the vessel as the *Nosta Seignora del Choro* of Balboa.[23]

By means of Dutch and Danish merchant houses, the Franco-Irish connection reached deep into the Atlantic. In June 1756, for example, a New York captain saw five ships arriving at Saint Eustatius with provisions from Ireland. Two years later, a Waterford merchant admitted that 50,000 to 60,000 barrels of provisions had been sent to the tiny Dutch island, nearly all of it for transshipment to the French. "Upon her arrival in the road of St. Eustatius," according to an Irish report on the activity of a Dutch galley, "the principal part of the cargo was put on board several barks and carried to the adjacent French settlements."[24]

The rapid expansion of North America's trade with the French through the neutral islands was, in part, a response to the flood of Irish exports. By the spring of 1756, Governor Hardy had become alarmed at the growing involvement of the mainland colonial ports. "If this trade be suffered," he wrote, "prohibitory laws will be to little purpose, nor indeed will it be in the power of the governors to bring their assemblies to pass such, while they can use the argument, if we do not trade with those islands the Irish will."[25]

The first phase of the city's trade with the enemy—direct voyages to Cape Breton—had reached its peak the year following George Washington's skirmish with the French at Fort Necessity in July 1754. Later, military defeats and Indian massacres on the North American frontier made such direct assistance unpopular and distasteful. The strict prohibitions against doing business with the French enacted by the New York General Assembly in the summer of 1755 further reduced the northward flow of goods.[26]

The second phase—indirect, circumspect trade conducted through Dutch and Danish intermediaries—accelerated after the French defeated Braddock's army in July 1755 and was at a high pitch when the king declared war in May

1756. According to an American writing in the *London Evening Post,* "Our very good friends the Dutch are, according to their wonted custom, contriving every scheme and practicing every method to engross the trade and supply our enemies." Dutch sloops carried North American flour to the Dutch settlements in the West Indies and even called at Barbados "to practice the same method of trade." " 'Tis said," he added, "3,000 barrels of flour had been shipped off in less than a week for the Dutch settlements, for whose use and service is but too evident, the thing being in its own nature too obvious to admit of any dispute."[27]

"There is [a] great number of French vessels here waiting for provisions," wrote a Connecticut merchant at Saint Eustatius in December 1755. "Northward provisions must command a great price here," he told his correspondent at home after learning that Irish salted provisions were being held up at Dublin and Cork by embargo. "Molasses rum sugar &c. are very plenty and the new crop now coming in will make them more so."[28]

Because of its clandestine character, it is impossible to establish the size of this trade. But it was significantly larger than the direct trade of the first phase. Driven by expanding wartime demand and the success of British privateers interdicting long-distance French and neutral shipping, exchanges were expedited through North American, Irish, and French intermediaries on Saint Eustatius, Curaçao, and Saint Croix. In Canada, Governor Hardy was informed, the French "depend on what can be sent from Europe and what they can purchase at the Dutch islands of St. Eustatius and Curaçao." Lewis Morris, judge of the New York court of vice-admiralty, observed that the Dutch islands had become little more than "public factors for the enemy."[29]

Saint Eustatius was the most important of these entrepôts. Comprising just eight square miles, it is located six miles northwest of Saint Christopher in the Leeward Islands, part of the Lesser Antilles in the eastern Caribbean. "Though very inconsiderable in extent and produce, yet [Saint Eustatius] drives a great smuggling trade," wrote one observer. At Oranjestad, the principal town, and for a mile along the crowded shore of Orange Bay, about two hundred warehouses offered an astonishing array of goods.[30]

"From one end of the town of Eustatia to the other is a continued mart, where goods of the most different uses and qualities are displayed before the shop doors," wrote a woman visitor with a shopper's eye. "Here hang rich embroideries, painted silks, flowered muslins, with all the manufactures of the Indies. Just by hang sailor's jackets, trousers, shoes, hats, etc. [The] next stall contains most exquisite silver plate, the most beautiful indeed I ever saw, and close by these iron-pots, kettles and shovels."[31]

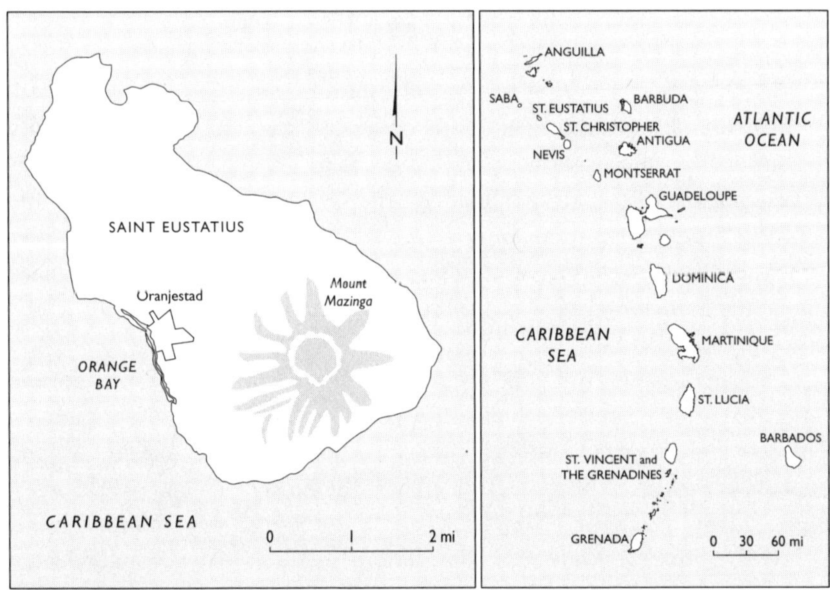

Saint Eustatius and the Lesser Antilles

"Never did I meet with such variety," she added. "Here was a merchant vending his goods in Dutch, another in French, and a third in Spanish." English speakers—North Americans, Irish, Scots, and some English—were the most common, but language skills were an asset to merchants doing business directly with French agents or French ship captains shuttling cargoes among the islands. In September 1755 a North American on Saint Eustatius wrote home asking for a book of French grammar, "as I propose to make myself master of the language."[32]

New York was one of as many as ten ports in the middle colonies and New England active in trade with the French via Saint Eustatius. Resident factors were a feature of trade there. The factor Thomas Allen—a New Londoner in partnership with Francis Goelet (the former Provincial Grand Master of the Masons in New York)—maintained a correspondence from Saint Eustatius with Salem, Newburyport, Boston, Newport, New London, New York, Philadelphia, and Savannah.[33]

Cargoes sent to Saint Eustatius differed according to the regional identity of the exporter. Whereas imports from New England were highly variegated and could include anything from apples to horses, New York and Philadelphia characteristically shipped bread and flour, sometimes supplemented with lumber and salted provisions. The island's free-port status, large and fluid market, tolerant Dutch governance, and convenient navigation made it the crossroads of the Caribbean.[34]

By the spring of 1756, it had become customary for New York ships to clear customs for Nevis or Saint Christopher and then head straight for Saint Eustatius. Securing paperwork was no problem. Merchants at Orange Bay worked closely with correspondents on the North American mainland and had little trouble procuring forged certificates to cancel provisions bonds. "The end and intent of the law that those same provisions shall not be carried among the French is evaded and rendered ineffectual," wrote a New England ship captain.[35]

The small New York contingent that engaged in this trade comprised "men that may be depended upon," according to Waddell Cunningham. They were experienced and well connected politically and socially. Among the best known were Nathaniel Lawrence, the brother-in-law of Alderman Philip Livingston; Robert Stewart, a partner in the Irish-Dutch firm Stewart and DeGraaff; and Francis Goelet, Thomas Allen's partner and George Harison's predecessor in Masonry.[36]

Though not as large a trading center, Curaçao had even closer ties with New Yorkers. The tiny Dutch island was a flourishing trading station in the southern Caribbean Sea perched at the edge of the Spanish New World. A crossroads of transnational trade, it had been an irritant to British and Spanish mercantilists through much of the eighteenth century, the model of an open, accessible Atlantic marketplace. Especially grating was its easy accessibility to British, Irish, and North American traders, on the one hand, and French West Indian planters, on the other. Saint Eustatius did more business in the French Caribbean than Curaçao—most of whose trade was with markets in New Spain—but there were Curaçao merchants at Cape François and other French ports who managed a steady flow of traffic.[37]

Curaçao ranked second only to Jamaica in New York City's West Indian trade. And New York was Curaçao's most important North American connection during the Seven Years' War, a particularly busy time for the island's commerce. The ties to New York ran deep, the close and long-standing relationship rooted in a common Dutch past and the eclectic character of New York commerce. At various times, the trading community at the port of Willemstad included Crugers, Cuylers, Depeysters, Franklins, Gouverneurs, Livingstons, Van Cortlandts, Van Ransts, Wallaces, and Waltons, all prominent New York mercantile names. During the war years, the partnership of Nicholas and Isaac Gouverneur, of New York and Curaçao, was particularly

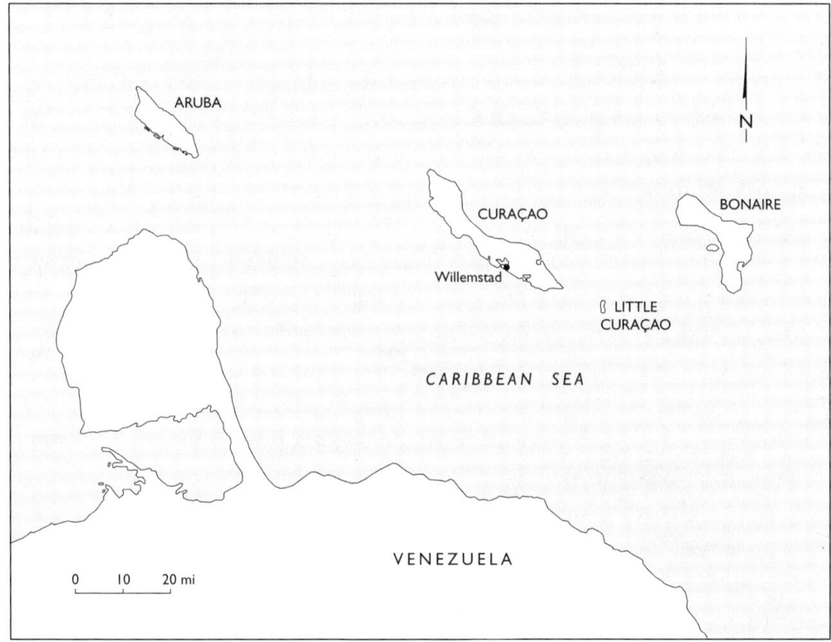

Curaçao and the Spanish Main

active. As one pamphleteer noted, "The merchants of New York have gotten their estates by the Curaçao Trade."[38]

Like the roadstead at Orange Bay on Saint Eustatius, Willemstad was open to ships of all nations. But trading vessels approached and departed with caution. In October 1756, a New York mariner reported seeing a half-dozen French sloops lying at Curaçao "afraid to stir out of port, being told that the seas swarmed with English privateers."[39]

The hazards came from both sides. In January 1757, Balthazar Kipp, a New York ship captain, lost his schooner to a French privateer "under the command of the cannon of the forts of Curaçao." Occasionally, privateer captains on both sides were jailed at Willemstad in retaliation for depredations against neutral shipping.[40]

Neutral Denmark likewise had a presence in the wartime Caribbean. Saint Croix, Saint Thomas, and Saint John in the Danish Virgin Islands were tiny sugar islands in the Lesser Antilles where British subjects occasionally settled "upon the invitation and the encouragements offered them by the Danes." As naturalized Danish citizens, resident English, Scottish, Irish, and

North American merchants traded directly with the French islands or indirectly through the Spanish free port of Monte Cristi in Santo Domingo. Although the Dutch islands far outstripped the Danish in financial resources and commercial expertise, Saint Croix, particularly, was a source of supply to the French throughout the war, and a touch point for New York vessels active in indirect commerce.[41]

New Yorkers were concentrated at the port of Christiansted, on the northeastern coast of the island, and the group included familiar names such as Beekman, Cruger, and Aspenwall. But the best-known New York firm was Kortright and Lawrence, a partnership established in 1756. Like other New York enterprises in the neutral islands, Kortright and Lawrence exchanged bread, flour, and salted provisions for "foreign" sugar, most of it destined for transshipment to the European continent. "I propose shipping you something in every vessel from hence," wrote a correspondent from home in April 1756, "if you give me proper encouragement."[42]

Ships were frequently captured within sight of the Danish harbors. Saint Croix and Saint Thomas, in particular, were magnets for privateers. In October 1756, according to the *New-York Mercury,* "five French privateers were then lying at the island of St. Thomas." The French seized anything without a French passport, and, with few French merchantmen at sea after 1757, British privateers—particularly those based in the West Indies—took a keen interest in every North American vessel carrying "foreign" sugar.[43]

New York City's trade with the Dutch and Danish Islands was typically part of a flow of commerce, rather than a distinct activity, and continued so throughout the war. This is illustrated by the voyage of the snow *Recovery* in the spring and summer of 1760. It was the property of William and Jacob Walton of New York and Waddell Cunningham's firm Greg and Cunningham of New York and Belfast.

The 69-ton vessel left New York City in March carrying flaxseed and lumber to Belfast, where it loaded Irish salted provisions and linen, along with a variety of British manufactured goods suitable for the French West Indies. The owners intended to exchange most of the cargo for "foreign" sugar and coffee at Monte Cristi after a brief stop at Curaçao.[44]

A few days after departing Ireland, the *Recovery* picked up the Canary Current below the Madeira Islands. The vessel then steered southwest until it met the North Equatorial Current, which carried it south of Barbados and west along the northern coast of South America. The captain, Robert Castle, had orders to steer for "the Margaritas on the Spanish Main," and there follow a course along the coast of Venezuela "till you think you can fetch

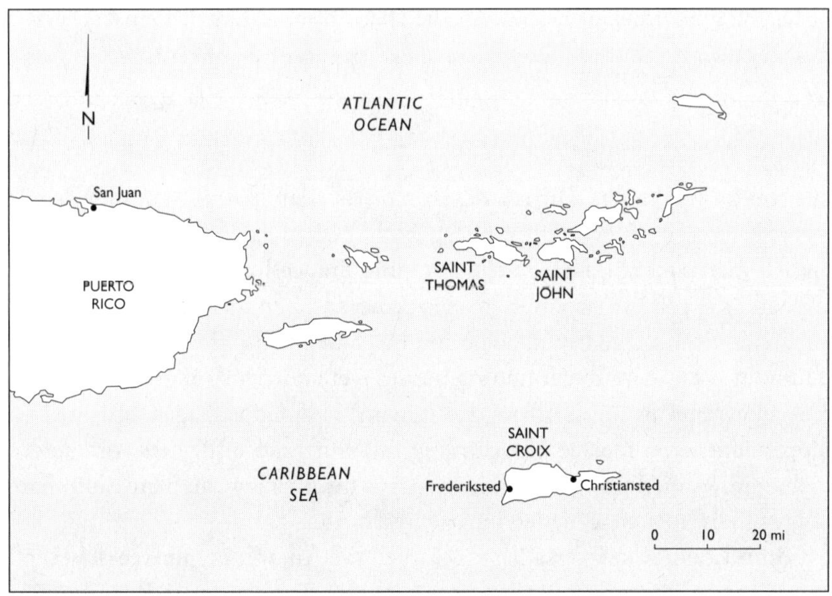

Danish Virgin Islands: Saint Thomas, Saint John, and Saint Croix

Curaçao without running [the] risk of falling to Leeward" and missing the island altogether.[45]

Upon making the island of Margarita, Castle moved through waters patrolled by Dutch privateers and Spanish Guarda Costas protecting local shipping from the depredations of English and French privateers. When it reached Curaçao, the *Recovery* dropped anchor in Saint Anna Bay, seventy days after its departure from the north of Ireland. The snow's owners had instructed Captain Castle to put the cargo in the hands of Isaac Gouverneur. "If [he] can sell it for cash, and to advantage," they said, "receive cash from him for what he sells, and proceed with it, and the remainder of your cargo, to Monte Cristi." Prices were low at Willemstad, and Gouverneur sold all of *Recovery*'s beef and about half its herring and tallow, articles in demand on the sugar plantations of Saint-Domingue.[46]

On August 27, *Recovery* cleared customs at Curaçao, weighed anchor, and began to work its way north toward the Mona Passage separating Hispaniola and Puerto Rico on a course for Monte Cristi Bay. The snow was crossing the Caribbean Sea at the height of the hurricane season, defying the collected wisdom of experienced mariners and London underwriters. But Captain Castle had a more pressing concern. Since the declaration of war four years earlier, merchantmen of every nation had become open targets for naval vessels and privateers in the most heavily patrolled waters of the West Indies.[47]

Just weeks before the British declaration of war in 1756, Antoine-Louis Rouillé, the French foreign minister, had brushed aside the dangers facing French merchant shipping in the Atlantic. France had a powerful navy, he said, and the privateer crews were aggressive and hungry, more than a match for the British. There would be no need to hide behind the flags of neutrals. Behind this facade, French trading houses were quietly strengthening ties to correspondents in Amsterdam, Rotterdam, and Copenhagen prepared to supplement, even replace, the carrying trade of France. And as commerce-raiding intensified from the summer of 1756 through 1757, an increasing share of French cargoes were loaded into neutral bottoms.[48]

Both London and Versailles monitored the Atlantic commerce of neutral powers. Spanish neutrality—a concern of the highest priority to British policy makers—challenged the forbearance of the Royal Navy while presenting unparalleled opportunities to North American merchants. The Dutch and Danes were subject to continual interference, however.[49]

The relation between the Dutch Republic—more properly, the United Provinces of the Netherlands—and Great Britain was the more complex of the two. The Anglo-Dutch Treaty of 1674 upheld the free movement of Dutch ships, but that of 1678 required that the United Provinces come to England's aid in the event of war. However, the Dutch were reluctant to enter into a conflict with France. In consequence, the British were "determined to show no respect to their flag, and not to allow it to cover French effects," according to the Prussian minister in London in August 1755, "still less [to allow] that the Dutch should freely trade with the French."[50]

In his declaration of war, George II had warned citizens "of what nation soever" that any vessel carrying "soldiers, arms, powder, ammunition, or other contraband goods" to any territory of the French king, "shall be condemned as good and lawful prize." So much for neutral rights and the doctrine of "free ships, free goods." In addition, Britain had asserted the doctrine of continuous voyage as a means of extending its prohibition to goods transshipped through Saint Eustatius, Curaçao, and other neutral islands.[51]

France, predictably, had responded by insisting that neutral shipping must not be put in the service of its adversaries. "Every power at war is naturally attentive to prevent its enemies from carrying on a free trade under the protection of neutral colors," declared the *Mémoire Instructif,* "delivered by the Court of France to the States General of the United Provinces" in the summer of 1756. "As the Hollanders are neutral in the present war," threatened the French in thinly veiled language, "it is their interest to conform to the regulations of France."[52]

The Dutch were thus in an impossible position. From the British they risked destruction of their commerce at sea; from the French they faced the possibility of invasion through porous borders that were indefensible against the armies of Louis XV.[53]

Perhaps it was not disingenuous for the French to insist on strict neutrality in the early weeks of the war. France still had a merchant fleet in the Atlantic and was not yet dependent on Dutch and Danish intermediaries. From the British perspective, however, the neutral shipping and entrepôt services provided by the Dutch and Danes had the potential of turning the war on its head. "What signifies our being masters at sea," wrote a London businessman early in the conflict, "if we shall not have liberty to stop ships from serving our enemy?"[54]

British public opinion demanded that the French be deprived of the protection of neutral flags. But this meant abandoning the Anglo-Dutch Treaty of 1674 and risking an enlargement of the war. The solution came in the form of "the Rule of 1756," the British assertion that a trade prohibited in peacetime could not be allowed in a time of war.[55]

"All the European nations exclude foreigners from their American colonies," wrote Lord Hardwick, the Lord Chancellor, in September 1756. "The question is whether England shall suffer [the Dutch and the Danes] to trade thither in time of war, without seizure, when the French themselves will not suffer them to trade thither, in time of peace, on that very account." In a stroke, Great Britain set down a sweeping dictum that took on the force of international law.[56]

New York's pragmatic governor, Sir Charles Hardy, was determined to deprive the French of the cover of neutral flags. Dutch treaty rights, loopholes in the laws governing British commerce, and the uncertain legal status of the New York statutes prohibiting trade with the French were of secondary concern to Hardy. A career naval officer, he demanded results. There was little he could do outside of his own jurisdiction, but he could ensure that New York, at least, did nothing to assist the enemy. "The French islands must be greatly distressed if we keep our provisions at home," he wrote in the summer of 1756.

And under his leadership the province of New York would set a proper example. "I took some pains on this point this spring," he told the Board of Trade.[57]

On May 22, 1756—based on an informer's tip—New York attorney general William Kempe had brought charges against Samuel Stilwell for trading with the enemy through the neutral islands, the first prosecution under New York's July 1755 statute prohibiting trade with the French. The case concerned the shipment of flour and bread that Stilwell and his partner John Burroughs had sent to Saint Eustatius aboard the *Catherine.* The sloop had not cleared customs, nor had Stilwell taken out the provisions bonds required under New York's Act to Prevent Exports of Provisions and Other Goods from New York to the French.[58]

Stilwell pleaded not guilty and published a string of affidavits in his defense. "It has been frequently reported, that since the commencement of the present operations against the French, I have exported provisions from hence, to some one or other of the [neutral] islands in the West-Indies, . . . for the use of the subjects of the French king," Stilwell told newspaper readers in New York. But, he insisted, he was an honorable man who, though "requested by a French gentleman, to export provisions to the island of St. Eustatia," had "absolutely refused to enter into a trade which he thought prejudicial to the interest of his country."[59]

The government was unmoved, however, "the defendant, Mr. Stilwell, having long, it seems, carried on this collusive and destructive practice," as Kempe told the court. At his trial in October a New York jury found Stilwell guilty of "putting flour and bread on board a vessel with intent to transport the same out of the colony, before the master or owner had entered into bond as directed by an Act of Assembly." He was briefly imprisoned pending payment of a fine of £500 (New York currency).[60]

Stilwell's troubles worsened. On September 13, shortly before the case of the *Catherine* went to trial, he was rearrested and jailed, charged with "a high misdemeanor in furnishing the King's enemies with provisions." Stilwell was accused of giving aid and comfort to one Monsieur Grael, a French ship captain who had brought a vessel loaded with West Indian produce from Cape François into New York Bay. Hardy—concerned about the infiltration of enemy agents and spies into the city—had begun rounding up French nationals, and the government accused Stilwell of hiding Grael in his home.[61]

According to Stilwell, who was released on £10,000 bail (New York currency), Grael had been on his way to New London when he entered New

York harbor in distress. At his hearing in January 1757, Stilwell told the court that he had provided the Frenchman with barreled beef and other supplies (including two ducks) out of a "motive of compassion joined with a sense of honor." Although "imprudence and misapprehension may have led him into some deviations from the letter of the law," Stilwell admitted, he had not "knowingly act[ed] contrary to the principles and obligations of a loyal and dutiful subject." His secretive behavior, he argued, had been "rather indiscreet than criminal." Stilwell having confessed, Attorney General Kempe called for a small fine, "whereupon the court set a fine of thirteen shillings and four pence on the defendant, and ordered that he be discharged."[62]

Shortly after Stilwell's arrest, Hardy alerted his superiors in London to the huge flow of provisions from North America and Ireland into the French West Indies and Canada through neutral islands in the Caribbean. The New York governor was frustrated by the lack of intercolonial and Irish cooperation in dealing with the problem and urged strong action at the center of government.[63]

"What you have thrown out, with regard to Ireland, and the West India islands, will be immediately taken into consideration," wrote Henry Fox, the Cabinet official responsible for the American affairs, "but I fear, meet with great difficulty in the execution." In September 1756, the government ordered an embargo in Ireland, but its effectiveness was undermined by Irish politicians who cast it as heavy-handed British interference in their nation's commerce. "The apprehension that [Ireland's trade with the French] may not be entirely put a stop to, should be no reason for the provision colonies, not following the good example you have set them," Fox told Hardy.[64]

A month later the Board of Trade approved a strict embargo in colonial ports on all vessels carrying provisions, except "to any other of His Majesty's colonies or plantations." It went into effect in New York City at the end of December 1756 and was accompanied by steep fines and penal bonds of £1,000 or £2,000, depending on the size of the ship, to force compliance. The American provisions embargo reflected Fox's determination to curb trade with the enemy in a war that was going badly for the British. The measure was necessary, according to the *New-York Gazette*, "to prevent the French getting such large supplies of provisions for their colonies and troops in America as they have hitherto obtained through the channel of the Dutch islands."[65]

In March 1757, with the provisions embargo in force, Lord Loudoun imposed a general embargo "on all vessels whatsoever outward bound" from any of the British-American ports. The British commander, in the midst of assembling an expeditionary force against the French fortress at Louisbourg, was determined to keep flour, salted provisions, and other vital goods out of the hands of the French. Loudoun's action, according to Benjamin Franklin, "deranged all our mercantile operations, and distressed our trade by a long embargo . . . on pretense of keeping supplies from being obtained by the enemy." The general embargo had the effect of beating down provisions prices to the benefit of the government, but it failed in its stated purpose. Blanket embargoes were ruinous to commercial interests. Even the provisions embargo had not been intended to continue through the end of the war.[66]

In January 1757, the Board of Trade, "upon consideration of the prejudice arising to His Majesty's service from the enemy's obtaining supplies of provisions" from British-American ports, had introduced a bill into the House of Commons that would—for the duration of the war—prohibit the exportation of all grain, flour, bread, and salted provisions "from any of His Majesty's colonies or plantations in America," except to Great Britain, Ireland, and other British colonies in America. The legislation moved swiftly toward passage. The bill was presented to the House of Commons on January 19, debated on January 27, amended February 2, and passed on February 7. Approval in the House of Lords came just a week later, and the Flour Act (also known as the Provisions Act) of 1757 received the royal assent on Tuesday, February 15.[67]

A copy of this "severe act of Parliament with regard to shipping off of provisions," so described by Alexander Colden at the customhouse, arrived in New York City on July 9. The Governor's Council immediately lifted the provisions embargo (the general embargo had been lifted on June 21), and two days later, on July 11, the Flour Act was published in the *New-York Gazette*. To force compliance, shippers were required to take out onerous provisions bonds —"in treble the value of such commodities"—and violators faced heavy fines.[68]

The Flour Act of 1757 was the sole piece of parliamentary legislation directed at Britons trading with the enemy during the Seven Years' War. If it was to be effective, the law would require broad support on both sides of the Atlantic. But the restrictions and penalties contained in the act applied only to colonial America. Cargoes dispatched from Great Britain and Ireland were unaffected. The discriminatory character of the act was immediately apparent. The ill-conceived legislation was one of the great blunders of the eighteenth-century British Parliament. Before a decade had passed, there would be others.[69]

In the early months of 1757, New York privateers waged their own war against neutral shipping. Disregarding the rights of the Dutch guaranteed by the Treaty of 1674, Lewis Morris, the elderly judge of the New York court of vice-admiralty, condemned nearly every captured neutral vessel brought before him. That most of these condemnations would later be reversed on appeal was of no concern in the heady days of the privateer war.[70]

In the West Indies, the interdictions of hungry British warships and privateers were making it ever more difficult to run the gauntlet to Saint Eustatius, Curaçao, Saint Croix, and Saint Thomas. Ships got through, of course, but the cost of doing business with the French through that channel undermined its advantages.[71]

With the navy's success, the handsome British warships at anchor off the tip of Manhattan must have seemed ever more inviting to Governor Hardy. From the parapet of Fort George, when gentle breezes picked up the clang of a watch bell or the chantey of sailors around a capstan, he must have pined for the congenial wooden world he had known since childhood.

Charles Hardy had been bred in a navy family for service on a quarter-deck, not in a political cockpit. He longed to be relieved of his responsibilities as governor and returned to shipboard command. He had begun to hint—perhaps more than hint—as much to his superiors in London in the late summer of 1756.[72]

The strongest candidate to replace him, Lieutenant-Governor James DeLancey—no longer a spokesman for the loyal opposition in the New York General Assembly—would face the daunting challenge of harnessing the fragmented politics of his colony behind the efforts of the British military in the darkest hours of the war. Under DeLancey, there would be no need to bother the ministry with the indiscretions of New York commerce, especially when culprits were so easy to find in Rhode Island and Connecticut, colonies already suspect for their independent ways. With Hardy out of the picture, doing business with the enemy would become just one more item in a long list of concerns facing the new administration.[73]

The ministry in London finally responded to Hardy's request for reassignment. On June 2, 1757, in a ceremony in the Council Chamber at Fort George, Rear Admiral Sir Charles Hardy presented James DeLancey, the colony's most powerful political figure, with a commission to serve once again as lieutenant-governor of the province of New York. Toasts were drunk to the king, the commanding general, the admiral, the lieutenant-governor, and the success of British arms in the forthcoming struggle against the French. The affable naval officer bid farewell to colleagues and friends and worked late into the night wrapping up what business he could. As commander of naval operations, Hardy would now join the British expeditionary force gathering in New York Bay for the campaign against the fortress at Louisbourg on Cape Breton Island.[74]

At midnight, Hardy's barge crossed the choppy water off Manhattan to HMS *Nightingale,* riding at anchor in the Hudson River. By 4 A.M. the last of the admiral's baggage had come aboard. A fifteen-gun salute echoed through the awakening city as the warship moved toward the Narrows and lower New York Bay where it found "His Majesty's ships *Sutherland, Kennington* and *Ferret* sloop with 79 sail of transports." By the following day, the admiral's stores had been transferred to the 50-gun HMS *Sutherland,* and his broad blue pennant flew high atop its mainmast.[75]

British commanders were impatient to be on their way. But an air of foreboding hung over the assembling Louisbourg expedition. Aboard *Sutherland,* Admiral Hardy, Lord Loudoun, and Major-General James Abercrombie, Loudoun's second-in-command, agonized over their predicament. Although it was late in the campaigning season, immediate departure would bring disaster if they should cross the path of a powerful French squadron that was thought to be sailing to the relief of Louisbourg. The squadron, composed of five ships of the line and their accompanying frigates under the command of Joseph de Bauffremont, had been sighted at Saint-Domingue in April and May. The British fleet of more than 100 ships carrying close to 6,000 men would be protected by just five escorts with a combined firepower of 120 guns. Characteristic of Loudoun, caution prevailed. On June 6—a Monday evening—Hardy sent HMS *Kennington* and *Ferret* on broad sweeps, one to the north, the other to the south, to reconnoiter the seas through which the expedition would pass.[76]

Waiting for their return, Charles Hardy began his final letter from New York to the Board of Trade in London. Nothing of what he wrote in the privacy of *Sutherland*'s great cabin on June 14, 1757, dealt with the Louisbourg campaign. He made no mention of politics, the state of finances, or the defense of the province. Instead, he voiced a single concern: supplies badly needed by British land and naval forces were being siphoned off by the French.[77]

The Royal Navy's interdiction of Dutch and Danish trading vessels and the close monitoring of North Americans doing business with Saint Eustatius, Curaçao, Saint Croix, and Saint Thomas had been intended to bring an end to this activity. In spite of Hardy's efforts and the occasional cooperation of other colonial governors, merchants in British America continued to ignore the king's declaration of war and statutes meant to curb commerce with the French. Worse still, the trade had taken on a more ominous and brazen form.

CHAPTER FOUR

Mountmen

HMS *Sutherland* strained at its anchorage as Admiral Hardy and Lord Loudoun awaited news of the whereabouts of Bauffremont's squadron. Early in June 1757, two sailors taken by a navy press gang off an incoming Rhode Island sloop had been brought aboard *Sutherland* for questioning. In their interrogation, they disclosed details of their vessel's trade with the French enemy through an obscure Spanish port on Hispaniola. Their story corroborated that of Martin Garland, an Irishman aboard a New York privateer, the brig *Hawke*, recently arrived from a cruise in the western Caribbean.[1]

Garland had been on the crew of a Spanish sloop that called at Cape François in the autumn of 1756. Along with other British and Irish subjects, he had been arrested by French authorities on suspicion of being a spy. During his confinement, Garland learned that North American vessels regularly entered the harbor at Cape François manned by Spanish crews, flying Spanish colors, and carrying Spanish passports. The American ships, he was informed, brought provisions and other articles that were in short supply at the Cape to exchange for French sugar, molasses, indigo, coffee, and cotton.

The North American cargoes were arriving from Monte Cristi Bay, a neutral Spanish shipping point about sixty miles to the east on the north coast of Hispaniola. At Monte Cristi, some American goods were transferred onto Spanish coasting vessels. In other cases, resident British merchants put Spanish captains and crews aboard the North American ships, which were then taken to Fort Dauphin, Cape François, Port au Prince, and other French ports while the American captains or supercargoes traveled overland to look after the affairs of their vessels. According to Garland, the man who managed this business at the town of San Fernando de Monte Cristi "is one Gambauld a Frenchman, who has a wife and a family at New York."

In April 1757, Garland had escaped from the jail at Cape François and, passing for a Spaniard, had secured a berth aboard a French schooner awaiting a convoy for Bordeaux. From his new vantage point, the Irishman discovered that shortages of equipment and supplies were so severe that French warships were having difficulty putting to sea. Garland saw, for example, the mast from a chartered Newport sloop taken out to be used as a bowsprit on a man of war, "which the king of France was to pay for," as well as the charges the shipper would incur until the sloop "could be fitted out again for Rhode Island."[2]

On May 4 the convoy of twenty-seven French merchantmen had departed the Cape for Bordeaux. A few hours later, Garland's schooner was taken by the *Hawke* and sent to Bermuda. But before the vessels separated, Garland had revealed his identity, gained his release, and joined the crew of the privateer. After two days, the privateer *Hawke* attacked a rich French merchantman—"deep loaded with sugar, coffee, cotton, &c. and . . . between 80 and 100,000 wt. of indigo." Following "a hot engagement of some hours," the *Hawke* escorted the prize to New York, where it entered the Sandy Hook channel on May 27. Not long afterward, Martin Garland appeared before Sir Charles.[3]

All of this Admiral Hardy reported to the Board of Trade in his final letter from New York in mid-June 1757. With him at sea aboard HMS *Sutherland*—after HMS *Kennington* and *Ferret* had found no trace of Bauffremont's squadron—was Lord Loudoun, commander of the British expedition against Louisbourg, who revealed his frustrations in a letter to the earl of Cumberland: "The truth is no rule or law has any force in this country, and all of them, . . . have carried on a trade with the enemy the whole time. They take clearances to the British islands and give security; they trade notwithstanding with the Dutch and Spaniards at Hispaniola; . . . and now that the embargo is off, the French will be supplied with everything they want in spite of all the regulations." Hardy's efforts to block trade with the French through the neutral islands had done little more than force commerce into a new channel.[4]

The scale of New York City's involvement with Monte Cristi was masked by technical compliance with the Flour Act's requirement that colonial exporters post provisions bonds at their customhouses to guarantee that their goods reached only British-controlled destinations. The financial strains created by these bonds—"in treble the value of such commodities"—had the effect of diverting cargoes destined for Monte Cristi to nearby ports in Connecticut and New Jersey (even Rhode Island) where customs enforcement was lax and false clearances to British West Indian ports were readily available. By this means, reported a British officer, "the master is enabled to show a certificate, that the provisions, were landed agreeable to his bond."[5]

Beginning in 1757, shipments to New Haven, New London, Perth Amboy, and Newport steadily grew as suppression of New York City's trade with the French through the neutral islands took hold. In the twelve months ending October 1, 1758, New Haven took just 114 barrels of New York flour. The following year, shipments exceeded 2,000 barrels. And in the year ending October 1, 1760—when the Monte Cristi trade was in full bloom—New Yorkers shipped more than 10,000 barrels of flour through Long Island Sound to New Haven, with New London, Perth Amboy, and Newport taking equally impressive amounts. Not everything found its way to the French, of course, but most of it did.[6]

Trade between British North America and Spanish Monte Cristi—known to contemporaries as "The Mount"—was not illegal. Spain was a neutral power at peace with Great Britain. Throughout the war, vessels regularly cleared customs in New York for the Spanish West Indian port carrying a broad array of goods. Under the terms of the Flour Act, however, it was illegal for shippers in British America to send provisions to any market outside the British Empire. (The restrictions did not apply to merchants in Great Britain and Ireland, several of whom traded in partnership with correspondents in New York.)[7]

If exporters cleared their cargoes according to the terms of British navigation laws (giving due regard to the Flour Act), did business exclusively with Spanish merchants at Monte Cristi (avoiding contact with Frenchmen), and scrupulously maintained the fiction that they were purchasing Spanish West Indian produce rather than French, they were safe. But that was a fine line to walk and explains why the Monte Cristi trade took a variety of forms.[8]

Cautious participants preferred to send cash and British manufactured goods, such as linens and hardware, in exchange for "Spanish" sugar, "there being no law or act of Parliament prohibiting this trade." Men of this stripe—respectable New Yorkers like David Van Horne—persuaded themselves that the Mount trade was "vastly beneficial to the nation, and would undoubtedly, if they were fully acquainted with it, be greatly encouraged by them." Whether it was beneficial or not, Van Horne and his associates recommended "dispatch . . . in the strongest manner," in their instructions to the captain of their snow *London* in September 1759.[9]

A less cautious—but not entirely reckless—arrangement is exemplified by a busy Mount-trading sloop owned by John Bogert, Jr., the New York City alderman who had played a role in the punishment of the informer George Spencer in November 1759. In 1760, Bogert's younger brother, Captain Nicholas Bogert, routinely loaded flour, bread, beef, and other provisions for New Haven, where he fictitiously entered his cargoes and purchased clearances for British West Indian ports.

Returning from the Mount, Bogert would bring his French West Indian sugar, rum, and coffee to a Connecticut port or to Perth Amboy, New Jersey, where he procured customs documents declaring that his cargo consisted of prize goods taken by one of the privateers of that port—"though perhaps no privateer ever belonged to or sailed from thence," wrote a cynic. Paperwork in hand, Bogert would then take his sloop the short distance to New York City, legally entering at the customhouse. In three such voyages in 1760, the Bogerts shipped over 1,600 barrels of flour to Monte Cristi, returning with about 400 hogsheads of sugar.[10]

The brig *Sea Flower* of New York took a more audacious approach. Its principal owner was Samuel Stilwell, who had been imprisoned and fined in 1756 for shipping bread and flour to the French through Saint Eustatius. Now more cautious, he sent his brig *Sea Flower* to Monte Cristi in 1759 and 1760 loaded with lumber, coal, grindstones, and assorted dry goods such as linens and lace—all legal exports. But buried deep in the hold, beneath the lumber, coal, and grindstones, were the barrels of flour and salted provisions that constituted the most sought-after cargoes in the trade. A shrewd businessman, Stilwell sent his sugar, coffee, indigo, and rum to the German port of Hamburg, where prices were better than in New York, a city awash in French West Indian produce.[11]

A striking feature of New York's Mount trade is the prominence of the city's commercial, political, and social elite: men with names like Bayard, Chambers, Cruger, Gouverneur, Jones, Harison, Kortwright, Livingston, Marston, Van Dam, Van Horne, and Walton. Figures close to the lieutenant-governor, the Governor's Council and provincial assembly, and the Supreme Court, city hall, and customhouse were deeply involved. Even military contractors, firms such as Walter and Samuel Franklin of New York, which supplied the British forces, shipped provisions to Monte Cristi. "We are well informed," wrote a South Carolinian after the seizure of the Franklins' sloop *Sarah* in 1758, that "the French, who were during the late embargo almost starving throughout Hispaniola, are now plentifully supplied."[12]

Well over one hundred New York City merchants did business with the

French through Monte Cristi. This does not include ship captains, supercargoes, countinghouse staff, warehousemen, carters, and the myriad of others involved in the busy work of the port. Activity on this scale had been inconceivable during the administration of Governor Hardy when Samuel Stilwell was arrested for spiriting 180 barrels of flour and 50 casks of bread out of the city under cover of darkness.[13]

The trickle of 1756 had become the flood of 1759. Lieutenant-Governor James DeLancey was too close personally—and politically—to the trading establishment in New York to do more than express concern, shift the problem onto the shoulders of his collector of customs Archibald Kennedy, and blame Rhode Islanders, whose lack of regard for king and country went unquestioned.[14]

Among those who embraced the Mount trade, one group stood out: New York City's Irish merchants. Others participated, of course—the Dutch, French Huguenot, Scottish, and Jewish communities were well represented. But the Irish were a major force. This can be explained in part by the longstanding commercial ties between Ireland and France. Irish firms in New York became adept at getting around the Flour Act by shipping Irish salted provisions—the best in the Atlantic world—direct to Monte Cristi from Dublin, Cork, and Belfast.[15]

Expatriate Irish merchants also benefited from their close ties to New York's political, social, and economic elite. George Folliot, for example, a Derry native who emigrated to the city in 1752, married the daughter of George Harison, a high-ranking customs official and the brother-in-law of Alexander Colden, son of Cadwallader Colden, president of the Governor's Council and later lieutenant-governor.[16]

James Thompson, who arrived from Newry in 1748, married Catharine Walton, perhaps the city's wealthiest young heiress, whom the *New-York Mercury* singled out for her beauty, charm, and intelligence:

> A lady blooming with every noble pride,
> Meet to adorn, or grace her consort's side;
> Truth, innocence and wit, mildly expressed,
> And sweet good nature, innates of her breast;
> These leagued with youth, endear her mental store,
> Their hands were joined;—neither demanded more.

One of eight children, Catharine had been reared by her politically powerful uncle, William Walton, Sr., following the death of her father in 1745. Her sister Mary was the wife of Lewis Morris, Jr., son of the judge of New York's court of vice-admiralty and a rising political star, and her brother William (named in honor of his uncle) married the daughter of James DeLancey. William and another brother, Jacob, Jr., were deeply involved in the city's trade with the French.[17]

But Folliot and Thompson were not the only Irish traders to have married well. As a group the city's Irish merchants were young and ambitious, determined to make their mark, and they had come to New York to get rich. Thomas White, a Dubliner; Hugh Wallace, a Waterford man; Thomas Lynch of Galway, and John Torrans of Derry all found brides among the city's wealthiest and best-connected families.[18]

As George Spencer was being humiliated on the streets of New York in November 1759, a 140-ton brig lay at a wharf on the east side of Manhattan taking on a cargo for Monte Cristi. The owners—Waddell Cunningham, William Kelly, and Samuel Stilwell—each played a role in the conspiracy to silence the man threatening the city's trade with the French. On Thursday, December 6, with the informer safe in the New York City Jail, the *Charming Polly* cleared customs for Kingston, Jamaica.[19]

The following day, in "the hard frost that [had] set in," Captain Nicholas Horton steered his deep-laden vessel through the Narrows, past Sandy Hook, and into the Atlantic. The twenty-nine-year-old Dublin native drove the *Charming Polly* hard along a 1,600-mile route, sailing southeast in the direction of the Greater Antilles but well west of Bermuda. Horton took advantage of seasonal northerlies as he pushed past the Caicos Islands just north of Hispaniola. Then, instead of continuing south toward Kingston through the Mona Passage separating Hispaniola and Puerto Rico, the *Charming Polly* swung west along Santo Domingo's northern coast, passed through waters made dangerous by reefs, outcroppings, and enemy privateers, and finally fetched up at Monte Cristi.[20]

Monte Cristi was an unlikely Atlantic seaport. There were "no keys, wharfs, or cranes of any kind by which goods may be landed or shipped," reported a British naval officer. On the beach stood a tiny village—home to a few fishermen and their families—containing "a guard house, three sutling huts [for the sale of provisions], and five sheds for coopers and carpenters to work under." During heavy rains, "this village is overflowed two feet deep and

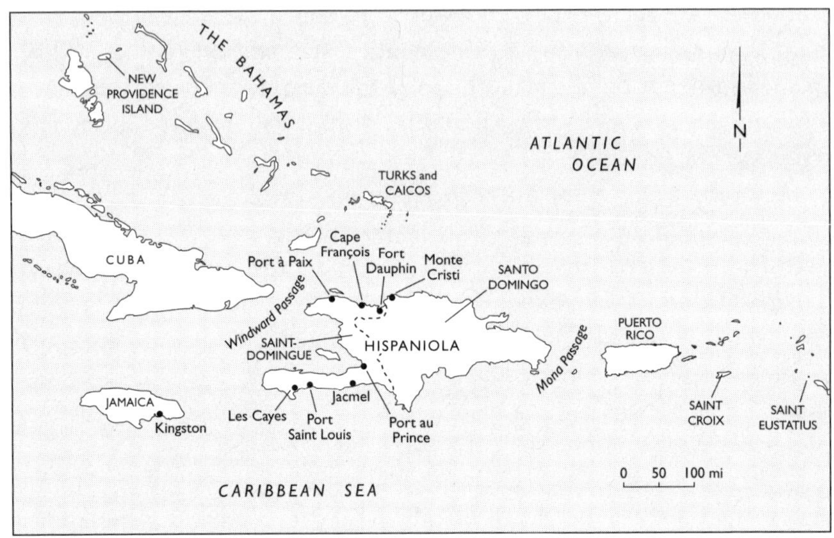

Hispaniola and the Greater Antilles

the country about it, for about five miles from east to west." Its most dramatic landmark is a massive rock known today as El Morro de Monte Cristi. The 900-foot mesa emerges out of the sea on land jutting into the Atlantic at the north end of Monte Cristi Bay. Named in 1493 by Christopher Columbus, who saw in the stone formation the face of Jesus Christ, it is visible from far out at sea. The height and size of the great rock are dramatized by the flat, stark barrenness of its setting.[21]

Eighteenth-century Santo Domingo (like its descendant, the Dominican Republic) was a land of climatic and geographic contrasts. Its eastern region was lush and tropical, with heavy rainfalls, impenetrable jungles, and exotic wildflowers. West of an imaginary line running from the mouth of the Nizao River on the south coast to Cape Isabella on the north, the climate became increasingly arid. In the far northwest, the area surrounding Monte Cristi Bay, desertlike conditions prevailed.[22]

This was a desolate but beautiful land of cloudless skies, scorching heat, cactus, mesquite, and tumbleweed, much like the American Southwest. Settlement in this inhospitable region was possible because the largest river in Santo Domingo, the Yaque del Norte, emptied fresh water into Monte Cristi Bay. This unlikely crossroad of commerce was situated just a few miles east of the border with French Saint-Domingue.[23]

During the Seven Years' War, Monte Cristi Bay was among the busiest shipping points in the Western Hemisphere. As many as 150 ships rode at anchor there at a single time. The broad, open bay had excellent anchoring ground, "well secured from the trade winds." But the reefs that protected the bay presented a hazard to mariners, as did the extraordinarily high surf. The shallowness of the water obliged trading ships to stand well off shore, subjecting them to the vagaries of weather and the depredations of enemy privateers.[24]

Just off El Morro stood "Englishman's Key," known today as Cayo Cabrita, a tiny island that served as a gathering point for some of the goods traded in the bay, though most never touched land. Above Monte Cristi, on higher ground about three miles inland, stood the larger town of San Fernando de Monte Cristi, the seat of Spanish regional authority. Here was the residence of "the officer of His Most Catholic Majesty" and a weakly defended fortress. Spain established the municipality in 1749 to halt encroachments by the French eastward along the northern coast of Hispaniola.[25]

Such was the seat of the official charged with overseeing commerce in the bay: Don Francisco de Cabrejas, "Lieutenant Colonel of the Militia, and Lieutenant Governor of Arms of the Town of San Fernando de Monte Cristi, and of the Territory thereof." Beyond his impressive title and seals attesting to the authority of the state, there was little evidence of imperial power in this shadeless desert town.[26]

In 1750, by royal dispensation, the Spanish Crown granted San Fernando de Monte Cristi the right to conduct trade for ten years with ships of all nations at peace with Spain. In spite of this, local agriculture remained primitive, and there was little evidence of sugar, coffee, or indigo production, the staple exports of Monte Cristi Bay. Indeed, there was little to suggest that Monte Cristi was a proper Atlantic seaport. There were "no tribunal of justice, no officers of customs or duties of any kind, to receive an account of the imports and exports made to and from this pretended free port," according to a report by the Royal Navy; "no royal registers kept; nor no house or office for transacting the public business; no settled merchants of any denomination whatever; no magazines, weighing houses, store houses, cellars, or conveniences of any kind; for the reception, preservation, and regulation of trade and commerce."[27]

Charming Polly arrived at Monte Cristi along with "the Norths, which blow here very strong in the latter part of the year." Set for a three-month visit, the brig anchored well off shore. Watches were relaxed, a few of the

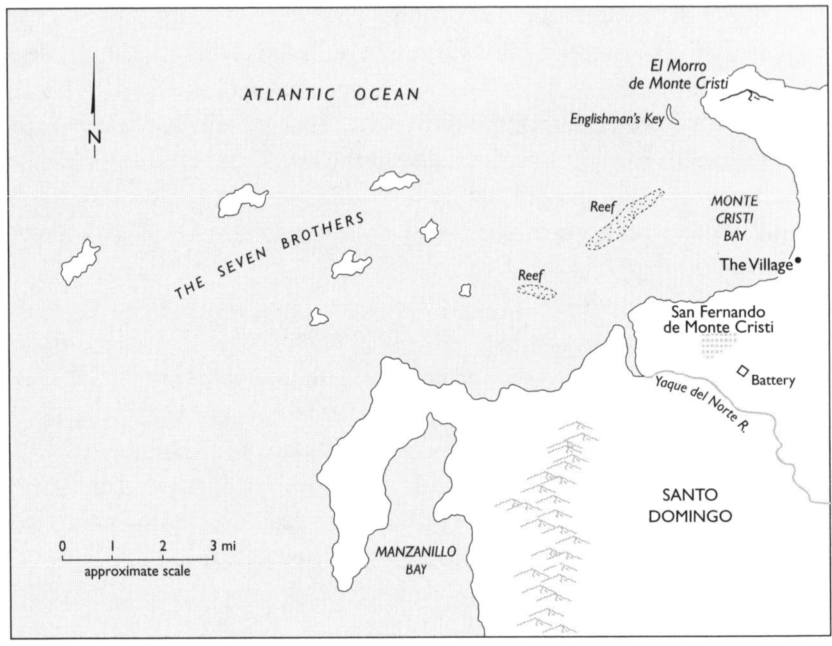

Monte Cristi Bay, c. 1760

sailors paid off and discharged, and repairs begun that would lessen the tedium of shipboard life. Shortly after *Charming Polly*'s arrival, its longboat brought Captain Horton through the choppy surf to the watering place at the head of the bay. From there he made his way inland to San Fernando de Monte Cristi, where he reported *Charming Polly*'s arrival, paid the entry fee, declared his incoming cargo, and received permission "to trade with His Most Catholic Majesty's subjects residing there."[28]

Monte Cristi Bay was a floating city. The coasting vessels, merchantmen, privateers, and occasional British warships that crowded into the bay housed as many as six thousand souls representing all the trading peoples of the Atlantic. North America accounted for the largest number of ships. Those from Massachusetts specialized in fish, an important component in the diet of slaves at Saint-Domingue. Vessels from Rhode Island and Connecticut carried more mixed cargoes, some of which included flour shipped from or taken aboard in New York. Philadelphia was also active in the trade, as was Charleston, much of whose Mount trade was conducted in concert with New

York merchants like Nathaniel Marston and Waddell Cunningham. New York City had a hand in as much as 40 percent of the North American trade at Monte Cristi, as well as a good deal of what came from Ireland.[29]

Commerce at Monte Cristi was a thinly veiled exchange of North American, Irish, British, and neutral European provisions, lumber, and "warlike stores"—along with slaves and a staggering variety of manufactured consumer goods—for the produce of the plantation economy of French Saint-Domingue. Spanish hides and other local goods played no significant role.[30]

A large share of the gold and silver being sent to North America by the British government to finance the war was also finding its way to Monte Cristi. "English provisions, are not sufficient to purchase French sugars," wrote an officer on the staff of army headquarters in New York. The balance was paid in specie. "Instead of returning to the mother country in payment for its produce, and manufactures, [it] is, by this iniquitous trade, transferred into the hands of Your Majesty's enemies," the Board of Trade told King George in August 1759.[31]

Resident agents—known as Mount merchants—conducted most of New York's trade at Monte Cristi, with no fewer than a dozen having "the management and direction of cargoes sent to that port." Some remained at Monte Cristi for just a few months, but many were there for long stretches between 1757 and Spain's entry into the war in early 1762.[32]

Captain Horton had orders to put *Charming Polly*'s cargo and a French prize—"in case you have the good luck to take [one]"—into the hands of Messrs. Gill and Amiel, "who will make more of her there than she will fetch at any other market." Gill and Amiel, active from 1758 through the summer of 1761, was the partnership of John Gill, an Irish merchant from New York, and John Amiel, a Frenchman with a wife in Boston. "John Gill does not reside on shore at Monte Cristi," reported a witness, "but stays afloat on board of a vessel, where he attends the loading of cargoes." He and other New York factors—men such as Richard Mercer, soon to marry Waddell Cunningham's sister Grace—spent most of their time aboard the trading vessels that rode in the bay.[33]

Gill, Amiel, Mercer, and other Mount merchants typically worked through Spanish intermediaries. Goods were sometimes loaded onto pack animals and carried overland to Fort Dauphin and Cape François, but the rough terrain rendered this option inconvenient and expensive. Cargoes were most often transferred from oceangoing vessels anchored in the bay onto single-masted Spanish sloops and luggers shuttling between Monte Cristi and nearby French ports, as well as to Port au Prince, Port Saint Louis, Les Cayes, and Jacmel, "which are the more distant."[34]

There were, according to one report, "60 or 70 families of fishermen who subsist by having large boats always ready to take out a ship or vessel's cargo and carry it to Cape François and return with sugar, coffee rum and molasses." A few Spanish traders speculated in French produce, which they collected on shore or at Englishman's Key. But most goods moved from vessel to vessel without ever touching land.[35]

Nature dictated the rhythm of commerce. The Monte Cristi coasters—forty or more shallops, sloops, and schooners, ranging from 15 to 30 tons each—made one round trip a day, and all had "Spanish colors hoisted," according to a witness. "They go in the morning with the land wind from Cape François to Monte Cristi and return in the afternoon with the sea breeze," wrote a British naval officer. The small ships passed between "reefs of rocks, some under water, some above" and the "Seven Brothers," treacherous outcroppings farther out to sea, staying as close to shore as possible to avoid the reef fields off Fort Dauphin and at the entryway to Cape François.[36]

Each coaster carried from 4 to 20 hogsheads of French produce, all of which was certified as Spanish by the governor of Monte Cristi after payment of one piece of eight per hogshead. Some vessels conveyed goods purchased in advance. Others trucked their wares from ship to ship in search of the highest bidder, with "people almost fighting for the sugars" when the bay was crowded with ships. But the risks and capital requirements of the sugar trade put it out of the range of most local dealers to do more than serve as intermediaries for French merchants at Fort Dauphin, Cape François, and Port au Prince. Except for the largest players, the availability of cash was critical in a trading environment that was incompatible with settled relationships and commercial credit.[37]

Since the beginning—in the most carefully hidden feature of the Monte Cristi trade—North American ship captains, supercargoes, and resident agents had been slipping across the border to do business with French merchants at Fort Dauphin and elsewhere. Such contact was in direct violation of the king's declaration of war. But sustained commerce depended upon mutually beneficial exchanges and amicable relationships between the citizens of warring powers. "Whatever you do," a New York captain was reminded in 1759, "do not give any offence to the Frenchman as our voyage depends on him."[38]

Eighteen months after Admiral Hardy broached the subject of Monte Cristi to his superiors in London, the Royal Navy finally took notice. Although the British succeeded in destroying the French carrying trade in the Caribbean, they appeared to be oblivious to Monte Cristi. This changed in January 1759 when Rear Admiral Thomas Cotes, commander of the British squadron at Port Royal, Jamaica, was informed by his sea officers that "the French at Cape François were supplied with provisions and plantation stores from North America by way of Monte Cristi." Cotes sent Arthur Usher, commander of the sloop of war *Viper*, into the bay to investigate.[39]

Admiral Cotes was dismayed by what he learned. "At present [the French] have plenty of everything by the way of Monte Cristi," he told the Admiralty. Without provisions and other articles from North America, "they could not fit out any privateers." And it was obvious that Spanish vessels calling at Monte Cristi Bay were in the service of France and that their owners expected little interference from the Royal Navy.[40]

The bay also attracted northern European neutrals. "The Dutch and Danes from St. Eustatius and St. Thomas now clear out for that port to avoid being seized by our cruisers," Cotes told the Admiralty. Some of this neutral shipping was secretly British. In 1760, for example, the Danish ship *Ravenes,* the quintessential mid-eighteenth-century transnational trading vessel, was under the management of Greg and Cunningham of New York and Hugh White and Company of Dublin. Even the Norwegian captain was a straw man. The *Ravenes*'s true commander—James McLaughlin, an Irish sea captain—had orders to proceed from Cork "to Monte Cristi, Port au Prince, the Cape or wherever you judge best."[41]

"There will be no possibility of putting a stop to this trade except we are permitted to seize the vessels in Monte Cristi Bay," Cotes insisted. When London replied with silence, he increased his patrols and began harassing Mount traders as they exited the bay. Wary of drawing Spain into the war, that was all he could do without hard evidence of British subjects doing business with the enemy or North Americans violating the Flour Act.[42]

Deprived of French merchant shipping on which to prey, British and colonial privateers became a regular sight in the traffic outside the bay. New York privateers, many of whose owners were heavily involved in trade with the French, targeted the Dutch and Danish competition at Monte Cristi, and—until the diplomatic repercussions became too great—Spanish competition as well.[43]

British West Indian privateers, particularly those from the port of Nassau on New Providence Island in the Bahamas, "cruise about Monte Cristi, and plunder any vessel that they meet with," according to a New Yorker at the Mount. The seizure of North American ships doing business with "our good friends the French" deepened the resentment independent-minded North Americans felt toward their British West Indian cousins. Inevitably, this led to reprisals, with a good many West Indian merchant vessels being carried into New York and other mainland ports.[44]

Even so, friendly privateers were an important feature of New York's Mount trade. When they could, vessels sailed home "under convoy of an English privateer, the commander of which was to have a considerable premium for conducting them safe to a certain latitude." North Americans took this a step further and entered into collusive captures—the capture of their own trading vessels by their own privateers or privateers hired for the occasion.[45]

This sleight of hand, impressive by any standard, deprived British warships and Nassau privateers of the right to make prizes of vessels departing Monte Cristi Bay loaded with French sugar, coffee, and indigo. Timing was everything, however, and the rule "first come, first served" applied. Whether the sham prizes ever appeared in vice-admiralty courts in New York and elsewhere is another matter.

Such collusive captures were common. In the autumn of 1760, for example, Stephen Snell, master of the schooner *Rose,* was among the New York ship captains ordered to remain at the Mount "till you have the convoy of some vessel that will take care of you." Help arrived in the form of the privateer sloop *Harlequin,* one of whose owners, Waddell Cunningham, had a stake in the schooner and her cargo. Snell and *Harlequin*'s commander worked out the details of a collusive capture.[46]

When *Rose* was ready to sail, *Harlequin* slipped out of Monte Cristi Bay "to wait in the offing." The following morning, *Rose* was formally taken and a member of the privateer's crew sent aboard to "take upon him the office of a prize master." This ensured that if the *Rose* were detained by a British warship or a Nassau privateer, it would be unable to claim the schooner as prize: the New York prize master would present a copy of his commission and demand his rights to the vessel he was carrying to a British port for condemnation before a court of vice-admiralty.[47]

Privateer commissions sometimes masked a vessel's true function. Such was the case of the privateer brig *Sally* of New York, also at the Mount in 1760. The commander, Morley Harison, was the brother of one of the privateer's owners, George Harison (the other was Thomas White). Earlier, another New York vessel, the schooner *Gideon* (owned by George Folliot, Samuel Stilwell, and Thomas White), had carried flour from New York to Fort Dauphin with no more protection than a clearance for Kingston, Jamaica, from New London, Connecticut. *Gideon*'s captain had spent six months at Fort Dauphin loading sugar and awaiting the arrival of his protector.

In September, *Sally* entered Monte Cristi Bay and the supercargo, Andrew Caldwell, traveled overland to Fort Dauphin to purchase sugar for water carriage to Monte Cristi and to arrange a collusive capture. A few days later, without firing a shot, Morley Harison seized the *Gideon* as it departed Fort Dauphin. He placed a prize crew aboard and carried the prize to nearby Monte Cristi Bay. Anchored close by its sister ship, the *Sally* took on 106 hogsheads of sugar and a few barrels of coffee. Then the two trading vessels waited for a break in the British patrols off the Mount to head north through the Keys and set a course for home.[48]

As Mount traders became more ingenious, British sea officers began questioning the intentions of every ship entering and departing the bay. Occasionally, they ignored their instructions to respect Spanish neutrality. In late 1760, for example, when three New York vessels "were chased by the men of war to windward of the Mount," the niceties of international diplomacy became a casualty of war. "It falling calm, the man of war sent their boats to board them," reported a witness, and one of the New Yorkers fired upon them. "A breeze sprung up, and they got into the Mount. The man of war followed, and sent ashore and demanded them."[49]

Most British commanders respected Spanish sovereignty, however. That—and limits on the capacity of the Jamaican squadron to monitor traffic—allowed a significant number of Mountmen to depart undetected. In March 1760, Captain Horton and the *Charming Polly* slipped out of Monte Cristi Bay and steered northwest through the Turks Island Passage. He then set a course for the Bay of Gibraltar, where he was to pick up orders and refit before heading into the Mediterranean. Documents signed by the lieutenant-governor in the "city of St. Fernando de Monte Cristi" certified that the sugar and indigo aboard *Charming Polly,* consigned to the firm of a Frenchwoman at Leghorn (the modern Italian port of Livorno), "were the effects of Spaniards, and of no other nation whatsoever."[50]

Charming Polly's exit coincided with steps by Philip François Bart, governor of Saint-Domingue, to expand trade with North America. In mid-February 1760, he issued orders that vessels bound for Monte Cristi were off-limits to French privateers swarming off Hispaniola. "I am credibly informed that flour and all sorts of provisions is 50 percent cheaper at Hispaniola than at Jamaica, and money plenty," wrote Admiral Cotes, "all occasioned by the trade to Monte Cristi and flags of truce."[51]

The huge flow of goods through Monte Cristi Bay—the principal venue for New York City's wartime trade with the French—continued to be a source of frustration at Port Royal. Despite misgivings over the legality of the Mount trade, the Royal Navy had little choice but to respect Spanish neutrality. Like it or not, Spain had to be kept out of the war. Far more odious, from the perspective of the admiral's mess or the quarterdecks of His Majesty's fighting ships patrolling off Hispaniola, was the thriving trade carried on by North Americans shamelessly entering the seaports of the enemy flying flags of truce.

CHAPTER FIVE

Flag-Trucers

During the summer of 1759 fighting ships of the Royal Navy gathered in the Saint Lawrence River to support General James Wolfe's assault on Quebec. As the North American coast lay exposed and vulnerable, a powerful French squadron appeared in the western Caribbean. News filtered into army headquarters in New York City that warships of the comte de Bompar refitting at Cape François were taking in supplies drawn from New York, Philadelphia, and ports in New England. At the head of a British force advancing up Lake Champlain—in an operation coordinated with Wolfe's at Quebec—General Jeffery Amherst urged the provincial government in New York to be watchful of the Crown's wayward colonial subjects.[1]

Meanwhile, just north of Hispaniola, the snow *Speedwell* of New York was sailing cautiously toward the coast of Saint-Domingue. Flying a white flag of truce, Captain William Heysham guided his two-masted trading vessel beneath the heavy guns guarding the channel between the tip of the Cape and "La Coqueville," the great bank of reefs and rocks that protected the entry to Cape François's busy harbor. "All along the coast, [the French] had erected 3, 6, and 8 gun batteries with alarm lights, and watchmen blowing conchs."[2]

With a French pilot aboard, *Speedwell* moved under light sail toward Ville du Cap. In the languid summer heat, steep purple mountains rose in the distance, and lemon trees lined the road that followed the snow's path from the Cape battery to the northern edge of the city. An officer on horseback or a slave working in the heat of the day might have caught a glimpse of the modest ship and its watchful crew as they slipped deeper into enemy territory.[3]

Riding in the crowded harbor at Cape François, so "admirably well suited for ships," Heysham found *Le Défenseur,* a 74-gun ship of the line and flagship of Bompar's squadron of eight heavy French warships. *Speedwell* came to rest in the company of as many as thirty North American trading vessels, representing every port from Salem in the North to Savannah in the South.[4]

From their anchorage, the Americans could hear the Angelus bells of the Jesuit college and Ursaline convent, as well as those of the sisters of Saint-Jean de Dieu, mixing with the cacophony of the busy harbor. Not far from the wharves and warehouses, the boardinghouses, taverns, billiard halls, and brothels of the waterfront offered an entry point into the dangerous underworld that characterized every Atlantic port. Some visitors found Ville du Cap unhealthy and its streets narrow and dirty. But others discovered in its whitewashed buildings and tree-lined walks "a very fine town" and "a civil well disposed people."[5]

Having exchanged its flour, butter, fish, and smoked hams for high-quality white sugar, *Speedwell* began the homeward journey to New York about the third week in August. In early September, Heysham entered the snow's 143 hogsheads of sugar at the New York customhouse as "prize" goods imported from New Haven, Connecticut. But he had arrived without a plantation bond that would attest to the origin of his cargo.[6]

The government waited about two weeks to act. Then, on September 22, 1759, Lieutenant-Governor DeLancey announced the receipt of information, given under oath, that "William Heysham, master of the snow Speedwell, of the port of New York, hath been guilty of high treason, in adhering to His Majesty's enemies, giving them aid and comfort" by carrying a cargo of flour and other provisions to Cape François. With a warrant out for his arrest, the thirty-eight-year-old New York sea captain fled the city.[7]

DeLancey ordered "all magistrates, justices of the peace, sheriffs, constables, and other civil officers, within this province" to begin a diligent search for "the said William Heysham." When discovered, the fugitive was to be "committed to the jail of the city or county where he shall be so apprehended."[8]

Heysham was never brought to justice on charges related to the *Speedwell*'s voyage, unlike the owners, James Depeyster and George Folliot, who later appeared in a New York courtroom—before a judge whose nephew was deeply involved in the same trade. For his trouble, however, William Heysham earned immortality in eighteenth-century verse:

> Poor Fysham formly, we' re told,
> Sold goods to France for Sake of gold,
> 'Tis true he did, in Time of War,
> Yet he escaped from Rope or Tar.[9]

Indirect trade with the French through the neutral islands and Monte Cristi Bay operated on the fiction that New Yorkers were innocently shipping goods meant for Dutch, Danish, and Spanish West Indians, who were providing the produce of their sugar, indigo, and coffee plantations in return. Officials at Saint Eustatius, Curaçao, Saint Croix, Saint Thomas, and Monte Cristi encouraged this fantasy with documents that bore their formal seals of state.

Direct trade sanctioned by the state depended upon an even more subtle sleight of hand: prisoner-of-war exchanges protected by flags of truce. To financially strained colonial governments, it was far more advantageous to exchange prisoners of war than to maintain them. The legislatures rarely bore the cost of such exchanges, however. At one time or another, nearly every British colony issued licenses to ship captains for this purpose. During the Seven Years' War, merchants who sent French prisoners to the West Indies for repatriation and brought back liberated British subjects did so at their own expense. To cover their costs, overseas merchants were permitted to carry trade goods aboard the cartel ships, as they were called, and to profit by doing so.[10]

New York City played an important role in "flag-trucing," a contemporary name for this activity, which accounted for as much as a quarter of the city's trade with the enemy. (Indirect trade through the neutral islands represented about 20 percent, indirect trade through Monte Cristi Bay about 40 percent, and unprotected direct trade about 15 percent.)[11]

As defended by its participants, the flag of truce trade was justifiable on the grounds that shipowners could not be expected to perform so costly, necessary, and patriotic a service for nothing. But the reality of flag-trucing was another matter. By the end of 1758, when the practice came into prominence, it had little to do with prisoner-of-war exchanges but was rather a pretext for the large-scale exchange of re-exported British manufactured goods (along with colonial provisions when they could slip through) for French West Indian sugar, sugar products, indigo, coffee, and cotton.[12]

From the outset, the licenses, called flag of truce commissions, were more difficult to obtain in provincial New York than in Pennsylvania and Rhode Island, the colonies most commonly identified with the practice. "It is a piece of justice due to the lieutenant-governor [in New York] to tell you, that he deviates from the ways of his neighbors and sells no flags of truce," wrote the quartermaster-general of the British Army in March 1760. DeLancey was more comfortable with passive acquiescence to the Mount trade than with public endorsement of state-sponsored trading with the enemy, a subject of intense public debate.[13]

That said, flags of truce were occasionally issued by the Governor's Council to well-connected New Yorkers like John Bogert, Jr. (a justice of the peace and alderman of Montgomery ward), James Jauncey (a political ally of the lieutenant-governor), and Richard Jeffery, Sr. (master of the port of New York). Although never in abundant supply, it was more "customary and usual in the province of New York" for flags of truce to be procured through Lewis Morris, the aged judge of the court of vice-admiralty.[14]

The voyage of the brig *General Amherst* in the spring of 1760 opens a window onto New York flag-trucing. Like the *Charming Polly,* the *General Amherst* belonged to Samuel Stilwell and William Kelly, men experienced in every phase of trading with the enemy. In February 1760, the 70-ton brig began loading a cargo of hoops, snuff, linen, calico, cutlery, sealing wax, candles, earthenware, and "4 boxes Tunbridge ware," colorful articles finished in wood mosaic at Tunbridge Wells in Kent, England.[15]

Stilwell and Kelly had intended to send their brig to Monte Cristi, and on March 8, 1760, they took out a false clearance at the New York customhouse for Kingston, Jamaica. Just two days later, they procured a commission from vice-admiralty judge Morris that allowed Obadiah Hunt, the brig's master, "to go with a flag of truce from this port to Cape François in the island of Hispaniola in order to carry some French prisoners."[16]

As it happened, there were none to be had; the last six prisoners had been taken the previous week on a similar voyage aboard James Thompson's brig *Achilles.* Undeterred, on March 11, the day after Stilwell and Kelly obtained their commission, the *General Amherst* departed the city carrying no French prisoners.[17]

The *General Amherst* spent nine days at Monte Cristi, where Hunt waited "for a favorable opportunity of getting to Cape François without being molested by the Providence privateers." In early April he saw his chance and made a dash west along the coast of Saint-Domingue, following the route of the Spanish Monte Cristi coasters. As the *General Amherst* approached the battery at the Great Pass, a sailor unfurled a large white flag, and the New York vessel passed under the guns protecting the entry to the harbor at Cape François.[18]

Twenty-eight North American cartel ships rode at anchor off Ville du Cap. (By way of comparison, "seventy loaded with provisions were said to be trading among the French Islands last January," wrote a British officer in

March 1760.) McCarty and Company—a Franco-Irish firm that did a large business with New York—managed the sale of the *General Amherst*'s cargo and purchased 158 hogsheads and 5 barrels of brown sugar.[19]

At the Cape, as in New York, there was a scarcity of prisoners. However, Hunt was able to locate four British prisoners of war, although one was lured aboard a Philadelphia-bound vessel and another ran away. With the cargo stowed, the *General Amherst* prepared to depart the Cape in company with seven other flag of truce vessels, including the brig *Achilles* (which had picked up no British prisoners in exchange for its six Frenchmen). On June 9, with his "truce colors" hoisted, Hunt used the ebbing tide to carry his brig out of the harbor, mindful of avoiding "le Grand Mouton" and other dangerous outcroppings.[20]

Most New York flag of truce ventures relied upon the cooperation of merchants in Boston, Newport, Philadelphia, and even Perth Amboy, New Jersey. "Be so good [as] to inform me if there is any vessel to be chartered with you that could carry 2 or 300 hogsheads sugars to go from hence [on] a flag-trucing voyage with a regular flag to Cape François, Port au Prince, Port Louis, or any of the French islands," a New Yorker asked his Boston correspondent in 1760. "I am concerned in a vessel flag truce which is daily expected at Rhode Island from the Mississippi with a large quantity [of] Indian dressed deer skins and furs on board."[21]

Compliant governors, particularly in Rhode Island and Pennsylvania, stimulated investment in cartel ships far beyond their borders. In Rhode Island, Governor Stephen Hopkins saw trading with the enemy (if it adhered to the letter of the law) as not only good for his small colony but in the interests of the British Empire as a whole. And he was not afraid to state his point of view to the ministry in London.[22]

The results were predictable: "I shall take it a very particular favor [if] on receipt of this you would purchase one or as many flags [as] you can, even should it cost two hundred pounds each flag," a merchant in New York wrote his Newport correspondent in September 1759, "and if possible get a certificate to carry flour." The two cities had a history of cooperation. After passage of the Flour Act in 1757, and before the rise to importance of flags of truce, New York had sent large amounts of flour and provisions to Newport, much of which found its way into enemy hands.[23]

Not surprisingly, after 1758 New York firms invested heavily in Newport cartel ships. Some of these ventures were underpinned by family ties, such as the 1759 voyage of the brig *Brawler* (owned by the brothers Napthali and Isaac

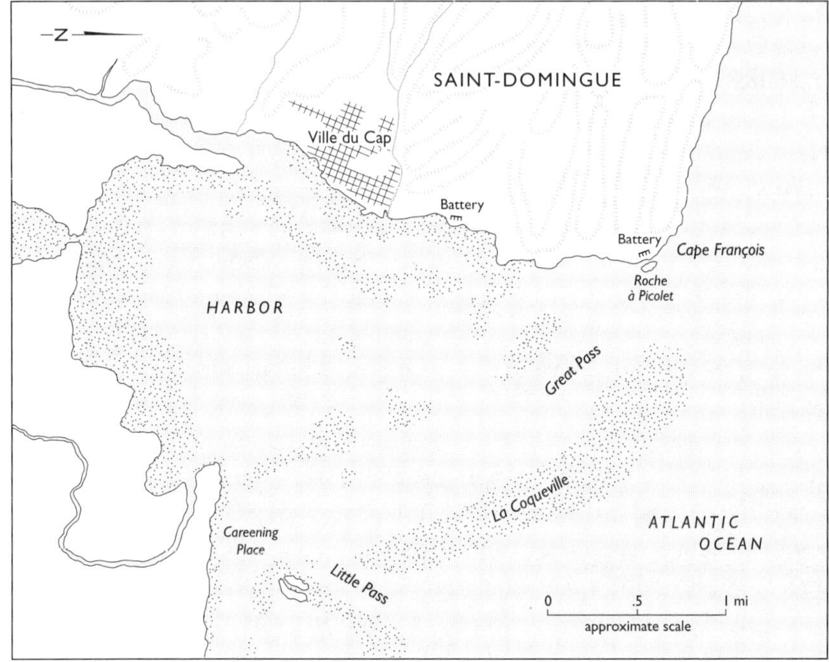

Cape François, c. 1760

Hart of Newport, Abraham Hart of London, and Stephen Hart of New York). *Brawler* left Newport for Port au Prince in September carrying lumber, dry goods, prize French wine, and a commission from Governor Hopkins—but no French prisoners—and headed home with 208 hogsheads of white sugar and 20 barrels of indigo. Many returning vessels (with or without repatriated British subjects) entered their "foreign" West Indian produce at the New York customhouse.[24]

In 1759 New York was in the grip of a flag-trucing fever, fueled partly by the city's ties to Rhode Island. The frenzy, magnified by rumors of huge profits at both ends of the trade, led to a collapse of common sense, and it became routine to write in the names of imaginary prisoners on the blank forms trading from hand to hand. "I should think they might give the flag and . . . leave those vacancies to be filled in here, for which I will give them my honor it shall be done in a very proper manner before the vessel leaves this," wrote a desperate New Yorker to his kinsman in Newport.[25]

New York probably edged out Philadelphia in sheer volume of trade with the enemy over the entire war. But in the flag-trucing business, the Pennsylvania capital was the undisputed leader. The Delaware River "swarms with shallops, unloading their illegal cargoes, . . . [and] carrying provisions, and ready money to the enemy," an informer told Thomas Penn, the proprietor of Pennsylvania, in 1759. This thriving trade was due to the efforts of one man, the Honorable William Denny, Pennsylvania's lieutenant-governor from April 1756 to November 1759.[26]

The last six months of Lieutenant-Governor Denny's term were the golden age of flag-trucing. A protégé of the duke of Cumberland, Denny was a self-proclaimed dilettante who "showed that he lacked the temperament for serious business." Denny's venality was impressive, even in an age in which there was nothing extraordinary about mining public office for personal gain.[27]

A letter from Deputy-Governor James Hamilton, Denny's successor, to William Pitt in November 1760 speaks for itself: "Mr. Denny, now in England, . . . about the month of May in the year 1759, began the practice of selling flags of truce; at first indeed in smaller numbers, and under the pretence of transporting French prisoners, of whom, 'tis well known we have not had more during the whole war more than might have been conveniently embarked in one, or at most, two small ships."

"Yet Mr. Denny or his agents," Hamilton continued, "received for each flag so granted, a sum not less than from three to four hundred pistolen, and having once relished the sweets of this traffic, he became more undisguised, and as it were opened a shop at lower prices to all customers, . . . [including those] of the neighboring provinces, to which they came and purchased freely."

A model for corrupt politicians everywhere, Denny even conducted a going-out-of-business sale. "Towards the end of his administration, the matter was carried to such a pitch, that he scrupled not to set his name to, and dispose of great numbers of blank flags of truce, at the low price of twenty pounds sterling or under; some of which were selling from hand to hand at advanced prices, several months after my arrival. In consequence of this iniquitous conduct, by which he amassed a great sum of money," Hamilton added, "I found at my arrival . . . a very great part of the principal merchants of this city, engaged in a trade with the French islands in the West Indies."[28]

Large New York merchant houses took full advantage of the cheap flags. In one of many examples, Waddell Cunningham, William Walton, Jr., and Jacob Walton, Jr., purchased a flag of truce commission for a Port au Prince venture through their Philadelphia correspondent, Scott and McMichael, an

Irish firm on Water Street. On November 4, 1759, just two days after the Spencer riot in New York, Captain Bartholomew Rooke weighed anchor off "Riddy Island, on the river of Delaware" and took their ship *Nancy* downriver through Delaware Bay into the Atlantic. The commission signed by Lieutenant-Governor Denny permitted the *Nancy* to pass on its journey "without let, hindrance, or molestation . . . so there may not any impediment be put to the mutual relief of prisoners."[29]

The *Nancy*'s captain carried "a license to take on board eight French prisoners, which," he later recounted, "he was prevented from doing by blowing weather and the extremity of the season." The truth was that there were no prisoners. Flag-trucing was so brisk in Philadelphia in the autumn of 1759 that merchants bid against one another for prisoners to carry to Saint-Domingue.[30]

For a voyage of their own, Scott and McMichael hired four French speakers to impersonate prisoners of war. In addition to receiving high wages, the men were allowed to ship sugar home to Pennsylvania, and their wives were paid forty shillings a month for the duration of their absence.[31]

Philadelphia shippers even placed orders for "prisoners" in New York. "I have obtained a flag and desire you will procure some Frenchmen for that purpose," wrote Jacob Van Zandt's Philadelphia partner in April 1759. "Let me [know] the terms and cost to get them to the ferry opposite Philadelphia and how many we must have for a snow about 150 or 160 tons."[32]

Francis Lewis and Thomas Lynch, conspirators in the punishment of George Spencer, were among the many New Yorkers who held shares in Philadelphia cartel ships. And George Folliot, half-owner of William Heysham's snow *Speedwell,* had a long-standing relationship with George Bryan of Front Street, the politically active son of a wealthy Dublin merchant deeply involved in Ireland's trade with the French.[33]

In mid-March 1760, Folliot and Bryan's brig *John and William* sailed from Philadelphia carrying dry goods and provisions (along with a clearance for New Haven, Connecticut) and dropped anchor off Ville du Cap flying a white flag. On Monday, June 9, after the disposal of its cargo by McCarty and Company, the brig departed for New York carrying 109 hogsheads of brown sugar in company with seven other North American flag-trucers, at least two of them New Yorkers—Stilwell and Kelly's brig *General Amherst* and James Thompson's brig *Achilles.* The following day, making their way under an overcast sky toward the Turks Island Passage, the little fleet sailed into the waiting arms of three British warships.[34]

The British navy had made occasional seizures of cartel ships in the summer of 1758. At first the captured vessels—such as the brig *L'Union* carrying rum and sugar from Port au Prince to New York—were as likely to be sailing under French flags of truce as under British North American or West Indian flags. These early interdictions appear to have been on the initiative of individual naval officers rather than the execution of a policy to stamp out prisoner-of-war exchanges as a pretext for trading with the enemy. Such action, as often as not, expressed the frustration of British commanders who suspected—correctly—that flags of truce not only were a cover for the transfer of goods but also provided a means for passing intelligence to the French regarding the intentions of the British fleet. Even so, as late as November 1759, most seizures were made by private ships of war based at Nassau on New Providence Island in the Bahamas.[35]

In 1758 and the early months of 1759, British men of war based in the Caribbean were fixated on the Dutch. This was a constant theme in the letters of naval commanders. "The French at Hispaniola are supplied with provisions and stores of all sorts by neutral vessels," wrote Admiral Thomas Cotes from Port Royal, Jamaica, in May 1758. They receive goods "either from the islands of Saint Eustatius or Curaçao in small sloops and brigantines, or from Holland in very large ships, who carry back their sugars, indigo and coffee."[36]

It was not until the beginning of 1759 that Cotes realized the full significance of Spanish Monte Cristi in the French chain of supply and began directing his thinly stretched warships to cruise off Monte Cristi Bay. But in spite of the navy's overbearing presence, Spain's fragile neutrality and the ministry's reluctance to widen the war by provoking Spain put severe restraints on what Cotes could accomplish.[37]

The Royal Navy's concern with Dutch, Danish, and Spanish neutrals was heightened by fighting in the eastern Caribbean. In January 1759, as part of William Pitt's strategy to weaken French power in the Caribbean, British land and sea forces began a daring amphibious assault on Martinique and Guadeloupe, the most important of the French Leeward Islands.[38]

On January 16, supported by thirty men of war—ten of them ships of the line—under the command of Commodore John Moore, the British put six thousand soldiers on Martinique under the command of Major-General

Thomas Hopson. In the face of heavier than expected resistance, the British withdrew on the 22nd to the less well defended island of Guadeloupe.[39]

The cautious but competent Hopson enjoyed initial success in taking control of key coastal positions and driving the French inland. But the campaign bogged down, and his men began to sicken in the tropical conditions. On February 27, Hopson himself succumbed to disease, and command fell to Brigadier-General John Barrington, a younger and more vigorous soldier. Then, on March 12, as Barrington and Moore were planning their campaign, word arrived that a powerful French squadron (eight ships of the line and three frigates) under the command of the comte de Bompar, was sailing to the relief of the French Leeward Islands.[40]

Within a few days, Bompar and Moore's squadrons had taken up cautious defensive positions: the French at Fort Saint Pierre on Martinique and the British at Prince Rupert Bay on the neighboring island of Dominica. Bompar, with the weaker force and no French naval bases in the West Indies, did not have recourse to established supply depots and repair facilities. Commodore Moore, many of whose vessels had been damaged supporting the campaign, believed that preserving and concentrating his force was the best check to French designs.[41]

Bompar made the most of his circumstances. With Moore tied down at Prince Rupert Bay, the large and voracious fleet of French privateers on Martinique feasted on British shipping in the Leeward Islands, seizing eighty to ninety vessels in just eleven weeks. Many were heavy-laden supply ships bound for the English islands. And although Moore sent his cruisers to blockade Saint Eustatius, merchants there continued to play a role supplying Bompar with goods from Europe and British North America.[42]

The absence of British naval support off Guadeloupe did not deter Barrington. He pressed ahead, engaging in a war of attrition against French property, as well as a war of containment against the French military. With the arrival of reinforcements from Antigua—ordered by Hopson just days before his death—momentum on the ground fell to the British.

In late April, the planters of Guadeloupe, facing the destruction and confiscation of their property, negotiated with Barrington for a cessation of hostilities even as the French governor and military commanders urged continued resistance in the face of overwhelming odds. On May 1, 1759, with the French commander accepting the inevitable, separate civilian and military capitulations were signed that gave control of Guadeloupe to Great Britain.[43]

The next day, with the ink hardly dry on the surrender documents, Bompar

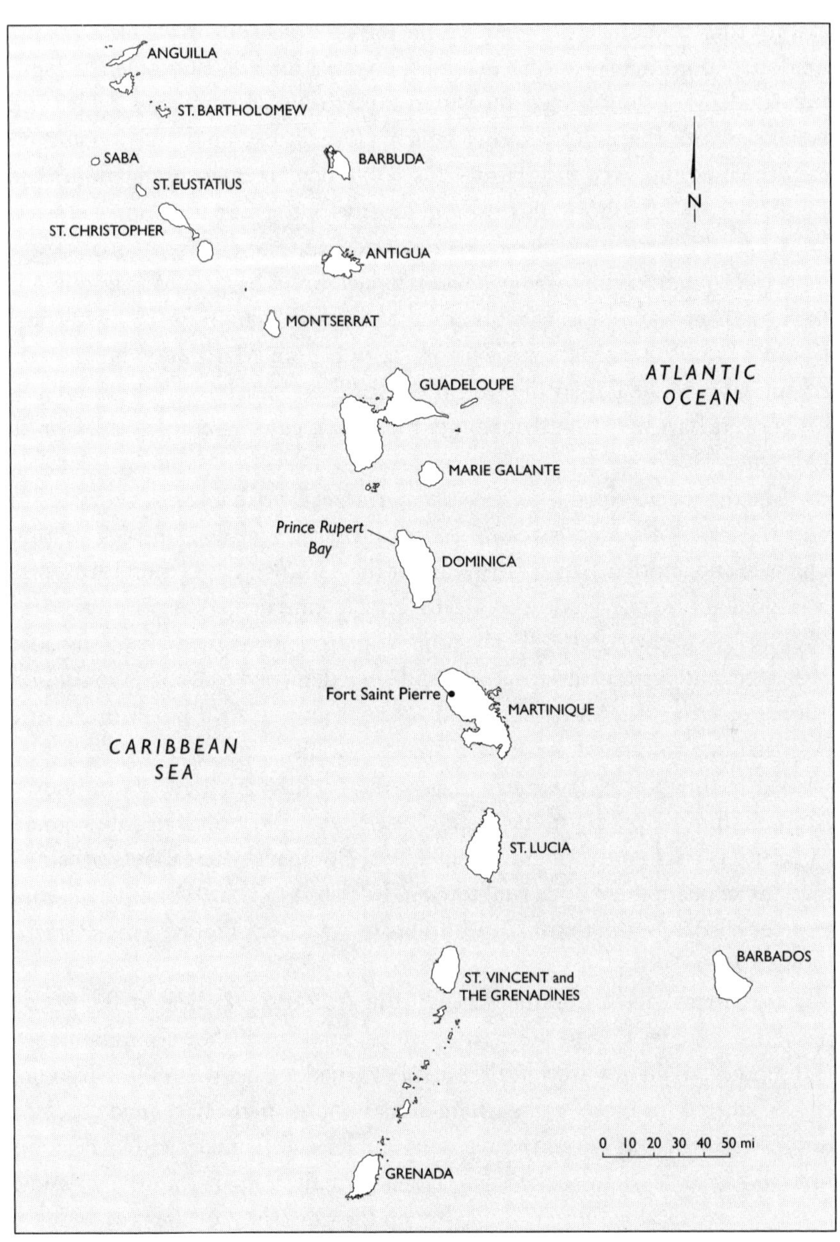

Martinique, Guadeloupe, and the Lesser Antilles

and his squadron of eleven warships, having decisively out-maneuvered Commodore Moore, appeared off Guadeloupe with a force of 2,600 men. Despite this sudden and unexpected turn in events, the inhabitants of Guadeloupe, beneficiaries of Barrington's terms, which allowed freedom of religion and full rights to their property, steadfastly refused to repudiate their capitulation.[44]

After some desultory skirmishing, mostly for the sake of honor, the sixty-one-year-old Frenchman declined the opportunity to engage Moore's more powerful squadron and by May 6 had returned to his base on Martinique. On the 27th, Bompar's ships were observed departing: "I am informed Monsieur Bompar is sailed with seven ships of the line from Martinique but not yet certain whether he has entirely left these seas," wrote Moore, "but as none of my cruisers have seen him, I am apt to think he is either gone to Europe or St. Domingo."[45]

Meanwhile, in North America a much larger British force was converging on the Saint Lawrence River to join in General Wolfe's campaign against Quebec, and another British army, under the command of General Amherst, was moving into position for an assault on Ticonderoga, to be followed by an attempt on Crown Point. Forty-nine warships, along with 119 transport, ordnance, and commissariat vessels, had been deployed to Canada to support a force of 8,500 British regulars and colonial militia. And north of Albany, Amherst had command of 11,000 men under arms.[46]

With the North American coast only lightly guarded, Commodore Moore's ships tied down in the eastern Caribbean, and Admiral Cote's Jamaican cruisers chasing the phantom squadron, Bompar's whereabouts became a pressing concern in every coastal town in British America. "Where he is gone uncertain; some think to the Cape, others for Quebec," reported the *Pennsylvania Gazette.*[47]

The threat to North America was real. According to Robert Beatson, a naval historian writing in the eighteenth century, "had M. de Bompar, when he found he could not prevent the island of Guadeloupe from falling into our hands, steered for New York with his squadron, he might have made such an impression there, as [would] have obliged General Amherst either to come himself, or at least to make such a detachment from his army, as would perhaps have disabled him from acting on the offensive, for the remainder of the campaign."

"From New York, M. de Bompar might have gone to Halifax or Saint John's, Newfoundland, or both," Beatson added. "An attack on either of these places, would have obliged Admiral Saunders [in command of British naval forces off Quebec] to make such a detachment from his fleet, as might have greatly diminished our force before Quebec, and, perhaps in the end, would have proved the ruin of the enterprise; while, before such detachment could have been able to overtake M. de Bompar, he might have done his business, and sailed for Europe."[48]

As the summer wore on, British cruisers in the Caribbean had trouble picking up the scent. Patrolling along the southern coast of Saint-Domingue in late July, HMS *Cerberus* received intelligence that Bompar had slipped into Port Saint Louis. On August 3, Captain Charles Webber sent his second lieutenant and a mate "to Orange Quay to reconnoiter the ships." They learned that Bompar had come and gone. He was, in fact, at Cape François. Discovered, the men from the *Cerberus* "were fired upon by a Dutch armed sloop who took them prisoners and carried them to the governor of Port Louis." The French accused the British officer of being a spy but returned the mate "on Captain Webber's sending a boat."[49]

In the midst of all this, HMS *Cerberus* seized a New York flag-trucer coming into Port Saint Louis. Following Captain Webber's return to Port Royal in mid-August—delayed by long days of "very little wind" along the south coast of Hispaniola—his report of the capture of the snow *Hercules* was an epiphany for Admiral Cotes.[50]

The vessel carried a clearance from Connecticut and nearly seven hundred barrels of flour, which, the British admiral reported to London, "I have reason to believe . . . was ordered for the supply of Monsieur Bompar's squadron." Cotes learned that New Yorkers were getting an exorbitant amount for flour and beef in the ports of Saint-Domingue at the very time a visitor at Port au Prince saw a Jamaican flag of truce "land quantities of gunpowder, which was disposed of at a very great price."[51]

"These trading flags must certainly be very lucky in escaping His Majesty's ships," editorialized the *New-London Summary,* "for we have not yet heard of so much as one of their number being seized and sent to Jamaica; the Monte Cristi men appear to be the only objects of their pursuits." For the flag-trucers, the bubble was about to burst.[52]

In spite of the extraordinary opportunity that lay at his feet—and his unparalleled access to military intelligence by way of North American flag-trucers—Bompar allowed his powerful squadron to devolve into a flotilla of merchantmen. Throughout the summer their lower gun decks filled with West Indian produce after Bompar posted announcements "in several parts of Hispaniola, giving notice, that the vessels of his squadron will take in sugar,

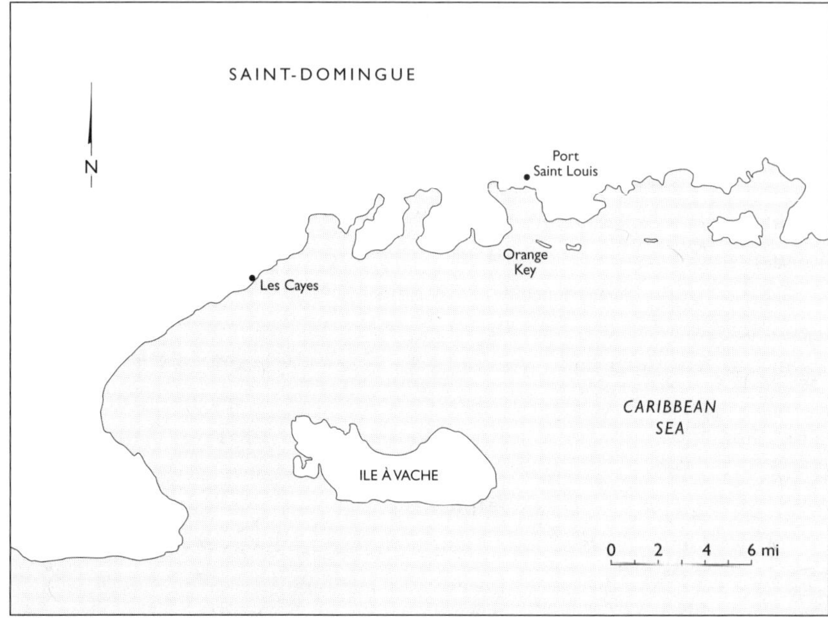

South Coast of Saint-Domingue: Les Cayes and Port Saint Louis

indigo, &c. for Old France." The French warships loaded cargo at Cape François early in July, at Port Saint Louis and Port au Prince later in the month, and were back at the Cape in September. "Monsieur Bompar sailed from Cape François the 10th of October with his whole squadron for Europe," Cotes told the Admiralty in November. "There is not at present one ship of war at that island and very few merchant ships, their commerce being entirely carried on by neutral vessels and flags of truce."[53]

With Bompar gone and the close of the hurricane season, Rear Admiral Thomas Cotes declared war on flags of truce. Rankled by the absurdity of a powerful French force being sustained "by cartel vessels from North America," Cotes added flag-trucers to his inventory of targets and repositioned his forces. "Since the departure of Monsieur Bompar's squadron," Cotes told the Admiralty, "I have stationed His Majesty's ships under my command . . . to block up the French ports of Hispaniola."[54]

Cotes sent HMS *Marlborough* (70 guns) and *Hampshire* (50 guns) to cruise along the south coast of Saint-Domingue, put *Edinburgh* (64 guns) and *Harwich* (50 guns) off Cape François, and placed his smaller, more nimble ships—*Trent* (28 guns), *Cerberus* (28 guns), and *Lively* (20 guns) and the sloop-of-war *Port Royal* (12 guns)—in the Gulf of Gonâve to intercept vessels entering and leaving Port au Prince and Leogane.[55]

Cotes's campaign had an inauspicious beginning. Working mostly off the Ile à Vache and along the stretch of coast from Les Cayes to Jacmel, Captain Coningsby Norbury, commander of HMS *Hampshire,* stopped twenty-one vessels, most of them Spanish sloops and schooners. He took three prizes on his two-and-a-half month cruise, one of which, *La Madamma,* was a 10-gun privateer sloop. "On the approach of our boats she hauled down the Dutch and hoisted French and fired at them," after which "[we] stood with her and fired a broadside, then hauled off in order to fetch again." When *Hampshire* fired a second time, the plucky French privateersman struck his colors. But though Captain Norbury kept the Hampshires busy, five flag-trucers slipped through his fingers.[56]

On January 6, 1760, his officers "examined a sloop and found her a cartel from and belonging to Rhode Island for Les Cayes." Later in the day they met one from New York bound for Port Saint Louis. Both vessels were soon on their way, and before it returned to Port Royal, HMS *Hampshire* had stopped and released three more flag-trucers, including another from New York City. In light of Admiral Cotes's determination to stamp out flag-trucing, it is hard to imagine that he was entirely pleased.[57]

Captain John Lindsay in HMS *Trent* did much better. In mid-January, operating off the Ile de la Gonâve, the twenty-two-year-old officer—the nephew of the earl of Mansfield, Lord Chief Justice of England and Wales—picked up eight flag-trucers coming out of Port au Prince and Leogane carrying 1,600 hogsheads of sugar. Seven of the flag-trucers were from North America (Philadelphia, New York, and Newport), and one was from the British West Indies (New Providence in the Bahamas). News that William and Jacob Walton's snow *Desire,* a prize they had purchased at Port au Prince and loaded with sugar, had been captured by the Royal Navy raised an alarm in New York City.[58]

At least two dozen flag-trucers remained at Port au Prince, and there were others at Cape François and elsewhere in Saint-Domingue. Among them was the 250-ton ship *Nancy.* In November, Captain Bartholomew Rooke brought *Nancy* into the Port au Prince roadstead carrying—according to sworn testimony—an innocuous cargo of lumber, barrel staves, beeswax, beer, cider, apples, onions, and soap. The truth, if we could know it, would be far more interesting.[59]

To reduce the danger of a sure condemnation should a curious naval officer discover even a single barrel of flour that might be construed as cargo, flag-trucing captains buried contraband deep in the bowels of their ships. "I request you may have her loaded in the following manner," instructed a merchant at Port au Prince: "Four hundred barrels of light flour to be put in the bottom and afterwards some thousands of bricks to be stowed on the top of them," which should be covered over with hoops, staves, and boards. In light of Waddell Cunningham and the Waltons' long involvement with the French, it is unlikely that the lading of their ship *Nancy* was any different. With the British seizing flag-trucers, *Nancy* and its 330 hogsheads of French West Indian sugar would need all the protection they could get for the journey home.[60]

On Wednesday, January 30, the privateer brig *Eagle* "appeared off the harbor of Port au Prince, and hoisted a white jack at the main-top-gallant-mast-head, and an English jack or ensign at the fore-topgallant-mast-head, upon which some boats came out of the harbor." One of these carried Bartholomcw Rooke, master of the *Nancy,* and Edmund Vaughan, master of the ship *Friendship.* "They both stayed on board to dinner, about three hours," planning the events of the next day.[61]

At two o'clock the following morning, a "musket fired from the *Eagle,*" and both flag-trucers, having weighed anchor the previous evening, "stood out to join the brig *Eagle.*" *Nancy* and *Friendship* sent their boats across to the privateer and played out the charade of seizure, with a cooper unskilled in the art of navigation acting as prize master aboard the *Nancy.* By sunrise, the three ships were sailing northwest in the direction of Cape Saint Nicholas and the Windward Passage.[62]

Captain Frederick Maitland in HMS *Lively* had just cleared Cape Saint Nicholas and was heading into the Gulf of Gonâve. In light rain off Cape Saint Mark the following morning—with HMS *Cerberus* and a prize now in company—*Lively*'s watch sighted sails to the northeast. The two warships came about and gave chase.[63]

Aboard *Nancy,* Captain Rooke saw "three sail of vessels" and prepared to receive a boarding party. He instructed the sham prize master "not to be afraid, if stopped by any English men of war, and not to mind their threatenings." "At 10 A.M.," according to Maitland's logbook, *Lively* "came up with the chace which proved to be the letter of marque brig *Eagle,* with the ships *Nancy* and *Friendship.*" Maitland sent a petty officer and six seamen aboard each vessel to examine papers and rummage for contraband. The sailors from *Lively* and *Cerberus* spent the day sorting out the truth of what lay before

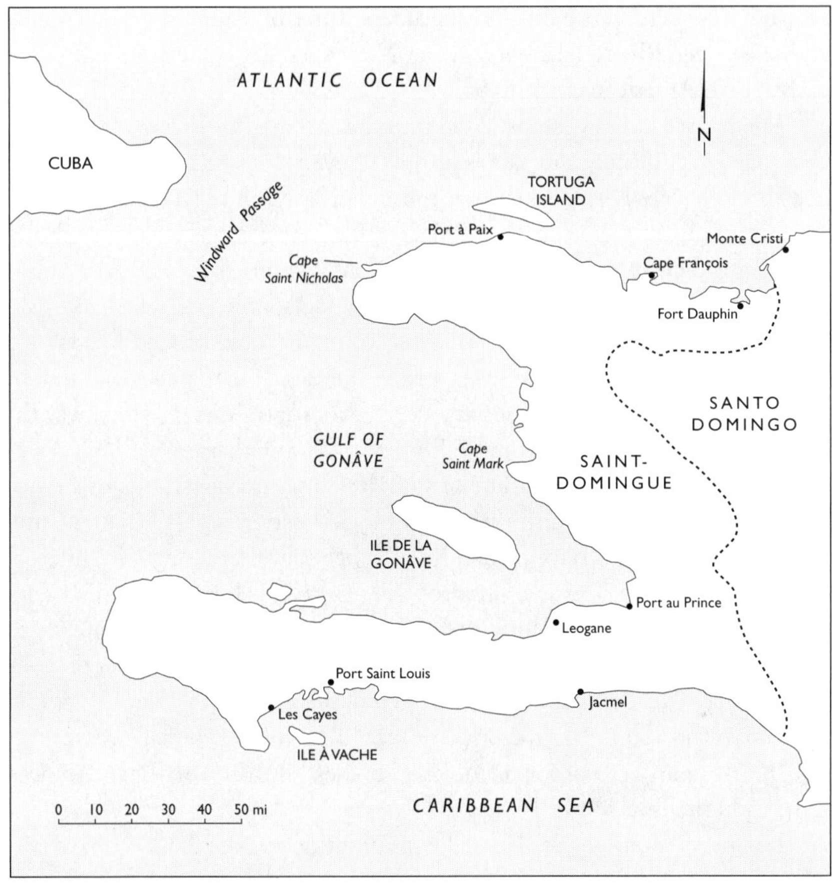

Saint-Domingue and the Windward Passage

them. The next morning, *Cerberus* bore away on seeing "a sail in the south-east," and *Lively* set a course for home.[64]

Maitland anchored off Jamaica where he quarantined his prizes and interrogated their crews. On February 11, 1760, HMS *Lively* entered Port Royal harbor with two deep-laden flag-trucers and a British privateer. *Cerberus* and the sloop of war *Port Royal* brought in another four. By the end of February, *Trent, Lively, Cerberus,* and *Port Royal* had delivered twenty-four flag-trucers to the Jamaican court of vice-admiralty: eighteen were North American and the remaining six from Jamaica and New Providence. Of the North Americans, ten were from Philadelphia, five from New York City, and three from

Newport. New Yorkers held shares in at least three of the Pennsylvania vessels and one of the Rhode Islanders, giving New York City a stake in half of the early North American captures.[65]

The parade of cartel ships lasted into the summer. In July 1760 the *New-York Gazette* published the names of thirty-seven flag-trucing ships that had been brought into Port Royal before the end of May. Of the twenty-six North Americans, there were fourteen Philadelphia ships, seven from New York, three from Newport, one from New London, and one from a port in Maryland, probably Annapolis. Of the Rhode Islanders, at least one, the *Brawler,* was partly owned by New Yorkers, as were as many as five of the Philadelphia ships. Verdicts came down in seventeen of the cases that had gone to trial by April 1760, with ten convictions and seven acquittals—one of which was the *Nancy,* much to the relief of the Waltons and Cunningham.[66]

"There is now in the harbor of Port Royal 4,000 hogsheads of French sugars and other commodities seized by His Majesty's ships," Admiral Cotes reported in March. "I have certain intelligence that there is now in different ports of Hispaniola near two hundred sail [of] English vessels loading with sugars and other produce," he added. This included the ships at Monte Cristi Bay, as well as cartel ships in the ports of Saint-Domingue. Wary of provoking the Spanish, the forty-eight-year-old admiral struck where he could—without authorization from London—intending to destroy flag-trucing before he turned over command of the Jamaica squadron to Rear Admiral Charles Holmes in May.[67]

The news from Jamaica created consternation in New York. "I have part of seven flags that went to Hispaniola by which I expect to lose two thousand pounds," a New York merchant told his kinsman in Liverpool. "Out of four that was coming home three is already taken by our men of war and fear they will be condemned." To his Rhode Island partner, the source of his expensive flag of truce commission signed by Governor Stephen Hopkins, he had a more pointed message. "I say damn them all."[68]

CHAPTER SIX

Mixed Messages

In May 1760, George Spencer was emboldened—even exhilarated—by the reports from Jamaica. In a cold and damp room reserved for insolvent debtors at the New York City Jail, the informer was spinning a legal web to ensnare his tormentors. "[They] imagine, that they have no other chance to reduce me to their own terms, but keeping me in jail," he wrote, "and, by that means, tire me out, if they can, . . . in order to put off the evil day."

His enemies would soon know both his wrath and the severity of the law. "Without any view to my own interest," he wrote—momentarily forgetting the reward for informing that would come his way—he would make them regret "that most barbarous inhumane treatment I met with, . . . for no other reason, than only endeavoring to serve my king and country."[1]

But first things first. In April, after declaring Spencer "destitute of help unless the court shall interpose," the New York Supreme Court of Judicature had appointed John Tabor Kempe, in his capacity as a private attorney, to act as Spencer's counsel and John Alsop, Sr., a prominent New York lawyer, "to assist him in carrying on the several prosecutions and suits."[2]

To obtain his release from jail, the informer appealed to the cupidity of his fellow New Yorkers. "In order that I may have an opportunity of doing that justice to my country which I am debarred of doing by being confined," he wrote, "I will give any person, properly qualified, who will be my special bail, five thousand pounds out of the first money recovered by any of [my] suits." As he awaited his freedom, Spencer put into motion his plan "to obtain satisfaction for that ignominious abuse, and [the] damages I have sustained."[3]

For the faint of heart in Hanover Square and its neighboring streets and alleys, Admiral Cotes's campaign against flags of truce was the exit point from a trade rife with legal and moral ambiguities and burdened with excessive risk.

But not everyone was faint of heart. In New York, there are always those who see opportunity where others see ruin.

In the drawing rooms, coffeehouses, and taverns of Manhattan, Spencer's impending prosecutions and the unsettling news from Jamaica made trading with the enemy an issue of grave public concern. "The trade carried on from these northern colonies, . . . which a formidable fleet has been industriously employed to obstruct, has long been the subject of conversation, and frequently of warm disputes," reported the *New-York Gazette* in May 1760.[4]

News that the navy had begun seizing flag-trucers fueled extreme positions in a debate that largely pitted New Yorkers against their West Indian rivals and the British military. "When we turn our thoughts, and consider the treatment the Northern merchants' interest, and the mariners employed in their service, meet with at Jamaica and New Providence," complained a New York newspaper later in the year, "the inhuman barbarities of Indian savages, and all that train of misery and sufferings attending a war with perfidious infidels, will appear as small evils."[5]

Those who did business—in all its incarnations—with the French were adamant in protesting loyalty to king and country. Samuel Stilwell, a man as involved as any in the city, had issued a string of public statements in 1756 defending his honor and countering "reports being spread abroad, insinuating that discoveries have lately been made of my carrying on an illegal trade with the French."[6]

Only trade with French Canada early in the war and, later, exports of "warlike stores" anywhere were impossible to defend. In the darkest hours of 1755 and 1756, shipments of flour and other provisions sent from New York to Cape Breton had fed French garrisons at Louisbourg, Quebec, Montreal, Crown Point, and posts along the Ohio River, "which greatly assists and puts them in a better condition to pursue carry on and support themselves in their encroachments on His Majesty's territories." There was no mistaking the subversive character of the trade at a time when New York City was vulnerable to attack from a French army poised to move down the Lake Champlain corridor into the Hudson River valley.[7]

The consequences of trade through the Dutch and Danish islands were not so immediate. But the aggressiveness of the navy's interdictions, the vulnerability of neutral shipping in British admiralty courts, and Governor Hardy's watchful eye reduced participation to a hardy few. In London, the Lords of Appeals—the court that heard appeals of verdicts in prize cases brought before courts of admiralty and vice-admiralty—condemned "without mercy" every Dutch vessel caught trading at a French island. "This the nation had spirit enough to put a stop to," remarked the *New-York Gazette*, expressing a widely held antipathy toward neutrals—except, of course, among New Yorkers who used the neutral islands as a channel to supply Saint-Domingue, Martinique, and Guadeloupe.[8]

Indirect trade with the enemy through Spanish Monte Cristi Bay, which rose to importance as commerce through the Dutch and Danish islands was suppressed in 1757, had the advantage of being legal. But it was legal only so long as British subjects avoided doing business directly with the French, and North American merchants adhered strictly to the terms of the Flour Act.[9]

To opponents of trade with the enemy in any form, this indirect trade was "a new invention," an insult to the king's proclamation, and a sham commerce that drained away the resources of the nation. "We have an odd kind of mongrel commerce here called the Mount Trade," wrote a member of the New York Governor's Council; "the lawyers say it is legal and contrary to no statute, the men of war say it is illegal and both take and condemn them at their own shops while they are acquitted at others. No two courts pursue the same measure."[10]

Proponents insisted that supplying the French in Saint-Domingue with British manufactured goods through Monte Cristi Bay had no military significance. In any case, it would be impossible to starve out the French. Unlike Martinique and Guadeloupe, both of which depended upon supplies from abroad, enemy troops on Hispaniola had the means to support themselves—or so it was argued. Taking off French sugar, indigo, and coffee at bargain prices in exchange for manufactures and colonial produce at inflated prices not only enriched the British nation, it added to the king's revenue and helped pay for the war. Even supporters acknowledged that there had been few Spaniards at Monte Cristi "until it became a kind of mart or fair, for the English and French, to exchange their goods at."[11]

In their trade with Monte Cristi, New Yorkers saw themselves as victims of "a hard and partial law," the Flour Act of 1757. While British and Irish merchants were at liberty to send provisions to any neutral port, North Americans were required to post large bonds guaranteeing that their goods would be shipped only to ports under British control. "It was generally believed this law was obtained by the contractors for victualing the army in America, to keep down the price of provisions," wrote the anonymous author of the privately circulated "State of the Case Touching the North American Trade to Monte Christo."

If that were the case, he argued, "it was not thought so great a crime to break it," especially as English and Irish provisions vessels arrived daily at Monte Cristi with proper clearances from home. Believing that merchants in London, Dublin, and Cork had been issued a license to supply the French through Monte Cristi—"as if it had been directly to Cape François"—New Yorkers felt that they, too, ought to share in "a trade greatly beneficial to England."[12]

This is all nonsense, snapped the author of "Reply to 'The State of the Case.'" Such justifications were the sophistry of men "so void of public spirit as to prefer their own to the nation's interest; and who, if unrestrained by law, will not be restrained by principle, from acting to the prejudice of their country and the advantage of the enemy." And, he added, New Yorkers benefited from official collusion. There were glaring irregularities in clearing and entering ships at the customhouse—"a general plan of perjury among the traders"—and the corruption of customhouse officers was "too well known to need explanation."[13]

By 1760 the pattern of deception underpinning the Mount trade had become "from its generality (to great shame be it said) rather the object of laughter than horror." If a crime against the state deserved punishment, the argument went, "it is hard to conceive one more punishable than the practice of this illicit trade."[14]

To its enemies, flag-trucing was even more pernicious, barely a step above trading with the enemy on the authority of a permission, or passport, signed by a French governor. "Did they not run directly into the enemy's ports?" "Did they not constantly, coming from the seat where the preparations for war were necessarily made, give the enemy the earliest and surest intelligence of our designs?" "Did they not discharge their cargoes into Monsieur Bompar's squadron?"[15]

Flag-trucers held their ground. The entire British nation benefited, argued a pamphlet in defense of doing business with the French on Hispaniola. Powerful interests in England "who trade to New York, or Philadelphia, . . . can neither be ignorant of the channel, through which their remittances come, nor of the extraordinary call that hath been made for goods of English manufacture, for those markets; insomuch, that all the manufacturers find it out of their power to supply the demand."[16]

Proponents argued that the huge returns from flag-trucing were widely shared: "On a moderate computation [based on prices in Saint-Domingue and the European continent], not so little as £400,000 sterling's worth of commodities of British manufacture, or the produce of our colonies, have, during this war, been thus sent to the French islands from North America; which must bring back into this kingdom, the enormous profit of £3,200,000." Why should the neutral powers—the Dutch, the Danes, and the Spaniards—have a piece of so lucrative and beneficial a commerce?[17]

"The condemnation of flags of truce [was] not only impolitic, but in the highest degree unjust," advocates added. From its outset, the trade had the implied consent of the government. "For it cannot be supposed that His Majesty's governors in North America, who granted flags of truce to private merchants to carry French prisoners to Hispaniola, and bring back others in return at their own expense, were ignorant that in doing so they had a view to their own private advantage." Surely, interference was motivated by greed. "How much is the public injured by the commanders of such of His Majesty's ships of war, as are employed in taking flags of truce, and enriching themselves at the expense of their fellow citizens, and the commonweal?"[18]

And so the accusations went back and forth. "A stranger to form judgment from them would imagine that the nation in its jurisdiction had neither rule [of] law or probity," wrote a New York politician to his friend in London, "and yet the evil is suffered to go on without any determination, the subject is tore to pieces by robbers, lawyers and all sorts of vermin."[19]

Even the Dutch Trade—the time-honored smuggling operation whose suppression in the spring and summer of 1756 had pushed New Yorkers into the waiting arms of the French—was once again flourishing. It was fueled by massive exports of "foreign" sugar to Amsterdam, Rotterdam, and Hamburg, and its leading practitioners were the same men George Spencer had fingered earlier: Cunningham, Depeyster, Folliot, Kelly, Stilwell, and Walton.[20]

In early 1760, according to a notice in the *Gazette,* informers were again being welcomed at the customhouse. "Whereas we the officers of His Majesty's customs, are given to understand, that the old illegal Dutch Trade, so prejudicial to the trade of Great Britain, and injurious to the fair and honest British trader, is again upon the revival. These are therefore to give the public notice, that whoever will discover the conduct, or any part of the conduct, of those unfair dealers in this affair, by a line directed to the collector, or comptroller of His Majesty's customs; shall, in due time, be amply rewarded."[21]

With George Spencer in jail merchants did not fear informers, ample rewards or not. "I'm not much afraid here, matters being pretty well fixed," wrote an Irish newcomer to the trade in January 1760. The city was being flooded with smuggled tea and manufactured goods from the European continent. "Mr. SS's part comes down in small craft which I suppose don't enter in the custom house on arrival," he told his contact in New London. "Would you approve ours should come so, or suppose it was stowed away in flaxseed or other goods?"[22]

As the merchants of New York stretched the limits of imagination to justify their behavior, George Spencer clogged the dockets of the Supreme Court of Judicature and the court of vice-admiralty to achieve revenge and end his financial nightmare. In the first four months of 1760, he initiated seventeen proceedings against the men he had accused of violating the Flour Act or of instigating the riot in which he had been abused on the streets of New York the previous November.[23]

At the time of Spencer's arrest, creditors had seized all his moveable property, "even to the very clothes on his back." In January 1760 he offered the deed to his house and land on Broadway as security against his outstanding debts, "provided they would have discharged him." But his tormentors "absolutely refused" and obstructed every attempt to resolve the claims. One declared that the informer "should never come out of jail till carted out in his coffin." "They intended him no less punishment than imprisonment for life," Spencer lamented, "for what he had said to the lieutenant-governor."[24]

Spencer counterattacked in the January session of the New York Supreme Court of Judicature. His court-appointed attorney John Alsop, Sr., had purchased the property on Broadway, and from the proceeds Spencer set in motion his barrage of lawsuits and prosecutions. He moved first against the instigators of the mob, expecting the "justice due to himself and family for the ignominious abuse he had received." In separate actions, he sought to recover personal damages from six men—Philip Branson, Waddell Cunningham, George Harison, William Kelly, Thomas Lynch, and Michael Wade—each of whom also faced criminal charges for the attack.[25]

Then, as an informer in the New York court of vice-admiralty, Spencer initiated actions against William Richardson, Samuel Tingley, and Francis Welsh, owners of the brig *Earl of Loudoun*. In September 1759 that vessel had carried 1,500 barrels of flour—each containing three bushels—from New York City to Monte Cristi Bay in clear violation of the Flour Act, which called for a fine of twenty shillings per bushel and forfeiture of the ship and cargo. The informer's one-third share in any of the prosecutions under the statute would have made him a wealthy man. But the wheels of justice turned slowly—and justice was expensive.[26]

In the April session of the New York Supreme Court, Spencer launched the third and most audacious part of his plan: a string of eight actions to recover the penalties allowed to informers in prosecutions "for exporting provisions contrary to the act of parliament." Locked away from the world, he anticipated earning more than £20,000 in these early cases. In just one, the case against Theophilact Bache, one of the bondholders keeping Spencer in jail, the informer expected to recover an amount "more than double the sum in the bond."[27]

While Spencer gathered evidence, planned further prosecutions, and awaited the judgment of the courts, British warships, having already interdicted many North American vessels in the Caribbean, began paying attention to Mount-men and flag-trucers in the waters off New England and the middle colonies. With French privateers operating in the vicinity of Sandy Hook in July 1760, Captain James Campbell in HMS *Nightingale* patrolled "close in shore of Block Island and Montague Point" in search of transgressing Americans. "The brave Captain Campbell," sneered the *Gazette,* chased three ships into New London harbor.[28]

Campbell took his prizes to Nassau on New Providence Island in the Bahamas, where "it is to be hoped, . . . he may carry at least one of the enemy's frigates with him; which, if not so agreeable to the judge of the admiralty and people of that island, will be more for the interest of the public than [the] numbers of vessels lately condemned there on the most frivolous pretences."[29]

Then, at the end of July, the city received more bad news. On Wednesday morning, July 30, 1760, the fifty-seven-year-old lieutenant-governor, James DeLancey, died suddenly at his estate in the Bowery. The unexpected event "threw the whole city into the deepest sorrow and amazement." Grieving New Yorkers poured forth their admiration: "He was for capacity and integrity equaled by few—excelled by none. Patient in hearing, ready in distinguishing, and in his decisions sound and impartial," claimed the *Mercury.* DeLancey was also a ruthless politician and the dominant figure in New York's factious political culture.[30]

The following evening, after the firing of the great guns aboard HMS *Winchester,* moored in the Hudson River, there began the largest funeral in the 150-year history of the city. The procession, more than half a mile in length, moved "in a very regular manner, and with a slow pace" from the Bowery to Trinity Church through streets thronged with mourners, there to mark the passing of a true friend of New York.[31]

Into the void stepped the seventy-two-year-old president of the Governor's Council, Cadwallader Colden, a physician, scientist, and long-time political rival of the DeLanceys. Where DeLancey had steered through the divisive politics of provincial New York with skill and discretion, collecting strong allies and cautious enemies, Colden, although attentive to the business of state, could be inflexible, rash, and imprudent, and he lacked altogether the popular touch. A staunch Royalist, he was—as his tenure in office would demonstrate—repeatedly caught between London's expectation of unquestioning subservience and the reality of what lay before him.[32]

New York adjusted to life without DeLancey, and far away in London, William Pitt, de facto prime minister, finally spoke out on wartime trade with the French. Although long aware of the problem, the ministry had been slow in responding. In August 1759, for example, Pitt had received documents from the Admiralty establishing a link between British North America and Spanish Monte Cristi, "from whence there is great reason to believe the French are supplied." And later that month, the Privy Council had urged the king to issue a proclamation demanding an end to all trade with the enemy and to punish offenders with the full severity of the law. Nothing happened until the navy's interdictions caught the attention of the public.[33]

On August 23, 1760, in response to reports by Admiral Cotes in Jamaica and Commodore Moore in Antigua, Pitt issued a stern statement to the colonial governors. He had received, he said, "repeated and certain intelligence of an illegal and most pernicious trade, carried on by the king's subjects, in North America, and the West Indies, . . . by which the enemy is, to the greatest reproach, and detriment, of government, supplied with provisions, and other necessaries, whereby they are, principally, if not alone, enabled to sustain, and protract, this long and expensive war."

The matter had reached the highest level, and it was time for an accounting. "It is His Majesty's express will and pleasure, that you do forthwith make the strictest and most diligent enquiry into the state of this dangerous and ignominious trade, that you do use every means in your power, to detect and discover persons concerned, either as principals, or accessories, therein, and that you do take every step, authorized by law, to bring all such heinous offenders to the most exemplary and condign punishment."

Pitt called on each colonial governor to "use your utmost endeavors to trace out, and investigate the various artifices, and evasions, by which the dealers in this iniquitous intercourse find means to cover their criminal proceedings, and to elude the law."[34]

The responses were predictable: "I beg leave to assure you Sir that since my arrival in this province, nothing of the kind has been connived at," wrote Thomas Boone of New Jersey. Francis Fauquier of Virginia admitted to having "been tempted by large offers" to issue flags of truce, "which I have never been prevailed upon to grant." After a colorful indictment of his predecessor, William Denny, James Hamilton of Pennsylvania assured Pitt "in the most solemn manner" that he had not consented in any way to "this iniquitous commerce." "I do not mean to answer for any other part of New England," said Francis Bernard of Massachusetts, "but I am informed that in those parts, where this trade has been practiced, it is now entirely ceased."[35]

And so it went—except in Rhode Island, where Governor Stephen Hopkins's candor shone through the fog, and New York, where Colden's obfuscation led to crisis as the war neared its end. Rhode Island, "though very small," Hopkins told Pitt, "hath always carried on a considerable trade by sea." He acknowledged that his legislature had authorized flags of truce, owing to the large number of French prisoners taken by the colony's privateers, and affirmed Rhode Island's participation in commerce with Monte Cristi, "to which it hath always been thought lawful to trade, provided nothing prohibited by law was carried thither."

Hopkins also confided about the difficulty of preventing vessels from altering legal voyages and then covering their tracks with false documents. But, he complained, many law-abiding Rhode Island ships had been seized by British naval officers and "promiscuously condemned" in the vice-admiralty courts of Jamaica and New Providence. Those in the West Indies who stood to make fortunes from North American prizes "set these matters in a partial and bad light, both against the parties immediately concerned, and the colonies to which they belong."[36]

Colden's tone was different. The lieutenant-governor—the naive (or perhaps disingenuous) father of a high-ranking New York customs official—declared himself "entirely a stranger" to the city's trade. Colden assured Pitt that he had directed John Tabor Kempe, the attorney general, and Archibald Kennedy, collector of customs, "to use all possible diligence in discovering what they can of this illegal trade." Although "none could be induced to inform," reported Colden in an astonishing lapse of memory, "the merchants in this place have been too generally concerned in this illegal trade." Colden had some good news, however. "All agree, that the trade with the French Islands is now effectually stopped, by the many seizures made by His Majesty's ships of war, by which some of the merchants have been entirely ruined, and all of them have suffered greatly."[37]

As the colonial governors were responding to Pitt's letter in late October 1760, George Spencer was expecting to reap court-awarded penalties of £4,000 in the first of his prosecutions based on the Flour Act. The case against the owners of the *Earl of Loudoun* had been tried in the New York court of vice-admiralty, but Lewis Morris, the aged judge, was in no hurry, and the matter lingered on his docket. Back in April, William Smith, Jr., representing the brig's owners, had asked Judge Morris to dismiss the matter on the cynical grounds that the crime had been committed in the East Ward of the city rather than on the high seas, the proper sphere for admiralty law.[38]

Morris's ruling on November 12 came as a shock to both sides. "The judge," Spencer recalled, "after having kept me in suspense above six months," now refused to hear the case, claiming that only the "high court of admiralty" was mentioned in the Flour Act, not the "court of vice-admiralty." Meanwhile, Spencer's eight prosecutions in the Supreme Court of Judicature also became mired in jurisdictional wrangling.[39]

"I am debarred of the benefit of the laws of my country, by an overbearing people," Spencer told General Amherst, the highest-ranking British official in North America, in a letter dated November 29. "The merchants in this city," he charged, "have not only traded both directly and indirectly with the enemy, but still carry it on, to the greatest prejudice of the nation: and have defrauded His Majesty of the duties on sugars brought into this port from Monte Cristi and other foreign ports since the commencement of the war . . . [by] an immense sum, not less, I dare say, than two hundred thousand pounds sterling."

Then Spencer metaphorically threw himself at the British commander's feet, begging Amherst to send him to England, where the bankruptcy case would be immediately resolved and his suits against the violators of the Flour Act would be heard by an impartial court. "I should have been discharged long ago had I not entered prosecutions against two gentlemen in the city, who are nephews to two of the justices of the Supreme Court of Judicature."[40]

General Amherst "with the utmost impatience" forwarded Spencer's letter to Cadwallader Colden. With it he included a letter from a second informer, Augustus Bradley, an itinerant West Indian trader who had recently been accused of forgery and was now incarcerated at the New York City Jail. Bradley claimed to have been "sent to this place by a set of people who it is notoriously known have been concerned in an illicit trade." He parroted many of Spencer's accusations, even including a list of offending ships, but added colorful flourishes of his own. Amherst demanded an immediate inquiry. "I shall not trouble you any further on the subject," wrote the exasperated commander.[41]

The Spencer-Bradley inquiry—more properly, "examinations before [the] Council concerning illegal trade"—began on Monday, December 8, 1760, in the Council chamber of the governor's house at Fort George. The special committee of inquiry consisted of councilors thoroughly versed in the affairs of the city—John Tabor Kempe, Archibald Kennedy, Supreme Court Justice John Chambers, the attorney William Smith, Sr., and the merchants William Walton, Sr., and John Watts.

The probe, which concluded with a full report on Christmas Eve, was presided over by William Smith, Sr. Council President Cadwallader Colden began the proceedings by reading General Amherst's directive of December 6 and presented the six charges leveled against the city by George Spencer and Augustus Bradley: that great quantities of provisions were being sent to the French West Indies; that massive amounts of French sugar were entering the flow of New York exports; that New Yorkers were shipping gold to the enemy that had been sent from London to finance the war; that the city was supplying the French with naval stores, gunpowder, and other warlike articles; that trade with New Orleans was sustaining the French on the North American continent; and, finally, that all these illegal activities depended upon the cooperation of neighboring colonies. Given the severity of the charges, the board had little choice but to examine Spencer and Bradley "in order to find what proof they had or could give in support of their allegations."[42]

Augustus Bradley, the first to be called, appeared on Tuesday morning at eleven o'clock. He was a fountain of information. There were, he said, four vessels in the harbor owned by Allen Popham, a West Indian merchant, that were currently loading flour for Saint Eustatius under false clearances for Saint Christopher. The informer named the vessels and their captains, mentioning that Popham, who was then in the city, was in league with one of New York's most powerful figures, Nathaniel Marston.

Bradley accused Marston of shipping provisions and naval stores to the enemy "in upwards of 20 different vessels" by way of Saint Eustatius and Monte Cristi and of exporting flour directly to Saint-Domingue aboard his privateer ship *Hunter*. The witness also told the board that another prisoner in the New York City Jail—a sailor named John Cox—had been part of the privateer's crew when the vessel outran two British warships before delivering a large cargo of flour at Leogane in the Gulf of Gonâve, returning to New York with 300 hogsheads of French sugar.

Warming to his role, Bradley described how the captain of one of Marston's schooners—the *Little Esther* carrying 90 hogsheads of French sugar—had brought it through Sandy Hook, "then proceeded in his boat to [Perth] Amboy and entered his cargo and obtained a clearance for it, for which he paid a dollar a hogshead," before sending the vessel to New York and landing his goods. Sometimes ships returning from the Mount transferred their goods into "a small craft in the Amboy channel . . . in order to avoid the men of war, and came afterwards to New York in ballast."

Bradley then told the board that Popham and Marston had invented the charge of forgery in order to keep the informer "fast" in jail and obstruct justice. On and on Bradley went, pouring out what he knew (or suspected), anxious to prove his worth as a witness and earn a fair reward for honorably serving his country "on behalf of His Majesty."[43]

But Bradley had gone too far. On cue, four witnesses appeared on Tuesday, one on Wednesday, and five on Thursday to undermine his testimony and attack his character. Among them were John Cruger, the mayor of New York; aldermen John Bogert and Philip Livingston; representative merchants and ship captains; and one of the objects of Bradley's attention, Allen Popham of Saint Christopher. Nathaniel Marston, however, did not appear.[44]

The witnesses spoke with a single voice: William Coventry, a merchant, referred to Popham's "fair and unblemished character." Popham, of course, swore that he had never "ordered any provisions to be sent to any French port" and that the vessels in New York harbor were "bona fide bound to St. Christopher's." According to John Stevenson, captain of Popham's sloop *Postilion,* "he never landed one ounce of provisions in any French or neutral port."[45]

Now it was time to expose the informer as vindictive and mean-spirited. Livingston and Cruger revealed that in their examination Bradley had expressed anger at Popham and Marston for ordering him confined in the city jail for forging a bill of exchange. Bradley "did not like to be an informer," he had told his interrogators, but "revenge was sweet."[46]

Augustus Bradley understood what was happening. Following Wednesday's session, he urged Attorney General Kempe to subpoena John Cris, a sailor aboard the *Postilion* on its voyages from New York to Monte Cristi. "He is going to leave the place this day or tomorrow," Bradley told Kempe; and he "does not choose to say any thing of the matter." On Thursday he warned

Kempe that "some of the gentlemen that are concerned in shipping provisions contrary to [the] act of parliament will be for getting out of the way shortly."[47]

It was Spencer's turn on Friday morning. George Spencer had spent thirteen months confined in the city jail awaiting this moment. With Amherst's shadow over the proceedings, the informer expected a full and open inquiry. Instead, Spencer's questioners focused narrowly on New York City's unprotected direct trade with the French. They allowed nothing else. To his interrogators, Saint Eustatius, Curaçao, and Monte Cristi were irrelevant.[48]

In contrast to Bradley's bravado, Spencer's manner was reserved, his flat responses suggesting a tightly controlled—possibly ill or even threatened—witness. "Of his own knowledge," he told his interrogators, "he knoweth nothing of any trade carried on with the king's enemies." He had heard a rumor that Alderman Bogert once loaded a vessel with naval stores and ammunition for the Mississippi, but "he cannot now recollect the particulars." Spencer admitted having no knowledge of gold bullion sent to the French beyond what had appeared in newspapers—or of any "artifices or evasions, by which any person or persons trading with the king's enemies, find means to cover their criminal proceedings."[49]

In the afternoon, brushing Spencer aside, the committee turned to Monte Cristi. For sheer mendacity, the most memorable witness was Balthazar Kipp, a New Yorker who had resided at the Mount from September 1759 to April 1760 and before that was active in New York's trade to the neutral islands. During his time at Monte Cristi, Kipp had seen no evidence of French involvement; "the whole trade there appeared to him to be carried on between the English and the Spaniards." His imagination hit full stride when he told his interrogators that goods sent to Monte Cristi were intended for inland Spanish settlements to be "expended by the Spaniards." After seven months at the Mount, Kipp did not know "of any trade carried on with the king's enemies from Monte Cristi or elsewhere by the king's subjects."[50]

On Sunday, December 14, a reinvigorated George Spencer wrote a long, impassioned letter to William Pitt in London. He described how, just two days before, he had been brought before the New York Council, which "I thought intended to have examined me on every point relative to this affair." Instead, the Council had confined him to "trade carried on by the king's subjects with the subjects of the French king. . . . They would not permit me to say any one thing relative to that pernicious, ignominious trade carried on from hence to Monte Cristi; nor of the fictitious clearances brought hither from the neighboring provinces, by which the sugars brought into this port from the Mount, &c. are admitted to an entry at this customhouse."

In his letter Spencer lashed out at his interrogators, nearly all of whom, he claimed, were somehow connected to the city's trade with the French enemy. Cadwallader Colden's son Alexander, second-in-command at the New York customhouse, was a man "who never refuses a bribe when offered." John Chambers, a justice on the Supreme Court, was the uncle of one of the men "I have commenced a prosecution against in that court, for exporting provisions contrary to the act of parliament." William Walton, Sr., "in particular, has been, and I believe is still, greatly concerned in this illicit trade." And the daughter of William Smith, Sr., perhaps the most respected attorney in the city, was married to Jack Torrans, "a great Mount trader" and a close associate of Waddell Cunningham's.

"These were the gentlemen of the Council," the informer told Pitt, "who, together with His Majesty's attorney general, examined me on this point only, to wit: Whether I knew, of my own knowledge, any persons who traded with His Majesty's enemies. This was all they asked me."[51]

"I am quite impoverished," he added, "reduced to the lowest ebb of fortune" and kept in jail "purely to prevent me from going to the ministry on account of this illicit trade the merchants here have been, and are still carrying on, to the greatest prejudice of the nation." Spencer had been confined for six months before a court-appointed attorney would speak in his defense, "as none would take a fee against the people of the town, as they called it."[52]

The following week the committee heard from "the people of the town." Cunningham was an expert on both the Mount trade and Spencer's incarceration. He described Ireland's involvement with Monte Cristi and explained that ships carrying flour were regularly given clearances for the Spanish port by customs officers in London. But the task of attacking the informer's credibility fell to Francis Lewis and George Harison, both of whom had played leading roles in Spencer's imprisonment—and both of whom had a long history of doing business with the French.[53]

Lewis began by asserting the innocence of his sloop *Rachel,* which had carried twelve French prisoners to Hispaniola on a flag of truce license from the governor of New Jersey. The witness emphatically denied knowing "of any arms, ammunition, warlike stores or naval stores, being put on board the said sloop." As for Spencer, Lewis had been with him in London in 1757, and it was he who had secured Spencer's release from debtors' prison and "procured a passage for him in a vessel for New York."[54]

Harison—the choreographer of the November 1759 riot—had a startling revelation. Spencer, according to Harison, had been involved in treason "against the government." Harison had also been in London in 1757 and was with Spencer and Lewis on the return voyage to New York. Aboard ship, Spencer had bragged that on a visit to France in 1755 he had "exhibited to the French minister a plan of the harbor of New York with the number of the inhabitants and strength of the place" in exchange for the promise that if the "French should succeed in the reduction of New York, he should be appointed governor."[55]

Spencer's reaction to the accusation is not recorded. But he must have been shocked. In April 1756, Spencer, then in London, had written to the earl of Holdernesse, a high-ranking British official involved in intelligence gathering. The financially straitened Spencer had been in Calais on business in August 1755 when he heard rumors of French intentions to capture the principal seaports of British North America.

"I was animated by a dutiful regard, and sincere intention to serve my king and country," he had told Holdernesse, "and to prevent the French, if possible, from ravaging those places which I have particular esteem for." Spencer had concocted a scheme to discover "what towns His Majesty intended to attack; and, at the same time, to endeavor to induce, or draw the French fleet to a certain place, at so great a distance from any of their own ports, that our fleet might fall upon them in such a manner, that not one of their ships might escape, as such a blow might probably determine the dispute between the two nations."

In his report to Holdernesse, Spencer described how he had ingratiated himself with the French officials who had interviewed him at Versailles. Spencer had offered to provide a plan of New York harbor and map out an overland route by means of which the city might be easily captured and serve as a base from which to stage the French conquest of British North America. When offered "a present of a thousand louis d'ors" to travel with the invasion fleet and "a pension of five thousand louis d'ors per annum" on their success, he had demurred, preferring instead, he claimed, to be at the service of the invaders when they arrived at New York.

"This was only a finesse," explained the self-made double agent. "I was fully determined no sum should tempt me to betray my country in any respect whatever, and much less to a perfidious nation, who are the common disturbers of the repose of Europe, and more particularly of this kingdom." He reassured Holdernesse that "the greatest part [of what] I wrote to the Court of France upon this occasion was fictitious, . . . and entirely calculated to decoy the French, who would deceive all the world if they had it in their power."[56]

George Spencer's patriotism was of the highest order—almost. He expected to be compensated for his trouble. In a letter to Holdernesse's secretary in June 1756, the New Yorker had recalled how he had been assured that "I should be well rewarded for the service I had done, . . . and if His Lordship thinks I have merited a place, or any other favor, I shall gladly accept of it as a recompense." The earl had needed a character reference, and how fortunate it was that a fellow New Yorker—and good friend—was close at hand. "One George Harison, Esq., who is searcher and surveyor of His Majesty's customs in the City of New York, is now in London; and as that gentleman has been intimately acquainted with me above seventeen years, I make no doubt he will be so kind to give you an impartial account of me."[57]

Harison, perhaps wary of entanglement in the affair, had made himself unavailable. "I find, that gentleman is lately gone into the country," wrote an embarrassed Spencer the following day, "and will not return to town for a considerable time." Uncompensated for his service to the state but freed from debtors' prison, Spencer had returned to New York with Lewis and Harison. Four-and-a-half years later, he must have been numbed by the realization that his daring scheme had been so artfully turned against him.[58]

George Spencer was finished. His arch-nemesis had destroyed the last traces of his reputation. In addition to conspiring to hand New York over to the French enemy, Harison told the committee, Spencer had shown him documents that revealed other "treasonable practices." And—a final thrust—the informer had become a Roman Catholic, having done so solely "to serve his own particular interests." With Spencer demolished, the Spencer-Bradley inquiry neared its conclusion.[59]

But Augustus Bradley was not quite finished. "You and the gentlemen of the Council seemed angry with me (when I was before you) for writing to General Amherst before I let you know of the informations I had to make," he wrote Colden. "By what I can learn Your Honor omitted (by which I imagine it slipped your memory) to examine Mr. Spencer . . . with regard to the Monte Cristi trade and false clearances which was the most material point of [his] evidence."[60]

There was contempt in Bradley's challenge: "I mentioned this fearing you had forgot it, although I am thoroughly sensible it is in the power of Your Honor and Council to examine them to those articles or not as you shall see fit." Bradley's remarks were impertinent, snapped Colden, who refused to respond.[61]

On Christmas Eve, William Smith, Sr., chairman of the committee examining the allegations of George Spencer and Augustus Bradley, presented a full report in the Council chamber at Fort George. One by one, he dismissed each of their claims and attacked "the assertion, that a considerable trade has been carried on from this port to the French ports on Hispaniola." Smith stressed that trade with Monte Cristi was legal, as was commerce with Saint Eustatius and Curaçao, and that respectable merchants had testified that their ships carried no provisions or "warlike stores" to any of those places. The allegations of collusion with customs officials in neighboring colonies were likewise set aside: "As this charge only affects the conduct of officers of other governments, the board were of opinion it did not properly fall under their consideration."

"Mr. Spencer has already commenced several actions," Smith went on, "not less than eight, against divers merchants of this city, for exporting provisions contrary to the act of parliament, [and] . . . these suits are still depending though commenced nearly a year since, and not one of them brought to trial, probably from the want of proof."

However, Smith concluded, "the committee are humbly of opinion" that in all cases of trade with the enemy, the government should assert its authority, "whenever it shall appear necessary for the discovery of the offence, or the bringing [of] the offenders to justice."[62]

On Saturday, December 27, Cadwallader Colden prepared a report for William Pitt. The acting governor explained that he had received a communication from General Amherst early in December containing letters from an insolvent debtor and an accused forger, both of whom were confined in the city jail. Because the letters "contained general information of illicit trade carried on in this place," Colden had laid them before the Council, which "spent a considerable time in examining witnesses" and responding to the charges.

"The gentlemen of the Council distinguished between trade with the enemy's colonies and trade with neutral ports," wrote Colden. "All trade with the enemy was allowed to be prohibited; but that the trade with the neutral ports in the West Indies is only illegal under certain circumstances and in certain commodities, and that this trade came not under the view of His Majesty's orders of the 23rd August [is] signified by your letter of that date."

"I have nothing further to say," wrote New York's acting governor, "than, that I shall do my utmost to discourage all illegal trade, of every kind, wherever I can discover it, and to prosecute vigorously those who shall be found trading with the enemy."[63]

On the day Colden finished his report, Captain Samuel Partridge, master of the ship *Racehorse*—just arrived from London—dropped anchor in Boston harbor after a grueling winter crossing of forty days. "By him we have the melancholy news of the death of our most gracious sovereign, King George the Second," reported the *Boston Evening Post.* The British monarch had died "in the 77th year of his age, and in the 34th of his reign" at Kensington Palace on October 25, 1760. Far out at sea, HMS *Fowey,* the British warship carrying formal instructions for proclaiming the new king, was pushing hard for New York City.[64]

CHAPTER SEVEN

Business as Usual

New Yorkers expected that their city would be the first in colonial America to proclaim the young monarch King George III. But the warship carrying the documents from London was still at sea on December 30, 1760, when Governor Francis Bernard of Massachusetts announced that he had received "certain advice of the death of His Late Majesty King George the Second, and the accession of His Royal Highness the Prince of Wales to the imperial throne of Great Britain." Reading his own draft, Bernard proclaimed the new king before the Massachusetts Council, after which it was "repeated with a loud voice from the balcony of the courthouse [before] . . . a vast concourse of people of all ranks."[1]

New York City could still get in ahead of Newport, Philadelphia, and other colonial rivals. Awaiting the warship's appearance, the Council set aside Sunday, January 11, 1761, as a day of public mourning. With houses of worship draped in black and muffled bells tolling, "funeral sermons were preached in all the churches in this city, on the death of His Late Majesty."[2]

On the afternoon of Friday, January 16, HMS *Fowey* came to anchor in the East River within sight of Saint George's steeple, three blocks inland on Beekman Street. The captain, George Anthony Tonyn, hove his vessel "within a ship's length of the wharf out of the way of the ice." As crewmen unbent the sails and secured their ship, Tonyn made his way to the governor's mansion at Fort George carrying a packet thick with London newspapers, military dispatches, and documents bearing the scarlet seals of His Majesty's Privy Council.[3]

At noon on Saturday, a twenty-one-gun salute announced the new king to New Yorkers bundled against the sleet and snow and gathering along lower Broadway. In the warmth of the Council Chamber, Acting Governor Colden read from the proclamation: "[We] do hereby with one full voice and consent of tongue and heart, publish and proclaim, that the high and mighty, Prince George, Prince of Wales, is now, by the death of our late sovereign, of happy and glorious memory, become our only lawful and rightful, liege lord George the Third, by the grace of God, King of Great Britain, France, and Ireland, defender of the faith, supreme lord of the . . . province of New York, and territories depending thereon, and all other His Late Majesty's territories and dominions in America."[4]

The document was subscribed "by His Honor the president, the members of His Majesty's Council, the mayor and corporation, and most of the principal gentlemen of the city, who were present at the solemnity." Among the fifty-six signatories were fifteen merchants and perhaps a dozen public officials complicit in the city's wartime trade with the French. John Bogert, Jr., Waddell Cunningham, Francis Lewis, and Jacob Walton—and perhaps others—had even taken a hand in inciting the riot against George Spencer in November 1759.[5]

At the conclusion of the ceremony, the dignitaries, many in colorful regalia, braved the weather to march in solemn procession up Broadway escorted by "the company of grenadiers, with their bayonets fixed, and [a] troop of horse." Redcoats, barely visible through swirling snow, lined the route to Wall Street and City Hall. "His Majesty being again proclaimed, three huzzas were given," and a second royal salute echoed through the city. "The procession returned in the same order from City Hall to the fort," as the guns aboard the *Fowey* fired a third salute. "Notwithstanding the severity of the weather, the whole began and concluded with great order and decency."[6]

Buoyed by British victories, particularly the French surrender at Montreal in September, the snowbound city was in a festive mood. With windows illuminated by candlelight and taverns bursting with merrymakers singing "God Save the King," New Yorkers congratulated themselves through the night as "loyal healths" were drunk to the young king "and all the brave and gallant generals, admirals, officers, seamen and soldiers, in His Majesty's service."[7]

No doubt the toasts of the men embroiled in trade with the French were loyal. But their allegiance was complex—and carefully nuanced—especially after the whitewashing of the Spencer-Bradley inquiry in December. With Spencer safely behind bars as a warning to informers, there ought to have been a renewal of confidence in the city. Instead, there was uncertainty. The merchants of New York were becoming "chagrined at the interdiction of their commerce with the French and Spaniards of Monte Cristi." Two signatories to the proclamation declaring the new king, Waddell Cunningham and Jacob Walton, had received disturbing news from John Harris Cruger, nephew of the mayor and an attorney in Kingston, Jamaica.[8]

Admiral Charles Holmes had taken over as commander of the British naval base at Port Royal, Jamaica, in May 1760. His predecessor, Admiral Cotes, had spent the previous six months disrupting "northward" flag-trucers and driving the most timid participants out of North America's trade with the French. Even so, large quantities of goods—some made in English workshops to French specifications—continued to get through, largely by way of Monte Cristi Bay and "contraband Dutchmen." The huge flow led to shortages throughout the British Caribbean and—most frustrating to the admirals—enabled French privateers to operate with impunity. "Thirty English vessels, bound for several West Indian ports, have lately been taken and carried into Martinique," reported the *New-York Gazette* on May 12, 1760, the day Holmes arrived at Port Royal.[9]

Cotes had been slow to intervene as the Mount trade grew to huge proportions. His squadron had been over-extended, and London had ignored repeated requests for instructions regarding Monte Cristi. Then, in the summer of 1759, his sea officers had brought in hard evidence that North American flag-trucers were provisioning the marquis de Bompar's squadron at Cape François, Port-au-Prince, and Port Saint Louis. From September 1759 to May 1760, British cruisers had seized close to fifty flag-trucers, and the New Providence privateers took at least another dozen. The condemnation of North American ships and cargoes in Jamaica's court of vice-admiralty for violations of the king's proclamation led to panic in New York, Philadelphia, Newport, and Boston.[10]

Behind the scenes, wealthy men like William Walton, Sr., brought their influence to bear. Thomas Bullock, chief judge of the vice-admiralty court of Jamaica, announced ten acquittals just two days after Holmes took command. New Yorkers responded with relief to news that their "unjustly detained" flag-trucers had been cleared, but Cotes and Holmes were furious.[11]

For months, Bullock had been skirmishing with both Cotes and Jamaica's lieutenant-governor, Sir Henry Moore. The dispute with the navy reached its climax when Bullock displayed a letter from Cotes demanding condemnation of the captured flag-trucers. "He was not to be instructed by Mr. Cotes," snapped the judge, "knowing his business as well as him." With Moore, the dispute was about prize money. Bullock preferred to prosecute under the Prize Act of 1756, which granted those aboard the capturing vessel full value of all prizes. The governor of Jamaica, on the other hand, favored prosecutions under the Flour Act, which put the officers and men involved in a capture into the role of informers, with the king's share flowing into the hands of well-situated politicians. And the sugar planters—the basis of the island's political establishment—resented the easy access to the British market now enjoyed by North American merchants shipping "foreign" sugar acquired aboard their flag-trucers.[12]

Bullock's acquittal of ten flag-trucers in mid-May had driven the politicians and naval officers together. In June, Judge Bullock was dismissed by the governor and Council of Jamaica and replaced by the twenty-six-year-old Edward Long, Moore's brother-in-law. "This stretch of power shows the extravagance and tyranny of the people in that island in the strongest light," wrote a Philadelphia merchant, "and renders it hardly probable that a new judge appointed by them or their governor will listen to any arguments that can be offered by the claimants in any future trial."[13]

He had reason to be concerned. Admiral Holmes was determined to put an end to the Monte Cristi trade. "The gentlemen of North America, have long attempted to cover themselves under flags of truce to Hispaniola," he wrote, "but the little regard that has been paid to them in the judicial courts and the vigilance of the king's ships, in seizing them as well as the ships of neutral powers, coming directly from the enemy's ports, have brought them to place their chief hopes of security in the pretended free port of Monte Cristi." As many as five hundred British, Irish, and North American ships had called there during the previous twelve months. The British ministry did not demand an end to the trade, however. On the contrary, complained Holmes, "it has been lately reported here that . . . Monte Cristi is admitted, by the government and courts at home, to be a free port and that all His Majesty's subjects, as well as others may trade to and from it with impunity."[14]

"If this trade be permitted," he warned, "it is altogether impractical to hinder the enemy being supplied by ourselves, with provisions and everything else, they may want. Their trade will go on in the briskest manner, in our own or other bottoms; and this island, as well as our other settlements, must continue to starve. I shall therefore think it my duty to impede the enemy's progress, that way, as much as possible, by seizing such ships as may come from Monte Cristi with the enemy's produce on board until I receive orders to the contrary."[15]

Cruisers from Port Royal began interdicting Mountmen in the summer of 1760, with Holmes himself directing operations from aboard HMS *Defiance* in September and October. In addition to making prizes of "all the Monte Cristi and Cape traders, no matter where they belong," according to a Boston newspaper, the cruisers began impressing sailors off British ships riding in the Bay. By December, few dared cross the paths of HMS *Boreas, Defiance, Edinburgh, Hussar, Renown, Zephyr,* and the other warships patrolling off the north coast of Hispaniola. As a result, Holmes told the Admiralty, at Cape François "provisions begin to grow dear, notwithstanding the glut they had some time ago."[16]

Monte Cristi Bay became a refuge for stranded vessels. "The men of war taking all the ships from this place puts us into the greatest dilemma," worried an English ship captain in December. "The place is well guarded by seven of His Majesty's ships of war who seem determined to destroy the trade," wrote a North American merchant. Holmes's squadron was stretched thin, however, and his warships were in bad repair from constant sea duty.[17]

One of those stranded vessels was the snow *Recovery* of New York, owned by Walton and Company and Greg and Cunningham, which from mid-October to early December 1760 sat waiting at Monte Cristi Bay "until some good opportunity offers" before attempting the return home. "[We] might have sailed twenty days ago," Richard Mercer, the firms' agent, wrote home in November, "only for the men of war" of Admiral Holmes's squadron.[18]

Help arrived in the form of Waddell Cunningham's sloop *Harlequin,* one of New York's most successful private ships of war. On December 4, after Robert Castle, master of the *Recovery,* and James Oman, the privateer's commander, had planned a collusive capture, *Harlequin* stood off Monte Cristi to await its prey. The next morning—a Friday—Oman carried out the charade and placed a prize master aboard the *Recovery.* Somewhere north of Hispaniola, the privateer veered away as its prize steered for Turks Island Passage and the open sea.[19]

Then *Recovery*'s luck ran out. On Saturday afternoon, the 6th of December, it was spotted by a lookout high atop HMS *Hussar,* a 28-gun British frigate patrolling midway between Cape François and the southernmost entry point of Turks Island Passage. At five o'clock, Captain Robert Carkett sent out his boats, and an hour later British sailors were aboard the *Recovery.* During the seizure, George White, a crewman aboard *Hussar,* was discovered "offering to assist the master in taking her from the midshipman on board." By eight o'clock, the officers had "exchanged the people and [taken] possession." The warship already had two prizes in its care.[20]

HMS *Hussar* had left Port Royal on October 17. Off the eastern end of Jamaica, it had spoken with HMS *Lively,* returning home with a rich French prize. A few days later, in the Windward Passage between Cuba and Hispaniola, *Hussar* had sighted HMS *Glasgow* with another two prizes, both North Americans. Patrolling off northwestern Hispaniola, Carkett's frigate had crossed paths with four more British warships—*Defiance, Hampshire, Renown,* and *Trent*—all escorting vessels taken in the vicinity of Cape François and Monte Cristi. The day after *Recovery*'s capture, *Hussar* picked up yet another New York ship and began the return to Port Royal. As the warship approached Cape Dame Marie at the far southwestern point of the Gulf of Gonâve, Captain Carkett "read the Articles of War . . . to the ship's company [and] punished George White with 24 lashes for mutiny (on board the prize Recovery snow)."[21]

On December 14, with the weather worsening, *Hussar* chased an enemy privateer under the guns of a small French fort, where the British "fired several shot and left her." The next day, in driving rain, Carkett picked up his fifth and final prize when he seized a small French privateer schooner at anchor near the Navassa, an abandoned rock between Saint-Domingue and Jamaica.[22]

During its final hours at sea, HMS *Hussar* sailed through a violent storm. Gale-force winds "rolled away the main mast which carried away the mizzen top mast and swept the yawl overboard." Two sailors—John Cary and Duncan Coats—"being on duty aloft went both overboard with the mast and were lost." The damaged frigate limped into Port Royal harbor, where it found HMS *Cambridge* riding at anchor. The 80-gun warship displayed the broad pendant of Rear Admiral Charles Holmes, the nemesis of the Mount traders.[23]

Admiral Holmes ordered the *Recovery*'s captain, Robert Castle, brought before the vice-admiralty court of Jamaica. His bail, set at £200, was posted by John Harris Cruger, the Kingston attorney who was a nephew of New York's mayor and a Walton in-law. According to Castle's deposition, he had done business at Monte Cristi exclusively with subjects of the king of Spain; the sugar and coffee aboard the *Recovery* had been "brought from Monte Cristi shore"; and he had no knowledge whether the Spanish at Monte Cristi acted as "agents, factors, or trustees for the French king, or his subjects and vassals, for the disposal of their goods." Furthermore, no ship's papers had

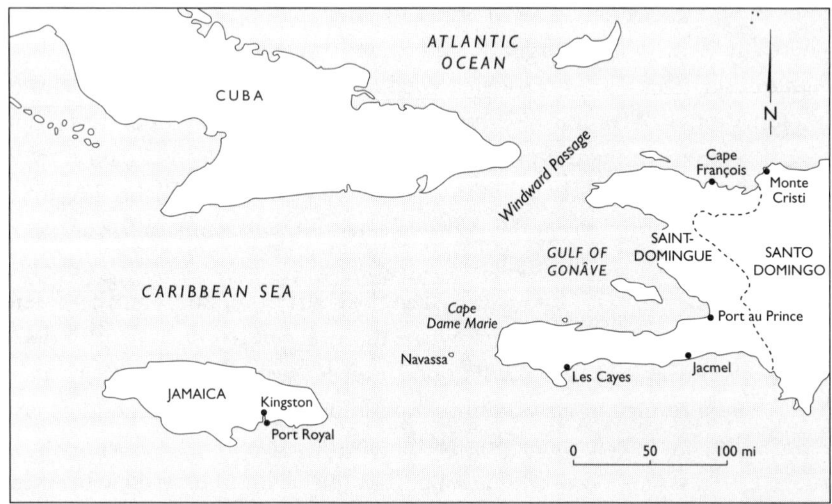

Cuba, Jamaica, and Saint-Domingue

been in any way "destroyed, made away, secreted, concealed, or altered." Then the second lieutenant of the *Hussar* discovered sixteen incriminating documents in the sea chest of the snow's boatswain.[24]

On Tuesday, December 22, Judge Edward Long convened Jamaica's court of vice-admiralty at the town of Santiago de la Vega to hear the case against the New York ship. James Innes, advocate general for Jamaica, spoke for the captors. He began by telling the court that before he reached Monte Cristi, Captain Castle had put a large part of *Recovery*'s cargo into the hands of Dutch intermediaries on the island of Curaçao who transported it "to the French king's territories." Thus did Castle and the vessel's owners "aid assist, strengthen and enable the said French king his subjects and vassals to carry on and prolong the present war."

At Monte Cristi, Innes continued, papers seized aboard the *Recovery* revealed that Castle's agent, Richard Mercer, "did actually hold correspondence with the subjects of the French king," contrary to the "declaration of war expressly prohibiting the same." The advocate general challenged the integrity of Spanish documents, showed the snow's capture by the privateer *Harlequin* to have been collusive, and argued that Castle had perjured himself when he stated that he alone had conducted his ship's business as it rode in the bay at Monte Cristi.[25]

Recovery's owners were in a difficult position in an unfriendly court. Their defense was in the hands of George Lumsden, a Kingston lawyer who emphatically denied the charges and protested the snow's "illegal and unjust capture and detention." Lumsden argued that Castle was innocent of delivering provisions and contraband goods "to the subjects and vassals of the French king" indirectly through Dutch intermediaries at Curaçao and Spanish traders at Monte Cristi or directly through the owners' factor, Richard Mercer. The defense asserted the authenticity of certificates attesting to the purchase of the cargo from Spanish traders.[26]

In mid-January 1761, Lumsden asked the court to conduct a further interrogation of Robert Castle following the discovery of the documents hidden aboard his vessel in Port Royal harbor. Lumsden argued that Castle had not had an opportunity to answer "the imputation laid to his charge . . . [that there were] no papers belonging to the snow or her cargo." According to Judge Long, Castle's depositions supporting his claim to have done business with "Spaniards only" were "irregular and inadmissible."[27]

On March 2, nine weeks after the case was brought before him, the judge rendered his verdict. The snow *Recovery* and its cargo were to be "confiscated and condemned" and the value "distributed and divided among the captors." Judge Long had found sufficient evidence of direct contact between the owners' agent and the French at Cape François, of a collusive capture, of perjury by Captain Castle, and of promiscuous use of "fictitious bills of parcel, receipts and certificates from the Spanish lieutenant governor."[28]

The *Recovery* would probably have been condemned even on far weaker evidence. According to a Newport captain facing the same prospect, "if but one barrel of provisions has been sold to the French they say that the cargo will be condemned." Few North American prizes brought into Port Royal by the warships of Admiral Holmes's squadron escaped condemnation; "the people here are such villains and so united in these affairs," wrote another North American awaiting a verdict.[29]

Despite the vigilance of Admiral Holmes's cruisers and the inevitability of Judge Long's guilty verdicts, Monte Cristi had returned to business as usual by the spring of 1761. At the time of *Recovery*'s condemnation, "69 sail of English merchant vessels employed in shipping" rode at anchor in the bay. A quarter were English, Scottish, and Irish. A third of the rest were from New York City. They included *Recovery*'s sister ships, the sloop *Little David* and the snow *Kingston.* There were, as well, vessels owned by James Depeyster, Phillip Livingston, and David Proovst, men with a long history of doing business with the French.[30]

The spirit of New York was exemplified by the ubiquitous Captain William Carlisle. Following the outbreak of fighting, he shuttled between New York City and the Danish islands of Saint Croix and Saint Thomas, calling intermittently at Monte Cristi Bay and French ports in the Leeward and Windward Islands. Like other long-term participants, Carlisle adapted to changing circumstances and found protection where he could.[31]

Sometimes this involved pure charade. "In a new sloop bound from hence for Jamaica," reported the *New-York Mercury* in January 1760, Carlisle was "taken by a French privateer, and carried into Cape-François," just as Admiral Cotes's cruisers deployed against the flag-trucers. Miraculously, four months later Captain Carlisle entered 58 hogsheads of sugar at the New York custom house, declaring it to be imported from Perth Amboy, New Jersey. In September, he brought in another 101 hogsheads, this time purportedly from New Haven.[32]

On October 31—his third visit to Hispaniola in 1760—Carlisle was greeted at the Mount by the boarding party of a British man of war, HMS *Defiance.* "They took 700 pounds of butter out of him, and gave an order on [the navy] for it," Richard Mercer wrote home. A close call, perhaps, but British naval officers had little interest in seizing flour and salted provisions when, with patience, they could have French sugar, coffee, and indigo, far more valuable cargoes. They had to make their captures at sea, however, and Carlisle was elusive.[33]

In February 1761, at a wharf in the ice-clogged East River, Captain Carlisle exchanged an unknown quantity of French sugar for 714 barrels of flour and "sundry gammons and hams, and a quantity of linens, woolens and canvas" loaded aboard the brig *Polly.* He cleared Sandy Hook on March 2, the day Judge Long in Jamaica handed down his verdict on the *Recovery,* and he was in Monte Cristi Bay on the 20th. On his arrival, Carlisle put his cargo into the hands of Isaac Van Dam, a New Yorker resident at the Mount, who sent it on Spanish coasters to Cape François, where the canvas—good quality sailcloth—found its way aboard "a frigate belonging to the French king."[34]

Returning through Sandy Hook early in May with yet another cargo of sugar, *Polly* was detained by a British warship pressing sailors off incoming merchantmen. "The more effectually to conceal his collusive and fraudulent proceedings," according to a British officer, Carlisle destroyed incriminating documents as HMS *Greyhound*'s boat approached his brig, "burning some and causing others to be thrown into the sea, with a shot and spike nails fastened thereto in order to sink the same." But Carlisle had become overconfident and reckless. The brig's cargo of flour, hams, and canvas had not been properly cleared from the New York customhouse—nor had the owners posted the bond required by the Flour Act. There was, in addition, no clearance from Monte Cristi for New York, nor any record of the voyage in the *Polly*'s logbook or, for that matter, records of the two previous voyages to Monte Cristi. Doubting that he would receive justice in a New York courtroom, Thomas Francis, *Greyhound*'s commander, took his prize to Halifax, Nova Scotia, for trial before an admiralty judge friendly to the navy.[35]

Pressure from British cruisers and the Bahama privateers continued through 1761. In April, the *Boston Post-Boy* reported that British warships out of Port Royal had "taken several English flags of truce and Mount traders which were all condemned." The month before, a brig belonging to James Depeyster bound from Cape François to New York was brought into Nassau by two New Providence privateers. "The business of privateering is the most beneficial and almost only profitable trade carried on in these islands," wrote the merchants of New Providence in 1760.[36]

New Yorkers responded by sending additional privateers to the West Indies to stage collusive captures and keep the Nassau men at bay. Cunningham alone commissioned two privateers in April, one commanded by the nephew of a New York Supreme Court justice, and the other by a kinsman of his busy Monte Cristi agent. But financial ruin was always close at hand. "Consider[ing] how many vultures are out in quest of prey," wrote an Irish merchant in Philadelphia to his kinsman at Cape François in May 1761, "I cannot find that the profits of this trade [are] at all adequate to the risk."[37]

James Thompson may have wondered the same thing. In June 1760, his brig *Achilles* had been seized coming out of the Cape and tried in the Jamaican court of vice-admiralty under the Flour Act. Thompson's business began to unravel following condemnation of his vessel and cargo, together with a fine of twenty shillings for every bushel of flour brought into the French port. He managed to hang on through the autumn and winter but was jailed in the spring of 1761 as an insolvent debtor. In May, a New York court invited his creditors (many of them doing business with the French) to show cause "why an assignment of the estate of the said James Thompson, should not be made and he thereupon be discharged from his imprisonment." Then William Walton, Sr., allowed Thompson, the husband of his niece Catharine, to draw against her legacy and settle his affairs "with great reputation." By September, James Thompson was back in business, this time at Monte Cristi. Before the end of the year he was representing the family's interests at Cape François.[38]

In New York, the government's complacency regarding trade with the enemy was beginning to break down. In June 1761 army headquarters advised Cadwallader Colden, now lieutenant-governor, to be watchful of Frenchmen moving freely about the city—especially paroled French officers. "By the company [Captain] McCarthy generally keeps," responded Colden, "I suspect that he is upon some scheme of illegal trade." General Amherst was growing uncomfortable with "the negligence and carelessness, in letting French officers and men come into New York, from on board privateers, and other vessels, without anybody's knowing from whence, or what they are doing."[39]

Madame Jerome—"the French milliner in New York"—tipped off Amherst that one of her countrymen had slipped out of town aboard a trading ship bound for the Mississippi. He had sailed "in partnership with one Mrs. Willett, of New York." The offending vessel carried twenty-two tons of provisions through the East River to New London, where Mrs. Willet gave bond that it was being shipped to a British port. "I strongly suspect that she has not landed them, because she has carried off privately a Frenchman who lives at the Mississippi and is suspected to be a spy," reported Colden. "His name [is] Renaud, and [he] has been at Boston and some months in this place."[40]

This "open and barefaced" infringement of the law required a response, insisted Amherst, as though discovering the problem for the first time. Colden, who nine months earlier had initiated the Spencer-Bradley inquiry, experienced a similar epiphany. "I have received some information of illegal trade carried on from this port by means of the customhouse officers of New London," he wrote Governor Fitch of Connecticut. The investigation had to be conducted quietly, Amherst warned, "for there is no doubt, if the affair should get wind, and the owners have room to suspect their being discovered, they would prevent our obtaining the legal proofs, and order the vessel, and Renaud, not to return to New York."[41]

As officials in New York City attempted to tighten controls on wartime trade, admiralty courts in Great Britain were upholding the rights of British subjects to trade in neutral ports, so long as that trade conformed to the

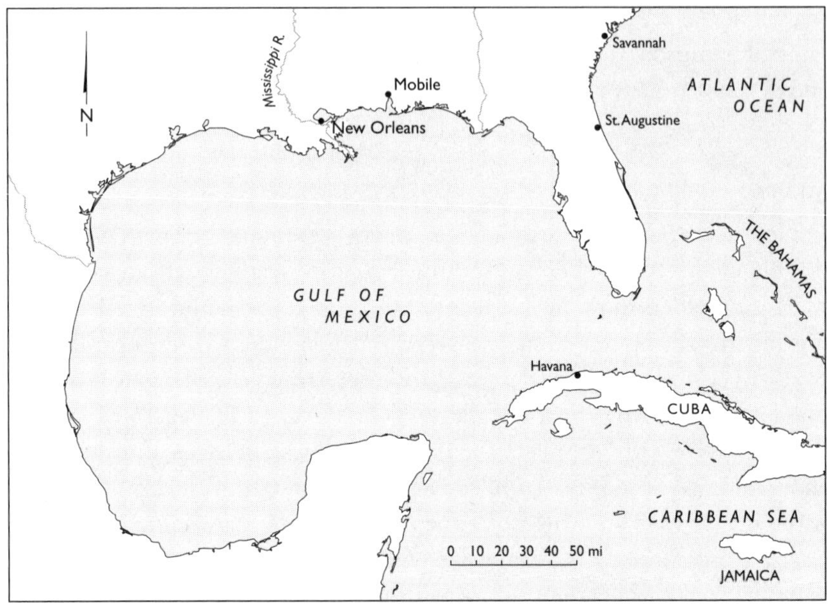

New Orleans, Mobile, and the Gulf of Mexico

requirements of the king's declaration of war, the British Acts of Trade and Navigation, and the Flour Act of 1757. In April 1761 the *Connecticut Gazette* reported the release by an admiralty judge in London of an English ship taken coming out of Monte Cristi Bay by one of Admiral Holmes's men of war. The vessel had been seized with papers showing that its cargo had been "bought of the Spaniards on English account." The documents protected it from condemnation, according to the *Gazette,* "as if she had come from Jamaica, or from the enemy, as being a neutral ship and going to a neutral port."[42]

Then in September, the *New-York Gazette* published an "extract of a letter from a gentleman in London, to his friend in this city, dated July 4, 1761, the authenticity of which is out of doubt." This gentleman wrote, "I have the pleasure to acquaint you, that last Saturday was determined by the [Lords] Commissioners of Prize Causes, the several appeals depending upon the English ships from Monte Cristi, taken by our men of war and condemned at Gibraltar, when their lordships reversed the sentences of that vice admiralty court, and ordered restitution of ships and cargoes to the appellants, or the full value."[43]

In their decision, the Lords Commissioners for Appeals in Prize Causes (better known as the Lords of Appeals) affirmed the status of Monte Cristi as a neutral port open to Dutch and Danish, as well as British, merchantmen. "They further declared, that every British subject had an undoubted right of purchasing French produce in every neutral port in America, or Europe; and as the appellants swore that they had not corresponded directly or indirectly with the French, the Lords ordered restitution." Before the end of July, the Lords of Appeals had overturned condemnations of six New York vessels by vice-admiralty courts on Jamaica and at Gibraltar.[44]

Such news had little impact on Admiral Holmes, whose letters home seethed with contempt for admiralty judges and politicians who committed the "most outrageous acts of injustice" with the "intention of defrauding the officers and seamen of His Majesty's squadron, as well as of encouraging and protecting the trade carried on with the enemy at Monte Cristi." He stepped up the British navy's interdictions, and French planters, desperate to get their produce home, increased their dependence on French warships pressed into service as merchantmen. In June 1761, Holmes had been aboard HMS *Hampshire* when it fell in with and took "a French man of war of 74 guns in the Bite of Leogane, very richly laden with sugar, coffee, indigo, &c. &c. bound from Port au Prince to Old France." In spite of Holmes, trade flourished, and in September, HMS *Pembroke* "found riding [at the Mount] 70 or 80 sail of English vessels." During the summer, provisions were cheap at Saint-Domingue, "insomuch, that the best Irish beef was at one pistole a barrel, and flour a perfect drug."[45]

In New York, Monte Cristi was a heated topic. "Great clamors have, without the least foundation, been raised concerning the shipping of provisions to that port," according to the *New-York Gazette* in mid-October. "It is said, the French have been supplied, who otherwise must have been starved out of Hispaniola; let any man in his senses think of the folly and absurdity of such arguments." The argument that France benefited was dismissed out of hand as British intervention in the commerce of New York became a local grievance against the British Parliament.

"By false reports and unjust representations," continued the *Gazette,* "an Act of Parliament was obtained [in 1757] to prohibit the shipping of provisions from North America; which act, for want of proper representations to His Majesty and Council, is still in force—notwithstanding the severe and cruel hardships it laid on His Majesty's loyal subjects in America, who were prevented from exporting their staple commodities, while their fellow subjects in Great Britain and Ireland, enjoyed the privilege of sending every kind of provisions to Monte Cristi and every other neutral port in Europe and America, . . . at the time when our men of war and privateers from Jamaica, Providence, and other places, were distressing the trade of these colonies to a degree very little different from robbery and piracy."[46]

New York's response to the British navy's interdictions had taken on a tone and a vocabulary that would soon become familiar. "The day seems approaching when they will be obliged to give up their ill got plunder, and very probably smart for their tyranny and great abuse given to subjects more loyal and much better than themselves; who, though they are so unhappy as to be at a distance from Britain's happy shores, will find a way to get justice, while a George reigns and a Pitt advises."[47]

Merchants in London were in an even greater uproar. Their spokesman was James Bourdieu of Lime Street, styled a "French merchant" in the London directories of the 1760s. With "concerns at the Mount exceed[ing] seventy thousand pounds sterling," Bourdieu succeeded in obtaining intervention at the highest level of government to protect property "invaded and plundered, by these very men of war, whose duty it is to grant us protection." In December the ministry dispatched a sloop of war to the Mount "with orders to protect, and not molest His Majesty's subjects on a legal trade to that place."[48]

Rumors spread that Admiral Holmes was soon to be recalled. "Every department of government disavows his wanton and extraordinary conduct," wrote one observer. To powerful London merchants with a stake in the Monte Cristi trade—and insurance underwriters faced with huge losses—the commander at Port Royal was a tyrant running roughshod over the liberties of British citizens. Driven by the lure of prize money, his enemies intimated, Holmes was disrupting a legal trade based on "a wrong interpretation of Mr. Pitt's remarkable letter last year."[49]

Holmes's departure did come that fall, but it took an unexpected form. As merchants and politicians in North America and the British Isles plotted against him, the rear admiral's health deteriorated. After a few days "in a dangerous way," Charles Holmes died on the evening of November 20. He was laid to rest Monday afternoon three days later at Halfway Tree churchyard (in present-day Kingston) as the great guns on "all His Majesty's ships in the harbor" at Port Royal marked his passing.[50]

His replacement, Commodore Arthur Forrest, complained bitterly about the diversion of North American provisions to the French. But his cruisers desperately needed repairs, forcing him to relax the prohibition against flags of truce and end the blanket interdiction of Mount traders. By mid-December, "the men of war [had] entirely desisted from taking any vessels in this trade," wrote a wary Connecticut ship captain at Monte Cristi.[51]

North America's trade with the enemy remained a problem for the Royal Navy. But there were more pressing concerns. "The Spaniards," Forrest told the Admiralty in December, were "strengthening their squadron in these seas which may escape their Lordships' notice, as they drop them out ship by ship." HMS *Viper,* which had recently called at Havana, reported the arrival there of "seven sail of the line with 4,000 troops," and more expected. According to Forrest's intelligence, there were then at the Spanish stronghold eighteen to twenty ships of the line and several frigates, "a squadron very unusual for them."[52]

Meanwhile, George Spencer languished in the New York City Jail. His resources depleted, he could no longer afford one of the rooms reserved for gentleman debtors. Crowded into damp and filthy quarters with common criminals, the celebrated informer struggled to maintain his veneer of respectability as his health worsened. Spencer had contracted a disorder of the eyes that he could not "get the better of, having been much indisposed for many months." Despised and abandoned, he lived in constant fear for his life and, late in his imprisonment, reported a plot "by two villains, to murder him."[53]

By the autumn of 1761, not one of the cases he had initiated against New Yorkers trading with the enemy had been brought to trial. Unknown to Spencer, his court-appointed lawyer John Alsop, Sr., owned shares in at least three vessels doing business at the Mount and Cape François, among them Captain John Easton's brig *Polly* of New London, "taken by His Majesty's ship, *Hussar,* and condemned in the admiralty court of Jamaica, without appeal."[54]

To the delight of his enemies the informer's confinement had been prolonged by a constitutional crisis. The office of chief justice of the province of New York had gone unfilled since the death in July 1760 of the incumbent, James DeLancey. In the past justices sitting on New York's most important court, the Supreme Court of Judicature, had held their commissions "during good behavior" (in effect, for life) not at "His Majesty's pleasure," as the ministry now insisted. By the autumn of 1761, the matter had come to a head. Cadwallader Colden, determined to follow the directives of his superiors in

London, was unbending. Standing together against the lieutenant-governor —whom they detested—the New York judges were unwilling to curry favor with the ministry in order to hold their commissions. As a result, the courts closed, and "many prisoners [were] long confined, at New York, without any trial." The Supreme Court of Judicature reopened in January 1762 only after Benjamin Prat, a compliant but competent Boston lawyer, agreed to assume the post of chief justice.[55]

On Saturday, January 23, on condition that Spencer adhere to the terms of his bankruptcy settlement of 1757 (a point never in doubt), Judge Prat released him from his confinement of 813 days in the New York City Jail. Soon after, Spencer was warned by his tormentors that "if he intended to prosecute those actions which he had commenced, he would be much worse treated than he had been." Not surprisingly, the informer "thought it most prudent to leave [New York] as soon as he conveniently could."[56]

In June, a broken man appeared at the London doorstep of none other than Benjamin Franklin: "One Spencer," wrote Franklin's clerk, "formerly a merchant of figure and credit in North America, being by various misfortunes reduced to poverty, is here in great distress, and would be made happy by any employment that would only enable him *to eat,* which he looks as if he had not done for some time."[57]

CHAPTER EIGHT

Crackdown

French agents moved with ease in the shadows of wartime New York. They were there well before the king's declaration of war in May 1756, faceless among the transients of the waterfront and innocuous in boardinghouses tucked into cobblestoned alleys. Occasionally the government paid attention to them, but there was no sustained effort to root them out—or even to monitor their activities. Agents and spies entered and departed unseen aboard vessels shuttling between New York City and French settlements in Maritime Canada, the western Caribbean, and the Gulf of Mexico. In the busy Atlantic seaport, with its large Dutch-, French-, German-, and Spanish-speaking communities, they were hardly noticed.

New York City had an obvious appeal to curious Frenchmen, as well as to those with business to transact. There was much to see, hear, and accomplish in a city crowded with soldiers and sailors for whom rum and camaraderie were a convenient escape from harsh military and maritime life. Collecting information was easy in dockside bars or the brothels bordering the New York Common. Meanwhile, French gentlemen—some claiming to be in town to recover their health—ingratiated themselves into polite society and established contacts within the merchant community.[1]

Britain's disruption of the Monte Cristi trade had the unintended effect of increasing French dependence on commercial agents embedded in North American cities. "Frenchmen were settled here in order to promote this intercourse," noted John Tabor Kempe. "So beneficial was it to the enemy that they sent blank passes to the Frenchmen here to be by them dealt out to such persons as they should think were fit." According to an informer, the passes were "signed by two principal secretaries of France and sealed with the king's seal, directed to all the generals, intendants, governors, admirals, captains of men of war, captains of privateers, and indeed to any French subject in the service of the French king, to countenance [and] give aid and assistance to all such masters of vessels with provisions, that they are not to be molested or interrupted on any account."[2]

The revival of New York's trade with the enemy in September and October 1761 was fueled by favorable rulings of the Lords of Appeals, sharply higher demand on Saint-Domingue, and the ready availability of French passports "for any vessel that shall carry provisions to any of their settlements."[3]

The new ventures made no pretense of legality. The sloop *Dove,* for example, pulled away from its East River mooring in early December 1761, just twelve days after the death of Admiral Holmes. The captain, William Carlisle, was cleared for Jamaica but steered directly into Cape François. The *Dove* carried 24 tons of provisions, along with a passport signed by the governor of Saint-Domingue, Philip François Bart, acquired through Jean Baptiste Rieux, "a Frenchman from the Cape, . . . [who] has resided some months in this place, as a factor for the French." Aboard were letters for William Walton's nephew James Thompson, the recently established Mount trader who had become a familiar figure in the countinghouses of Cape François and Port au Prince.[4]

On January 25, 1762, the crew of a British warship anchored at Spithead on the south coast of England worked into the night completing preparations for an urgent Atlantic crossing. The captain had been whistled aboard carrying secret dispatches for the commanders of British land and naval forces in North America, as well as orders from the Lords of the Admiralty, which were to remain sealed until the vessel stood off the entrance to New York harbor. The 44-gun frigate took on the last of its officers and marines, as ships' carpenters made final repairs and sailors adjusted masts and shrouds. With the wind picking up, a channel pilot guided HMS *Enterprise* out of the Solent, "through the Needles," and into the open sea.[5]

Off the Lizard, the most southerly point on the island of Great Britain, Captain John Houlton set the fighting ship on a course for the Madeira Islands. It pushed hard through "fresh gales and squally" weather, sighting Porto Santo Island in the Madeiras on February 9. A few days later, the warship picked up the North Equatorial Current and began the difficult passage west on a path approximating the Tropic of Cancer. When the weather cleared on the 23rd and 24th, the *Enterprise*'s well-seasoned crew exercised the great guns and practiced small arms fire, and on Thursday, the 25th, the ship took the captain and four crewmen off a New Hampshire sloop, the *Seaflower,* "being waterlogged on the 27 January by her steering in[to] a violent gale of wind." "They had been 20 odd days almost famished," remarked the *New-York Mercury* in a later report.[6]

On February 28, according to the same newspaper, "Captain Houlton fell in with an English brig" that had been taken and released by a large French squadron under the command of Rear Admiral the comte de Courbon-Blénac. An officer "informed the English captain they were bound to the relief of Martinique; that in case it was invested by the English, they were to proceed to the Havana, and there join the Spanish squadron."[7]

In mid-March, somewhere south of Bermuda, HMS *Enterprise* swung broadly to the northwest and began working its way toward the North American coast through gale-force winds and high seas. It was off Cape Hatteras on March 24, and by the 29th had sighted Cape Henlopen at the mouth of Delaware Bay. On March 30, 1762, the British warship rode out a violent storm off Sandy Hook and, as it awaited a pilot to guide it into lower New York Bay, pressed twenty sailors off a New York sloop bound for Saint Croix. On the rainy Thursday afternoon of April 1, *Enterprise* settled into its mooring off Staten Island. Sailors lowered the barge as Captain Houlton prepared to cross over to Manhattan carrying dispatches for Major-General Sir Jeffery Amherst and documents proclaiming war against Spain.[8]

Britain's declaration of war on January 2, 1762, had followed confirmation that Spain was soon to enter the larger conflict on the side of France. Spain's grievances had been festering since early in the war, most notably against British violations of Spanish neutrality on the high seas, especially in the Caribbean, where Spanish merchant vessels were frequent victims of North American and West Indian privateers. By August 1761, pride and frustration —fueled by fear that the French would make peace with Britain before Spain's grievances were redressed—had led Charles III to enter into a Bourbon "family compact" with his first cousin Louis XV. Their agreement asserted that any state that became the enemy of one ruling Bourbon was the enemy to all. The document contained a secret clause declaring Spain's intention of going to war against Great Britain by May 1, 1762.[9]

When they heard the news, war-weary Britons and their colonial cousins did not celebrate in the streets, especially in the West Indies. At Port Royal, Commodore Arthur Forrest read captured letters describing the buildup of forces at Cape François and reports of a combined French and Spanish expedition on its way from Europe "intended for a descent on the island of Jamaica." "The island is in no state of defense," Forrest wrote Lord Anson, First Lord of the Admiralty. Jamaica lacked an adequate force of British regulars, and militia regiments were seriously undermanned. In addition, the planters of Jamaica had neglected to maintain the island's fortifications or to provide a sufficient supply of ordnance. "They consider His Majesty's ships as the sole protection," noted Forrest. For six years, the British navy had prevented the French from gaining any advantage in the western Caribbean and, in cooperation with North American and West Indian privateers, had swept the French carrying trade from the sea.[10]

But in early 1762, with victory in the long and costly war tantalizingly close, Forrest's squadron was in no condition to engage a large and well-equipped naval force. Constant sea duty had left his fighting ships in bad repair, and provisions were so low at Port Royal that Forrest had placed sailors on half rations. Stocks of essential articles—some as common as sheathing nails—were now depleted, preventing the completion of critical repairs. Forrest had been promised resupply from Britain and North America, but he was disappointed in that as well.[11]

On February 4, for example, Captain Isaac Sears, in a sloop from New York, "loaded with king's stores for the fleet at Jamaica, was taken in sight of Port Royal" by a small French workboat "of 4 swivel guns, and 26 men, and carried into Port au Prince." At the same time, huge quantities of provisions, along with masses of British manufactured goods, flowed into French hands. At the time of Sears's capture, there were at least ninety North American, British, and Irish vessels anchored in Monte Cristi Bay, in addition to "fifty or sixty sail of flags of truce from the northern colonies" moored in the harbor at Cape François.[12]

In mid-February, Forrest informed London that two large French ships had appeared at the Cape carrying as many as sixteen hundred troops. When they arrived, "an embargo was laid on all the English flags of truce, and orders given out to have them close hauled in to make room for their fleet."[13]

At the end of February, trade between British North America and the French on Hispaniola took a dramatic turn. Tensions between the British and Spanish at Monte Cristi had been rising since September 1761, when one of Admiral Holmes's cruisers, HMS *Defiance*, seized as many as thirty Spanish coasting vessels coming into the bay. Long resentful of insults to their neutrality, the Spanish had been building up their strength at Monte Cristi and during the summer of 1761 had replaced their compliant governor, Don Francisco de Cabrejas. The new lieutenant-governor, Las Sobras, was far less accommodating than Cabrejas and occasionally threatened North Americans doing business in the bay. By the time news of the war between Great Britain and Spain arrived at San Fernando de Monte Cristi, the Spanish had enlarged the garrison and built up a battery of fifty cannon. On February 27, Las Sobras declared war on Great Britain, and the fort "immediately began to fire on the English vessels," reported the *New-York Gazette*. In the "confusion and danger," British ships moored in the bay were barely able to get "safe out of the reach of their guns."[14]

"Our Mount traders and underwriters are much dejected by the bad news that was this day confirmed by the arrival of Captain Bethell from the Cape," wrote an Irish trader in New York in early April. "All the vessels at the Mount have been obliged to depart in an hour's warning, many without water &c., and some of them were in great danger of being sunk by shots from the fort, particularly Mr. Cunningham's ship *New Grace,* who got a shot between wind and weather."[15]

"At the time the Spaniards fired at the English vessels in that bay," Waddell Cunningham later recalled, "he had several vessels there. One of them—being a vessel of force"—mounted "16 four, six, and nine pounders." Captain Alexander Kerr, a regular in the Irish-American trade, "was of great service in protecting the English vessels in that port, and by the assistance [he] gave, with some other armed vessels, they all got safe away," as did Cunningham's agent Richard Mercer, "the factor that did his business the most of this war at Monte Cristi [who] in the confusion went to Fort Dauphin with a considerable value in cash and goods."[16]

A month later, following a week of wet and blustery weather, the Manhattan sky was a deep and glorious blue as a crowd gathered outside City Hall. On Saturday, April 2, 1762, resigned but weary New Yorkers heard the public reading of the king's declaration of war against Spain. The city's confidence belied the anxiety that hung over the commander of British military operations in North America.[17]

HMS *Enterprise*'s protracted, nine-and-a-half-week crossing had put General Amherst far behind schedule. At the beginning of January, King George III had approved a massive amphibious operation against Havana, the symbol of Spanish power in the Americas. The sole purpose of Houlton's Atlantic crossing had been to deliver orders relating to Amherst's role in the campaign. "I wish from my heart these dispatches had arrived sooner," he confided, "that I might put in execution some commands, which His Majesty has been pleased to lay on me, earlier than I now can possibly do."[18]

The plan called for landing a force of eighteen thousand troops supported by fifteen ships of the line and no fewer than thirty lesser warships, not including transports, supply ships, and ordnance vessels. By express rider to Boston and a fast sloop to Halifax, Amherst had forwarded London's orders to Commodore Alexander Colville, commander of the North American squadron, to dispatch all available fighting ships to New York as rapidly as possible in order to convoy the troops to a rendezvous point off Cape Saint Nicholas in northwest Hispaniola. Amherst immediately set to work assessing his needs and ferreting out sources of shipping and provisions.[19]

The North American contingent was to consist of four thousand men (half regulars and half provincials), "the whole to be victualed for four months and fitted up with bedding and every other requisite." London expected no less than half this force to arrive off Havana sometime in April, "or at the farthest the beginning of May." To come even close to his deadline, Amherst would need the full cooperation of colonial politicians, shipowners, and provisioning merchants.[20]

The British commander issued orders stripping two thousand British regulars from thinly manned duty stations throughout North America, including two regiments in Canada. "Please to order the 46th regiment to march with all possible dispatch to this place," he wrote Major-General Gage at Montreal, "by the route of Crown Point, Ticonderoga, Fort George, Fort Edward and Albany, bringing all their tents, camp equipage and necessaries." It was an even greater challenge putting together the provincial troops, each component of which required negotiating with a colonial governor and legislature. At this stage of the war, few Americans were eager to board troop transports for "secret expeditions" to undisclosed places.[21]

Amherst anticipated problems. He had organized the New York component of the seaborne army sent against Quebec in 1759 and, more recently, the force sent from North America against Martinique. Experience had taught him that merchants in New York and Philadelphia, the busiest provisioning ports, would be wary of tying up their trading vessels in lease agreements with the army and reluctant to liquidate inventories of provisions at prices only loosely linked to market conditions.[22]

But the difficulties he faced in early April 1762 challenged even Amherst's administrative skill. Governors and legislatures dawdled when pressed to raise soldiers; once-plentiful shipping space evaporated; and the mountains of beef, pork, flour, and other articles the general needed to victual his soldiers became unavailable to his purchasing agents, though the city's warehouses and storerooms were well stocked.[23]

Meanwhile, twenty-one miles from Amherst's headquarters, small sailing craft from HMS *Enterprise* stood off Sandy Hook examining the papers of incoming vessels and impressing sailors for the Havana campaign. On Tuesday, April 13, in a routine operation, British sailors stopped a sloop purporting to be from Kingston, Jamaica, carrying a cargo of coffee, sugar, and rum. Rummaging through the ship they discovered a packet of papers that told a much different story. Captain Carlisle's sloop *Dove* was returning to New York City to reload for the French West Indies having delivered provisions and naval stores to the comte de Courbon-Blénac's squadron of heavy French warships anchored at Cape François.[24]

Amherst examined the documents the following evening. Before him was the reason he was unable to outfit the expeditionary force to Cuba. In the captured letters, accounts, bills of lading, and invoices were references to New York merchants with goods in transit, the names of their correspondents in the French West Indies, and the identities of French agents in the city supplying passports and coordinating the movement of goods. The documents included plans "for furnishing the French and Spaniards with the means of fitting out vessels . . . with every necessary they can require for carrying on the war against us."[25]

Amherst faced the shattering realization that—exactly as he had been told by George Spencer in November 1760—New York City was cooperating with the king's enemies and sustaining their efforts to wage war. "Such infamous practices," he wrote, must come to an immediate end. "There is the greatest reason imaginable, to think that without supplies from this continent the enemy could not subsist their fleets in the West Indies." Without supplies from North America, the French and Spanish "must decline any intended offensive operations, and be obliged to abandon their coasts." The British commander was determined to keep supplies out of enemy hands that were meant for his own forces.[26]

At Cape François, more than sixteen hundred miles away, James Thompson prepared to return to New York and his beautiful wife, Catharine. He had been at the Mount since September 1761 and had survived the expulsion of

British traders with his property intact. "It has pleased the Divine Providence that I have been continually more successful than I even hoped, since I have been here, not having lost the least value through so many continued dangers," he told Catharine. "I am full of the pleasing thought of seeing you," he added, "which give me more joy than the profits of so long a stay could purchase."[27]

In mid-March, he alerted his wife—a woman as comfortable on the New York waterfront as in the fashionable homes of lower Broadway—to forthcoming shipments of high-quality Saint-Domingue sugar. "[It] is the fruits of many risks both of my life and health, with the severest exercise at the same time of body and mind," he confided.[28]

The first of these consisted of 64 hogsheads of "fine white" sugar purchased through McCarty and Company. When the vessel—the sloop *Prosper* —arrives at New London, he told Captain Dishington in early April, "give out that you are come from the Grenadines, lately conquered by the English, and deliver your letter to Mr. Joseph Chew who will do the needful in that place, and will clear out your vessel and cargo for New York." Dishington was "to follow the orders of Mrs. Thompson . . . in case you find any letter for you at New London." Everything must be managed with the greatest discretion: "Be cautious and do not permit any of your sailors to enter into conversation with the country people, as they are very inquisitive, and may hurt you."[29]

"Immediately on your arrival . . . send off my letters for Mrs. Thompson by express to New York, and make all possible dispatch to go from New London to New York where you are bound, as I don't suppose Mr. Chew will detain you twenty-four hours," instructed Thompson. "Take a pilot with you and go to Cruger's Wharf in New York, where you must unload and proceed according to the directions of Mrs. Thompson."[30]

In the city, Dishington was to "make no answers to the questions of anybody there; and take care your sailors proceed in the same manner." Catharine would manage everything. She was to sell the sugar immediately on the sloop's arrival and then "discharge the sailors and sell the vessel." "I shall see you in 20 or 30 days after you receive this," James wrote his wife the first week in April. Unbeknownst to the Thompsons, the *Prosper* was sailing into the middle of the government's crackdown on New York's trade with the enemy.[31]

It began on April 15, 1762, with publication of a stern proclamation by Lieutenant-Governor Cadwallader Colden. New York politicians could no longer look the other way. Colden had had a taste of power, and he had no wish to compromise his relationship with General Amherst, who was as close to a viceroy as Britain's North American colonies ever knew, in order to protect in-laws and acquaintances in the city's errant merchant community. Colden's proclamation announced his intention to prosecute anyone "within this government, who shall send, carry or transport any provisions, ammunition, or stores of any kind, either directly or indirectly, to His Majesty's enemies, or to the ports, harbors, rivers, creeks, or bays belonging to any neutral prince or state, or be any ways acting, aiding, or assisting therein." Offenders, Colden emphasized, would be "punished with the utmost rigor that can be inflicted by law."[32]

The Council then authorized the impressment of provisions and appointed Mayor Cruger and four prominent merchants, among them Nathaniel Marston, to assist the military by identifying inventories and establishing prices. "I hope Your Excellency believes that I am solicitous to do every thing in my power for providing the king's service," Colden wrote Amherst late in the day. [33]

A busy week followed. Colden spent much of Saturday the 17th with Chief Justice Prat and Attorney General Kempe determining whether the documents taken from the *Dove*—seized off Sandy Hook the previous Thursday—could serve as the basis for a criminal proceeding. In Kempe's opinion, they were unlikely to lead to a conviction unless supported by oral testimony. He and Prat advised rounding up and detaining members of the sloop's crew for examination aboard HMS *Enterprise.* But law officers must be careful not to alert French agents or tip off the *Dove*'s owners and captain, who, they felt, could not be charged without stronger evidence.[34]

Discretion was everything, Colden told Amherst, lest the people of New York "be influenced to favor" those accused of corresponding with the king's enemies. In 1759, the government's case against Depeyster and Folliot had fallen apart when frightened witnesses refused to come forward. "It was impossible to guard against the collusive and shocking perjuries that are made use of on such occasions, to screen offenders from detection," Deputy-Governor Hamilton of Pennsylvania told Amherst in response to the general's urging that a crackdown get under way in Philadelphia as well.[35]

On Monday, April 19, Archibald Kennedy published a blunt announcement in the *New-York Gazette.* "It is apparent," wrote the seventy-seven-year-old customs collector, "that some of our traders have for some time carried on, and do at this time carry on, a correspondence with the enemy at the Cape, and have from time to time supplied them with provisions." This "scene of iniquity," promised Kennedy, "will soon be laid open with all its circumstances." Pushed forward by events—and an angry British commander—the government was slipping out of its lethargy. "Whoever will assist in detecting such scandalous and infamous practices, they need not doubt of the protection of the government, or of being thankfully rewarded."[36]

Aboard HMS *Enterprise,* Chief Justice Prat began his examination of three sailors from the *Dove* who had been rounded up over the weekend. In his sworn statement, George Moore, the *Dove*'s first mate, told Prat of "being informed by . . . William Carlisle that the said sloop the Dove was bound to Jamaica" and having "not then any suspicion of her being bound to any other port."[37]

According to Moore, Carlisle had carried papers "concealed, by being sowed in the hinder part of his breeches or drawers," and had been on the lookout for English privateers cruising off Saint-Domingue. The *Dove* had entered two French ports—Port à Paix and Cape François—"under French and English colors." At Port à Paix, another sailor testified, they saw "a brig belonging to Rhode Island, commanded by one Mr. Hopkins, son to the governor of that island." When they arrived at Cape François, Moore continued, they were neither detained nor searched, and the captain "was mostly on shore during the time the . . . sloop the Dove lay there" doing business with "one Mr. Loree a French merchant at Cape François."[38]

They found a great number of English vessels, among which were several from New York, including the sloop *Prosper.* "Provisions were very plenty and cheap at Cape François," Moore added as an afterthought. By the end of the week, Judge Prat had issued a warrant for the arrest of Captain William Carlisle—whose visit to the Cape had been authorized by the governor of Saint-Domingue—on a charge of treason.[39]

At the same time, Amherst was receiving mixed reports from colonial governors regarding the availability of men and supplies. A search by the attorney general for a statute empowering the government in New York to seize provisions revealed only the authority to impress "boats carriages artificers &c." Although Kempe had had misgivings about the Council's decision of April 15 to issue impress warrants, he advised Colden that "extreme necessity will justify taking these provisions paying their worth."[40]

The link between the scarcity of provisions and the city's thriving trade with the French was now obvious. "So many people, I suspect, have been concerned in this illicit trade from this place," a discouraged Colden told Amherst on April 23, "that it is very difficult to find persons to execute any orders, who have not connections with them, or are not afraid of their resentment, so that however solicitous I be to bring the guilty to condign punishment, and to put an entire stop to the pernicious trade, my endeavors may not have the desired effect."[41]

That evening, in the midst of the deepening crisis, Jeffery Amherst hosted a lavish ball at the New Assembly Room on Broadway. "The entertainment was the most elegant ever seen in America," reported New Haven's *Connecticut Gazette.* There were nearly two hundred guests, "all very richly dressed," the women in gowns of fine silk, their jewelry reflecting the soft candlelight; the gentlemen handsomely tailored, bedecked in wigs of the latest fashion. The crowded dance floor was a cascade of color and sound—with highlights of army scarlet and navy blue—as couples performed stately quadrilles beneath the great chandeliers. Amherst's guests represented the political and commercial elite of New York, as well as the upper echelon of the military. For a moment, in conversations around silver punch bowls or in the intermingling of laughter and strings, the tension gripping the city was forgotten, or at least put aside.[42]

The roundup of French agents took place ten days later. Planning had begun shortly after the seizure of the *Dove,* but Amherst, Colden, and Kempe moved with caution. The government had no idea how many Frenchmen were in the city or the extent of their involvement. The warrant issued by the lieutenant-governor to the New York sheriff, John Roberts, identified only "A.B.C.D. and divers others[,] subjects of the French king," who were "in this city of New York at large, there transacting matters prejudicial to the interest of His Majesty and his Dominions." The Frenchmen were to be taken into custody—together with "their effects and papers"—and confined "in the common jail of the City of New York there to be taken care of as prisoners of war."[43]

Sheriff Roberts and two British Army officers fluent in French struck just after noon on Monday, May 3. Working from a list of names culled out of documents taken from the *Dove,* they set out to apprehend one Monsieur Rieux at the boardinghouse of Monsieur Valade; a Monsieur Fougere at his lodgings "on Brewer's Hill"; a Monsieur Veruil at a rooming house "opposite the Coffee House"; a Monsieur Tetard at a house "near the Old English Church"; and Messrs. Langardiere, Gillet, and Marqui "at Monsieur Jerome's" near the Oswego Market on Broadway. The residence of Jean François Cartoe, a shadowy figure linked to McCarty and Company of Cape François, "is not known, but is in New York," wrote Amherst.[44]

By Monday evening, Gillet, Langardiere, Marqui, and Rieux were behind bars, along with Pascal LeComte, a surprise catch. Another French subject living in New York was picked up, but when "there was nothing material found," Amherst ordered him released. In addition to the five French prisoners deposited in the New York City Jail, the raids yielded nineteen documents, all but one taken from the rooms of Jean Baptiste Rieux and Pascal LeComte. The British officer in charge of the operation, an aide to General Amherst, delivered translations the following day, after which the commander-in-chief ordered the release of Gillet, Langardiere, and Marqui for lack of evidence, leaving only Rieux and LeComte in jail. The evidence against them was likewise an indictment of the city of New York.[45]

Rieux had been shuttling between Cape François and New York City since at least 1759. He was a source of French passports and an experienced facilitator of commerce. Among his papers was a letter of introduction from the governor of Saint-Domingue to Lieutenant-Governor William Denny of Pennsylvania written at the height of flag-trucing in 1759. An undated letter from a merchant at the Cape to Lewis Pintard—brother-in-law of George Spencer—included "proposals for opening a trade to this port."

The correspondence contained "account[s] of sundry cargoes shipped thither from New York," most of which, "it appears, were provisions," Amherst noted in his report to London. Some of the names were familiar, such as James Depeyster; others were not, including Monsieur Vergareau, a discreet French merchant operating out of New York.

LeComte's papers were even more interesting. A recent arrival, the Frenchman had traveled extensively in New England, visiting Salem, Boston, Newport, and New London in March and April. He brought letters of introduction to the governors of Connecticut, "La Nouvelle York," and "La Caroline," signed by the governor of Port Saint Louis, "some of which mention his having business of interest to transact."

The LeComte seizure was a mixture of business correspondence and commercial documents, such as Stilwell, Kelly and Company's invoice for 60 hogsheads of sugar (mentioning "an obligatory note" for the unpaid balance) and six French passports, three of which licensed "the importation of Negroes from Guinea." Amherst could not fail to notice a bill of exchange drawn by John McConnell, an Irish merchant at Les Cayes, against Waddell Cunningham and Thomas White of New York. The "memorandum of letters wrote by Mr. LeComte to his several correspondents by name; relative to illicit trade," was damning. More damning—by a high order of magnitude—

was a "letter from Messrs. Raby Freres, dated at the Cape 25th March 1762, giving an account of a French fleet of men of war and troops arrived there, and containing proposals for sending provisions to victual them."[46]

As the government probed deeper into the dark side of wartime New York, Colden faced his own darkness and grief. In January 1762 he had "met with the heavy affliction of [his] wife's death" and, in late April, that of his daughter Alice, her namesake. "My misfortune at this time in losing a daughter I was very fond of and the danger another is in," were too much to bear. "I cannot think properly," he confided to Amherst on May 2, as his youngest daughter, Catherine, lay "dangerously ill" in the governor's mansion at Fort George. The suffering of one so "gentle and engaging in her manners," in the midst of perfidy and double-dealing, "really discomposes my mind."[47]

"I was in hopes I should not have had any occasion of troubling you with [the] illicit trade carried on from this port," responded Amherst four days later, "but I must confess there appears to me to be no end to it." The general was at last turning his attention to the Havana expedition when Captain John Houlton of HMS *Enterprise* delivered another round of revelations. Between April 26 and May 2, four New York vessels had been seized by "the tender of the *Enterprise* man of war" as they made their way home from Saint-Domingue.[48]

The first, the snow *Johnson,* had been taken on Monday the 26th "off of the east end of Long Island" heading toward New London. The *Johnson* had not bothered to clear customs in New York City before departing for Cape François in November 1761 with provisions and lumber.[49]

The sloop *Industry,* also returning from Cape François, was intercepted on Saturday, May 1, "near Sandy Hook." The sloop *Susannah and Anne*—taken the same day—had cleared New York customs six months earlier for Jamaica but had made for Port Saint Louis on the south coast of Hispaniola with lumber, dry goods, and cash. *York Castle,* seized on May 2, had done much the same thing but called at Les Cayes as well. On its return home, the Thompsons' sloop *Prosper* had somehow slipped through or had been waved off as it approached Montauk Point. "I need add no remarks on the foregoing to show the height to which this iniquitous trade is arrived," wrote Amherst, "and the absolute necessity of crushing it."[50]

The British general pressed Colden to establish even stricter controls on the export of provisions, and he ordered sailors from the detained vessels to be held aboard the *Enterprise* to await formal examination. "I have already seen some good effects," Amherst told Colden on May 6. "One of the merchants mentioned as the owner of the snow *Johnson,* viz. Waddell Cunningham, has this day offered a quantity of beef, which I can have no doubt he intended to have shipped for the enemy." Colden warned Amherst of the difficulties that lay ahead: "The merchants concerned in the illicit trade will do everything in their power to prevent that any evidence appear against them."[51]

To Lord Amherst the behavior of the merchants was treasonous, inexcusable on every count. It angered him to see men freely walking the streets of New York who had grown rich at the expense of the British war effort. "It appears extraordinary to me, [that] anyone, who enjoys the benefits of a British subject, should, with impunity, be permitted to transgress the known laws of the kingdom, whilst a Frenchman, whose principles may naturally lead him to assist his own country, is punished according to the nature of the crime."[52]

Though distracted by the crisis within his family, Colden edged closer to confrontation with the city. "We have lately discovered a most pernicious trade carried on from the colonies to the French settlements on Hispaniola," he told the Board of Trade. "I am now collecting all the proofs I can obtain, . . . [and] shall communicate them to the attorney general that he may take the proper steps to prosecute the offenders." On May 12, Colden imposed a limited embargo. "As the enemy have several squadrons in the West Indies I have, at Sir Jeffery Amherst's request, put a stop to the exportation of provisions from this port, lest the enemy should be supplied by our traders who consider nothing but their own profit."[53]

"Too great care cannot be taken" to keep the investigation as quiet as possible, urged Kempe. The Rieux and LeComte documents, together with the new seizures, provided "the highest reason to be assured that an illegal correspondence with the king's enemies has been carried on from this port," but the evidence may not be strong enough to convict. If the government were to prevail, it would need corroborating testimony from the sailors held aboard the *Enterprise*.[54]

The examinations took place before Justice Daniel Horsmanden on May 14 and 15, 1762. In a dozen detailed depositions—signed by men more fearful of the repercussions of not cooperating than the ire of the merchants—the captain and two sailors from each of the four vessels provided a rich store of evidence. Several remarked on the role British trading vessels played in outfitting the comte de Courbon-Blénac's warships at the Cape.[55]

Meanwhile, Amherst continued to face frustration in putting together the provincial component of the expedition against Cuba. Colonial governors balked at his troop requisitions, and he was far behind schedule collecting transports and supplies. The assembly in Pennsylvania refused outright to impress shipping, and although Governor Fitch of Connecticut was now assisting with preparations for the expedition, he reported that four vessels loaded with provisions had recently departed New London for the French Islands.[56]

Then, on May 22—three days after the death of his beloved daughter Caty—an exhausted Cadwallader Colden faced further disturbing revelations. He had just been informed, he told Amherst, of the involvement of local merchants in a contract to supply the Spanish garrison at Havana. The new trade was to be channeled through New Providence Island in the Bahamas. That discovery was followed by news from the governor of Massachusetts that a New York vessel had been brought into Boston loaded with flour for Cape François, never having cleared customs in New York City.[57]

In an extraordinary example of bad timing, Rieux and LeComte petitioned on May 25 to be released from the New York City Jail, "a place where vermin and insects torment us, where we sleep not and where we are fearful of contracting a grievous disease." "If we erred in any respect," the prisoners affirmed, "it was through ignorance and not through malice, of which we are incapable."[58]

During the last week of May, the self-confidence that had so long characterized the merchant community in New York finally collapsed. A general embargo, along with news that the four vessels recently seized by HMS *Enterprise* had been condemned in the New York court of vice-admiralty, had a devastating effect. The "severities upon trade of late have intimidated people from meddling with shipping," wrote a member of the Council. The vice-admiralty cases were entirely separate from criminal proceedings against the owners of the condemned vessels now going forward in the New York Supreme Court of Judicature. Eighteen men—among them, such prominent merchants as Waddell Cunningham, William Kennedy, Godardus Van Solingen, Jacob Van Zandt, and Thomas White—faced criminal charges as "persons trading to the enemy from the port of New York."[59]

"Strong gales with thunder, lightning, and rain" lashed at the city all day Friday, May 28, as those with a history of trading with the enemy braced for the fury of the government. "From the discoveries I am daily making of the schemes that have been formed for supplying the enemy with provisions from this continent," Amherst wrote, "I doubt almost every vessel, and I must desire the embargo may be continued for some time longer." Trade in New York City was at a standstill.[60]

Then came a desperate plea from the merchants of New York. On May 29, 1762, fifty-four signatories of a petition to Lieutenant-Governor Colden—most likely debated and signed at the Merchants' Coffee House that evening—expressed their "utmost concern, that some merchants in this city, have incurred the censure of the government, on account of the commercial intercourse which individuals may have had, during the present war with the French West Indian settlements."

The merchants urged the lieutenant-governor to "abate the rigor of that resentment, which some of our fellow citizens at present labor under" and to consider the motives that "induced them to enter into that trade." It had long been known that "great numbers of European vessels both from Great Britain and Ireland, did constantly keep open a trade in the article of provisions, with St. Eustatius and Monte Cristi, and that from the quantities which those vessels alone must have furnished (being vastly more than could be consumed at St. Eustatius and Monte Cristi) it was apparent that the French on the island of Hispaniola, if not immediately, yet through that channel had considerable supplies."

Neither the government in London—nor that in New York—had ever spoken out against the trade. The petitioners even believed that wartime trade with the French was in the nation's interest, "especially as it also furnished opportunities of exporting large quantities of British manufactures, the invaluable staple of our Mother Country, and thus of profitably exchanging with our enemy, the luxuries of life, for sugars, a commodity of great and general demand throughout all Europe." It was therefore reasonable to suppose that "those that have been concerned in that trade, thought no detriment to the nation, could arise from such a mercantile intercourse with the enemy."

The signatories were, however, "not insensible, that this trade puts on a very different appearance, from the present state of things with respect to the war in America." Employing an argument that applied throughout the conflict—particularly the dark early days—the merchants admitted that "while the enemy's settlements in the West Indies, call loudly for succors, from their naval force," the prosecution of trade with them "might be of the most dangerous consequence to the public." Patriotic and penitent, the merchants of New York gave the lieutenant-governor "the strongest assurances, of their resolution not only to disavow the trade themselves, but [to] endeavor as far as they are able, totally to suppress it, during the continuance of the present war in America."[61]

"I have received a memorial from the merchants," Colden told the Board of Trade in June. "After some excuses for their having been drawn into that trade without any bad intentions," they had promised solemnly "to abstain from it for the future."[62]

"I think them sincere," he added. But apologies or no, the government intended to punish the offenders. "Great quantities of provisions have been carried from this and the neighboring colonies to the French on Hispaniola," Colden wrote the earl of Egremont, the ministerial official responsible for American affairs. "I have ordered the attorney general to prosecute the offenders in this province, and I hope an effectual stop is put to this pernicious trade."[63]

CHAPTER NINE

The Trial

On July 1, 1762, Captain John Houlton took HMS *Enterprise* through the Sandy Hook channel into the open Atlantic. With the firing of a signal gun on that mild summer evening, *Enterprise*—in the company of HMS *Lizard* and *Porcupine*—began nudging transports and supply ships toward a West Indian rendezvous off Cape Saint Nicholas at the far northwestern tip of Hispaniola. There they would join a large British force gathering for the assault on El Morro, the Spanish citadel at Havana. The departure of the first contingent of the North American expeditionary force was shrouded in mystery. "Their destination we leave our readers to find out," reported a Connecticut newspaper.[1]

As the ships cleared Sandy Hook, a New Yorker writing to an Irish newspaper described a crisis unfolding in the city. "Several persons in trade of considerable rank in these parts, have been taken up," he wrote, "being charged with high crimes and misdemeanors little short of treason." Most were out on bail, "which was not taken without difficulty, and even then for very large sums. It is said there is undoubted intelligence and proof," he continued, "that not only provisions, but all sorts of naval and warlike stores have been sent from these parts to the enemy's islands, and that naval and warlike stores have been sold at Cape François out of English vessels to the French fleet there."[2]

A parade of chagrined New Yorkers had passed through the Supreme Court of Judicature since the end of May. Eighteen men accused of "illegal correspondence with His Majesty's enemies" were arraigned before Justice Daniel Horsmanden and incarcerated in the New York City Jail. To gain their release, Horsmanden took notes of recognizance totaling £50,500 (New

York currency)—a huge sum—together with £43,250 pledged by seventeen others willing to stand as sureties.[3]

The arrests related to six ships seized by *Enterprise* at the height of General Amherst's crackdown on New York's trade with the enemy. To Attorney General John Tabor Kempe, the most promising cases were those against two New York Irishmen, Waddell Cunningham and Thomas White, owners of the snow *Johnson*. They were ornaments of the city's merchant community—and among the instigators of the Spencer riot in 1759—as were their associates, George Harison and Jacob Walton, who posted sureties worth £21,000 on behalf of the men charged in connection with the snow's voyage to Cape François. Horsmanden set bail for Cunningham and White at £10,000 each, five times that of the men involved in other vessels.[4]

Waddell Cunningham was the personification of New York's wartime swagger. In December 1760 he had appeared as an expert witness at the Spencer-Bradley inquiry, defending the propriety of the Monte Cristi trade while facing criminal charges for his role in the riot. Owing to numerous delays and continuances, the Spencer matter remained unresolved. In London, meanwhile, Cunningham's attorneys stood before the Lords of Appeals challenging the decisions of vice-admiralty judges in at least four cases related to trading with the enemy. As always, the Irishman was confident. But in a resolute John Tabor Kempe, Waddell Cunningham had met his match.[5]

In colonial America, the criminal prosecution of British subjects during the Seven Years' War for trading with the enemy was exceedingly rare. Rather, when vessels were seized by the Royal Navy or British privateers, the offending ships and cargoes were subject to forfeiture in noncriminal prize hearings held in courts of vice-admiralty. In a prize case, the ship and its cargo, not the owners, captain, or crew, were on trial. The claimant (or libellant)—the naval officer or privateer captain who had seized the offending vessel—sought a share of the value of the ship and cargo in the form of prize money distributed by the court.[6]

The first round of the snow *Johnson*'s encounter with the British judicial system took place in New York's court of vice-admiralty. There, on May 3, 1762—eight weeks before *Enterprise* left New York for the campaign against Havana—Captain Dennis McGillicuddy, commander of the privateer brig

Mars, claimed the *Johnson* as a French prize. He was not the only suitor, however. The same day Captain John Houlton initiated a second action against the *Johnson.* Houlton made his claim on behalf of the officers and men of HMS *Enterprise,* arguing that the snow had never been French and that its capture by the *Mars*—owned by Waddell Cunningham—had been collusive.[7]

Within a fortnight, the *Mars* had departed New York to cruise against the Spanish, and McGillicuddy's attorney withdrew his client's claim, "the libellant and witnesses being so remote, that they can't be examined within the [time allowed]." Before the end of May, the court took up the case once again and declared "the snow and lading as lawful prize to John Houlton, Esq., in behalf of himself and those for whom he claims." On June 1, the snow *Johnson* and its cargo of 63 hogsheads of white and 90 hogsheads of brown sugar were on the auction block at the Merchants' Coffee House.[8]

The arrests and arraignments of May, June, and July 1762 had not ended clandestine links between New York City and "His Majesty's enemies." Though sporadic, they remained a distraction for the British military well into autumn. In August, for example, Bartholomew Sandilands—"a Frenchman born, [who] speaks good English, was at this place a twelvemonth ago, went to Hispaniola and is returned"—entered the city via Long Island Sound aboard William Kelly and Samuel Stilwell's brig *Monckton.*[9]

About the same time, General Amherst received intelligence that French forces occupying Newfoundland had sent "a double-decked schooner commanded by an Irishman, whose name is not known, to some part of the continent for a cargo of flour." New York was the likely destination, and Amherst alerted customhouse personnel in the city, as well as along the entire North American coast, to be on the lookout. The vessel might be identified by "another Irishman on board, whose name is Casey," who had been "employed by the French to get flour, &c." But these were the last gasps of the trade.[10]

In New York City and London the ground was shifting—imperceptibly at first. A new governor of the province of New York, Robert Monckton, arrived in the city on June 12, 1762. And Lewis Morris, the aged judge of New York's court of vice-admiralty, died on June 25. A week later, George Harison wrote to the archbishop of Canterbury, a member of the Privy Council, to offer himself as a candidate for the judgeship. Then Harison ran headlong into New York politics. Determined to curb the influence of the autocratic Cadwallader Colden (a Harison in-law), New York's popular new governor, a British general and a wounded hero of the Battle of Quebec, preempted

London by appointing Richard Morris, son of the deceased, to the vacant post. Monckton did so "by virtue of my commission of vice-admiral," he later informed the Board of Trade, the body in London that supervised colonial affairs.[11]

By chance, William Smith, Sr., a member of the New York Council and no supporter of Colden's, happened to be in London when the archbishop received Harison's request. "Yesterday, when Your Grace spoke of his desire of a public office that requires the most unimpeached integrity and mentioned the fairness of his character, I could not in duty, as it seemed a kind of appeal to me, help hinting to Your Grace that it might be well to inquire a little into his character." "By the general account," Smith confided, "it had been much the reverse of fair in his last public office."[12]

Until the spring of 1756, Harison had functioned as a kind of gatekeeper for the port of New York. Serving simultaneously as surveyor and searcher of customs, he had approved or rejected the paperwork of every entering and departing vessel. "The rectitude of his principles, and the integrity of his conduct (which was ever directed by honor, virtue and religion)"—qualities cited by a eulogist at his death in 1773—were more theoretical than real. Harison had been the embodiment of laxness and high-handedness in the American customs service, maddening officials in London and making them eager for reform. Change was already under way in New York.[13]

On the opening day of the October 1762 session of the New York Supreme Court of Judicature, Waddell Cunningham and Thomas White appeared before Justice Horsmanden to face criminal charges related to the voyage of the snow *Johnson*. The Crown accused the two of "devising and intending unlawfully wickedly and corruptly to have keep and maintain an illegal correspondence and communication in time of open war with the enemies of our said Lord the king that is to say the subjects of the French king." Attorney General Kempe characterized the defendants as devious, lawless, and unrepentant, men who thumbed their noses at government and the rule of law. "Contrary to the faith and duty of good subjects, . . . [they] aid comfort assist and furnish them—these enemies of our said Lord, the king—with divers kinds of provisions naval stores and other necessaries of which they stood in great need of."[14]

Cunningham appealed for clemency to Governor Monckton. The besieged merchant hoped that "Your Excellency will consider with your unwonted [*sic*] clemency [my] present situation." Cunningham assured Monckton that he had "not been concerned directly or indirectly in any correspondence with the enemy, since the memorial presented [by the merchants of the city] to His Honor Cadwallader Colden" on May 29.[15]

Monckton was unimpressed. In late June, at a meeting of the Council, he had heard the owner of a schooner that had recently returned from Cape François and New Orleans implicate prominent New Yorkers in a long-standing operation to supply the French. Disturbed by the revelations, Monckton had demanded action. The evil must be extirpated, he insisted, the memorial of frightened merchants notwithstanding.[16]

With the backing of Monckton and General Amherst—the two most respected military figures in British America—the attorney general intended to make an example of Cunningham and White. "I beg leave to acquaint Your Excellency with what has been done in regard to the persons charged with illegal communication with the king's enemies," Kempe told Monckton. From the customhouse, the attorney general had learned that the owners of five of the six vessels seized in April and May 1762 had posted provisions bonds. The *Johnson* was the sole exception. In the case of Cunningham and White's ship, "no mention [was] made in the customhouse books . . . but a bond not perfected; and she laded in this port a very large cargo of provisions, some naval stores and other merchandise without the notice, and I am inclined to think without the knowledge of the customhouse officers."[17]

During the war, few merchants—or customhouse officers—paid scrupulous attention to the requirements of the hated Flour Act. Even so, if provisions were laden before the prerequisites of the act had been performed, or the ship left without having completed the bonding process, or the cargo was not delivered in exact conformity with information stated in the bond, "besides the loss of the provisions and the vessel," the shipper risked a severe fine, the amount of which would be calculated according to a formula contained in the statute.[18]

"It can hardly be conceived the *Johnson* ever could have carried out that cargo, or even laded it half, without being discovered and seized, unless those outdoor officers were extremely negligent of their duty," Kempe told Monckton. "I think I cannot in duty also omit mentioning to Your Excellency, that I have the greatest reason to believe that many of these provisions bonds have been illegally canceled at the customhouse after they have become forfeited to the Crown, and that they still are so, to the no small detriment of the king's interest."[19]

Wishing to avoid an intercolonial imbroglio, Monckton and Kempe had no intention of prosecuting delinquent customs officials, many of whom had political connections in Britain. But the arrogant owners of the *Johnson,* its wary captain, and a few hapless clerks in the Hanover Square offices of Greg and Cunningham—that was a different matter. With Monckton's approval, the attorney general added a violation of the Flour Act to charges pending against Cunningham and White. Their trial, which appeared on the docket for April 1763, was meant to be the first of a string of proceedings against hitherto inviolable figures in New York City.[20]

Prosecuting Waddell Cunningham and Thomas White was not without risk. They were well-connected members of a close circle of wealthy New Yorkers with a long history of skirting the law. Although their ships and cargoes were vulnerable in vice-admiralty courts—particularly in the West Indies—the two remained personally unaccountable. Furthermore, the government's case was circumstantial, as no witness would admit to having seen the actual transfer of goods from the *Johnson* to French merchants.[21]

The two men, particularly Cunningham, approached the legal system with a boldness characteristic of their trade with the French. In the days leading up to the trial, Cunningham occupied himself with rehabilitating his reputation, shoring up his alibi (that he had been in Philadelphia when the snow departed New York), and bribing and strong-arming witnesses. When "six rogues . . . threatened to inform against Mr. Cunningham" at the time of the crackdown, "their mouths were stopped at a small expense," wrote an admirer, and when Captain Williams began to vacillate on the eve of the trial, Cunningham withheld his wages, declaring "I will pay you according as you behave at court."[22]

Then, on January 24, 1763—with the Cunningham-White trial three months away—the city's trade with the enemy came to an abrupt end. Two days earlier, news had arrived from Europe that the warring powers had signed a truce. With France and Spain exhausted and defeated, victorious Britain stood at the pinnacle of its eighteenth-century power. The long and bloody contest was now a chess match among diplomats to determine the shape of the final treaty. In New York, the public celebrated as a procession of dignitaries carried the "royal proclamation declaring a cessation of hostilities with France and Spain" up Broadway to City Hall.[23]

On Tuesday morning, April 19, 1763, sunlight streamed through the tall windows of the wainscoted courtroom on the second floor of City Hall. On a motion of James Duane, the lead attorney for the defense, Justice Daniel Horsmanden "ordered that the defendants' appearances be entered" into the record of the court. The Cunningham-White trial was finally under way. At jury selection the next day, the defense moved that jurors be determined by lot rather than chosen by the court.[24]

The dispute over jury selection "being argued on both sides," the court handed down its ruling on a rainy Thursday morning: "Having considered the arguments on the motion of the defendants' counsel that the jury might be balloted, [the court] is unanimously of opinion that the motion be overruled and that the jury be sworn without balloting." With a jury to his liking, and the opposition unsettled, prosecuting attorney John Tabor Kempe was ready to begin.[25]

"It is a fact known almost to all," Kempe told the jury in his opening remarks, "that during the war a correspondence has been carried on with [the king's] public enemies from this port, as well as many other ports in North America, by means whereof the enemy have received continual supplies from His Majesty's subjects contrary to the laws as well as His Majesty's declaration of war.

"This communication was carried on with the enemy for some time without interruption, until His Majesty's ships of war and the West India privateers, having somehow got knowledge of it, cruised against these ships supplying the enemy." Though law officers in New York City had long known what was going on, he continued, "without any proofs appearing of it sufficient to ground a prosecution," they could not act.

"It was almost an accident that opened a full discovery of the means [whereby trade was conducted], and [the identities] of some of the persons concerned," explained Kempe. "I mean the taking of some of those vessels by Captain Houlton in His Majesty's ship *Enterprise* coming into this port. Among others thus discovered are the present defendants. And this brings me to their particular case." Charged with maintaining an illegal correspondence with the king's enemies and violations of the Flour Act, "the defendants," said Kempe, "have pleaded not guilty and have put themselves on their country to be tried."

In his opening remarks, Kempe also made a general reference to natural law—unchanging moral principles that were regarded as a basis for human conduct—and what he termed "the law of nations." "The very nature of war, supposes all communication and correspondence [with an enemy] to be at an end," he told the jury, "as it must in all cases be dangerous in the highest degree." By means of trade the enemy gains intelligence, "but it also serves to enrich them, supplies them with necessaries and softens to them the rigors of war." This being a British court of law, however, he, as New York's attorney general, intended to base his prosecution on the king's declaration of war, English common law, and relevant parliamentary statutes.

The Crown had explicitly prohibited doing business with the enemy in its declaration of war of May 1756. "The king's proclamation declaring war, strictly forbids any correspondence or communication whatever with the enemy," explained Kempe. He then presented a defense of "the king's power of declaring war and making peace by his royal proclamation": it could not "be doubted, nor his power thereby to regulate the conduct of his subjects toward the enemy, and also of foreign states so far as it relates to the good of the realm. The subject is bound to observe such proclamation—hence it is law."[26]

Kempe asserted a broad prohibition against trading with the enemy based on common law. He admitted, however, that "there are very few instances in our law books of persons charged with offences of this kind." Even so, Kempe cited a seventeenth-century precedent of "some merchants being prosecuted for trading with the Scots in time of war, although they had a license from the guardians of the truce." As a principle of common law, the attorney general reiterated that "trading with the enemy is punishable, and that no person (the king perhaps excepted) can license it."[27]

A third justification for the prosecution of Cunningham and White lay in statutory law. The definition of treason under English law had been established by Parliament in 1351. Among treasonable offences cited in the fourteenth-century statute were actions "adherent to the king's enemies in his realm, giving to them aid and comfort in the realm or elsewhere." By this definition, according to Kempe, "merchants [were] restrained from selling merchandise and provisions to the enemy."[28]

The prosecutor called the jury's attention to a more recent statute, the Correspondence with Enemies Act of 1704. This law served a very different purpose. Its intent had been "to restrain foreigners only from bringing into the realm the produce of the enemy." In the recent war, there had been no need for a law to prevent commerce with the enemy, he argued, the offence being "punishable enough before."[29]

In February 1757, Parliament had passed a statute (the Flour Act) meant to curb the shipment of provisions via neutral intermediaries from British North America to ports in the French West Indies and French North America. "Although it was unlawful for the subject to have any intercourse with the enemy," Kempe told the jury, "yet foreigners at peace both with the enemy and us, might lawfully trade with both nations and so might introduce into either of those nations the produce and manufactures of the other." The Flour Act applied only to goods shipped from British colonial ports in North America and the West Indies.[30]

New York City's trade with the enemy had been, essentially, the exchange of articles mentioned in the Flour Act—along with dry goods, lumber, and naval stores—for French West Indian produce. If British men of war or privateers seized vessels carrying the goods mentioned in the statute anywhere but to British ports, the owners were subject to ruinous fines and the confiscation of their ships and cargoes.

The attorney general's interpretation of the intent of the 1757 law suggested that most of New York's commerce with the Dutch and Danish islands, as well as with Spanish Monte Cristi, was illegal. It was a bold assertion in defense of an unpopular measure. The case at hand, however, dealt only with the voyage of the snow *Johnson* to Cape François, and Kempe intended to show how the requirements of the act had been repeatedly violated. "That the enemy received great benefit by it, is not to be doubted, when it is considered (as will appear in evidence on this trial) what great care they took to promote this communication and correspondence by granting passes to such as would venture among them with cargoes for their use, and take off their produce that lay useless on their hands."

Trading with the enemy was tempting, and "without doubt . . . made beneficial to these bold adventurers," suggested the prosecutor. "No person would run the risk of offending the laws of his country, or drawing punishment on himself in a [trade] so extremely dangerous as supplying the common enemy of his country, or having any correspondence with him, unless lured by a prospect of more than common interest." He then told the twelve men before him, "In order for your better understanding this case it may be proper I should in some measure open to you the ways and means and the covers used in carrying on this correspondence."

The Crown's case against Cunningham and White lay embedded in the *Johnson*'s voyage, the details of which "highly aggravate the fact the defendants are charged with," said Kempe, his confidence building. "Shipping a large quantity of provisions naval stores and other commodities, with intent they should be delivered to the enemy for their aid and comfort, . . . is the fact to be tried," said Kempe, and the matter "to which I now proceed." Kempe took the jury back to October 1761, when William Williams, a New York ship captain with experience in the French islands, took command of the *Johnson*. As Captain Williams prepared the snow for departure, Waddell Cunningham, one of the owners, had "opened a bond (as they called it) for the shipping provisions on board the said snow." But he had neglected to fill in the kinds and quantities of the goods to be shipped.[31]

To underscore the significance of this omission, Kempe offered a brief course on customhouse procedure, explaining how officers, "to ease the shippers and themselves from the trouble of entering into, and taking more bonds than were necessary, . . . contented themselves with opening a bond for the vessel at the customhouse, and when she was laden complete, in taking the bond for the whole cargo at once." By means of Cunningham's manipulation of customhouse procedure, "the out-of-doors officers were stopped from seizing the vessel as soon as any provisions were put on board."[32]

In contrast to New York City's trade with the neutral islands and Monte Cristi Bay, as well as trade conducted under cover of flags of truce, Cunningham and White's venture to the Cape had made no pretense of legality. Early in November 1761, "Captain Williams, in pursuance of [his] orders, sailed from hence without ever clearing out" or "the bond being completed." In addition to its cargo, Kempe pointed out, the *Johnson* carried a passenger, Jean François Cartoe, "one of the emissaries of the enemy" and a source of "blank permissions" for New Yorkers wishing to do business with the French.[33]

The snow had arrived in New London harbor a few days later without documents. With the assistance of Joseph Chew, a customs officer with close ties to New York, Williams had received a certificate of entry and a clearance for Jamaica. By mid-November, the snow was "bound to Cape François," Kempe told the jurors, carrying "a French paper" that served as both permission to trade at the Cape and protection "from being taken by the enemy."[34]

On December 3, 1761—after being detained by a French privateer—the snow *Johnson* appeared off "Roche à Picolet," the distinctive rock formation at the tip of Cape François. Colors prominently displayed, the snow passed beneath the guns of the formidable "castle which commands the entrance of the harbor." By one report, there were sixty North American, British, and Irish vessels riding off the "Ville du Cap" at the time of the snow's visit but just "two French merchant ships."[35]

The arrival of the *Johnson* had coincided with Commodore Forrest's decision to reduce the number of British warships patrolling off Hispaniola. The effect was immediate, and the rebound in wartime trade with the French was felt in ports from New England to the upper South. "Dry goods . . . are in pretty good demand, especially Irish linens," wrote a merchant at Cape François to his correspondent in New York early in February 1762. And a Philadelphia firm that did business with the French in cooperation with New York companies learned that their vessel had "met with a most glorious market at the Cape; all the flour &c. there was spoiled, and theirs sold monstrously; [and] that they should make a great voyage and be soon here full loaded with sugar in the hold and coffee between decks." This was before the arrival of the news of London's break with Madrid. "In case of a Spanish war," the Cape merchant promised, "all sorts of dry goods will immediately take a very great turn."[36]

At Cape François, Kempe told the jury, Captain Williams had put his cargo into the hands of David McCarty "who though he has an Irish name is a subject of the French king." McCarty and Company loaded 57 hogsheads of white and 87 hogsheads of brown sugar aboard the *Johnson,* and "a French gentleman there" shipped 6 hogsheads of white sugar "consigned to one Monsieur Cartoe." In late February 1762, with their cargo complete, Williams and his crew attended to minor repairs and awaited the appearance of Waddell Cunningham's privateer brig *Mars.*[37]

Meanwhile, British warships were monitoring a powerful French squadron under the command of the comte de Courbon-Blénac. It had left Brest in late January for the relief of Martinique. Early in March, "speaking with some fishing boats as they were steering for St. Pierre," Blénac had learned that the island had just fallen into the hands of British forces under the command of General Robert Monckton. Blénac's seven ships of the line and four frigates had then made their way to Cape François, where according to British intelligence they were either to refit before joining a Spanish fleet at Havana for an attack on Jamaica or return to France loaded with French West Indian produce. At the Cape, the French admiral had delivered three thousand troops and a new governor, but his fighting ships were in desperate need of repair. The French men of war "heeled and boot-topped," the prosecutor told the jury, and were refitted with lumber and other supplies from British North America, of which "there was a vast plenty."[38]

On the last day of March 1762—with Cunningham's privateer in the offing—the New York trading vessel slipped beneath the great guns at the entryway to Cape François. The next day, about twenty-five miles east-southeast of Great Inagua Island, the snow *Johnson* "fell in with the Mars privateer, belonging to this port," said Kempe. The commander, Dennis McGillicuddy, had a colorful reputation. Just ten days earlier, he had attacked —simultaneously—two enemy sloops "mounting 10 and 12 guns whom he was obliged to engage full four glasses."[39]

His encounter with the *Johnson* was more peaceful. "They were brought to by the privateer Mars, Captain McGillicuddy, who hailed them, and when he knew who they were, and from whence they came he told Captain Williams . . . that he would send him a prize master." According to court documents, "Captain Williams seemed pleased." He told his crew that "in case they should thereafter be brought to, by any English vessel of force that they should say they belonged to the privateer *Mars,* and were put on board that vessel to carry her into port as their prize."[40]

"This contrivance had the desired effect," said Kempe. By chance, a 16-gun British sloop of war, HMS *Bonetta,* was just then crossing through the Bahamas on its way from New Providence Island to Cape Saint Nicholas. Its captain, Lancelot Holmes, had been ordered to enlist pilots to guide the British fleet gathering there through the treacherous Old Bahama Channel north of Cuba for the attack on the great fortress at Havana. On April 6—the *Mars* having resumed its cruise—the *Johnson* steered north toward the Mariguana Passage and the open sea, ready to begin the voyage home. In the "light airs" and variable winds off "the center of Crooked Island," its path crossed that of the *Bonetta.* "This was unexpected and in all probability unforeseen," said the prosecutor, "and promised fair for putting an end to this illegal correspondence."[41]

As the boarding party approached, Williams reminded his men how to behave. "If the man of war should examine them," they were to say that "the snow's crew were on board of the *Mars.*" The *Johnson*'s captain and "the pretended prize master" were then taken aboard the *Bonetta.* In his examination by Captain Holmes, Williams offered a creative account of the snow's seizure by the *Mars,* and the sham prize master presented his commission. Convinced by their performance, "the commander of the *Bonetta* after such examination did not think proper to detain the [New York] vessel" and, said Kempe, "let them go."[42]

"The next day the *Mars* came up to them again." McGillicuddy "hailed the snow *Johnson*" and "made himself very merry with the sweating, as he termed it that Captain Williams had had the day before." "How finely they had flung the man of war," McGillicuddy had crowed, calling Holmes, "green as an Irish leek." "Captain McGillicuddy wished Captain Williams a good passage" until they met once again in New York City. "The privateer *Mars* then hoisted her colors, and gave the *Johnson* snow three cheers."[43]

The *Johnson* was carried north by the Gulf Stream, touching the western edge of the seaweed-entangled Sargasso Sea, a mid-ocean graveyard of ships. Williams steered for the eastern end of Long Island and in the last week of

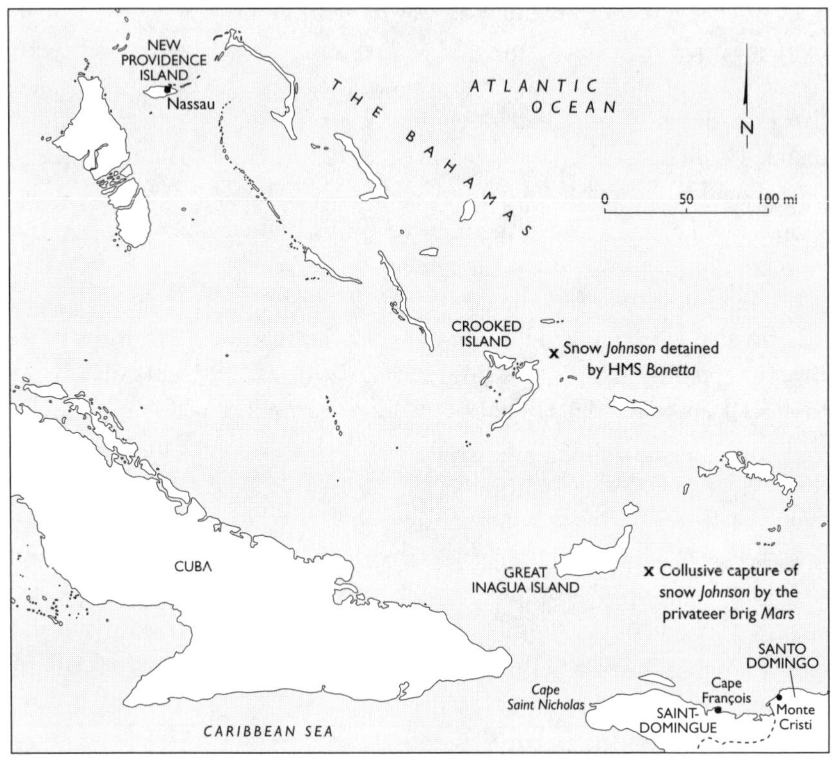

Points Where the Privateer Brig *Mars* and HMS *Bonetta* Detained the Snow *Johnson,* April 1 and 6, 1762

April swung to the northwest at Montauk Point, intending to enter Long Island Sound through the Race. "Captain Williams had orders to carry his cargo of sugars to New London," Kempe told the jury, "where there was no doubt of his having an entrance." There, the snow's captain was to "receive further orders from one Mr. Chew."[44]

On April 26, as it approached Fishers Island, the *Johnson* was brought to and boarded by the tender of HMS *Enterprise.* The auxiliary warship had been cruising off the east end of Long Island to enforce General Amherst's ban on the export of provisions, as well as to impress sailors for the campaign against Cuba. Unconvinced by Williams's story and the privateer's commission, the commanding officer had seized the snow in the name of Captain Houlton and placed a prize crew aboard. Unnoticed, a canvas bag weighted with shot and the trading vessel's papers had been slipped over the side. On

Friday, April 30—a beautiful spring day in New York—a British prize crew brought the *Johnson* through Sandy Hook to an anchorage off Staten Island.[45]

Details of Kempe's account of the voyage were corroborated by eight witnesses: the vessel's captain, first mate, and a sailor, along with three members of the staff at Waddell Cunningham's firm Greg and Cunningham. The witnesses answered questions relating to the composition of the cargo and its conformity to "the orders of the owners to Captain Williams." Hamilton Young, Cunningham's clerk, testified that "Captain Williams had a French pass delivered him before he sailed from New York," and that "Captain Williams by order of his owners carried one Mr. Cartoe with him to land him at the Cape." Even New York's elderly collector of customs, Archibald Kennedy, now in failing health, was put on the stand (along with a customhouse clerk) "to prove Captain Williams did not clear out here, but was nevertheless admitted to an entry at New London."[46]

There is only a fragmentary record of the trial from the perspective of the defense. In notes taken by Kempe, James Duane and his team (which included William Smith, Jr., and John Morin Scott) appear unprepared for the aggressiveness of the Crown's prosecution. They tried to argue that with "no proof of the shipping [and] particulars of the cargo," the attorney general had no proof that anything had been loaded aboard the snow and thus had no case. According to Duane, there was no evidence of written orders, nor of a French passport, nor that "the cargo was delivered at the Cape." Kempe's evidence was circumstantial, and his case was riddled with conjecture. "Belief [is] not evidence," said Duane; it is "not legal evidence to convict them."

Duane told the jury that Cunningham and White were being "charged equal to high treason" for acts that had been commonplace in the ports of North America since the beginning of the war. The defendants were being forced "to answer not only for themselves, but the whole continent"; "Had the gentlemen only been guilty, there might be some reason in your convicting them, but as many others have been guilty, there ought to be more evidence."[47]

The defense particularly objected to the prosecution's reliance upon coerced testimony and challenged its admissibility. It is impossible for us to know whether William Williams, John Martin, and Harry Henry Crowder, all of whom had sailed aboard the *Johnson,* testified unwillingly. There can be no doubt, however, that James Jones, Edward Forbes, and Hamilton Young—employees of Greg and Cunningham—had been reluctant to share what they knew.[48]

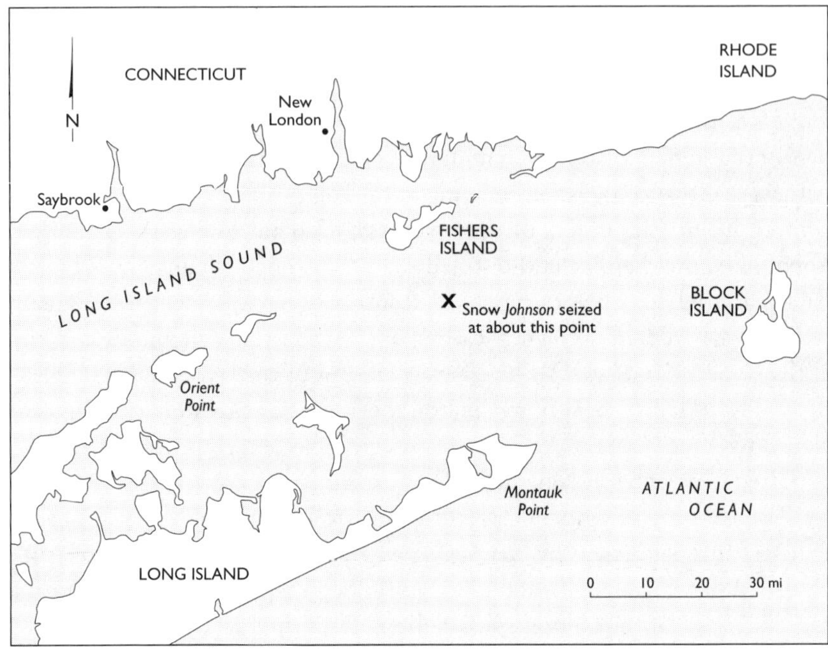

Point Where the Tender of HMS *Enterprise* Seized the Snow *Johnson*, April 26, 1762

"It will be insisted on," responded Kempe, "that no person interested can be a witness." On the contrary, "he is a good witness, it being supposed he will not for his own sake, say more than the truth." "In a case like this, no man can be interested in such a manner as to disqualify him for a witness—not even if he was a *particeps criminis* [an accessory to a crime]—for the conviction of the person on trial will be attended with no punishment corporeal or pecuniary to the witness, and he is not obliged to accuse himself."[49]

As he brought the proceeding to a close, Kempe assured the jury that the defendants before them, the owners of the snow *Johnson,* had knowingly and willfully entered into a correspondence with the king's enemies and—by written orders—had set in motion a scheme to violate a parliamentary statute meant to protect the nation in a time of war. The Crown demanded the conviction of Waddell Cunningham and Thomas White for crimes that the prosecuting attorney equated with high treason. "This offence was in manifest contempt of the king and his laws, to the great assistance aid and comfort of the . . . enemies of our said Lord the king, to the great damage and injury of the king and all his liege subjects, to the most pernicious example of all others in like case offending, and against the peace of the king."[50]

Justice Horsmanden delivered his charge to the jury, reviewing facts in the case and clarifying relevant points of law. The twelve men then withdrew under the watchful eye of a constable instructed to "keep every person sworn of this inquest together in some private and convenient room without meat, drink, fire or candle light" until they came to a decision on the guilt or innocence of the accused.[51]

Sometime before the end of the day, "the jury being returned to the bar say they find the defendants guilty" on both counts. This was not the outcome anticipated by the defense. Waddell Cunningham was outraged. He and White had been, he later wrote, prosecuted with a "rigor altogether unexampled." The verdict was, furthermore, "oppressive, contrary to the spirit of government and the dictates of law and reason." The Irishmen were being made scapegoats for the transgressions of an entire city.[52]

Two days later, on Saturday, April 23, 1763, Justice Horsmanden handed down the punishment prescribed by the Flour Act of 1757. Cunningham and White were each fined £1,568, a staggering amount in mid-eighteenth-century New York. Shocked by the severity of the penalty, Duane filed motions for arrest of judgment. The court responded the following Monday: "It is ordered," recorded the clerk, "that the defendants have leave until Wednesday in the next term to argue in support of their reasons in arrest of judgment, that the said reasons be then argued on the part of the defendants and that in the meantime judgment be stayed."[53]

The verdict in the Cunningham-White trial had an unsettling effect on the trading community in New York, especially as "Cunningham was convicted upon the fullest proof and on the testimony of the most reluctant witnesses." In the weeks that followed, a long shadow fell over the city.[54]

CHAPTER TEN

Fruits of Victory

Peace came at a price. Throughout the long conflict, New York had been self-assured and aggressive, benefiting from its geographic advantages and privileged status in the chain of military command. In addition to "an extensive trade to many parts of the world, particularly to the West Indies," the city had "acquired great riches by the commerce which it has carried on, under flags of truce, to Cape François, and Monte Cristi."[1]

Now all that was over. British expenditures had fallen off sharply after the surrender of Montreal in the autumn of 1760, and the departure of Monckton's army for Martinique in November 1761 had taken away thousands of free-spending British regulars and their officers. Preparations for war against Spain in the spring of 1762—and a sharp increase in spending by the French on Hispaniola—had merely postponed the inevitable. By April 1763 at moorings around Manhattan ships were waiting longer for cargoes as commissions became scarce and provisions prices rose in the wake of a devastating drought the previous summer. Down winding streets and alleys, warehouses groaned under the weight of unsold imports. There were bargains everywhere for customers with cash—but there was no cash. By summer, New York harbor had become a forest of idle ships.[2]

The postwar slump, felt throughout the contracting Atlantic economy, was accompanied by despair and foreboding. Unemployed sailors and day laborers found refuge in the haunts and dives of the docklands, where alcohol was cheap and life cheaper. At the height of the war, over three thousand men had found work aboard New York privateers, and the wages of ordinary seamen—some with little to offer but their youth—had risen to extortionate levels. With the return of privateersmen to maritime trades, wages plummeted.[3]

New York mariners shared the fate of their much-hated antagonists on

New Providence Island in the Bahamas: "a great number of seamen were consequently discharged" when "the privateers of that place, said to be about 12 sail, were converted into trading vessels." In April 1763 sailors in Nassau "were so destitute of employ that they were glad to go on board vessels begging to work for their victuals."[4]

In New York City, the laboring poor had been among the beneficiaries of the heady wartime prosperity. Now hungry men, women, and children—sometimes in bands numbering as many as two hundred—took to the roads north of the city to forage for food. "There is scarce a farmer, or gentleman's seat . . . [that has escaped] having their orchards and cornfields plundered," reported a newspaper late in the year.[5]

Adding to the uncertainty were rumors of far-reaching reforms in the enforcement of British laws governing overseas trade, the lifeblood of the city's economy. In April 1763, following passage of a tough new statute—"An act for the further improvement of His Majesty's revenue of customs; and for the encouragement of officers making seizures; and for the prevention of clandestine running of goods into any part of His Majesty's dominions"—the Admiralty allowed its naval officers to be deputized as customs enforcement agents in American ports.[6]

Continuing a practice established during the war, the customs enforcement act of 1763 stipulated that the proceeds from peacetime seizures made by ships of the Royal Navy were to be divided into half-shares between the king, on the one hand, and the officers and men aboard the seizing vessel, on the other. Before the war, the king, the governor, and the informer had each received a third. But there had been few seizures.[7]

Between the late 1680s and the outbreak of the Seven Years' War, a broad "salutary neglect" characterized British governance of colonial America. From the administration of Robert Walpole in the 1720s through that of the duke of Newcastle in the 1750s, *quieta non movere* (roughly, "let sleeping dogs lie") was set policy. In British America, it bred haphazard enforcement of commercial regulations and indifference to trading with the enemy by customs officials who were increasingly dependent upon the bribes of merchants.[8]

"Salutary neglect" had stimulated commerce and fostered expansion, but it had done so at the expense of tariff revenue payable to the Crown. To British politicians facing a staggering postwar debt—£137 million—the continuation of such a policy was unthinkable. Corruption must be rooted out and the customs service put on a paying basis. So it was that the free-flowing Atlantic economy that had functioned so well for much of the eighteenth century failed to survive the Peace of Paris. Neither did the delicate accommodations that held the empire together.[9]

Calls for reform predated the Seven Years' War. During the Anglo-French conflict of the 1740s, Rear Admiral Sir Charles Knowles, the British naval commander at Port Royal, Jamaica, had urged that London rein in "the base and illegal trade that is carried on by the Northward vessels." In their trade with the enemy, he had reported, North Americans covered their tracks with false documents, flags of truce, and every imaginable ruse. "I wrote to His Grace the duke of Newcastle some time ago," Knowles had complained in 1748, "desiring the several governors of the colonies might be under some restrictions, . . . but hitherto I have received no answer." Others, including Governor William Shirley of Massachusetts, had called for an act of Parliament prohibiting trade with the enemy. But nothing was done.[10]

What had been an annoyance during the War of the Austrian Succession had become a serious issue with the renewal of fighting in the mid-1750s. From New York, Governor Charles Hardy had complained bitterly about North Americans—especially in the charter colonies of Connecticut and Rhode Island—supplying the enemy at a time of military crisis. His charges had led to support on the Board of Trade for the Irish and North American provisions embargoes (1756–57) and lightning passage of the Flour Act in February 1757.[11]

But the Flour Act had had an inauspicious beginning. By the time it arrived in New York, in June, Hardy had already handed over the seals of office to Lieutenant-Governor James DeLancey and—still complaining—was with the fleet aboard HMS *Sutherland* "moored in Halifax harbor." DeLancey, a popular figure who was closely allied to the trading community, had no intention of prosecuting New York merchants under the new law. On the other hand, when he reported to the Board of Trade that summer on the situation at Monte Cristi—emphasizing the involvement of Rhode Island—the lieutenant-governor had expressed outrage over the "illegal and unwarrantable [exchanges] . . . by which the enemy are supplied."[12]

In November, acting on reports from Hardy and DeLancey, the Board of Trade had called for a close examination of North American trade. But the wheels of government turned slowly. Wartime demands had gotten in the way of action, and it was more than a year before the Board took up the report of its secretary, John Pownall. In February 1759 the Board of Trade's findings were presented to the Customs Board, which in May passed them along to the Treasury in the form of a summary report on customs abuses in colonial ports.[13]

The Treasury Board, ever in search of new sources of revenue, had opened a separate line of inquiry in 1757 into the inefficiencies of the American customs service. The May 1759 report by the Customs Board had corroborated the Treasury's findings that the core of the problem lay in three activities: the clandestine landing of cargoes from continental Europe (the Dutch Trade), the importation of "foreign" West Indian produce disguised as "British," and "the pernicious practice of supplying the French colonies and plantations with provisions." Meanwhile, angry dispatches about North American vessels trading at Monte Cristi Bay and the ports of Saint-Domingue had been flowing from Admiral Thomas Cotes, the naval commander at Port Royal, Jamaica, into the Admiralty and through the labyrinth of official London.[14]

In August 1759 the Board of Trade submitted its report to the Privy Council. The findings were damning. According to the Treasury, all the North American colonies were involved in some aspect of trading with the enemy; the most flagrant offenders—the charter colonies of Connecticut and Rhode Island—possessed powers that subverted British law; and the corruption of customs officials throughout the colonies undermined enforcement of the Acts of Trade and Navigation, the parliamentary statutes that regulated trade in the first British Empire.[15]

Continuing wartime distractions—and the caution of the ministry in dealing with neutral Spain—ensured that systemic reform would not take place until the fighting stopped. Even so, a stream of blistering reports from Admiral Charles Holmes (Admiral Cotes's successor at Port Royal) and General Amherst's furor over abuses he confronted in New York City kept the possibility of reform alive, as did George Grenville's rise to power in April 1763 as First Lord of the Treasury and Chancellor of the Exchequer, the king's prime minister.[16]

As it happened, George Spencer, now ensconced in rooms at 8 Hatton Garden, was also prowling London's corridors of power in the spring of 1763. In March, he had written to the earl of Bute, the political figure closest to King George III, with "a list of vessels, which have been employed from the port of New York, in that illicit trade, from time to time during the late war." In a long petition to the Treasury Board in June, Spencer spelled out in detail the ways the interest of the Crown had been subverted—and justice turned on its head—by a cabal of powerful politicians and wealthy merchants in New

York City determined to wring the last farthing of profit out of war with France.[17]

Spencer believed that justice, however elusive, was still possible. The informer had, he told the commissioners, received word that Waddell Cunningham and Thomas White—"the former of which was one of the principals concerned in the riot"—had been convicted "at New York, for exporting provisions, &c." contrary to an act of Parliament, "Sir Jeffery Amherst having ordered His Majesty's attorney general to prosecute."[18]

Spencer's petition to George Grenville, dated July 4, 1763, arrived as the prime minister was formulating a comprehensive reform of the American customs service. Spencer urged Grenville to take decisive action in New York while it was still possible to collect evidence. If cases there were brought to "a final end and determination," the penalties would be substantial, "amounting to near forty thousand pounds, if not above."[19]

Five days later, Grenville's brother-in-law, the earl of Egremont—William Pitt's successor as secretary of state for the Southern Department—sent off a stern letter to colonial governors demanding strict enforcement of the Acts of Trade and Navigation. Failure to do so in the past had resulted in "the diminution and impoverishment of the public revenue," which could no longer be tolerated in a nation laboring under a huge wartime debt. "The commanders of His Majesty's ships, stationed in America, will . . . be vested for the future, with the necessary and legal powers from the Commissioners of the Customs, for carrying into execution the several acts of Parliament relative to the seizing and condemning [of] any ships that shall be found transgressing against the said acts." "Salutary neglect" was a thing of the past.[20]

On July 17, 1763, the packet boat *Pitt* dropped anchor in the East River after an Atlantic crossing of seven weeks. The newspapers aboard contained no stories of armies on the march or bloody engagements at sea or even of recalcitrant statesmen locked in tentative peace negotiations. In the cities, towns, and villages of British North America, the news from Europe that a settlement had been reached—signed in Paris on February 10—was a welcome break in the clouds of postwar recession. Two days later yet another colorful parade of dignitaries marched up Broadway, with soldiers lining "the way from the Fort gate to the City Hall." A huge crowd on Wall Street gave three cheers after Sheriff John Roberts read the king's proclamation announcing "the definitive treaty of peace and friendship."[21]

By the terms of the agreement, France gave up all claims to North American territory east of the Mississippi River except the tiny islands of Saint Pierre and Miquelon off the south coast of Newfoundland. Spain ceded Florida to the British but retained Cuba, and the French islands of Martinique, Guadeloupe, and Saint Lucia were returned to France. There were other transfers, as well, nearly all to the advantage of the victorious British. Cheers went up as the proclamation characterized the settlement as bringing "a peace founded on real and solid advantages; effected on terms the most honorable; and distinguished by that equity and moderation, which afford the fairest prospect of its permanence and stability."[22]

On July 26 the New York Supreme Court of Judicature began its summer session. In a proceeding watched closely by the city's trading community, Justice Daniel Horsmanden postponed his decision on James Duane's motion for arrest of judgment in the Cunningham-White case. Waddell Cunningham, one of the principals, was involved in four other cases on the summer docket. He was a co-defendant—along with James Jauncey and Philip Livingston—in a prosecution under the Flour Act unrelated to trading with the enemy. In another case, he was being sued by the new commander of the privateer *Mars* for prize money that allegedly belonged to the captain and crew. Cunningham, in his turn, was suing the master of the snow *Prince of Wales* for frauds committed on a 1762 voyage from New York to Martinique. On top of this, there were criminal charges pending against Cunningham and four others for their roles in the Spencer riot.[23]

Three days later, Cunningham's troubles became even more serious. "I do and shall always look upon the 29th of July as the most unfortunate day of my whole life," he later told a friend. Returning from court at midday—"distracted by the most unfortunate coincidence of fretting circumstances that ever befell any man at one time"—the hot-tempered Irishman became involved in a violent altercation with a fellow merchant, Thomas Forsey. The two were locked in a dispute over a bill of exchange. By the end of July, the disagreement had become mean-spirited and personal. Cunningham's decision to sue for nonpayment "made me very angry," wrote Forsey, "well knowing our credit was as good as Cunningham's, and character much better."[24]

Forsey retaliated by passing around the response to a scurrilous letter he had sent to Jack Torrans, a former New York merchant and a native of Ireland now doing business in Charleston, South Carolina. Cunningham's behavior, Torrans had written Forsey, "was by no means consistent with our inclinations or wishes; and we must rather be led to think it proceeded from some private pique, indeed, we think it rather uncouth than otherwise."[25]

The explosion was inevitable. Cunningham confronted Forsey on the evening of Thursday, July 28, demanding that he "go immediately into the Coffee House, and there publicly under [his] hand retract what [he] had wrote in that letter." When Forsey refused, Cunningham demanded satisfaction and to that end appeared at the Coffee House at noon the next day. The heated exchange that followed spilled into the crowded street. Then Cunningham drew his sword.[26]

"Damn you," he said.

Forsey attempted to flee, but he was no match for Cunningham. Near Queen Street, he turned and faced his assailant. "He made a thrust at me with the sword," Forsey recalled. He tried to defend himself, "but [Cunningham] making a second thrust, run his sword into my breast about eight inches." Crying, "Stop the murderer," Forsey lay bleeding on the cobblestoned street before a crowd of astonished New Yorkers.[27]

Now Cunningham fled. He ducked through the home of his good friend and attorney James Duane, making his way into an alley and the home of another friend, Anthony Van Dam, where he found refuge "concealed in his garret." It was three hours before Cunningham was discovered and committed to jail, "attended with the shouts of an incensed populace."[28]

For weeks, Thomas Forsey lingered near death. His antagonist, sobered by the experience, publicly apologized. "I am very far from justifying the severity of my conduct to you," he wrote. "I think myself bound to confess that fault." But Forsey rejected Cunningham's entreaties. As the dispute rekindled, neither man could have foreseen the constitutional crisis—involving the king himself—that would erupt fifteen months later in the aftermath of their showdown in the New York Supreme Court of Judicature.[29]

Meanwhile, as the summer dragged on New Yorkers continued their search for the fruits of victory. On July 29—Cunningham's "most unfortunate day"—war-weary soldiers arrived at Sandy Hook from Cuba following the return of the island to the Spanish as required by the Peace of Paris. "These brave men," wrote the *Gazette,* "having gone through (full of success) great fatigues in a hot climate," immediately embarked for Albany to begin the first leg of a long journey west to join General Amherst and the British Army in putting down a vicious Indian uprising in the vicinity of Detroit.[30]

Still, there was much to be thankful for. Throughout the province, Thursday, August 11, "was observed here as a Day of Thanksgiving to Almighty God, for the great blessings of peace." Lieutenant-Governor Colden made the rounds of the city's churches, where he heard clergymen speak of God's hand in Britain's victory over the French and Spanish. The services were "extremely well adapted to the purport of the day," reported the *Gazette*. "After the different congregations had broke up, and His Honor the governor had returned to the Fort, His Majesty's, and other healths, were drank under the discharge of the cannon."[31]

In spite of the blessings of the Almighty and public expressions of goodwill, trade languished, unemployment rose, and "the prices of all manner of victuals daily brought to market . . . are grown excessively great." The postwar economy had become "not only ruinous to families of the poorer sort, but intolerable even to people of better estate," declared the New York Common Council in August. "Whosoever wishes to behold this declining city resume her ancient luster and opulence," wrote "Plebeanus" in the *Gazette* in September, must support whatever is necessary "to prevent the greatest part of this populous and (till lately) flourishing city, from beggary and ruin."[32]

Exacerbating the economic difficulties were twenty-one British warships —half of them fast and nimble sloops of war—that far out at sea were moving westward, fanning out toward the ports of North America. The squadron's commander, Rear Admiral Alexander Coville, a cynical and battle-hardened Scot headquartered at Halifax, Nova Scotia, had been ordered to tighten enforcement of the British navigation acts in colonial America.

This complex set of laws—the earliest dating from the mid-seventeenth century—restricted colonial trade to British ships manned largely by British sailors. Under the Acts of Trade and Navigation, American-bound transatlantic shipping was required to load at ports in Great Britain (even if it meant off-loading and reloading goods acquired elsewhere). Trading with nations that were at peace with the Crown was allowed, but there were prohibitive tariffs on articles such as tea from the European continent or "foreign" sugar and sugar products from the West Indies. Taken together, the navigation acts attempted to secure a protected British market for colonial produce (such as sugar, tobacco, and other "enumerated" articles) as well as a protected American market for British manufactured goods. The duties on colonial commerce—if actually collected, as the government now intended—would make a significant contribution to the British Treasury.[33]

Tighter enforcement of the navigation acts was already under way in New York City. In September 1763, three schooners and a sloop, along with a quantity of tea and tobacco—"lately seized by the officers of His Majesty's customs, for breach of the laws of trade, and condemned in the court of admiralty"—were auctioned off "at the king's storehouse near the Battery" at the tip of Manhattan. The tough new posture at the New York customhouse added to the gloom pervading the city.[34]

Merchants who had flown high during the war now faced bankruptcy as markets contracted and credit evaporated in the continuing postwar depression. In August, James Depeyster liquidated personal property to raise cash. Thomas Lynch and William Kennedy—two of the nine shipowners indicted in July 1762 for trading with the enemy—declared themselves "under the necessity at present, of settling and discharging all [their] accounts."[35]

The first of the British cruisers appeared off Sandy Hook in the second week of October. The sloop of war *Sardoine,* with a crew of ninety, arrived on Tuesday the eleventh, followed four days later by the station commander, Archibald Kennedy, Jr.—a native New Yorker and son of the late collector of customs—aboard the 28-gun frigate HMS *Coventry.* "We hear," speculated the press, "that the *Hornet* sloop, Captain Montgomery, and a cutter are expected, and that there will be four vessels kept continually cruising on this station" ready to seize violators of the navigation acts.[36]

British warships moored off Manhattan were an ominous presence. Their mission—"effectually to crush the contraband trade" with the European mainland and the "foreign" West Indies—bred deep resentment. Captain Kennedy and the officers under his command—like Colville, distrustful of the "well known mobbish disposition of the inhabitants"—were determined to bring the rule of law to the wayward port. But there was more at stake than principle. Out of their half-shares of condemned ships and cargoes, the men in blue stood to make fortunes.[37]

John Tabor Kempe intended to build on his successful prosecution in April of the owners of the snow *Johnson.* On the opening day of the Supreme Court's October session, he presented the Crown's arguments against arrest of judgment in the Cunningham-White case. Justice Horsmanden then ordered the defendants "to reply and conclude the argument" in the January 1764 session.[38]

Kempe was now ready to prosecute the owners of the three other vessels seized by Captain Houlton in April 1762. The first trial took place on Wednesday morning, October 19, 1763. The defendants, John Keating and William Kennedy, "both Irishmen," were charged with "lading provisions &c. on board a vessel with intent to send them to the enemy and open a communication with them in time of war." Their sloop *Susannah and Anne* had cleared

New York customs in January 1762 for Kingston, Jamaica, with provisions, dry goods, and lumber. Captain William Dobbs then set a course for Les Cayes and Port Saint Louis on the southern coast of Saint-Domingue, where he exchanged his American cargo for sugar and indigo. On his way home, as he approached Long Island Sound to pick up covering documents from Joseph Chew at the customhouse in New London, the *Susannah and Anne* was stopped by the tender of HMS *Enterprise*.[39]

Kempe built his case on three depositions taken before Justice Horsmanden aboard the *Enterprise* in mid-May 1762. One of the deponents, a sailor named Samuel Caraway, had long since left New York. And on the day of the trial, Captain Dobbs refused to answer the questions put to him by the prosecution—"which the court were of opinion were pertinent to the said issue." So did William Paulding, the first mate.[40]

"On the book being offered and the oath repeated by the clerk," records the court minute book, "[Paulding] said he understood he was not to declare anything that might affect himself. He was then told he had the king's pardon whereupon he declared he would not accept the pardon." Dobbs and Paulding were jailed for contempt and fined. But Kennedy and Keating went free. "The jury without going from the bar find the defendants not guilty."[41]

An even stronger case against Abraham Lott, Thomas Lynch, and Jacob Van Zandt, owners of the sloop *Industry*, was scheduled for Thursday, October 27. Two of the defendants, Lott and Lynch, had had a part in the Spencer affair. The third, Van Zandt, was a veteran of every phase of wartime trade with the French.[42]

Attorney General Kempe had a straightforward case. In October 1761 the owners of the *Industry* had taken out a provisions bond according to the requirements of the Flour Act. A few days later, the sloop had cleared New York customs for North Carolina and Jamaica. On verbal orders from the owners, Captain Theunis Thew had set a course for Cape François, where he delivered the cargo to Michael La Roche, a Franco-Irish merchant, "who shipped in return a cargo of sugars" for New York. Thew had been ordered, "in case he arrived safe from the Cape . . . [to] enter at the Sound and touch New London, and there enter the cargo . . . [which] he endeavored to do but was intercepted."[43]

What ought to have been an open-and-shut case slipped through the prosecutor's hands. The Crown's argument rested on the uncanceled provisions bond, for which Kempe had issued a subpoena, as well as on the oral testimony of witnesses, three of whom had given depositions in May 1762. But on October 19—the day of the Keating-Kennedy trial—Van Zandt informed Kempe that the *Industry*'s bond had, in fact, been canceled by Lambert Moore, comptroller of the customs in New York, now acting at cross-purposes with the attorney general in support of the besieged merchant community.[44]

"I did not credit the fact," a shocked Kempe told the lieutenant-governor. In the spring of 1762, customhouse officers had been explicitly instructed by Colden not to cancel the bonds of vessels seized by the *Enterprise* on their return from Saint-Domingue. Such bonds could only be fraudulent. On Friday, October 21—"determined to enquire into it"—the attorney general called upon Lambert Moore at the customhouse to ask "whether that bond was cancelled."[45]

"He told me it was," Kempe told Colden. "I asked him whether he had cancelled it after he had been served with a subpoena to bring it into court as proof against the defendants?"

"He said he had."

"I told him I thought it a very extraordinary step, and asked him if he had any orders for doing so from the surveyor-general?"

"He said he had and expressed his displeasure that I should trouble myself so far about it."[46]

Then the rest of the case fell apart. Captain Thew, though offered a pardon on the day of the trial, refused to testify against the owners of the sloop. Like Dobbs and Paulding, he was jailed and fined for contempt. Lott and Van Zandt were acquitted (charges against Lynch having been dropped on the eve of the trial). Lessons learned at the White-Cunningham trial had not been lost on the merchants of New York City.[47]

Attorney General Kempe, angry and frustrated, confronted John Temple, surveyor-general of customs for the Northern District of America. "Mr. Moore has just informed me," said Kempe, "that by your order he had cancelled a provision bond, which bond the lieutenant governor had ordered should not be cancelled; it having appeared before him on affidavit, that the cargo laden here on board that vessel, had been carried and landed in a French port."

"Sir," replied Temple, after a brief exchange asserting the superiority of his rank over that of the attorney general, "You have no business with anything done in the custom house until you receive an order from me."

"An order from you, Mr. Temple!" sneered Kempe, "Give me leave to tell you, your order is nothing to me."

"My order is nothing to you, Sir?"

"No, Sir, nor shall I receive anything as an order from you."[48]

The prosecution had nothing further to fall back on. Before the close of the autumn session of the Supreme Court of Judicature, Justice Horsmanden dismissed charges against the remaining owners, Thomas Livingston and Godardus Van Solingen, in spite of irrefutable evidence that their vessel, the brig *York Castle,* had exchanged provisions for sugar at Port Saint Louis in the winter of 1761. Faced with obstructive customs officials, scattering witnesses, and hostile juries, Kempe found himself once again where he had been in the autumn of 1759. As though intended to dishearten him further, news arrived the first week in November of "a pardon for Mr. Waddell Cunningham, of New-York, which His Majesty was graciously pleased to grant, in case the wound given Mr. Thomas Forsey, on the 29th of July last, had proved mortal."[49]

As the civil administration distanced itself from his prosecutions, Kempe became increasingly dependent on the support of army and navy officers in New York intent on punishing wartime offenders and promoting the rigorous enforcement of the navigation acts. But even that support was spreading thin. On November 16, 1763, General Thomas Gage arrived in New York City from Montreal via Crown Point and Albany. The following morning, he and Sir Jeffery Amherst discussed strategy for putting down Pontiac's Rebellion, the bloody Indian uprising in the West, and went over a long agenda of military business. Then Amherst formally invested Gage with "the command of His Majesty's forces in North America." That evening—"under the discharge of the cannon on Fort George"—Amherst and his party boarded the sloop of war *Weasel,* moored in New York harbor since October 30 alongside the new station ships: HMS *Coventry, Sardoine,* and *Sir Edward Hawke.* The fast sloop cleared Sandy Hook on November 21 and began the long journey home.[50]

John Tabor Kempe had been among those at dockside wishing Amherst "an easy and agreeable passage [and] joy on returning to your native country and friends." Governor Robert Monckton—"very respectfully attended to the water side, and very affectionately taken leave of"—had left New York for England at the end of June after turning over his seals of office to the lieutenant-governor, Cadwallader Colden. Since the spring and summer of 1762, Amherst and Monckton had been Kempe's strongest supporters.[51]

Colden also stood behind his attorney general—at least in public. But on December 2, the lieutenant-governor ordered Kempe to prepare a formal response to an angry petition from Waddell Cunningham to the Council "praying relief against a double prosecution in the Supreme Court of this province respecting the snow *Johnson.*" The Irishman had protested the harshness of the Crown's prosecution, claiming that he had been charged twice for the same offence and that he and his partner were being punished for the wrongdoings of an entire city.[52]

"These being charges which equally affect me who am the prosecutor, and His Excellency Governor Monckton who ordered me to prosecute," Kempe told the Council, "it cannot be improper I should at least defend myself." "From the loud complaints of Mr. Cunningham and the vehemence of his expressions, it might be imagined he . . . was grievously oppressed," noted Kempe in his report; however, "it is no just conclusion that his offence is mitigated because many others are equally guilty, nor because many people might think it unblamable, nor because those whose duty should have suppressed it, did not."

"Mr. Cunningham might with as much reason and propriety," Kempe continued, "apply to Your Honor . . . and set forth that in consequence of having wounded Mr. Forsey he had suffered greatly, and that those sufferings strongly plead for a cessation of that prosecution also, and so might every person under prosecution for any crime whatsoever, for there is no doubt but suffering and trouble are the consequences of crimes." British naval officers stationed in New York harbor were soon to learn that "suffering and trouble" were also the consequences of enforcing the law in a city that had turned against them.[53]

On Friday, December 2, the day the Council ordered Attorney General Kempe to justify the Crown's stand against Cunningham and White, the aptly named snow *New York* made its way from Sandy Hook to Perth Amboy. Somewhere in lower New York Bay, the vessel was brought to and boarded by His Majesty's sloop of war *Sir Edward Hawke*. "When my lieutenant demanded her papers," remembered Captain John Brown, "the master only produced one written in French"—an inventory of his cargo consisting of rum, molasses, Bordeaux wine—"and I dare say many other things not mentioned," all shipped from Port au Prince.[54]

Brown took possession and sent the snow to New York City with a boarding party under the command of his first lieutenant. When the *New York* arrived in the East River, the owners, Walter and Samuel Franklin, came on board to demand its immediate return. The Franklins—prominent military contractors who had done business with both sides during the war—

asserted that their vessel had been bound for the Isle of Man and had stopped in New York merely to pick up orders. "What could be her business at Amboy, but to smuggle," insisted Brown.[55]

Though the Franklin brothers owned the ship, none other than Thomas White owned the cargo. With an arrest of judgment in the Cunningham-White trial pending before the Supreme Court of Judicature, White remained silent. He "has not, as I have yet observed, made any stir," Brown told Admiral Colville ten days after the seizure.[56]

"I have taken all the necessary steps with the attorney general," said Brown, "whose advice and opinion was, not on any account to give her up and that she certainly would be condemned." One can imagine the delight of John Tabor Kempe, then hard at work on his response to Cunningham's petition.[57]

As Brown calculated his portion of the navy's half-share of the condemned ship and cargo, civil authorities in New York City closed ranks. Charles Apthorp, the new collector of customs, deprived of his one-third informer's share of the seizure, refused to become involved, claiming that he lacked instructions from the surveyor-general of American customs, John Temple, regarding the role of the navy in the business of the customhouse.[58]

On December 7, in a letter to the Board of Trade, Lieutenant-Governor Colden spoke up in defense of New York City. The devastating implications of customs reform had left him politically vulnerable. "Without doubt much illicit trade is carried on in this place," he admitted, "though more of it has been detected and punished in this port than in any of the other colonies." New Yorkers complained, he added, that merchants elsewhere now undersold them, "and that this place will be impoverished while the others grow rich."[59]

Captain John Brown brought his case against the snow *New York* before the court of vice-admiralty on December 19. Judge Richard Morris immediately set in motion a Byzantine tangle of requirements and fees, which Brown was forced to pay out of his own pocket. Then Brown's suit went into slow motion.[60]

"Mr. Franklin has been seen, since this seizure, very busy with the judge of the admiralty," Brown complained, "from which I cannot help thinking him inclined to favor an illicit cause, and from their general combinations, what are we to expect but much perplexity and little justice, beside the hazard of our persons." Brown had reason to worry: "I am threatened to be arrested and, for want of security must undoubtedly be put in jail, and I am inclined to think the next letter I have the honor to write your Lordship, will be from thence," he told Colville, "the attorney general having told me, he was very certain not a merchant in the place would bail me, if so all proceedings against the *New York* must likewise cease."[61]

To complicate matters even further—if that was possible—because John Temple had not received orders from London concerning the relationship between customs officials and deputized naval officers, he would not allow Apthorp to cooperate with Brown. Worse still, if Captain Brown backed away from the prosecution now under way, he faced a stiff fine from Kempe and risked dismissal from the service for disobeying his written orders to prosecute violators of the navigation acts.[62]

Official New York appeared determined "to defeat the intent of the late act of parliament in favor of sea officers employed against the smugglers"—the customs enforcement act of 1763—wrote Colville in January 1764. "The merchants concerned in the illicit trade carried on in these provinces seem to bid defiance to both law and government."[63]

January 28, 1764, the last day of the Supreme Court's winter session, was an overcast Saturday in a city digging out from a mid-week blizzard. Two ships departed for Ireland with the tide carrying flaxseed, and more were loading at wharves along the East River. The city went about its business under the glare of hovering British warships. In the newly refurbished courtroom on the second floor of City Hall, Attorney General Kempe asked Justice Horsmanden for judgment in the case of "The King v. Waddell Cunningham and Thomas White." Eighteen men had been indicted in July 1762 for their "illegal correspondence with His Majesty's enemies." Nine owned shares in vessels seized by HMS *Enterprise* that April. Though all nine had been brought to trial, seven had been acquitted for lack of evidence. Kempe's sole success was the guilty verdict and steep fine in the Cunningham-White trial in April 1763.[64]

Sometime before noon, attorney James Duane presented his argument for arrest of judgment. Then he delivered a copy of the May 1762 decree of the New York vice-admiralty court against the *Johnson,* "whereby it appears that the vessel, and cargo . . . for which the defendants are prosecuted in this cause, were adjudged as prize." Duane spoke of punishments already inflicted and the high cost of his clients' prosecution, as well as the "great expense for counsel and otherwise in defending the same."

The records of the New York Supreme Court of Judicature do not contain Duane's remarks before Justice Horsmanden that Saturday morning. But whatever he said was enough: "The Court doth on consideration of the premises," noted the minute book, "set a fine of one hundred pounds on each of the defendants, which they paid in court, and thereupon the Court discharges the defendants from their recognizances."[65]

The New York establishment no longer intended to make an example of Cunningham and White for activities that had brought prosperity to the city. The "severity of [their] prosecution for trading with the enemy, notwithstanding its universality throughout the colonies" had been, in the words of Waddell Cunningham, "an instance of rigor unexampled . . . contrary to the spirit of government and the dictates of law and reason." The young attorney general—as always, "blameless in the execution of my duty"—had been bested once again. But to those of His Majesty's sea officers who had heard merchants in New York taking "every occasion of boasting they will bring sugar &c. from the foreign islands here, and we shall not oblige them to pay the duties," none of this was a surprise.[66]

Epilogue

Path to Revolution

Exactly a fortnight after Justice Horsmanden's decision in the Cunningham-White case, on February 11, 1764, George Spencer stepped out of his lodgings "at Mr. Cooper's Hat and Feather on Snow-Hill" near the Church of the Holy Sepulchre. He probably cut through the Fleet Market within earshot of the debtors begging for alms in Old Fleet Prison. At Fleet Street he would have headed west in the direction of the Strand, following the sweeping southwesterly bend in the Thames to Whitehall and the seat of government. At the Treasury—a handsome stone building facing Saint James's Park and the Horse Guards Parade—Spencer handed the porter a private letter addressed to Charles Jenkinson, secretary to the Treasury Board and a close ally of George Grenville's. As it happened, Grenville and the Board were just then working out details of a legislative package to achieve economic and administrative reform in British America and ensure that the colonies would share in the rising cost of imperial defense.[1]

A few days earlier, Sir Jeffery Amherst, back in London after a quick but harrowing passage from New York aboard the sloop of war *Weasel,* had given the Treasury Board an account of Spencer's long ordeal in New York City and had spoken out in behalf of the justice of his cause.

In his letter to Jenkinson, Spencer repeated earlier requests. "For that important discovery I made [in 1755] of the designs of the French against New-York," he wrote, "I hope Their Lordships will be pleased to grant me a small pension." He also asked for authority to prosecute—"though at my own expense"—violators of the Flour Act. The informer explained that he had been obstructed by a vice-admiralty judge who was in league with influential New Yorkers enriching themselves while jeopardizing the security of the nation.[2]

George Spencer was nothing if not persistent. He intended to return to America with evidence against the owners of eight vessels that had carried colonial produce to the enemy during the long and bloody war. "If 'tis agreeable," he told Jenkinson, "to be my friend therein, permit me liberty, most humbly, to make you an offer of two thousand guineas" out of the informer's share. "[If] you are favorably pleased to use your interest in my behalf, you may rely on my performance as above and the greatest secrecy therein."[3]

Since the spring of 1763, Spencer had delivered no fewer than seven such letters and petitions to men of influence in American affairs. In each, he offered a detailed account of what had gone on in wartime New York and recalled his suffering at the hands of rich and powerful men. Standing on the very doorstep of empire that Saturday in February 1764, the indefatigable George Spencer grasped at prizes just out of reach as he helped to push Great Britain and its recalcitrant American colonies along the path to revolution.[4]

For more than a year, the ministry had been struggling to determine "in what mode, least burthensome and most palatable to the colonies, can they contribute toward the support of the additional expense which must attend their civil and military establishments." An important step toward that goal—"An Act for Granting Certain Duties on the British Colonies and Plantations in America"—won approval in the House of Commons on April 5, 1764. The Sugar Act, which sailed through Parliament with little comment from representatives of American interests, reduced the duty on British West Indian molasses from sixpence to threepence per gallon but established prohibitive tariffs on foreign-produced sugar and sugar products imported into the British colonies after September 29, 1764.[5]

The new law reached far beyond sugar. There were prohibitive duties on foreign coffee and indigo, as well as on Spanish and Portuguese wines carried directly to British America. The latter tariff was a direct assault on an important component of colonial commerce, the Madeira wine trade. Other clauses added duties or eliminated drawbacks (the reduction or cancellation of British import duties on reexported goods) on American imports of a variety of European and East Indian fabrics.

The Sugar Act was an attack on entrenched abuses. Customs officials discovered taking bribes or conniving with merchants to get around the law faced heavy fines and dismissal. Owners of vessels seized for violations—even if found innocent—could no longer sue their accusers. And, to put an end to obstruction by local vice-admiralty courts, prosecutions could now be brought in any court of record, including a court of vice-admiralty which "shall be appointed over all America."[6]

Grenville's program included a stamp tax, but wary of pushing too hard, too soon, he delayed its introduction. He did push for currency reform, however. On April 19, 1764, at the behest of British merchants fearing payment in depreciated colonial scrip, Parliament passed legislation prohibiting the issuance of paper money in any of the American colonies after September 1. The timing of the Currency Act could not have been worse.[7]

Far across the Atlantic in New York, economic depression, quasi-martial law in the harbor, and rumblings of onerous legislation on its way from London had set the city on edge. "If ever the colony wanted a friend at home, it is now," William Smith, Jr., wrote Governor Monckton in April. "The fears of these provinces, are excited more, by the apprehension of the imposition of duties upon our trade and taxes upon our estates, than by all the horrors of an Indian war."[8]

When copies of the new legislation arrived in June, a vocabulary of resistance was in the air. And it grew stronger as the summer progressed. "History does not furnish an instance of a revolt begun by the people, which did not take its rise from oppression," editorialized the *Mercury* in August. Men who just twenty-four months earlier had freighted cargoes of desperately needed provisions and "warlike stores" to the enemies of the king were finding common cause in defense of their birthright as Englishmen and the liberties they enjoyed as colonial Americans.[9]

Less than a month after implementation of the Sugar Act, the Forsey-Cunningham civil trial finally got under way in the Supreme Court of Judicature. Nine months earlier, Waddell Cunningham had stood in the same courtroom facing criminal charges for his assault of Thomas Forsey in July 1763. Cunningham was found guilty, fined £30 (New York currency), and discharged.[10]

The civil trial opened on October 25, 1764, an overcast Thursday morning in a week of blustery autumn weather. Neither the plaintiff nor the defendant was in attendance. Forsey was in Puerto Rico negotiating the return of a vessel seized by the Spanish, and Cunningham had departed for London on

July 12, never to return. The courtroom on the second floor of City Hall was packed, "being a cause of much expectation," according to the *Providence Gazette*. Those attending were not disappointed. The first day's session lasted nearly twelve hours, with fifteen witnesses appearing on behalf of Forsey and seven testifying for the defense. The jury began its deliberations late on Thursday evening.[11]

It was raining in New York the next morning as HMS *Coventry*, moored in the Hudson River between Fort George and King's College, "fired 21 guns it being the anniversary of His Majesty's accession to the throne." At City Hall, Justice Horsmanden called the court to order. "The jury being returned to the bar," records the minute book, "say they find for the plaintiff one thousand five hundred pounds damages, and six pence costs."[12]

George Harison, at the head of a group of the defendant's loyal friends, pressed for an appeal. With no legal basis for a writ of error, the most Cunningham's lawyers—James Duane, William Livingston, William Smith, Jr., and Whitehead Hicks—would do was file a motion for retrial. Dumbfounded, "Harison stood up and begged the court to hear him." Cunningham had left specific instructions to appeal if the damages were "extravagant," he told Justice Horsmanden. Harison was reprimanded for his breach of decorum, and the following morning, "a motion was made by the defendant's counsel for a new trial, on account of the largeness of the damages."[13]

When the justices would "neither lay aside the verdict nor mitigate the damages," Harison and Robert Ross Waddell (acting as Cunningham's attorney) prepared a petition to "allow an appeal . . . before the governor and Council." The document was supported by an appeal bond signed by William Kelly, Jacob Walton, Hugh Wallace, and Theophilact Bache, all close allies of the absent Cunningham.[14]

Horsmanden did not bend. Neither would Harison accept defeat. If the Supreme Court would not cooperate, he would go directly to his powerful in-law, Cadwallader Colden. "Mr. Harison [is] my particular friend," Colden wrote, "by my eldest son Alexander and he marrying two sisters." Though advised by the attorney general not to meddle in the procedural affairs of the court, Colden issued a stay of judgment pending an appeal before the governor and Council. He based his authority to override established practice on ambiguous language contained in the instructions from the Privy Council under which he functioned as governor.[15]

The animosity between Colden and the New York legal establishment—as well as between Colden and the Council—now burst to the surface. Horsmanden refused to act upon Colden's writ; the Council refused to hear the appeal; and Colden refused to back down. Then all sides appealed to London. A procedural dispute in a routine civil case had turned into a showdown between the prerogative power of a royal governor and the rights of the people as embodied in established legal practice.[16]

Portraying Colden as an autocrat who was undermining the sanctity of jury verdicts, the legal community closed ranks against the lieutenant-governor. "Mr. Harison has got many enemies for doing his duty only," Robert Ross Waddell wrote Cunningham, now in London. The dispute lingered deep into 1765 as the city awaited judgment from the Privy Council and became enmeshed in a complex web of grievances against the arbitrary exercise of British authority in colonial America.[17]

The rising drumbeat against the governor—whose harangues against lawyers, judges, and members of the Council had become a source of entertainment for polite society—was driven by the angry popular press. In the popular imagination, there was nothing amusing about the dark and sinister old man stripping away the rights of a vulnerable people. "While wc have juries," editorialized the *New-York Gazette* in the spring of 1765, "we may be free, or if we are not, it is our own fault."[18]

In February and March 1765, as tensions rose in New York, Parliament completed work on its stamp tax for the American colonies. The measure, basic to Grenville's program to establish an American source of revenue, required a stamp on all legal documents, permits, commercial contracts, newspapers, wills, pamphlets, and playing cards. News of passage of the Stamp Act, which was due to take effect on November 1, arrived in New York in April. A year earlier, the *Gazette* had published a resolution of the House of Commons forewarning Americans that in addition to tighter enforcement of customs regulations, "it may be proper to charge certain stamp duties in the said colonies and plantations." By June 1765 printed copies of the Stamp Act were available in the city, and in July a New Yorker wrote that "associations are forming to which several thousands have subscribed, . . . to draw up remonstrances to His Majesty, &c., and to oppose this tremendous act by all lawful means."[19]

With each passing week, the vocabulary of resistance became more strident, and threats leveled at stamp agents appointed by the Crown turned to violence. In August a Boston mob hanged the Massachusetts agent in effigy and destroyed his home. A few days later, James McEvers, the New York agent and a former flag-trucer, resigned his post, claiming "by the present disposition of people here it appears that a stranger would be more agreeable than a native."[20]

In the midst of all this, George Spencer had returned to America. In August, writing from the safety of Philadelphia, he urged Attorney General Kempe to redress long-standing grievances. Spencer had been swindled, misrepresented, and denied justice since the beginning of his ordeal in the autumn of 1759. The informer demanded action against the estate of John Alsop, Sr., the court-appointed attorney who had sold Spencer's home in 1760 to cover legal expenses. Over the following two years, Spencer's defense against his creditors went nowhere, and his prosecutions of New Yorkers who had traded with the enemy stalled in both the court of vice-admiralty and the Supreme Court of Judicature. Worst of all, a third of the proceeds from the sale of the house on Broadway—the share belonging to Spencer's wife—remained in the Alsop family's hands, "which is now about five years and six months."[21]

Spencer also hoped to initiate a suit against Alexander Colden, son of the lieutenant-governor, for his share of "the net proceeds of a sloop and cargo which was seized through my information" in 1760. Kempe himself had conducted the prosecution—"as you may well remember," wrote Spencer. "With respect to the several actions which I commenced" to recover the penalties on provisions exported to the French during the war, the informer offered to share his earnings with Kempe if he would renew the prosecutions in the New York court of vice-admiralty.[22]

In a letter to London a few weeks earlier, Spencer had leveled a blanket indictment against New York City: "The people there," he wrote, "have such connections one with another, I apprehend no justice will be done, having been denied it already; not only by Mr. Horsmanden, one of the Council, and now chief justice in the room of Mr. Prat, deceased; but also by the present lieutenant-governor."[23]

The informer's frustration focused on his failure to bring down "one of the chief instigators of that mob at New York by which I was so cruelly abused." Though Waddell Cunningham had left New York for London the previous summer, Spencer demanded that the government "take proper means to bring that notorious offender to justice." Cunningham "had in the harbor of New York, at the time I gave that information, a snow laden with sugars from Monte Cristi, . . . waiting for a fictitious clearance, in order to enter the same at the custom house." That was soon accomplished, charged Spencer, "and the Crown was defrauded of the duty."[24]

Spencer's ordeal, not surprisingly, had taught him to be cautious in dealing with New York. "As it will not suit me to come thither," he told Kempe, "I should be proud of the honor to wait [on] you at . . . [a] place you may please to appoint." The informer had no intention of rekindling his protracted nightmare. "While these matters are carrying on at New York," he had urged the Customs Board in March, "you will be pleased to order that I may be protected on board one of His Majesty's ships in that harbor. Otherwise, as I have no commission, I shall incur a risk of being murdered."[25]

Spencer was wise to keep his distance. Taken together, the economic crisis, brought on by the collapse of the wartime economy and exacerbated by parliamentary interference in colonial commerce, and the political crisis, spawned by the Forsey-Cunningham controversy and the Stamp Act, had created a lethal mix of political posturing and street theater.[26]

American colonists "have for a long time enjoyed the privileges of British subjects, and tasted the sweets of English liberty," editorialized the *Mercury* in mid-September. "It is no wonder then, that the most distant approaches of arbitrary power should spread a general consternation among them." The announcement of the Stamp Act "raised the alarm and transmitted it through the whole continent, and it is generally considered as an encroachment, unprecedented and unconstitutional, pregnant of innumerable woes and uncertainties."[27]

Among the "sweets of English liberty" was the right to a jury verdict free from arbitrary interference. On October 9, 1765, Cadwallader Colden informed the Council that King George III had allowed Waddell Cunningham's appeal to go forward. For a second time, the king had intervened on Cunningham's behalf. The latest news came "like a thunderbolt," wrote John Watts, a member of the Council. But the lieutenant-governor's victory was submerged by events.[28]

At City Hall two days earlier, twenty-seven representatives from nine British North American colonies had gathered for the opening of the Stamp Act Congress. The meeting brought together a cross-section of colonial elites that prefigured the Continental Congresses of the mid-1770s. Four of the five New York delegates—William Bayard, John Cruger, Leonard Lispenard, and Philip Livingston—had done business with the enemy during the war, as had one of the Pennsylvania delegates, George Bryan, a Dubliner and close ally of

Waddell Cunningham's. Collectively, they embodied the alliance of mercantile and political power that had underpinned the energetic wartime trade with the French, nowhere more firmly than in New York City.[29]

In May 1762, three of the New Yorkers—Bayard, Lispenard, and Livingston (along with Mayor John Cruger's brother and business partner Henry Cruger)—had signed a petition to Colden asking that he "abate the rigor of that resentment, which some of our fellow citizens at present labor under" for their wartime trade with the French. Each man expressed "the firmest loyalty and affection for our most gracious sovereign and the most steady and fixed attention to the honor of his crown and dignity."[30]

On October 22, 1765, as the Stamp Act Congress put the finishing touches on its petition to that same king, Captain William Davis brought the ship *Edward* through Sandy Hook after a nine-week crossing from London. The following day, it stood off the Battery protected by two British warships. Along the shore, thousands of angry New Yorkers challenged the government to land the shipment of stamps.[31]

Handbills posted around the city signed "Vox Populi" left no doubt as to the intentions of the radicals and the fate of anyone who defied them: "The first man that either distributes or makes use of stampt paper let him take care of his house, person, and effects." No one familiar with the sordid treatment of the informer George Spencer would have misunderstood the threat. Under cover of darkness, a detachment of marines moved the hated stamps to the safety of Fort George.[32]

The Stamp Act Congress wrapped up its work on Friday, October 25. The delegates adopted a "Declaration of Rights" and prepared letters and petitions for the king and both houses of Parliament. The declaration called for repeal, leveled a broad attack on Grenville's program, and asserted the American colonists' rights as Englishmen. Although the document implicitly recognized Parliament's authority to regulate trade, it denied its power to impose internal taxes, being a body without colonial representation. "It is inseparably essential to the freedom of a people, and the undoubted rights of Englishmen," stated the third article, "that no taxes be imposed on them, but with their own consent, given personally or by their representatives."[33]

On the eve of implementation of the Stamp Act, the *New-York Gazette* published "A Funeral Lamentation on the Death of Liberty."

Who finally expires this
Thirty first of October,

In the Year of our Lord
M. DCC. LXV.
And of our Slavery
I.

At four that afternoon, "upwards of two hundred principal merchants" met at the New York Arms "to consider what was necessary to be done in the present situation of affairs." They agreed to halt all imports from Great Britain until the Stamp Act was repealed and to set up a committee of correspondence to coordinate with other colonies. "The lawyers are the source from whence the clamors have flowed in every province," wrote General Gage. "In this province, nothing public is transacted without them." At separate meetings, New York City shopkeepers pledged cooperation, as did tradesmen and laborers who met on the Common and afterward staged a peaceful march down Broadway.[34]

Protests continued late into the night. According to a captain in the British Army, "a mob in three squads went through the streets crying 'Liberty'" and smashing street lamps. "Some thousands of windows [were] broke," he added. "The sailors who are the only people who may be properly styled [a] mob, are entirely at the command of the merchants who employ them," wrote his commanding officer.[35]

As the sun inched over the horizon the following morning, the city held its breath. Fort George had been preparing for this day since late in the summer, when military engineers began strengthening defenses and General Gage called down a company of regulars from Crown Point to reinforce the garrison. "The governor had very injudiciously, for some time before the arrival of the stamps, made a great show of fortifying the fort, providing it with mortars, guns, ammunition, and all the necessaries for the regular attack of an enemy—and it was given out that he threatened to fire on the town if the stamps were molested," reported the press.[36]

True to his character, Colden remained obstinate and difficult but steadfast in his devotion to the Crown. Somewhere off the coast, the *Minerva,* nearing the end of a hard Atlantic crossing, carried his replacement, Sir Henry Moore. Until the new governor arrived, Colden was in command.[37]

The two sides made their final preparations under a clear November sky. At the fort, there were adjustments to the cannons now facing Broadway, and soldiers worked through the day shoring up the gates and removing fences and obstructions to a clear field of fire. In the city, defiance was on open display. "Many placards [were] put up threatening the lives, houses and properties of anyone who shall either issue or receive a stamp," reported a witness. By evening, all was in place. An unruly crowd, "attended by a great number of lights, paraded through most of the public streets in the city, increasing as they went."[38]

Like the mob that had debased George Spencer six Novembers before, the crowd mocked and abused the object of its attention, a ribald effigy of the aged lieutenant-governor. Now as then, the city rose to reject interference in its commercial life. Along the way, rioters broke into Colden's carriage house, adding his handsome coach to their props.

A larger demonstration—at least two thousand strong—formed on the Common around a movable gallows bearing a sinister figure of Colden with the Devil himself whispering in his ear. "When the two parties met, and every thing was in order, a general silence ensued." Then the restless crowd flowed off the Common in the direction of the Drovers' Inn and moved toward the fort.[39]

Church bells tolled as British regulars, their red coats blending into the darkness, stood in silence along the parapet of Fort George. In the distance, tiny specks of light grew into a sea of torches and candle lamps. The angry demonstration on the Common became a mob as it surged down Broadway. "They knew the guns were charged, and saw the ramparts lined with soldiers," according to a newspaper account, but "they intrepidly marched with the gallows, coach, &c. up to the very gate." The jeering, taunting mob threw rocks at the soldiers and attempted to break open the gate—even scale the walls.[40]

Colden had been warned that he would "die a martyr to your own villainy, and be hanged, like Porteous, upon a signpost, as a memento to all wicked governors" if the soldiers fired a single shot into the crowd: "Every man, that assists you, shall be, surely, put to death." Colden, Gage, and the officers and men facing the insurrection held firm.[41]

Unable to provoke the guardians of the stamps, the mob set the governor's coach ablaze, along with the effigies and whatever else they could find. A breakaway group set out to sack the home of a British officer who had dared to belittle protesters against the Stamp Act. Then on a signal the rioters dispersed into the night, but their rage was unabated. "The engineers all on duty this night to fortify the Fort—its garrison between 150 and 200 strong," recorded a nervous officer. Public notices threatened the lives of citizens, and "stragglers throng[ed] in with arms from several parts even Connecticut, for plunder &c." For nearly a week, the city veered toward anarchy.[42]

On Tuesday, November 5, after "advertisements and many papers placarded throughout this city declar[ed] the storming of the Fort this night," Colden finally bent. "At last, by the advice of the Council, [the] opinion of the commander-in-chief and [the] earnest request of the corporation, the stamps were delivered up to the mayor and corporation."[43]

The crisis was over. "Perfect tranquility," recorded a witness. "It is expected that in a few days, all sorts of business will be carried on in all public offices as usual," wrote a New Yorker to a friend in London—"without stamps."[44]

A week later, Sir Henry Moore arrived in New York City after a voyage of ten weeks from Portsmouth. He was immediately "received at Fort George, by His Honor the Lieutenant Governor Colden, and saluted with 17 guns from the fort." After the formal reading of his commission in the Council chamber, Governor Moore led a procession of dignitaries "to the City Hall, where his commission was republished attended with loud acclamations of the people." And, according to the *Mercury*, "in the evening the city was handsomely illuminated."[45]

The following day—Thursday, November 14—heavy rain, damaging winds, and "a very high tide [that] overflowed the King's Wharf" kept the city indoors. The rain continued through much of Friday, but that evening the weather cleared and the city celebrated: "A very large bonfire was made in the Commons," reported the *Mercury*, "where many thousands of the inhabitants were assembled, who all demonstrated the greatest joy on the arrival of our new governor, by many loud huzzas, for, Long live Henry Moore, and a speedy repeal to the Stamp Act."[46]

On the eve of Moore's arrival, the New York's Supreme Court of Judicature had defied Colden once again. On November 12, Justice Horsmanden announced "that his court cannot comply with the king's order" and refused to hear Waddell Cunningham's appeal of the Forsey verdict. The controversy abruptly ended the following day with the arrival and installation of the new governor. Moore's instructions, unlike those of his predecessor, explicitly stipulated that only appeals based on writs of error could be brought before the governor and Council. And in December word arrived that the Privy Council, at the request of the Board of Trade—which was now fearful of establishing a dangerous precedent—had reversed its decision to allow the appeal.[47]

Colden had been defeated, and Cunningham, Harison, Kelly, and their friends had been forced to accept the jury's verdict. But the odor of autocratic rule lingered, as did a newly acquired taste for defiance. Its origins were deep and complex and, surely, manifest in the city's brazen trade with the enemy during the Seven Years' War. But the crush of events over the coming months and years, beginning with the nonimportation campaign and the movement to repeal the Stamp Act, obscured the links between political crisis in New York and the city's intoxicating wartime economy at the service of two masters.[48]

On January 8, 1766, George Spencer left his rooms at the Hat and Feather in central London and once again cut through the Fleet Market on his way to the Treasury. He had, at least for the time being, put aside ambitions to enrich himself at the expense of colonial merchants embroiled in wartime trade with the French. Ever resourceful, the expatriate New Yorker carried with him a brilliant new proposal to salvage the ministry's failed American policy. His scheme would raise at least £135,000, a sum equivalent to "what might be raised in America by the Stamp Act," which, he added, "will be repealed."

"With most humble submission to your Lordships," wrote Spencer, "permit me to mention, tea." "There is nothing produced in the British colonies, in America, that bears any resemblance," he continued. Tea "is used there by people of all denominations, from the gentleman even to the slave; and is so much in vogue, that the most menial servant will not be satisfied without it." Best of all, there could be no complaint at the American end. "There is at present a drawback of the [import] duties on the exportation of tea," he reminded the commissioners. Even with Spencer's tax, tea exported from Great Britain to the colonies would be "much cheaper than the consumer in England pays for that commodity."

"This, my Lords, is the scheme, which I humbly . . . lay before you," concluded Spencer. It "must of consequence be an annual increase to the revenue; and, I am persuaded, will greatly appease the clamors of those people, and answer the end proposed by the Stamp Act, at which they so loudly murmur."[49]

Conclusion

The early 1760s were a high-water mark in the history of trading with the enemy. Large-scale trade between belligerents would rarely again be so open and bare-faced as it was during the Seven Years' War. The world was undergoing profound changes. Great Britain, having conquered on a global scale, emerged from nine years of war as an eighteenth-century superpower. Its peacetime navy had the command of the oceans, and its economy was on the cusp of an industrial revolution. Trading with the enemy, when it challenged the interests of a nation with global reach, would not be tolerated in a modernizing world.

This does not mean that exchanges between nations at war—when they were expedient—wholly died away. In the first two years of the War of 1812, for example, American provisioners supplied roughly two-thirds of the beef rations for the British Army in Canada. "They also supplied the British fleet that blockaded the American coast and destroyed its capitol," according to Katherine Barbieri and Jack S. Levy, leading scholars of the subject. A persistent problem, trading with the enemy is a feature of modern war and remains a concern in the twenty-first century.[1]

British and American observers drew very different conclusions from the wartime experience of New York City and other colonial ports. It should not be surprising that the London government took a hard view of North Americans who traded with the French, seeing them as unpatriotic, even perverse. Most maddening for the ministry was that they got away with it and pushed hard at the limits of British forbearance in order to squeeze out the last farthing of profit. "To avoid the trouble of a double sale or to get a higher price," complained an officer on the army's headquarters staff in New York in 1760, New York ships "run for Cape François, and sell the provisions to

French merchants, nay it is well known that some New York vessels discharged their cargoes in Monsieur Bompar's squadron. They return laden with French sugars &c. generally unquestioned but always unpunished."[2]

Throughout the war, a steady flow of letters and reports reminded London of the disregard for British law that ran rampant in New York City and elsewhere in North America. To the men of the navy and army, there was nothing ambiguous about trading with the enemy. Admirals Cotes and Holmes in the West Indies and Generals Amherst and Monckton in New York, all outspoken, concurred with Attorney General Kempe that the king's declaration of war had made "any correspondence or communication whatever with the enemy" illegal.[3]

It did not matter that the trade had taken place under the cloak of commerce with Dutch and Danish neutrals or with the Spanish at Monte Cristi Bay, or even that it was conducted aboard government-sanctioned cartel ships. Trading with the enemy was trading with the enemy. Those who engaged in it were base and reckless, prepared to sacrifice the interests of the empire—and their own security—for financial gain in the midst of a bloody war.

From this perspective, the war had exposed the bankruptcy of the regulations that had governed British commerce through much of the seventeenth and eighteenth centuries. An ineffective customs service was at the center of the problem, made urgent in the immediate postwar period by the Crown's appetite for revenue and a national debt of unprecedented proportions. To policy makers now bent on top-to-bottom reform, it was easy to forget—or, perhaps, not to realize—that the "salutary neglect" of earlier decades had contributed mightily to the growth and prosperity of British North America and the empire as a whole. Regardless, Lord Grenville and those close to him—with a mountain of evidence before them (not the least of it from the pen of the irrepressible George Spencer)—were prepared to act and to act decisively. Wartime behavior in Boston, Newport, New London, New York, Philadelphia, and elsewhere in America pointed to a systemic problem. That problem would now receive attention.

There was little to debate. What other conclusion could one draw? Americans could not be trusted; they disregarded the rule of law; and they had—like recalcitrant children—turned their backs on king and empire at a moment of national peril. Worse still, their behavior was not confined to the lowest orders of society. In New York City, the evasion of customs duties (depriving the Crown of revenue), commerce with the enemy (prolonging the war and adding to its cost), and the subversion of law and order (evident in the abuse of informers and the reluctance of juries to convict) had found support among the political, mercantile, and legal elites. Seen this way, colonial Americans had failed to understand that their security and prosperity—as well as their rights as Englishmen—flowed from the common law, the wisdom of Parliament, and the ever-vigilant paternity of their king. Now they would learn to do as they were told.

New Yorkers saw all this in a very different light. If some in the city had engaged in commerce with the French enemy, they had done no more than their compatriots in Great Britain and Ireland. And it was well known that British bankers, financiers, insurance underwriters, and manufacturers of all kinds, along with Irish provisioners, had made their fortunes in the not-so-secret commerce. Most participants in British America, like those in the home islands, had done nothing technically illegal. But the law had been shaved close on both sides of the Atlantic.

Disdain on the British side was matched by distrust on the part of the Americans. To colonial Americans, the Flour Act of 1757 had been a blatant example of discriminatory British legislation. What it made illegal for American merchants remained legal for their British or Irish counterparts. And as cynics pointed out, keeping North American provisions out of the French islands had the added feature—to the delight of the West Indian lobby in Parliament—of depriving North Americans of a piece of the wartime sugar trade (though the sugar in question was French, not British).[4]

It was pure hypocrisy, from an American point of view, for colonial commerce to be subjected to harsh discipline in the midst of a postwar recession. In addition to the provisions forbidden by the Flour Act, New Yorkers had been shipping vast quantities of British manufactured goods to their French customers in the West Indies, sometimes made to French specifications in British workshops.

There were many in New York who were unwilling to acknowledge wrongdoing. For the king's North American subjects—especially those who had seen vessels from London, Bristol, Glasgow, Dublin, and Cork moored at Monte Cristi, Cape François, and Port-au-Prince—violating the Flour Act (that is, shipping provisions from ports in North America to non-British destinations) had never been a serious offence, and their treatment smacked of second-class citizenship. This was also a popular theme with the Irish, who, for very different reasons, complained that there was little equality in "the rights of Englishmen" across the British Empire. What was legal for one, they argued, must be legal for all.[5]

As the war progressed, Americans increasingly questioned the intentions of the naval officers who had pursued them on the high seas. With scarcely any French warships and fewer French merchantmen to hold their attention—though there were plenty of French privateers—the men in blue made their fortunes capturing North American vessels. Even Admiral Holmes was exercised by Jamaican politicians who attempted to deprive him of his fair share of prize money. One cannot question Holmes's zeal for clearing the seas of North American ships supplying the French, but his motives were mixed. This was, after all, the eighteenth century. He and his officers (along with the common sailors aboard his warships) stood to gain from the condemnation of their prizes in the Jamaican court of vice-admiralty.[6]

Most important, from the American perspective, the strident—and unwarranted—reforms and taxes that cascaded out of the Grenville ministry challenged both the liberties of Englishmen and the commercial arrangements that had brought prosperity to the colonies. Americans had a tradition of self-governance with only occasional interference from London, and the reform-minded British regime of the postwar period threatened colonial autonomy and long-established practices. In ports such as New York, Grenville's program was the opening gambit in a British conspiracy to strip colonial Americans of their cherished constitutional rights.

The view from the twenty-first century enjoys the benefit of hindsight. Trading with the enemy in New York City offered unparalleled opportunities to its boldest and best-connected participants. When conditions were favorable (as they often were), there was money to be made exchanging expensive North American provisions, lumber, and naval stores for cheap French West Indian produce and then undercutting British West Indian competition in European markets. But like any volatile trade, it could also bring financial ruin to an unlucky few.

Britain's muddled and contradictory response to the wartime commerce bred a distrust of royal authority that became a legacy of the Seven Years' War. From the beginning the government had sent mixed signals. Early in the war, the behavior of merchants and ship captains in Great Britain, Ireland, the British West Indies, and British North America had provided ample opportunity to prosecute the most egregious offenders. But the government remained silent, important British interest groups became involved, and the trade blossomed. The badly managed Flour Act, intended to curb trading with the enemy in North America, had little effect other than to breed resentment.

Even General Amherst vacillated. When he first encountered the problem in the spring of 1759, he did not insist that the trade end immediately. Amherst understood exactly why he faced difficulties supplying troops for the Quebec and Ticonderoga campaigns. He was also briefed on the situation in New York by George Spencer in the autumn of 1760. But, dependent upon the cooperation of the New York merchant community, Amherst had been reluctant to root out the trade. "Had General Amherst the power of laying on an embargo, he would not do it," wrote a staff officer in 1760, "unless he found it absolutely necessary." The crackdown that finally came in the spring of 1762 grew out of Amherst's embarrassment at being unable to meet the deadline imposed by London for the American component of the Havana expeditionary force.[7]

The most consistent opposition to the North Americans came from officers of the Royal Navy in the western Caribbean. Throughout the war, the fighting ships of the Port Royal squadron busied themselves interdicting and seizing vessels they suspected of doing business with the enemy. But British naval commanders in the West Indies never received a directive from London on the North American trade. The action they took was based solely on the initiative of the station commanders, Cotes and Holmes. The admirals had, in effect, taken the law into their own hands. This accounts for the large number of reversals when the Jamaican vice-admiralty condemnations were appealed before a London court.

In spite of the low opinion held in British military and political circles of the character and patriotism (or the lack thereof) of American provincials, colonial New Yorkers were not a set of lawless rogues trampling over the British commercial system. The myth of the prerevolutionary patriot working to subvert the British Empire from its colonial beginning in 1607 is not to be believed. Most of those involved in overseas trade played by the rules as they understood them. On balance, the system worked well and, under the umbrella of "salutary neglect," had allowed colonial commerce to intersect with that of the French, Dutch, Danes, Spanish, and Portuguese, largely to Britain's advantage. War changed all that, however, and made what had once been routine a punishable offence.[8]

The dramatic events in New York City during and immediately after the Seven Years' War underscore the centrality of trade to the story of the American Revolution. London's resentment over the lively wartime commerce contributed to the harsh, punitive tone of postwar reform. The heavy-handed response triggered widespread concern among Americans over the fragility of their rights and liberties as Englishmen. In New York, that anxiety led to confrontation—made inevitable by an impolitic and meddling lieutenant-governor. Through it all, no American city played a greater role than New York in defying arbitrary British authority and pushing colonial America toward revolution.

Postscript

For the men and women linked to the story of New York City's trade with the enemy, life went on, sometimes in surprising new directions. Ever the opportunist, George Spencer returned to North America in 1767 as a clergyman. Though "publicly carted through New York and . . . otherwise of very bad character to our prodigious astonishment we hear [he] is also ordained," wrote an Anglican official in Philadelphia, adding, "no church on this continent will receive him." Rejected by congregations in East Brunswick and Freehold, New Jersey, Spencer headed to North Carolina and then back to England. By the 1770s he had reestablished his wine business (and, perhaps, other pursuits) and was a man of means at the time of his death in London in 1784.[9]

Spencer outlived his nemesis, George Harison, by more than a decade. Until his death, Harison remained provincial grand master of the Masons in New York, expanding their influence and establishing lodges as far away as Detroit. Much loved—and feared—he had "the general esteem and regard of all who knew him," according to a eulogist in 1773. "Sincere himself, he looked with contempt on all dissimulations in others; and as his attachments were warm, so his resentments were free from perfidy, for they were undisguised, though not implacable." On the day of his death, "the colors of the several vessels in the harbor were hoisted at half mast."[10]

Harison's good friend Waddell Cunningham never returned to North America. When he retired from trade in 1783, he was the leading businessman in the north of Ireland, with involvements in shipping, manufacturing, and finance, in addition to extensive land holdings in North America and the West Indies. Cunningham was elected to the Irish House of Commons in 1784 and was periodically called upon by the Dublin government for advice on commercial affairs. His funeral in 1797 at Knockbreda on the outskirts of Belfast was attended by "a great concourse" of citizens.[11]

Joseph Chew, the helpful New London customs officer, experienced financial reverses as trade collapsed at the war's end. Facing bankruptcy, he was supported "almost wholly by [the] bounty" of his friend and patron Sir William Johnson, superintendent of Indian affairs in British North America. Johnson arranged for Chew's appointment as secretary to the Indian Department, and, after Sir William's death in 1774, Chew served as secretary under his successors, Guy Johnson and Sir John Johnson. Except for military service in and around New York City during the Revolution, Joseph Chew remained at his post as secretary to the Indian Department until his death in 1798.[12]

Samuel Stilwell died in 1766 at the age of forty-one, but his sometime partner, William Kelly, went on to cut a figure in the run-up to the American Revolution. Kelly had left New York after the Cunningham-Forsey trial and established himself in London, where he became "a gentleman well known in the commercial world for his respectable abilities and extensive connections." In 1773 those connections led the East India Company to award Kelly and his New York partner Abraham Lott the contract to distribute the company's tea in the province of New York. For this—and for allegedly remarking that Governor William Tryon ought to deal with obstreperous colonists by "cram[ing] the tea down their throats"—Kelly was vilified in the press, and in November 1773 his effigy was suspended from a gallows, carted through the principal streets of the city, and burned at the Merchants' Coffee House before a mob of thousands. William Kelly died at Bath, England, in August 1774, a year after his marriage to "a lady of exalted merit, and a fortune of thirty thousand pounds."[13]

Following the death of Sir Henry Moore in 1771, Lieutenant-Governor Cadwallader Colden once again drew the ire of the New York mob as the province awaited Moore's replacement. Opposition to British authority mounted during Tryon's administration (1771–80), and in 1774, with Tryon on business in London, Colden was presiding over the province when New Yorkers staged a tea party to prevent William Kelly's East India Company tea from being landed in the city. By the time Tryon returned in June 1775, royal authority had collapsed and a revolutionary government was forming. Distraught, Colden retreated to his country estate in Flushing. The British reoccupation of New York City occurred four days after Cadwallader Colden's death on September 20, 1776. He was eighty-seven years old.[14]

In contrast, the three British officers who strongly urged a crackdown on wartime trade with the French played no role in the American Revolution. Sir Charles Hardy was made Admiral of the White in 1778. Greatly outnumbered, Hardy had command of the Channel fleet when the French threatened —but did not follow through with—an invasion of England in August 1779. Robert Monckton, regarded as a friend of America after his term as governor of New York (1761–65), refused command of British forces in North America in 1773. He held a seat in the House of Commons until his death in 1782. Jeffery Amherst turned down the American command in January 1775. Gossip spread "that he could not bring himself to command against the Americans, to whom he had been so much obliged." But that was idle talk, for Amherst had no desire to return to North America. Though he expressed support for the government's policy and was raised to the peerage in 1776, Amherst refused the American command a second time in 1778.[15]

Many in New York City who had traded with the enemy suffered during the American Revolution for their loyalty to the Crown. George Folliot had been elected to the New York Provincial Congress in May 1775, but he declined to serve and became a Loyalist. Upon his return to England at the close of the war, he claimed losses of £66,000. Folliot was living at Chester at the time of his death in 1810, once again in possession of lands in North America, all of which he bequeathed to his Harison nephews and nieces at the request of his "late dear wife," the sister of Richard Harison, who was appointed the first U.S. attorney for the district of New York by George Washington in 1789. As U.S. attorney Harison laid the foundations of admiralty and maritime law in the United States. George Folliot's partner James Depeyster, though a Loyalist, retained his property after the war and died "an eminent merchant of this city" in July 1799.[16]

Nathaniel Marston suffered financial reverses during the war and died a Loyalist in New York in 1778, as did Thomas White in 1781. White had accumulated substantial property in New York and New Jersey. "Universally lamented," he was remembered as "a gentleman of great hospitality, benevolence and humanity; . . . he possessed those sympathetic feelings in an eminent degree, which characterize the good man." White's widow, Anne (the possible namesake of Ann Street in lower Manhattan), suffered from the posthumous confiscation of her husband's property, as did the heirs of Nathaniel Marston.[17]

John Tabor Kempe was the last attorney general of the province of New York. Kempe had become a wealthy man by the Revolution, amassing an estate worth £80,000 during his sixteen years as the Crown's chief law-enforcement officer in the colony. Though he profited handsomely from the privileges afforded by his position, he did so without tarnishing his reputation for integrity. In the aftermath of the Revolution, during which he had remained a Loyalist, Kempe took his large family to London, where he was unable to reclaim his vast fortune. He fared better than most Loyalists, however, and salvaged about a tenth of its value through compensation by the British government. Just as his struggles seemed to be ending, Kempe was killed in a carriage accident in 1791.[18]

On the Patriot side, James Duane, the attorney for the defense in the Cunningham-White trial, went on to a distinguished political career. As a conservative member of the Continental Congress, he opposed the issuing of a declaration of independence before the arrival of the commissioners appointed by the Crown to treat with the colonists. Duane served in the Congress throughout the war and returned to New York after the city was evacuated by the British in 1783. He became the first postwar mayor of New York in 1784, serving until 1789.[19]

Two of New York State's four signers of the Declaration of Independence had traded with the enemy during the Seven Years' War. Francis Lewis retired from business in 1765, having grown wealthy supplying both sides. He became active in politics in 1774 and entered the Continental Congress the following year. Philip Livingston joined the New York committee of correspondence following the Stamp Act crisis and, like Lewis, was selected as a delegate to the Congress in 1775. Though Livingston shared James Duane's misgivings about a declaration of independence, he signed the document in July 1776.[20]

No family in New York City was more divided by the trauma of the American Revolution than the Waltons. William Walton, Sr., patriarch of the powerful Walton family, died in 1768 at the height of his influence. His nephews carried on the family enterprise as William and Jacob Walton and Company and became active in New York politics. William Walton, Jr., sought to remain neutral during the American Revolution but veered toward the Loyalist side. His sister Mary Walton Morris was the wife of Lewis Morris, a signer of the Declaration of Independence, while his brother, Jacob Walton, Jr.—once an ally of Waddell Cunningham in his trade with the enemy—became an ardent Loyalist. Jacob's home on Horn's Hook in the East River, the present-day site of Gracie Mansion, was expropriated by Washington's army in 1776 and served as the headquarters of General Charles Lee before the Battle of Brooklyn Heights. Through the war, the more moderate William Jr. remained in the city, where he "devoted his time and large means to relieve the distress the war brought upon so many," including American prisoners of war.[21]

The Waltons' Irish brother-in-law James Thompson, had returned to Ireland with his wife, Catharine Walton Thompson, in 1770. There he became involved in the Irish emigrant trade to North America, among other activities. At the outbreak of the Revolution, James—"ever opposed to that republican spirit which began to show itself at the time of the Stamp Act"—set up in New York as a victualing agent for the British Army. As Loyalists, the Thompsons lost their property when it was confiscated after the war, and James departed for London in 1783 seeking compensation "at an advanced time of life with a large family depending upon him." Resilient as ever, James and Catharine were back in the city in 1785 with their Dublin-educated daughters, Catharine and Anne, at "the center of the gay and elegant society of New-York." In January 1786, nineteen-year-old Anne—remarked upon for her beauty and accomplishments—married Elbridge Gerry of Massachusetts, a signer of both the Declaration of Independence and the Constitution, and a vice-president of the United States of America.[22]

Chronology

1754

May 28 to July 4	Fighting begins when Colonel George Washington of the Virginia militia engages the French in present-day western Pennsylvania.
Autumn and winter	Ships from New York City and other British American ports deliver provisions and supplies to the French at Cape Breton.

1755

February 19	The New York General Assembly places temporary restrictions on provisions exports.
July 5	The New York General Assembly prohibits exports to the French.
July 9	Major-General Edward Braddock is defeated by a force of French and Indians at Monongahela, near present-day Pittsburgh.
September 3	Sir Charles Hardy is invested as governor of New York.

1756

May 8	A customs raid is carried out at Prospect Farm, the East River estate of Nathaniel Marston.
May 17	Great Britain declares war on France.
May 22	Samuel Stilwell is arraigned in New York City for exporting provisions to the French.
May–June	British forces are defeated on the island of Minorca, disgracing the Royal Navy.
June 9	France declares war on Great Britain.
July 23	Lord Loudoun arrives in New York City as commander of British Forces in North America, replacing William Shirley.
July 31	The declaration of war against France is read publicly at New York's City Hall.
August 14	Fort Oswego surrenders to the French.
October	A jury in New York City finds Stilwell guilty of violating the New York statute against trading with the French.

December 29	A provisions embargo ordered by the Privy Council on October 9 is implemented in New York.

1757

February 15	Parliament passes the Flour Act.
March 2	Lord Loudoun orders a general embargo in ports of British North America.
March–May	Trading vessels from British North America supply the comte de Bauffremont's squadron at Cape François.
June 2	Sir Charles Hardy, governor of New York, transfers the seals of office to Lieutenant-Governor James DeLancey.
June 20	The expeditionary force under Loudoun departs New York for Halifax to join the campaign against Louisbourg. The general embargo is lifted.
July 9	The Flour Act goes into effect in New York. An embargo ordered by the Privy Council on provisions exports in New York is lifted.
August 4	Loudoun learns that a superior French naval force has arrived at Louisbourg and abandons plans to land British forces. The marquis de Montcalm besieges Fort William Henry.
August 9	Fort William Henry surrenders to French.
November	The Board of Trade calls for further study of North American trade with the enemy.
December 1	William Pitt recalls Lord Loudoun. Major-General James Abercrombie succeeds him as commander-in-chief.

1758

January	British warships interdict North American vessels off San Fernando de Monte Cristi, a neutral Spanish free port on Hispaniola.
July 8	Abercrombie fails to take Fort Ticonderoga in bloody engagement.
July 27	The British Army under General Jeffery Amherst captures Louisbourg.
November 9	Amherst replaces Abercrombie as commander of British forces in North America.

1759

January 23	A British amphibious force lands on Guadeloupe after a failed attempt to capture Martinique.
February 24	The Board of Trade forwards a report (initiated in November 1757) on North America's trade with the enemy to the Customs Board.
March–April	Amherst encounters shortages in New York brought on by the Monte Cristi trade as he prepares British forces for campaigns against Quebec and Ticonderoga.
April 9	Archibald Kennedy, head of New York's customhouse, advertises for informers about the city's trade with the French.

May 1	Guadeloupe surrenders to the British. A French naval squadron under the comte de Bompar arrives too late to intervene.
May 9	The Customs Board reports to the Treasury on North America's trade with the enemy.
July–September	Bompar's warships put in at Saint-Domingue to refit and take in provisions and "warlike stores" from North American vessels carrying flags of truce to allow prisoner-of-war exchanges.
Mid-August	A New York vessel carrying provisions and naval stores for Bompar's fleet under cover of a flag of truce is seized by British cruiser off Saint-Domingue.
August 25	Admiral Thomas Cotes, the British naval commander at Port Royal, Jamaica, alerts the Admiralty to North American "flag-trucing."
August 31	The Board of Trade reports to the Privy Council on North American trade with the French through Monte Cristi.
September 13	General Wolfe defeats Montcalm at Quebec.
September 17	Kennedy repeats his call for informers.
September 22	The government in New York issues warrants for the arrest of the owners (James Depeyster and George Folliot) and the captain (William Heysham) of a New York ship recently returned from Cape François. Heysham flees and is sought as a fugitive.
October 10	Bompar departs Cape François for France.
October 12	New York City celebrates Wolfe's victory at Quebec.
October 15	About this time, Cotes launches a campaign against flag-trucers in the waters off Saint-Domingue.
October 16	New York attorney general John Tabor Kempe brings charges against Depeyster and Folliot. By the end of October, the case has fallen apart for lack of evidence.
October 31	George Spencer, a bankrupt New York wine merchant, meets with DeLancey and Kennedy to lay information about local merchants who trade with the enemy.
November 1	The men named by Spencer meet at the Merchants' Coffee House to plan his punishment for informing.
November 2	Spencer is publicly humiliated on the streets of New York, then jailed for having violated the terms of his London bankruptcy agreement; the charge is based on fabricated evidence.
November 8	DeLancey refuses to intervene on behalf of Spencer.
November 20	The British are victorious at the Battle of Quiberon Bay off the coast of Brittany, ending the threat of a French invasion of England.

1760

January–April	Spencer initiates lawsuits from jail against New York merchants for trading with the enemy in violation of the Flour Act.
March 18	The quartermaster-general of the British Army, in London following service in North America, reports to the Treasury on the large outflow of gold to the French resulting from New York City's trade with the enemy.

March 28	A report from the Customs Board to the Treasury expresses frustration over Britain's inability to curb North American trade with the French.
May 12	Admiral Charles Holmes succeeds Cotes at Port Royal, Jamaica.
July 30	Lieutenant-Governor DeLancey dies; Cadwallader Colden, president of the provincial Council, becomes acting governor of New York.
August 23	A circular letter from William Pitt, de facto prime minister of England, to colonial governors demands an immediate end to trading with the enemy.
September 8	Montreal surrenders to General Amherst.
October 25	King George II dies.
November 12	After months of delay, a New York vice-admiralty court claims no jurisdiction in the cases brought by Spencer in January and April 1760.
November 29	Spencer appeals to Amherst for help.
December 8–25	On Amherst's order, the New York Council conducts an inquiry into allegations by informers Spencer and Augustus Bradley.
December 27	Colden reports to Pitt on the outcome of the Spencer-Bradley inquiry. News arrives in North America of death of King George II.

1761

January 17	George III publicly proclaimed king at New York City.
July	Holmes steps up the navy's campaign against North American ships supplying the French.
August 15	France and Spain sign a "family compact," pledging the support of Bourbon monarchs for each other.
October 5	William Pitt resigns from the Cabinet.
November 20	Admiral Holmes dies at Port Royal, Jamaica.
December	London businessmen protest the navy's intervention in the Monte Cristi trade.

1762

January 2	Great Britain declares war on Spain.
January 23	Spencer is released from jail in New York.
February 13	A British force under General Robert Monckton captures Martinique.
February 27	The Spanish fortress at Monte Cristi opens fire on British shipping.
March 17	A French naval squadron under the comte de Courbon-Blénac arrives at Cape François; North American vessels deliver supplies to French warships.
April 1	Amherst receives orders to prepare the North American component of a British expeditionary force for attack on Havana.
April 3	Britain's declaration of war against Spain is read publicly at New York's City Hall.
April 13	Amherst is shocked by revelations of illicit trade with the French contained in documents seized aboard a homeward-bound New York trading vessel.

April 15	Unable to gather the ships and provisions he needs for the assault on Havana, Amherst initiates a crackdown on trading with the enemy in New York City.
April 26	HMS *Enterprise* seizes the snow *Johnson* off Fishers Island in Long Island Sound; *Enterprise* takes three other New York trading vessels into custody on May 1 and 2.
May 3	French agents in New York City are rounded up and jailed.
May 25–28	Amherst orders a general embargo in the port of New York. Eighteen New Yorkers, among them prominent merchants, are arrested and jailed for involvement in city's trade with the French.
May 29	In a petition to Colden, fifty-four New York City merchants beg forgiveness for their involvement in wartime trade with the French.
June	Spencer arrives in London.
July 1	The New York component of the British expeditionary force against Havana leaves the city.
August 14	Havana surrenders to the British expeditionary force.
Autumn	With the end of war in sight the buoyant New York economy collapses.
November 3	Preliminary articles of peace are accepted by Britain, France, and Spain.

1763

January 24	The truce ending fighting in the Seven Years' War is announced in New York City.
February 10	The Treaty of Paris is signed, ending the Seven Years' War.
March–July	Spencer establishes contact with leading British officials in London.
April 19	The Cunningham-White trial opens in the New York Supreme Court of Judicature.
July 9	The government in London demands that colonial governors strictly enforce all British laws respecting trade. Commanders of British warships stationed in North America to be deputized as customs enforcement agents.
July 19	The Treaty of Paris is publicly proclaimed in New York City.
July 29	In a dispute over a bill of exchange Waddell Cunningham stabs Thomas Forsey on the streets of New York.
October 11	British warships arrive in New York harbor to enforce customs regulations.
October 19	The Keating-Kennedy trial opens in the New York Supreme Court of Judicature.
October 27	The Lott, Lynch, and Van Zandt trial opens in the New York Supreme Court of Judicature.
November 17	General Thomas Gage takes over as commander of British forces in North America, replacing Amherst.
December 2	Lieutenant-Governor Colden orders Attorney General Kempe to justify the strenuousness of his prosecutions of Waddell Cunningham and Thomas White. The snow *New York* is seized by the Royal Navy in lower New York Bay.

1764

January 27	Cunningham, facing assault charges in the New York Supreme Court of Judicature, is fined £30 (New York currency).
January 28	Justice Daniel Horsmanden reduces the penalties in the Cunningham-White verdict.
April 5	Parliament passes the Sugar Act.
April 19	Parliament passes the Currency Act.
October 25–30	Jury verdict in Forsey-Cunningham civil trial favors Thomas Forsey. Cunningham's lawyers refuse to lodge an appeal based on size of penalty. George Harison presses Cadwallader Colden to allow an appeal before the Governor's Council.
November 1764–October 1765	In a standoff with Colden, the Governor's Council refuses to hear the appeal of the Forsey-Cunningham verdict. Colden forwards the matter to the Privy Council in London, inciting popular outcry in New York that an arbitrary government has undermined the rights of Englishmen to the verdict of a jury.

1765

March 22	Parliament passes the Stamp Act.
August 23	Now in Philadelphia, Spencer demands that Kempe move forward with prosecutions of New Yorkers charged with trading with the enemy.
October 9	News arrives in New York that the king is allowing Cunningham's appeal of the Forsey-Cunningham verdict.
October 7–22	The Stamp Act Congress convenes in New York City.
November 1	British forces attempt to unload the tax stamps in New York City, inciting the Stamp Act riot.
November 13	Sir Henry Moore takes over as governor of the province of New York.
December	Word arrives in New York City that the Privy Council will no longer allow Cunningham's appeal.

1766

January 8	Spencer, once again in London, proposes a tax on tea to the Treasury.

Glossary of Persons

ALSOP, JOHN, SR. (1697–1761) George Spencer's court-appointed attorney, he worked at cross-purposes with his client.

AMHERST, JEFFERY (1717–97) The commander of British forces in North America (1758–63), he orchestrated the crackdown in New York City on trading with the enemy.

BAUFFREMONT, JOSEPH DE (1714–81) The commander of the French naval squadron at Saint-Domingue in the spring of 1757 that threatened the New York expeditionary force against Louisbourg.

BOGERT, JOHN, JR. (1718–82) A New York alderman and merchant who, with his brother Nicholas, was a prominent figure in New York's trade with the enemy.

BOGERT, NICHOLAS (1725–1814) A ship captain who worked with his brother John Jr. in New York's trade with the enemy.

BOMPAR, MAXIMIN, COMTE DE (1698–1773) The commander of the French naval squadron that called at Saint-Domingue in the summer of 1759. He was dependent upon North Americans for supplies.

BRADLEY, AUGUSTUS (dates unknown) An itinerant merchant who was jailed in New York for forgery and then accused prominent citizens of trading with the enemy, blaming the government for failing to act against them.

BRANSON, PHILIP (dates unknown) The deputy sheriff of New York County, he cooperated with merchants to silence the informer George Spencer and was indicted as an instigator of the Spencer riot.

CARTOE, JEAN FRANÇOIS (dates unknown) A French agent in New York who traveled between the city and Cape François to coordinate the shipment of goods to Saint-Domingue.

CHEW, JOSEPH (c. 1725–98) A merchant and customs official in New London, Connecticut, who was a source of false clearances for vessels carrying provisions to neutral and enemy ports.

COLDEN, ALEXANDER (1716–75) The surveyor of customs in New York City, he enforced the law selectively. He was the son of Cadwallader Colden and the brother-in-law of George Harison.

COLDEN, CADWALLADER (1689–1776) The lieutenant-governor of the province of

New York (serving as chief executive in 1760–61, 1763–65, 1769–70, 1774–75), he vacillated between tolerating and suppressing trade with the enemy and fomented the political unrest that led to the Stamp Act riot.

COLVILLE, ALEXANDER (1717–70) From headquarters at Halifax, Nova Scotia, he commanded the Royal Navy's North American squadron (1759–62, 1763–66), which disrupted smuggling along the North American coast in the postwar years.

COTES, THOMAS (1712–67) The commander of the British naval squadron at Port Royal, Jamaica (1757–60), he disrupted the North American flag of truce trade with Saint-Domingue.

COURBON-BLÉNAC, CHARLES, COMTE DE (1710–65) The commander of the French naval squadron at Saint-Domingue in the spring of 1762, supplied by New York merchants who were later prosecuted for trading with the enemy.

CRUGER, JOHN (1710–91) The mayor of New York City (1757–66) and a prominent merchant, he promoted wartime prosperity, cooperating with the military while active in trade with the enemy. He was later a delegate to the Stamp Act Congress.

CUNNINGHAM, WADDELL (1729–97) The de facto leader of the Irish merchant community in New York City, he was a prime instigator of the Spencer riot and was prosecuted for trading with the enemy and assaulting a fellow merchant.

DELANCEY, JAMES (1703–60) The lieutenant-governor of the province of New York (serving as chief executive in 1753–55, 1757–60), he deflected attention away from the city's trade with the enemy.

DENNY, WILLIAM (1709–65) The lieutenant-governor of the commonwealth of Pennsylvania (1756–59), he was the principal source of North American flag of truce commissions.

DEPEYSTER, JAMES (1725–99) A New York merchant who was the son of the provincial treasurer. Along with George Folliot he was the subject of the abortive prosecution that led to the Spencer riot.

DUANE, JAMES (1733–97) A New York attorney, he defended Waddell Cunningham and others prosecuted for trading with the enemy.

FOLLIOT, GEORGE (1730–1810) An Irish merchant in New York, he was the son-in-law of George Harison and, along with James Depeyster, the subject of the abortive prosecution that led to the Spencer riot.

FORSEY, THOMAS (b. 1726) A merchant of New London, Connecticut, he was stabbed by Waddell Cunningham following a trade-related dispute.

GRENVILLE, GEORGE (1712–70) The prime minister of Great Britain (1763–65) who instituted reforms to improve customs enforcement and increase British tax revenue from colonial America.

HARDY, CHARLES (c. 1717–80) A British admiral and the governor of the province of New York (1755–57), he alerted London to the seriousness of North America's trade with the enemy.

HARISON, GEORGE (1719–73) A New York merchant and former customs official, he was provincial grand master of the Masons in New York and spearheaded the conspiracy to silence the informer George Spencer.

HEYSHAM, WILLIAM (1720–97) A ship captain in the service of Depeyster and Folliot, he fled New York City after being charged with high treason for his voyage to Cape François to trade with the enemy.

HOLMES, CHARLES (c. 1711–61) The commander of the British naval squadron at Port Royal, Jamaica (1760–61), he disrupted North American trade at Monte Cristi Bay.

HOPKINS, STEPHEN (1707–85) The governor of Rhode Island (1755–56, 1758–61, 1763–64, 1767), he defended indirect trade with the enemy and was a source of flag of truce commissions.

HORSMANDEN, DANIEL (1694–1778) A justice on the New York Supreme Court of Judicature (chief justice, 1763–75), he was a member of the Governor's Council and presided over the trials of New Yorkers charged with trading with the enemy.

HOULTON, JOHN (d. 1791) The commander of HMS *Enterprise,* he cooperated with General Amherst to suppress New York's trade with the enemy.

KELLY, WILLIAM (d. 1774) A prominent member of New York City's Irish trading community, he did a great deal of business with the French and was an instigator of the Spencer riot.

KEMPE, JOHN TABOR (1735–92) The attorney general of the province of New York (1759–82), he tirelessly prosecuted traders with the enemy in New York City.

KENNEDY, ARCHIBALD, SR. (1685–1763) The customs collector for the port of New York (1722–62), he favored light restrictions on Great Britain's Atlantic commerce and suppressed trade with enemy only when pressed by General Amherst.

LECOMTE, PASCAL (dates unknown) A French agent living in New York City who was arrested and jailed in the crackdown of 1762.

LEWIS, FRANCIS (1713–1803) A New York merchant who, as court-appointed referee, determined whether George Spencer should be jailed for bankruptcy. He was active in trade with the enemy and, later, a signer of the Declaration of Independence.

LIVINGSTON, PHILIP (1716–78) A New York alderman and merchant who was active in wartime trade with the French. He was a New York delegate to the Stamp Act Congress and a signer of the Declaration of Independence.

LOUDOUN, JOHN CAMPBELL, FOURTH EARL OF (1705–82) The commander of British forces in North America (1756–58), he arrived in New York at low point in war but was unable to improve the military situation.

LYNCH, THOMAS (1736–1814) An Irish merchant in New York with kinsmen in Ireland who were active in trade with the French, he helped instigate the Spencer riot and was charged with trading with the enemy.

MARSTON, NATHANIEL (1704–78) A New York merchant and slave trader whose East River estate was raided by customs officers suppressing the "Dutch trade." He was accused of trading with the enemy at the Spencer-Bradley inquiry.

MCCARTY, DAVID A partner in McCarty and Company, a Franco-Irish merchant house at Cape François that did a large business with New York City.

MERCER, RICHARD (1736–88) A New York merchant and the brother-in-law of Waddell Cunningham, he represented New Yorkers doing business with the French at Monte Cristi Bay.

MONCKTON, ROBERT (1726–82) A British general and governor of the province of New York (1761–65), he ordered John Tabor Kempe to prosecute New Yorkers for trading with the enemy.

MOORE, HENRY (1713–69) The lieutenant-governor of Jamaica (1756, 1759–62) and the governor of New York (1765–69), he restored calm to New York City following the Stamp Act riot.

MORRIS, LEWIS (1698–1762) A judge of the vice-admiralty court of New York, New Jersey, and Connecticut (1738–62) who allowed few cases involving trading with the enemy to be tried in his court. He was a source of flag of truce commissions.

MORRIS, RICHARD (1730–1810) The son of Lewis Morris, he succeeded to his father's position as judge of the vice-admiralty court of New York, New Jersey, and Connecticut.

PRAT, BENJAMIN (1711–63) The chief justice of the province of New York (1761–63), he released George Spencer from jail and supported General Amherst's crackdown on trading with the enemy.

RIEUX, JEAN BAPTISTE (dates unknown) A French agent living in New York City who was arrested and jailed in the crackdown of 1762.

SMITH, WILLIAM, SR. (1697–1769) A New York attorney and member of the Governor's Council, he wrote an exculpatory report on New York City's trade with the enemy at the conclusion of the Spencer-Bradley inquiry.

SPENCER, GEORGE (c. 1717–84) A New York merchant, self-styled double-agent, and government informer, he was jailed for twenty-seven months on fabricated bankruptcy charges as a warning to other would-be informers. On his release he deluged officials in London with details of his ordeal.

STILWELL, SAMUEL (1725–66) A New York merchant who was the first in the city to be prosecuted for trading with the enemy. He helped plan the Spencer riot and was active in trade with the French throughout the war.

TEMPLE, JOHN (1732–98) The surveyor-general of customs for the northern district of America (1761–68), he obstructed prosecutions in New York of merchants accused of trading with the enemy.

THOMPSON, CATHARINE WALTON (1729–1807) The wife of James Thompson and niece of William Walton, Sr., she managed the company's ships returning from Hispaniola with French cargoes.

THOMPSON, JAMES (1727–1812) An Irish merchant in New York who helped plan the Spencer riot and set up as a merchant at Monte Cristi and Cape François.

VAN ZANDT, JACOB (d. 1788) A New York merchant who was active in every phase of trading with the enemy, notably flag-trucing, for which he was prosecuted in 1762.

WALTON, JACOB, JR. (1733–82) A New York merchant and the nephew of William Walton, Sr., he helped plan the Spencer riot. He was protected by family connections from prosecution in New York City.

WALTON, WILLIAM, SR. (1705–68) The most powerful merchant in New York City, he was a member of the Governor's Council and related by marriage to Lieutenant-Governor James DeLancey. His firm, Walton and Company, had a conspicuous presence in the city's trade with the enemy.

WALTON, WILLIAM, JR. (1731–96) A New York merchant and the nephew of William Walton, Sr., he was married to eldest daughter of James DeLancey. William Jr. was active in wartime trade with the French but was never prosecuted.

WHITE, THOMAS (1724–81) An Irish merchant in New York City who helped plan the Spencer riot and was prosecuted for trading with the enemy in the Cunningham-White trial.

Glossary of Terms

The definitions below are taken from the following reference works, available in New York City in the 1760s: William Falconer, *An Universal Dictionary of the Marine* (London, 1769); John Harris, *Lexicon Technicum: An Universal English Dictionary of Arts and Sciences* (London, 1704); Samuel Johnson, *A Dictionary of the English Language,* 2 vols. (London, 1755–56); John Mair, *Book-Keeping Methodiz'd; or, A Methodical Treatise of Merchant-Accompts According to the Italian Form* (Edinburgh, 1749); *The Merchant's Ware-House Laid Open; or, The Plain Dealing Linnen Draper* (London, 1696); Malachy Postlethwayt, *The Universal Dictionary of Trade and Commerce,* 2 vols. (London, 1751–55); [Richard] Rolt, *A New Dictionary of Trade and Commerce* (London, 1756).

BALLAST "A certain portion of stone, iron, gravel, or such like material, deposited in a ship's hold, when she has either no cargo, or too little to bring her sufficiently low in the water" (Falconer). "Ships are said to be in ballast, when they have no other loading" (Rolt).

BARGE A boat rowed by a band of sailors "for the use of admirals and captains of ships of war." Such vessels "may be easily hoisted into, and out of the ships to which they occasionally belong" (Falconer).

BARREL "An oblong vessel, of a spheroidal or rather cylindrical figure, made of fir, oak, beech, or other timber, used for containing several sorts of goods, both liquid and dry. Barrel is also used for a certain quantity, or weight, of several merchandises, which varies according to commodities" (Rolt).

BILL OF EXCHANGE "A short note, or writing, ordering the payment of a sum of money, in one place, to some person assigned by the drawer, or remitter, in consideration of the like value paid to him in another place" (Rolt).

BILL OF LADING "An instrument signed by the master of a ship, acknowledging the receipt of a merchant's goods, and obliging himself to deliver them, at the place to which they are consigned, in good condition" (Rolt).

BOHEA TEA "The voui tea, or bou tea, of the Chinese [differs] from the green tea, by its being gathered in March, a month before it, and while in the bud; hence the smallness of the leaves, as well as the depth of the tincture it gives the water" (Rolt). "Many virtues are ascribed to the bohea" (Postlethwayt).

BOOT-TOP "The act of cleaning the upper-part of a ship's bottom, or that part which lies immediately under the surface of the water, and daubing it over with tallow" (Falconer).

BRIG, OR BRIGANTINE "A merchant-ship with two masts. . . . Amongst English seamen, this vessel is distinguished by having her main-sail set nearly in the plane of her keel; whereas the main-sails of larger ships are hung athwart, or at right angles with the ship's length" (Falconer).

BRING TO "To detain a ship . . . or to retard her course" (Falconer).

BURTHEN "The weight or measure of any species of merchandise that a ship will carry when it is fit for sea" (Falconer).

CAREENING YARD A place "for the laying a vessel on one side, to caulk, stop up leaks, refit, or trim the other side" (Rolt).

CARTEL "A ship commissioned in time of war to exchange the prisoners of any two hostile powers; also to carry any particular request or proposal from one to another" (Falconer).

CHACE "A vessel pursued by some other, which she apprehends or knows to be an enemy" (Falconer).

COLORS "The flags or banners which distinguish the ships of different nations" (Falconer).

CORDAGE "The ropes belonging to the rigging or tackle of a ship" (Mair).

CRUISE "A voyage or expedition in quest of vessels or fleets of the enemy" (Falconer).

CRUISERS "Such vessels as are employed by a government to sail, or cruise about, in appointed stations, for the interception of smugglers, the security of trade, the intimidating of enemies, and the suppression of pirates" (Rolt).

EMBARGO "A restraint, or prohibition, laid by a sovereign, or government, on merchant vessels, to prevent their going out of port; sometimes their coming in, and sometimes both, for a limited time: which are more usually done in time of war, in apprehensions of invasions, in times of scarcity, or pestilence abroad, and other extraordinary circumstances" (Rolt).

FACTOR "A correspondent or agent residing beyond seas, or in some remote part, commissioned by merchants (called his employers) to buy or sell goods for their account, or some way to assist them in carrying on commerce; and has wages allowed him for his pains" (Mair).

FATHOM "A measure of six feet, used for a variety of purposes at sea" (Falconer).

FIRKIN "An English measure of capacity, for liquids, containing the fourth part of barrel. The firkin of beer is 9 gallons, and that of ale only 8: . . . the firkins of soap and butter are on the footing of the firkin of ale" (Rolt).

FRIGATE "In the navy, a light nimble ship built for the purposes of sailing swiftly. These vessels mount from twenty to thirty-eight guns, and are esteemed excellent cruisers" (Falconer).

GREEN TEA "Singloe, or common green tea, is a small lead-colored leaf; the best sort has a fresh strong flavor peculiar to itself" (Postlethwayt).

GUARDA COSTAS "In America, the Spaniards constantly employ a great number of these armed vessels, to prevent the ships of another nation from enjoying a traffic with the American Spaniards: as also to search foreign vessels, in such latitudes, for what they esteem contraband goods" (Rolt).

HOGSHEAD "A measure of liquids containing sixty gallons." "Any large barrel" (Johnson). "A vessel containing 63 gallons" (Mair).

IMPRESS See "Press"

JACK "A sort of flag or colors, displayed from a mast erected on the outer end of a ship's bowsprit. In the British navy the jack is nothing more than a small union flag, composed of the intersection of the red and white crosses; but in merchant-ships this union is bordered with a red field" (Falconer).

LETTERS OF MARQUE AND REPRISAL "Letters under the privy seal, granted to subjects whose ships or goods have been seized or taken by the subjects of another nation, empowering them to retake, by force of arms, what, or to the value of what was injuriously taken from them" (Mair).

LIGHTER "A large, open, flat-bottomed vessel, generally managed with oars, and employed to carry goods to or from a ship when she is to be laden or delivered" (Falconer).

LONGBOAT "The largest and strongest boat belonging to any ship. It is principally employed to carry great burthens, as anchors, cables, ballast, &c." (Falconer).

MIZZEN "The aftermost or hindmost of the fixed sails of a ship" (Falconer).

NAVAL STORES "Comprehend all those particulars which are made use of, not only in the Royal Navy, but likewise in every other kind of navigation: as timber and iron for ship building, also pitch and tar, hemp, cordage, sail-cloth, gun-powder, ordnance, and fire-arms of every sort; also all ship-chandlery wares, &c" (Postlethwayt).

OZNABRIG "Germany [coarse] linen, called so in general from the countries of Osnabrug, Lunenburg, &c."(Postlethwayt). "Ozenbrucks [are] of more use than any one sort of coarse linen in England; the white is very much used for shirts and shifts. [If it is] not too much whitened and is thick after whiting and even threaded, [it] wears well for any use that [it] is proper for" (*Merchant's Ware-House*).

PENDANT "A sort of long narrow banner, displayed from the mast-head of a ship of war, and usually terminating in two ends or points" (Falconer).

PILOT "The person charged with the direction of a ship's course, on, or near the sea-coast, and into the roads, bays, rivers, havens, &c., within his respective district" (Falconer).

PRESS "To force into military service" (Johnson).

PRIVATEERS "Ships sent out in time of war, to seize the ships or goods of enemies" (Mair). "A vessel of war, armed and equipped by particular merchants, and furnished with a military commission by the Admiralty, or the officers who superintend the marine department of country, to cruise against the enemy, and take, sink, or burn their shipping, or otherwise annoy them as opportunity offers. These vessels are generally governed on the same plan with His Majesty's ships, although they are guilty of many scandalous depredations, which are very rarely practiced by the latter" (Falconer).

PRIZE "A vessel taken from the enemy by a ship of war, privateer, or armed merchantman" (Falconer).

ROAD "A bay, or place of anchorage, at some distance from the shore" (Falconer).

SCHOONER "A small vessel with two masts, whose main-sail and fore-sail are suspended from gaffs reaching from the mast towards the stern; and stretched out below by booms" (Falconer).

SHALLOP "A small light vessel with only a small main-mast and fore-mast, and lug-sails to hale up and let down on occasion. They commonly are good sailors [and] are used often as tenders" (Harris). "A sort of large boat with two masts, and usually rigged like a schooner" (Falconer).

SHIP "A general name given by seamen to the first rank of vessels which are navigated on the ocean. . . . It is more particularly applied to a vessel furnished with three masts, each of which is composed of a lower-mast, top-mast, and top-gallant-mast, with the usual machinery thereto belonging" (Falconer).

SHIP OF THE LINE "Usually applied to all men of war mounting sixty guns and upwards. Of late, however, our fifty gun ships have been formed sufficiently strong to carry the same metal as those of sixty, and accordingly may fall into the line in cases of necessity" (Falconer).

SHOT "In the military art, includes all sorts of ball or bullets for fire-arms, from the cannon to the pistol; but those for cannon are of iron; those for muskets, carbines, and pistols, are of lead" (Rolt).

SLOOP "A small vessel furnished with one mast, the main-sail of which is attached to a gaff above, to the mast on its foremost edge, and to a long boom below; by which it is occasionally shifted to either quarter" (Falconer).

SLOOP OF WAR "A name given to the smallest vessels of war, except cutters. They are either rigged as ships or as snows" (Falconer).

SNOW "Generally the largest of all two-masted vessels employed by Europeans, and the most convenient for navigation. The sails and rigging on the main-mast and fore-mast of a snow, are exactly similar to those on the same masts in a ship; only that there is a small mast behind the main-mast of the former which carries a sail nearly resembling the mizzen of a ship. The sail, which is called the try-sail, is extended from its mast toward the stern of the vessel" (Falconer).

SUPERCARGO "A person employed by merchants to go on a voyage, oversee the cargo, and dispose of it to the best advantage" (Mair).

TENDER "A small vessel employed in the king's service, on various occasions; as, to receive volunteers and impressed men, and convey them to a distant place; to attend on ships of war or squadrons; and to carry intelligence or orders from one place to another, &c." (Falconer).

WARLIKE STORES The equivalent of "naval stores" in time of war.

Statutes, Proclamations, and Orders in Council

Statutes are listed in order of their enactment.

Treason Act (1351) Among the treasonable offences listed in a parliamentary statute from the reign of King Edward III is "adhering to the king's enemies in his realm by giving them aid and comfort in the realm and elsewhere." At the time of the Seven Years' War, British North America's indirect trade with the enemy through neutrals did not constitute "adhering to the king's enemies," nor did doing business with the enemy under licenses issued by colonial governors. Conviction under the Treason Act required a high standard of proof of an intention to betray one's country.

Acts of Trade and Navigation (1651, 1660, 1663, 1673) The first of the statutes governing colonial commerce (passed by the Commonwealth Parliament in 1651 and reenacted by the Restoration Parliament in 1660) required that commodities imported into England be carried in English ships manned largely by British sailors. The act of 1660 stipulated that "enumerated" colonial goods (such as tobacco and sugar) be exported only to England or another English colony; by an act of 1663, European goods could be imported into the colonies only from England. The act of 1673—and subsequent acts—refined the system of duties and strengthened customs enforcement. Trading with nations at peace with the Crown was allowed, as long as it conformed to the requirements of the Acts of Trade and Navigation.

New York Revenue Act (1753) Passed by the New York General Assembly in December, this act—"An act for granting to His Majesty the several duties and impositions on goods, wares, and merchandise, imported into this colony therein mentioned"—established duties on imports and contained a provision to curb smuggling from the European continent and the foreign West Indies. Persons convicted of "the clandestine running" of goods were liable to the forfeiture of their cargoes, as well as fines of £20 (New York currency). Those unable to pay faced three months in jail. The second offence was punishable by six months in jail without bail.

Act to Restrain Provisions Exports from New York (1755) In February the New York legislature passed an act to stop provisions exports from New York City to Cape Breton and other French ports in North America. The statute—"An act to restrain the sending of provisions to Cape Breton, or any other French port or settlement, on the continent of North America, or islands nigh or adjacent thereto"—was rendered ineffective by its imprecise language and a weak enforcement mechanism. Its four-month duration reflected the distrust of New York lawmakers concerning the intentions of neighboring colonies. It was continued by a new act in May 1755.

Act to Prevent Exports of Provisions and Other Goods from New York to the French (1755) The Act to Restrain Provisions Exports from New York was replaced on July 5 by an act of the New York legislature—"An act to prevent the exportation of provisions, naval, and warlike stores from the colony of New York to Cape Breton, or to any other the dominions of the French king, or places at present in possession of any of his subjects"—prohibiting direct trade with France and its colonies. Merchants were required to post bonds of £1,000 (New York currency) to guarantee that shipments of flour, salted provisions, cordage, and other articles would not be sent to the French.

The declaration of war by Great Britain against France (1756) In his proclamation of May 17 declaring war against France, King George II forbade his subjects and "all other persons, of what nation soever" to correspond or communicate "with [the] French king or his subjects." The proclamation made it illegal to transport soldiers, arms, powder, ammunition, "or other contraband goods" to territory controlled by the French king. The proclamation depended on the Royal Navy and British privateers for enforcement: "Whatsoever ship or vessel shall be met withal, . . . the same being taken, shall be condemned as good and lawful prize."

The Irish and North American provisions embargo (1756–57) In October 1756, to prevent provisions from being sent to the enemy, the Privy Council ordered an embargo on provisions exports from Irish and colonial ports. In North America provisions could be shipped to other British colonies, provided that the masters or owners of ships entered into bonds (£1,000 or £2,000, depending on the size of the vessel) to ensure that goods would be sent to specified ports and nowhere else. In New York City, the Privy Council's provisions embargo ran from December 29, 1756, until July 9, 1757, the day the Flour Act went into effect.

Flour Act (1757) This piece of parliamentary legislation was an attempt to end North America's wartime trade with the French. The Flour Act received the royal assent on February 15 but did not go into effect in New York until July. Under the terms of the Flour Act—"An act to prohibit for a limited time the exportation of corn, grain, meal, malt, flour, bread, biscuit, starch, beef, pork, bacon, and other victuals (except fish and roots and rice, to be exported to any port of Europe southward of Cape Finisterre) from His Majesty's colonies and plantation in America, unless to Great Britain or Ireland, or to some of the said colonies and plantations; . . ."—shippers were required to take out provisions bonds, and there were steep fines for noncompliance. The Flour Act did not apply to goods shipped from ports in Great Britain and Ireland.

Customs Enforcement Act (1763) Passed in April, this was the first in a series of postwar parliamentary statutes designed to end abuses in the American customs service and increase British customs revenue from colonial trade. The law—"An act for the further improvement of His Majesty's revenue of customs and for the encouragement of officers making seizures and for the prevention of clandestine running of goods into any part of His Majesty's dominions"—allowed naval officers to be deputized as customs enforcement agents in American ports.

Sugar Act (1764) This legislation, approved in the House of Commons on April 5, reduced the duty on British West Indian molasses but established prohibitive tariffs on foreign sugar and sugar products imported into the British colonies after September 29. In addition to further restrictions on colonial trade, the Sugar Act attacked abuses in the American customs service and called for establishment of a North American vice-admiralty court.

Currency Act (1764) This act, passed by Parliament on April 19, prohibited the issuance of paper money in any of the American colonies after September 1. The Currency Act fostered anxiety over British intentions and brought unintended consequences, the most serious of which was a contraction of the money supply in British America at the height of the postwar recession.

Stamp Act (1765) Passed by Parliament on March 2, this act required a tax stamp on all legal documents, permits, commercial contracts, newspapers, wills, pamphlets, and playing cards after November 1. The Stamp Act created a political crisis throughout British America. It was widely seen as unwarranted external taxation and a threat to the liberties of British subjects. Nowhere in North America was reaction more severe than in New York City, where the Stamp Act went into effect during the height of local agitation over Lieutenant-Governor Colden's arbitrary interference in a jury verdict.

Notes

Abbreviations and Short Titles

Abstracts of Wills *Abstracts of Wills on File in the Surrogate's Office, City of New York*, New-York Historical Society, *Collections*, vols. 25–41 (New York, 1883–1909)

Allen Collection Allen Family Collection, American Antiquarian Society, Worcester, Massachusetts

Amherst Papers Jeffery Amherst Papers, 1758–63, William L. Clements Library, University of Michigan

ANB *American National Biography*, ed. John A. Garraty and Mark C. Carnes, 24 vols. (New York, 1999)

Beekman Papers *The Beekman Mercantile Papers, 1746–1799*, ed. Philip L. White, 3 vols. (New York, 1956)

BEP *Boston Evening Post*

BGCJ *Boston Gazette, and Country Journal*

BL British Library, London

BNL *Belfast News-Letter*

Board of Trade, *Journal* *Journal of the Commissioners for Trade and Plantations* [April 1704 to May 1782], 14 vols. (London, 1920–38)

BPB *Boston Post-Boy*

Cal. Coun. Mins. *New York (Colony) Council: Calendar of Council Minutes, 1668–1783*, ed. Berthold Fernow (Harrison, N.Y., 1987)

Cal. Hist. MSS. *Calendar of Historical Manuscripts in the Office of the Secretary of State, Albany, N.Y. (Part 2)*, ed. E. B. O'Callaghan (Albany, 1866)

Cal. NY Col. Comm. *Calendar of New York Colonial Commissions, 1680–1770*, ed. Edmund B. O'Callaghan (New York, 1929)

CG *Connecticut Gazette* (New Haven)

Chalmers: NY Papers Relating to New York, 1608–1792 (4 vols.), Chalmers Collection, NYPL

Col. Laws of NY *The Colonial Laws of New York from the Year 1664 to the Revolution*, ed. Charles Z. Lincoln, William H. Johnson, and A. Judd Northrup, 5 vols. (Albany, 1894–96)

Col. Recs. of NY Chamber *Colonial Records of the New York Chamber of Commerce, 1768–*

1784, with Historical and Biographical Sketches by John Austin Stevens, Jr., 2 vols. [bound as one] (New York, 1867)

Colden Letter Books *The Colden Letter Books,* New-York Historical Society, *Collections,* vols. 9–10 (New York, 1877–78)

Colden Papers *The Letters and Papers of Cadwallader Colden, 1711–1775,* New-York Historical Society, *Collections,* vols. 50–56, 67–68 (New York, 1918–37)

Commerce of Rhode Island *Commerce of Rhode Island, 1726–1800,* ed. Worthington Chauncey Ford, Massachusetts Historical Society, *Collections,* 7th Series, vols. 9–10 (Boston, 1914–15)

Coun. Mins. New York Council Minutes, vol. 25 (1755–64), New York State Archives, Albany

Court Min. Book (1754–57) Minute Book of the Supreme Court of Judicature of the Province of New York, April 1, 1754, to January 22, 1757 (engrossed), MS in New York County Clerk's Office, Division of Old Records

Court Min. Book (1756–61) Minute Book of the Supreme Court of Judicature of the Province of New York, April 20, 1756, to October 23, 1761 (rough), MS in New York County Clerk's Office, Division of Old Records

Court Min. Book (1762–64) Minute Book of the Supreme Court of Judicature of the Province of New York, October 19, 1762, to April 28, 1764 (engrossed), MS in New York County Clerk's Office, Division of Old Records

Court Min. Book (1764–66) Minute Book of the Supreme Court of Judicature of the Province of New York, July 31, 1764, to August 2, 1766 (engrossed), MS in New York County Clerk's Office, Division of Old Records

Cunningham-White Trial Miscellaneous Documents Relating to the Trial of Waddell Cunningham and Thomas White in the New York Supreme Court of Judicature, 1762–64, PL 1754–1837 K1023, NY/DOR

Cuyler Letter Book Philip Cuyler Letter Book, 1756–60, NYPL

Docs. Col. NY *Documents Relative to the Colonial History of the State of New York Procured in Holland, England, and France,* ed. E. B. O'Callaghan, 15 vols. (Albany, 1856)

"Exports. Coastways" "An Abstract of the Exportations Coastways at the Port of New York in America Commencing the 6 July 1757 and Ending the 10 October 1760," PRO/TNA, CO 5/19 (part 2), fols. 303–10.

Gage Correspondence *The Correspondence of General Thomas Gage with the Secretaries of State, 1763–1775,* ed. Clarence Edwin Carter, 2 vols. (New Haven, 1931)

GM *Gentleman's Magazine*

Harison Papers Richard Harison Papers, 1730–1920, NYHS

Holmes, "Memorial 1st" "Memorial 1st. Memorial, Respecting the Trade Carried on by His Majesty's Subjects, to the French Settlements in Hispaniola, Under the Colour of Flags of Truce," December 1760 (PRO/TNA, ADM1/236, fols. 147–55).

Holmes, "Memorial 2nd" "Memorial 2nd. Memorial Respecting Monto Christi in Hispaniola and the Correspondence and Trade Carried on with the Enemy from the Bay of Monto Christi by the King's Subjects and the Subjects of Neutral Powers Under the Pretense of this Place Being a Free Port and Protected by a Neutral Power," December 1760 (PRO/TNA, ADM 1/236, fols. 156–63)

Hough, *Reports* *Reports of Cases in the Vice Admiralty of the Province of New York and in the Court of Admiralty of the State of New York, 1715–1788,* ed. Charles Merrill Hough (New Haven, 1925)

HSP Historical Society of Pennsylvania, Philadelphia

"Imports. Coastways" "An Abstract of the Importations Coastways at the Port of New York in America Commencing the 12 April 1759 and Ending the 10 October 1760," PRO/TNA, CO 5/19 (part 2), fols. 311–16.

Independent Reflector *The Independent Reflector, or Weekly Essays on Sundry Important Subjects More Particularly Adapted to the Province of New-York* (New York, 1753)

Jefferys, *West-Indian Atlas* Thomas Jefferys, *The West-Indian Atlas; or, A Compendious Description of the West-Indies: Illustrated with Forty Correct Charts and Maps, Taken from Actual Surveys, Together with an Historical Account of the Several Countries and Islands Which Compose That Part of the World* (London, 1775)

Journal of Jeffery Amherst *The Journal of Jeffery Amherst: Recording the Military Career of General Amherst in America from 1758 to 1763*, ed. J. Clarence Webster (Chicago, 1931)

Journal of John Moore Journal of John Moore, 1760–70, Malcolm Papers, Public Record Office of Northern Ireland, Belfast, D3165/2.

Kempe Papers John Tabor Kempe Papers, 1678–1782, NYHS

LC Library of Congress, Manuscripts Division, Washington, D.C.

LEP *London Evening Post*

Letterbook of G&C (1756–57) *Letterbook of Greg & Cunningham, Merchants of New York and Belfast, 1756–57*, ed. Thomas M. Truxes, British Academy, Records of Social and Economic History, vol. 28 (London, 2001)

Letterbook of G&C (1764–65) Letterbook of Greg, Cunningham & Co. 1763–64, BV Greg, Cunningham & Co., NYHS

LM *London Magazine*

Loudoun Papers Loudoun Papers, Huntington Library, San Marino, California

MGBNL *Massachusetts Gazette, and Boston News-Letter*

Military Affairs *Military Affairs in North America, 1748–1765: Selected Papers from the Cumberland Papers in Windsor Castle*, ed. Stanley M. Pargellis (New York, 1936)

Mins. of NY Comm. Coun. *Minutes of the Common Council of the City of New York, 1675–1776*, 8 vols. (New York, 1905)

Montresor Journals *The Montresor Journals*, ed. G. D. Scull, New-York Historical Society, *Collections*, vol. 14 (New York, 1882)

NHG *New-Hampshire Gazette*

NLS *New-London Summary, or the Weekly Advertiser*

NM *Newport Mercury*

"Note of Recognizances" "Note of Recognizances Taken by Mr. Justice Horsmanden of Persons Accused of Illegal Correspondence with His Majesty's Enemies and Filed July Term 1762," Kempe Papers, Box 1, Folder 2, NYHS

NY Assembly Journal *Journal of the Votes and Proceedings of the General Assembly of the Colony of New-York*, 2 vols. (New York, 1766)

NY/DOR New York County Clerk's Office, Division of Old Records

NYG *Weyman's New-York Gazette* (first issue, February 16, 1759); retitled *The New-York Gazette* (August 13, 1759, to last issue, December 28, 1767)

NYGGA *New-York Gazette and General Advertiser*

NYGWM *The New-York Gazette, and the Weekly Mercury*

NYGWPB *The New-York Gazette, or, the Weekly Post-Boy* (known as *The New-York Gazette* between January 31 and February 21, 1757, and as *Parker's New-York Gazette, or, the Weekly Post-Boy* from March 19, 1759, to April 29, 1762)

NYGRWPB *New-York Gazette, Revived in the Weekly Post-Boy*
NYHS New-York Historical Society
NYM *New-York Mercury*
NY Marriages *New York Marriages Previous to 1784: A Reprint of the Original Edition of 1860 with Additions and Corrections,* ed. Kenneth Scott (Baltimore, 1968)
NYPL Manuscripts and Archives Division, New York Public Library
NY Vice-Adm. Recs. Records of the Vice-Admiralty Court for the Province of New York (1685–1775), Record Group 21, U.S. National Archives and Records Administration, Northeast Region (New York City)
NYWJ *New York Weekly Journal*
Oxford DNB *Oxford Dictionary of National Biography,* ed. H. C. G. Matthew and Brian Harrison, 60 vols. (Oxford, 2004)
PG *Pennsylvania Gazette*
PJWA *Pennsylvania Journal, and Weekly Advertiser*
PRO/TNA Public Record Office, the National Archive of the United Kingdom, Kew, Richmond, Surrey
Riché Letter Books Thomas Riché Letter Books, 1750–92, HSP
Siege and Capture *The Siege and Capture of Havana, 1762,* ed. David Syrett (London, 1970)
Watts Letter Book *Letter Book of John Watts, Merchant and Councillor of New York, January 1, 1762–December 22, 1765,* ed. Dorothy C. Barck, New-York Historical Society, *Collections,* vol. 51 (New York, 1928)
WMQ *The William and Mary Quarterly*

Introduction

1. *BNL,* Oct. 1, 1762 (quote).

2. Fernand Braudel, *The Wheels of Commerce,* vol. 2 of *Civilization and Capitalism, Fifteenth–Eighteenth Century,* trans. Sian Reynolds (New York, 1986), 209 (quote); Pauline Croft, "Trading with the Enemy, 1585–1604," *Historical Journal* 32:2 (June 1989): 281–302; G. N. Clark, "Trading with the Enemy and the Corunna Packets, 1689–97," *English Historical Review* 36:144 (October 1921): 521–39; Katherine Barbieri and Jack S. Levy, "Sleeping with the Enemy: The Impact of War on Trade," *Journal of Peace Research* 36:4 (July 1999): 463–79.

3. Carl and Roberta Bridenbaugh, *No Peace Beyond the Line: The English in the Caribbean, 1624–1690* (New York, 1972), 3–5. "The undeclared war in the Caribbean, in the sixteenth-century phrase, 'no peace beyond the line,' was enshrined in the Treaty of Cateau-Cambrésis of 1559 between France and Spain: 'west of the prime meridian and south of the Tropic of Cancer . . . violence by either party to the other side shall not be regarded as in contravention of the treaties'" (Eric Williams, *From Columbus to Castro: The History of the Caribbean, 1492–1969* [London, 1970], 73).

4. Cornelis Ch. Goslinga, *The Dutch in the Caribbean and in the Guianas, 1680–1791* (Assen/Maastricht, The Netherlands, 1985), 189–230 (quote on p. 190).

5. *BEP,* July 27, 1747 (quote).

6. *NYGRWPB,* June 6, 1748 (quote).

7. *NYGRWPB,* Sept. 26, 1748 (quote).

8. Lawrence Henry Gipson, *The Coming of the Revolution, 1763–1775* (New York, 1954), 1 (quote); *NYGRWPB,* Sept. 26, 1748 (quote).

9. Robinson to [Treasury], Mar. 18, 1760, PRO/TNA, T 1/403, fol. 94 (quote).

10. Edward Coke, *The Third Part of the Institutes of the Laws of England, Concerning High Treason, and Other Pleas of the Crown, and Criminal Causes,* 5th ed. (London, 1671), 2 (quote); *LM* (May 1756): 237 (quote); *Col. Laws of NY,* 3:1050–51, 1077, 1121–24 (quote on p. 1050).

11. Jacob M. Price, *France and the Chesapeake: A History of the French Tobacco Monopoly, 1674–1791, and of Its Relationship to the British and American Tobacco Trades,* 2 vols. (Ann Arbor, 1973), 1:393, 577–87 (quote on p. 393).

12. Coke, *Third Part of the Institutes of the Laws of England,* 2 (quote); S. C. Biggs, "Treason and the Trial of William Joyce," *University of Toronto Law Journal* 7:1 (1947): 162–95; Diane Parkin-Speer, "John Lilburne: A Revolutionary Interprets Statutes and Common Law Due Process," *Law and History Review* 1:2 (1983): 293.

13. Sanna Feirstein, *Naming New York: Manhattan Places and How They Got Their Names* (New York, 2001), 28, 41, 43–45, 52, 73.

14. Greg & Cunningham to Light, Sept. 12, 1756, *Letterbook of G&C* (1756–57), 204 (quote).

Prologue

1. *NYG,* Oct. 15, 1759.

2. See Frank McLynn, *1759: The Year Britain Became Master of the World* (New York, 2004). For broader perspective on the war, see Fred Anderson, *Crucible of War: The Seven Years' War and the Fate of Empire in British North America, 1754–1766* (New York, 2001).

3. Richard Pares, *War and Trade in the West Indies, 1739–1763* (Oxford, 1936), 265–325.

4. Anderson, *Crucible of War,* 108–9, 150–57, 185–201, 240–49; Virginia D. Harrington, *The New York Merchant on the Eve of the American Revolution* (New York, 1935), 289–315.

5. Andrew Burnaby, *Travels Through the Middle Settlements in North-America* (London, 1775), 66; Spencer to Amherst, Nov. 29, 1760, Spencer to Pitt, Dec. 14, 1760, PRO/TNA, CO 5/60, fols. 161, 168.

6. *NYM,* Apr. 16, 1759 (quote); DeLancey to Amherst, Aug. 24 and Sept. 10, 1759, PRO/TNA, WO 34/29, fols. 173, 193.

7. *NYG,* Sept. 17, 1759 (quote); Lawrence Henry Gipson, *The Coming of the Revolution, 1763–1775* (New York, 1954), 32 (quote); *NYG,* Sept. 24, 1759; *NYM,* Dec. 31, 1753, Sept. 28, 1761; *Abstracts of Wills,* 7:104–5, 308–10; Coun. Mins., 295; Harrington, *New York Merchant,* 23, 37; Ossian Lang, *History of Freemasonry in the State of New York* (New York, 1923), 29–32; Edward Coke, *The Third Part of the Institutes of the Laws of England, Concerning High Treason, and Other Pleas of the Crown, and Criminal Causes,* 5th ed. (London, 1671), 2; Court Min. Book (1756–61), 152.

8. List of Vessels, 13 Dec. 1760, PRO/TNA, CO 5/60, fol. 170.

9. *NY Marriages,* 367; *Col. Recs. of NY Chamber,* 2:156; Beekman to Spencer, July 1752, *Beekman Papers,* 1:145; *NYGWPB,* Aug. 13 and Oct. 1, 1750, Sept. 9, 1751, May 25 and Dec. 25, 1752, Aug. 9, 1756; *NYWJ,* Jan. 7, 1740; Spencer to Holdernesse, Apr. 1, 1756, BL, Eg. 3490, fols. 198–206.

10. The King v. George Harison, Waddell Cunningham, William Kelly, Thomas Lynch, and Philip Branson, NY/DOR, PL 1754–1837 K930 (hereafter cited as "King v. Harison et al."); Spencer to "the Printer," May 20, 1760, PRO/TNA, CO 5/60, fol. 165.

11. *NYM,* Apr. 16, 1759 (quote); Examination of George Spencer, Nov. 3, 1759, NY/DOR, PL 1754–1837 K980 (hereafter cited as "Exam. of Geo. Spencer"); Spencer to DeLancey, Nov. 8, 1759, PRO/TNA, CO 5/60, fol. 163.

12. Spencer to Pitt, Dec. 14, 1760, PRO/TNA, CO 5/60, fol. 163 (quote); Spencer to Cannon & Pintard, Oct. 29, 1759, PRO/TNA, CO 5/60, fol. 163.

13. Spencer to "the Printer," May 20, 1760, PRO/TNA, CO 5/60, fol. 165 (quote); HMS *Mercury,* logbook, Oct. 31, 1759, PRO/TNA, ADM 51/3904; *NYM,* Nov. 5, 1759.

14. Spencer to Pitt, Dec. 14, 1760, PRO/TNA, CO 5/60, fol. 161 (quote); Spencer to Monckton, Aug. 2, 1763, Chalmers: NY, vol. 4, fol. 3 (quote).

15. Spencer to "the Printer," May 20, 1760, PRO/TNA, CO 5/60, fol. 165 (quote); Spencer to Pitt, Dec. 14, 1760, PRO/TNA, CO 5/60, fol. 161 (quote).

16. Spencer to Pitt, Dec. 14, 1760, PRO/TNA, CO 5/60, fol. 161 (quote); Spencer to "the Printer," May 20, 1760, PRO/TNA, CO 5/60, fol. 165; Milton M. Klein, "Archibald Kennedy: Imperial Pamphleteer," in *The Colonial Legacy,* ed. Lawrence H. Leder, 2 vols. (New York, 1971), 2:95–97; Alex. Colden to Harison, Oct. 24, 1756, Harison Papers; King v. Harison et al.; Exam. of Geo. Spencer.

17. King v. Harison et al. (quote); Exam. of Geo. Spencer; Witnesses to be Subpoenaed, Nov. 9, 1759, NY/DOR, PL 1754–1837 K930; The King v. Branson and Wade, NY/DOR, PL 1754–1837 K978; Spencer to Kempe, Apr. 20, 1761, Kempe Papers; Spencer to Colden, Dec. 16, 1761, *Colden Papers,* 6:93; *Selected Cases of the Mayor's Court of the City of New York, 1674–1784,* ed. Richard B. Morris (Washington, D.C., 1935), 596–99, 608–11; Razer to West, May 1754, BL, Add. MSS 34,728, fols. 21–22.

18. King v. Harison et al. (quote); Exam. of Geo. Spencer.

19. Exam. of Geo. Spencer (quote).

20. King v. Harison et al. (quote).

21. John Roberts, high sheriff of the city and county of New York, was the brother-in-law of George Harison (NY/DOR, PL 1754–1837 K979). King v. Harison et al.; W. Harrison Bayles, *Old Taverns of New York* (New York, 1915), 179.

22. King v. Harison et al. (quote).

23. Ibid. (quote).

24. *NYG,* Sept. 24, 1759; Court Min. Book (1756–61), 158, 162–64.

25. King v. Harison et al. (quote); *NYGWPB,* Nov. 5, 1759 (quote).

26. The King v. John Lawrence, NY/DOR, PL 1754–1837 K976 (hereafter cited as "King v. Lawrence") (quote); King v. Harison et al.

27. King v. Harison et al. (quote); Spencer to Kempe, Oct. 20, 1760, Kempe Papers.

28. King v. Harison, et al. (quote).

29. Ibid. (quote).

30. Ibid.; Exam. of Geo. Spencer; King v. Lawrence; Spencer to Colden, Nov. 26, 1761, *Colden Papers,* 6:91; Spencer to "the Printer," May 20, 1760, PRO/TNA, CO 5/60, fol. 165.

31. Spencer to "the Printer," May 20, 1760, PRO/TNA, CO 5/60, fol. 165 (quote); Spencer to Monckton, Aug. 2, 1763, Chalmers: NY, vol. 4, fol. 3.

32. Spencer to Kempe, Nov. 3, 1759 (10:00 A.M.), Kempe to Spencer, Nov. 3, 1759, Spencer to Kempe, Nov. 3, 9, and 30, Dec. 1, 1759, Kempe Papers.

33. *NYM,* Nov. 5, 1759 (quote); Coun. Mins., 300–301 (quote); *Cal. Coun. Mins.,* 447 (quote). Indicted were George Harison, Waddell Cunningham, Philip Branson, William Kelly, Thomas Lynch, and Michael Wade (NY/DOR, PL 1754–1837 K981; *The New York City Court Records, 1684–1760,* ed. Kenneth Scott [New York, 1982], 84).

34. DeLancey to Spencer, Nov. 8, 1759, PRO/TNA, CO 5/60, fol. 163 (quote); Spencer to DeLancey, Nov. 7, 1759, cited in PRO/TNA, CO 5/60, fol. 163; Spencer to Amherst, Nov. 29, 1760, PRO/TNA, CO 5/60, fol. 168.

35. Spencer to Monckton, Aug. 2, 1763, Chalmers: NY, vol. 4, fols. 3–5; Spencer to Kempe, Aug. 23, 1765, Kempe Papers; "Imports. Coastways," fol. 313; *NYGWPB*, Jan. 7, 1760.

36. Affidavit of Francis Lewis, n.d., in "[List of] the Papers Produced and Read at the Hearing of This Cause," PRO/TNA, HCA 45/3 [snow *Greyhound*]; Spencer to Monckton, Aug. 2, 1763, Chalmers: NY, vol. 4, fol. 3.

37. Spencer to Amherst, Nov. 29, 1760, PRO/TNA, CO 5/60, fol. 168 (quote); Warrant, Dec. 31, 1759, PRO/TNA, CO 5/60, fol. 166; Spencer to Kempe, Oct. 24, 1760, Kempe Papers; Spencer to Monckton, Aug. 2, 1763, Chalmers: NY, vol. 4, fols. 3–5.

38. DeLancey to Amherst, Oct. 22, 1759, PRO/TNA, WO 34/29, fol. 237; Court Min. Book (1756–61), 152, 154, 158, 165; Spencer to Pitt, Dec. 14, 1760, PRO/TNA, CO 5/60, fol. 161.

39. DeLancey to Amherst, Nov. 5, 1759, PRO/TNA, WO 34/29, fol. 243 (quote).

CHAPTER ONE. A City at War

1. HMS *Nightingale*, logbook, Nov. 1756, PRO/TNA, ADM 51/3921; HMS *Sutherland*, logbook, Jan. 1757, PRO/TNA, ADM 51/952; HMS *Kennington*, logbook, Apr. 1757, PRO/TNA, ADM 51/499; HMS *Vulture*, logbook, Apr. 1757, PRO/TNA, ADM 51/1025; HMS *Mercury*, logbook, Oct. and Nov. 1759, PRO/TNA, ADM 51/3904; HMS *Winchester*, logbook, July 1760, PRO/TNA, ADM 51/1071; HMS *Enterprise*, logbook, Mar. 1762, PRO/TNA, ADM 51/313; HMS *Weasel*, logbook, Oct. 1763, PRO/TNA, ADM 52/1507; T[homas] Pownall, *A Topographical Description of the Dominions of the United States of America*, ed. Lois Mulkearn (Pittsburgh, 1949), 40–42.

2. HMS *Fowey*, logbook, Jan. 15, 1761, PRO/TNA, ADM 51/3845; HMS *Nightingale*, logbook, Feb. 26 and 27, 1759, PRO/TNA, ADM 51/3922; Pownall, *Topographical Description*, 41–42; Campbell to Clevland, Feb. 28, 1759, PRO/TNA, ADM 1/1607; *NYM*, Jan. 24, 1757.

3. "Remarks for Sailing from the Hook to New York and Some Observations on the Depths of Water, Made April 7th 1757," Loudoun Papers; J. F. W. DesBarres, *A Chart of New York Harbour with the Soundings, Views of Land Marks, and Nautical Directions* ([London] 1779).

4. Andrew Burnaby, *Travels Through the Middle Settlements in North-America in the Years 1759 and 1760* (London, 1775), 60–61; Peter Kalm, *Travels into North America*, trans. John Reinhold Forster, 2 vols. (London, 1772), 1:183–85, 193, 197; Pownall, *Topographical Description*, 42; "Five Recognition Views for Vessels Approaching New York City" (c. 1773) in J. F. W. DesBarres, *The Atlantic Neptune* (London, 1779).

5. HMS *Nightingale*, logbook, Nov. 1755 through Feb. 1756, July and Aug. 1756, Jan. and Feb. 1759, PRO/TNA, ADM 51/3921 and 3922 (quote on Feb. 7, 1759); HMS *Lizard*, logbook, Apr. and May 1759, PRO/TNA, ADM 51/549; HMS *Porcupine*, logbook, May and June 1762, PRO/TNA, ADM 51/706; HMS *Intrepid*, logbook, Jan. to May 1759, PRO/TNA, ADM 51/474; HMS *Fowey*, logbook, Jan. 1761, PRO/TNA, ADM 51/3845; HMS *Vulture*, logbook, Mar. 11, 1757, PRO/TNA, ADM 51/1025.

6. [Edward] Thompson, *Sailor's Letters: Written to His Select Friends in England During His Voyages and Travels in Europe, Asia, Africa, and America, from the Year 1754 to 1759*, 2 vols. (Dublin, 1766–67), 2:102 (quote); Kalm, *Travels*, 1:193–7.

7. *The New-York Pocket Almanack for the Year 1759* (New York, 1759), 4; Journal of John Moore, 29; Carl Bridenbaugh, *Cities in Revolt: Urban Life in America, 1743–1776* (London, 1955), 216; *New York City Population Projections by Age/Sex and Borough, 2000–2030* (New York, 2006), 4–5.

8. Journal of John Moore, 31 (quote); Thompson, *Sailor's Letters,* 2:102 (quote); Kalm, *Travels,* 1:191–92; Virginia D. Harrington, *The New York Merchant on the Eve of the American Revolution* (New York, 1935), 16–18.

9. Journal of John Moore, 31; *Cal. NY Col. Comm.,* 50; *Cal. Coun. Mins.,* 443; Kalm, *Travels,* 1:195–96; Joyce D. Goodfriend, *Before the Melting Pot: Society and Culture in Colonial New York City, 1664–1730* (Princeton, 1992), 187–221.

10. *NYM,* June 6, 1763 (quote); Burnaby, *Travels,* 61, 65–66; Pownall, *Topographical Description,* 43; *NYG,* May 12, 1760; *NYM,* Mar. 15, 1756, Jan. 8, 1759, Feb. 1, 1762; Paul E. Cohen and Robert T. Augustyn, *Manhattan in Maps, 1527–1995* (New York, 1997), 60–61; W. Harrison Bayles, *Old Taverns of New York* (New York, 1915), 165; Esther Singleton, *Social New York Under the Georges, 1714–1776* (New York, 1902), 291; Edwin G. Burrows and Mike Wallace, *Gotham: A History of New York City to 1898* (New York, 1999), 176.

11. Eliza Noel Pintard Davidson, ed., *Letters from John Pintard to His Daughter, 1816 to 1833,* New-York Historical Society *Collections,* vols. 70 to 73 (New York, 1940–41), 3:299 (quote); *NYM,* Mar. 8, 1756; *CG,* May 1, 1762; "Another Landmark Going," *New York Times,* Mar. 22, 1871; Singleton, *Social New York,* 301–7; Burrows and Wallace, *Gotham,* 177.

12. *Independent Reflector,* 210 (quote); William Smith, Jr., *The History of the Province of New-York,* ed. Michael Kammen, 2 vols. (Cambridge, Mass., 1972), 1:230 (quote); Burnaby, *Travels,* 60–62; Kalm, *Travels,* 1:197–201; John J. McCusker and Russell R. Menard, *The Economy of British America, 1607–1789* (Chapel Hill, N.C., 1985), 196–97; Jacob M. Price, "Economic Function and the Growth of American Port Towns in the Eighteenth Century," *Perspectives in American History* 8 (1974): 159; Smith, *History,* 1:230.

13. Smith, *History,* 1:230; *Independent Reflector,* 210–11.

14. Smith, *History,* 1:228 (quote); Pownall, *Topographical Description,* 43 (quote); Malachy Postlethwayt, *The Universal Dictionary of Trade and Commerce,* 2 vols. (London, 1751–55), 1:366 (quote).

15. *NYGRWPB,* Apr. 17, 1749 (quote); *Independent Reflector,* 38–40, 55–58; George William Edwards, *New York as an Eighteenth-Century Municipality, 1731–1776* (New York, 1917), 148–58.

16. *Independent Reflector,* 209–10; Smith, *History,* 1:201–3.

17. *NYM,* Jan. 21, 1754, Sept. 6, 1756, May 22, 1758, Apr. 23, 1759, Oct. 31, 1763; *NYGWPB,* June 12, 1758; Journal of John Moore, 29; Kalm, *Travels,* 194; Carl Abbott, "The Neighborhoods of New York, 1760–1775," *New York History* 55 (1974): 41–42; Philip L. White, *The Beekmans of New York in Politics and Commerce, 1647–1877* (New York, 1956), 337.

18. Harrington, *New York Merchant,* 191–200; Cathy Matson, *Merchants and Empire: Trading in Colonial New York* (Baltimore, 1998), 49–117, 146–49.

19. Harrington, *New York Merchant,* 14–18, 184–92; *Col. Recs. of NY Chamber,* 2:27–34, 55–68, 145–46, 156; Leon Huhner, "Daniel Gomez: A Pioneer Merchant of Early New York," in *The Jewish Experience in America,* ed. Abraham J. Karp, 5 vols. (New York, 1969), 1:175–93; *Oxford DNB,* 14:699–701.

20. *NYM,* Feb. 16 and Sept. 27, 1756; Goodfriend, *Before the Melting Pot,* 155–69, 195–96, 217–21; Gregory Palmer, *Biographical Sketches of Loyalists of the American Revolution* (Westport, Conn., 1984), 281.

21. *ANB,* 6:369–71, 12:564–65.

22. Smith, *History,* 1:208–10; Bayles, *Old Taverns,* 135–36; Burrows and Wallace, *Gotham,* 176; Edwards, *New York,* 28; Spencer v. Rutgers and Pennington, Nov. 20, 1760, PRO/TNA, CO 5/60, fol. 166b.

23. *NYGWPB,* Aug. 27, Sept. 17 and 24, 1759; *NYM,* Nov. 26, 1753, Jan. 5, 1756; Singleton, *Social New York,* 367–68; Bayles, *Old Taverns,* 140–41, 154, 253; Walter Barrett, *The Old Merchants of New York City,* 3rd series (New York, 1865), 274–76; Austin Baxter Keep, *History of the New York Society Library* ([New York], 1908), 151; Norreys Jephson O'Conor, *Servant of the Crown: In England and North America, 1756–1761* (New York, 1938), 81; Burrows and Wallace, *Gotham,* 176.

24. *NYGWPB,* Mar. 12, 1759 (quote); Peter Linebaugh and Marcus Rediker, *The Many-Headed Hydra: Sailors, Slaves, Commoners, and the Hidden History of the Revolutionary Atlantic* (Boston, 2000), 180–82.

25. *NYM,* Dec. 27, 1756 (quote).

26. Ibid. (quote); *NLS,* Feb. 2, 1759; *NYGWPB,* Mar. 12, 1759.

27. Harrington, *New York Merchant,* 289–315.

28. Aaron Burr, *The Watchman's Answer* (New York, 1757), 28–30 (quote on p. 29); Nehemiah Curnock, ed., *The Journal of the Rev. John Wesley, A.M.,* 8 vols. (New York, [1909–16]), 4:144 (quote); *BNL,* Jan. 13, 1756; *Daily Advertiser* (London), Apr. 14, 1756; *(Faulkner's) Dublin Journal,* Dec. 23, 1755; *NYM,* Jan. 5 and 19, 1756; Plumsted to Jackson, Mar. 12, 1756, Plumsted Letter Book; T. D. Kendrick, *The Lisbon Earthquake* (Philadelphia, 1957); Smith, *History,* 2:194.

29. Fred Anderson, *Crucible of War: The Seven Years' War and the Fate of Empire in British North America, 1754–1766* (New York, 2001), 86–175.

30. Lawrence Henry Gipson, *The British Empire Before the American Revolution,* 15 vols. (New York, 1939–70), 6: 3–61; Anderson, *Crucible of War,* 5–85.

31. Anderson, *Crucible of War,* 86–93; Michael Kammen, *Colonial New York: A History* (New York, 1975), 315; Francis Jennings, *Empire of Fortune: Crowns, Colonies, and Tribes in the Seven Years' War in America* (New York, 1988), 146–57.

32. Robert L. D. Davidson, *War Comes to Quaker Pennsylvania, 1682–1756* (New York, 1957), 150–53; Joseph F. Meany, "Merchant and Redcoat: The Papers of John Gordon Macomb, July 1757 to June 1760" (Ph.D. diss., Fordham University, 1990), 103; Jennings, *Empire,* 312–13.

33. Hardy, quoted in Kammen, *Colonial New York,* 319.

34. Anderson, *Crucible of War,* 108–23, 135–41.

35. Hardy to Halifax, Nov. 27, 1755, *Military Affairs,* 150 (quote); *NYM,* Dec. 15, 1755, Jan. 12, 1756, Mar. 1 and 8, 1756.

36. Burr, *Watchman's Answer,* 29 (quote); *NYM,* Jan. 5, 1756 (quote); Anderson, *Crucible of War,* 108–10.

37. *NYM,* Dec. 15, 1755 (quote); Alex. Colden to Harison, June 24, 1756, Harison Papers; *NYM,* Jan. 12 and Mar. 1 and 8, 1756.

38. Stephen Brumwell, *Redcoats: The British Soldier and War in the Americas, 1755–1763* (Cambridge, 2002), 137–50, 215–26; Anderson, *Crucible of War,* 140–42, 286–88.

39. Hardy to Halifax, May 7, 1756, *Military Affairs,* 171 (quote).

40. Stanley McCrory Pargellis, *Lord Loudoun in North America* (New Haven, 1933), 36–37; Anderson, *Crucible of War,* 136–46.

41. Patricia U. Bonomi, *A Factious People: Politics and Society in Colonial New York* (New York, 1971), 158–78; Mary Lou Lustig, *Privilege and Prerogative: New York's Provincial Elite, 1710–1776* (Madison, N.J., 1995), 78–80; Kammen, *Colonial New York,* 280, 305–7.

42. Lustig, *Privilege and Prerogative,* 93–94.

43. Alex. Colden to Harison, May 10, 1756, Harison Papers (quote); *NY Assembly Journal,* 2:496 (quote).

44. HMS *Nightingale,* logbook, July 22, 1756, PRO/TNA, ADM 51/3921; *Cal. Coun. Mins.,* 429–30; *NYGWPB,* July 26 and Aug. 2, 1756.

45. *BEP,* June 28, and Aug. 23 and 30, 1756; *NYM,* July 19, 1756, Mar. 7, 1757; "A List of All His Majesty's Transports, Ships, & Vessels at New York," May 17, 1757, Loudoun Papers, LO 5863; Burnaby, *Travels,* 66; Brumwell, *Redcoats,* 145–50.

46. Alex. Colden to Harison, Jan. 8, 1757, Harison Papers (quote); Pargellis, *Lord Loudoun,* 198–200; Smith, *History,* 2:210–11. George Harison's wife, Jane, and Alexander Colden's wife, Elizabeth, were the daughters of Richard Nicholls, a prominent New York lawyer and one of the earliest non-Philadelphia members of the American Philosophical Society. Another daughter, Mary, was the wife of the Reverend Dr. Samuel Auchmuty, rector of Trinity Church (Whitfield J. Bell, Jr., *Patriot-Improvers,* 2 vols. [Philadelphia, 1997–99], 1:109).

47. Pargellis, *Lord Loudoun,* 200; *Cal. Coun. Mins.,* 436; *Mins. of NY Comm. Coun.,* 6:111–12; *BGCJ,* Nov. 16, 1761; *NYM,* Oct. 31, 1757, Apr. 30, 1759, Nov. 2, 1761; Kalm, *Travels,* 196; C. M. Azoy, *Three Centuries Under Three Flags: The Story of Governors Island from 1637* (New York, 1951), 15–18; Brumwell, *Redcoats,* 91n, 104.

48. Journal of John Moore, 19 (quote); Burnaby, *Travels,* 66; Abbott, "Neighborhoods," 49–51.

49. *NYM,* Feb. 21, 1757 (quote).

50. *NYG,* Jan. 3, 1763 (quote); *BEP,* Oct. 26, 1761 (quote); *BGCJ,* Nov. 2, 1761; N. A. M. Rodger, *The Wooden World: An Anatomy of the Georgian Navy* (New York, 1996), 252–64; O'Conor, *Servant of the Crown,* 81–82; Brumwell, *Redcoats,* 87–93; *Oxford DNB,* 21:258; Kenneth Scott, comp., *Genealogical Data from Colonial New York Newspapers* (Baltimore, 2000), 90.

51. Richard Pares, *War and Trade in the West Indies, 1739–1763* (Oxford, 1936), 273–78, 276n.

52. Campbell to Clevland, Feb. 28, 1759, PRO/TNA, ADM 1/1607 (quote); Julian Gwyn, *The Enterprising Admiral: The Personal Fortune of Admiral Sir Peter Warren* (Montreal, 1974), 36, 47–48; William Laird Clowes, *The Royal Navy: A History from the Earliest Times to the Present,* 7 vols. (London, 1897–1903), 3:167–68; I. N. Phelps Stokes, *The Iconography of Manhattan Island, 1498–1909,* 6 vols. (New York, 1915–28), 4:682; *Cal. NY Col. Comm.,* 48; *Cal. Coun. Mins.,* 436; HMS *Hampshire,* logbook, May 3, 1758, PRO/TNA, ADM 51/426; *BEP,* June 28, and Aug. 23 and 30, 1756; *NYM,* Mar. 7, 1757; "A List of All His Majesty's Transports, Ships, & Vessels at New York," May 17, 1757, Loudoun Papers, LO 5863.

53. Rodger, *Wooden World,* 15, 64–65, 193. For the dress of merchant sailors, see Peter Earle, *Sailors: English Merchant Seamen, 1650–1775* (London, 1998), 34–35, 58–59.

54. HMS *Trent,* logbook, Apr. 18, 1759, PRO/TNA, ADM 51/3994 (quote); Rodger, *Wooden World,* 205–51; Earle, *Sailors,* 145–63.

55. *Alexander,* logbook, Oct. 5 and 6, 1761, PRO/TNA, HCA 15/53 (quote). For another perspective, see Marcus Rediker, *Between the Devil and the Deep Blue Sea: Merchant Seamen, Pirates, and the Anglo-American Maritime World, 1700–1750* (Cambridge, 1987), 205–53.

56. *The Journals of Hugh Gaine, Printer,* ed. Paul Leicester Ford, 2 vols. (New York, 1911), 2:8–9 (quote); Gipson, *British Empire,* 8:68; Pargellis, *Lord Loudoun,* 237.

57. HMS *Fowey,* logbook, Jan. and Feb. 1761, May 12, 1761, PRO/TNA, ADM 51/3845 (quote on May 12, 1761); Journal of John Moore, 7.

58. HMS *Lizard,* logbook, Apr. 13, 1759, PRO/TNA, ADM 51/549 (quote).

59. Cad. Colden to Board of Trade, Aug. 30, 1760, *Docs. Col. NY,* 7:446 (quote); Coun. Mins., 320–22, 326, 450–51; *NLS,* Aug. 29 and Sept. 5 and 12, 1760; Abbott, "Neighborhoods," 50–51.

60. "[List of] Papers Belonging to the French King's Subjects," May 4, 1762, PRO/TNA, WO 34/102, fols. 101–2.

61. Ibid.; O'Conor, *Servant of the Crown,* 55–56.

CHAPTER TWO. Admiral Hardy and the Smugglers

1. Alex. Colden to Harison, May 21, 1756, Harison Papers (quote); Alex. Colden to Cad. Colden, May 8, 1756, *Colden Papers,* 5:72.

2. Alex. Colden to Harison, May 21, 1756, Harison Papers; James Riker, *Revised History of Harlem, City of New York* (New York, 1904), 807.

3. Alex. Colden to Harison, May 10 and 21, 1756, Harison Papers; *NYM,* April 12, 1756; *BNL,* Oct. 25, 1754; William Smith, Jr., *The History of the Province of New-York,* ed. Michael Kammen, 2 vols. (Cambridge, Mass., 1972), 1:230; Basil S. Yamey, *Art and Accounting* (New Haven, 1989), 36; Naval Office Shipping Lists for New York, 1713–1765, PRO/TNA, CO 5/1227, fols. 232–33.

4. Alex. Colden to Harison, May 21, 1756, Harison Papers (quote); Alex. Colden to Cad. Colden, May 8 and 18, 1756, *Colden Papers,* 5:72–73, 78–80.

5. Alex. Colden to Harison, May 10 and 21, 1756, Harison Papers (quotes); Alex. Colden to Cad. Colden, May 8, 1756, *Colden Papers,* 5:72–73 (quote on p. 73).

6. Alex. Colden to Cad. Colden, May 18, 1756, *Colden Papers,* 5:73, 80 (quote); Alex. Colden to Harison, May 10, 1756, Harison Papers (quote); Alex. Colden to Cad. Colden, May 8, 1756, *Colden Papers,* 5:73 (quote).

7. Alex. Colden to Cad. Colden, May 8, 1756, *Colden Papers,* 5:73 (quote); Cunningham to Hope, May 10, 1756, *Letterbook of G&C* (1756–57), 99 (quote).

8. J. H. Parry, *Trade and Dominion: The European Empires in the Eighteenth Century* (New York, 1971), 51; Lawrence A. Harper, *The English Navigation Laws: A Seventeenth-Century Experiment in Social Engineering* (New York, 1939), 234–38, 387–414; John J. McCusker and Russell R. Menard, *The Economy of British America, 1607–1789* (Chapel Hill, N.C., 1985), 46–50.

9. Cad. Colden to Halifax, Aug. 3, 1754, *Military Affairs,* 21 (quote); Michael Kammen, *Colonial New York: A History* (New York, 1975), 306; Thomas M. Truxes, "The Case of the Snow *Johnson:* New York City's Irish Merchants and Trade with the Enemy During the Seven Years' War," in *Re-figuring Ireland: Essays in Honour of L. M. Cullen,* ed. David Dickson and Cormac Ó Gráda (Dublin, 2003), 151–52; Virginia D. Harrington, *The New York Merchant on the Eve of the American Revolution* (New York, 1935), 250–51; Victor L. Johnson, "Fair Traders and Smugglers in Philadelphia, 1754–1763," *Pennsylvania Magazine of History and Biography* 83 (1959): 126–28.

10. *BNL,* Oct. 25, 1754 (quote); *Letterbook of G&C* (1756–57), 66n, 67n, 239n.

11. Ludlow to Jeffery, Jr., Jan. 8, 1756, John Ludlow Letter Book, 1752–63, Rare Book and Manuscripts Library, Columbia University, New York (quote).

12. Hardy to Board of Trade, July 10, 1757, *Docs. Col. NY,* 7:271–72 (quote); Hardy to Board of Trade, July 15, 1757, BL, Add. MSS 32,890, fols. 507–10; James H. Levitt, *For*

Want of Trade: Shipping and the New Jersey Ports, 1680–1783 (Newark, N.J., 1981), 18–20, 119–23.

13. DeLancey to Board of Trade, London, July 30, 1757, *Docs. Col. NY,* 7:273 (quote); Alex. Colden to Harison, Mar. 21, 1756, Harison Papers; Gilliland to Shaw, Jan. 19, 1760, Nathaniel and Thomas Shaw Papers, Sterling Memorial Library, Yale University, New Haven, Connecticut; *Letterbook of G&C* (1756–57), 88–91; Malachy Postlethwayt, *Britain's Commercial Interest Explained and Improved,* 2 vols. (London, 1757), 1:422–23; Jacob M. Price, "Economic Function and the Growth of American Port Towns in the Eighteenth Century," *Perspectives in American History* 8 (1974): 149–50.

14. *Charming Sally,* logbook, Sept. 29, 1756, PRO/TNA, HCA 32/178 (1) (quote).

15. *Charming Sally,* logbook, Sept. 29 to Oct. 16, 1756, PRO/TNA, HCA 32/178 (1) (quotes on Sept. 29 and Oct. 16); Ports, Districts, and Towns in America, BL, Add. MSS 15,484, 4 (quote).

16. Ludlow to Jeffery, Jr., Jan. 8, 1756, Ludlow Letter Book (quote).

17. Ibid. (quote); *Letterbook of G&C* (1756–57), 67n.

18. *Charming Sally,* logbook, Oct. 17 to Oct. 21, 1756, PRO/TNA, HCA 32/178 (1).

19. "Report from the Committee Relating to Chequed and Striped Linens," *Reports from Committees of the House of Commons . . . Not Inserted in the Journals, 1715–1801,* 16 vols. (London, 1803–6), 2:292 (quote); Cunningham to Greg, May 10, 1756, *Letterbook of G&C* (1756–57), 110 (quote).

20. Greg & Cunningham to Mierop, Sept. 13, 1756, *Letterbook of G&C* (1756–57), 202–3; Ludlow to De Neufville, Jan. 10, 1756, Ludlow to Crommelin, Feb. 26 and July 16, 1757, Ludlow Letter Book; Smith, *History,* 1:230.

21. Plumsted to Ayrault, May 21, 1756, Plumsted Letter Book, 1756–58, MS in the University Library, Cambridge (quote); *NYM,* Aug. 30 and Sept. 13, 1756.

22. Harrington, *New York Merchant,* 199–200; *NYM,* June 11, 1753, Sept. 27, 1756; Alex. Colden to Harison, May 10 and 21, 1756, Harison Papers; Carr to Kelly, Sept. 29, 1756, American Papers of Ralph Carr, Merchant of Newcastle-Upon-Tyne, 1741–78, MS in Northumberland Record Office; *Letterbook of G&C* (1756–57), 134n.

23. Lane, Bensons, and Vaughan to Lopez, Mar. 8, 1766, Aaron Lopez Letters, MS in Newport Historical Society, Rhode Island (quote); *NYM,* Feb. 23, 1756; Thomas M. Truxes, *Irish-American Trade, 1660–1783* (Cambridge, 1988), 112–17; Thomas M. Truxes, "London's Irish Merchant Community and North Atlantic Commerce in the Mid-Eighteenth Century," *Irish and Scottish Mercantile Networks in Europe and Overseas in the Seventeenth and Eighteenth Centuries,* ed. David Dickson, Jan Parmentier, and Jane Ohlmeyer (Ghent, 2007), 283–88.

24. Cunningham to Mierop, Oct. 27, 1756, *Letterbook of G&C* (1756–57), 228 (quote); Naval Office Shipping Lists for New York, 1713–65, PRO/TNA, CO 5/1227, fol. 242, and CO 5/1228, fols. 25, 31; *Letterbook of G&C* (1756–57), 88–92.

25. *NYM,* Mar. 12, 1753 (quote); *Col. Laws of NY,* 3:967–68; *NY Assembly Journal,* 2:372.

26. Alex. Colden to Harison, May 21, 1756, Harison Papers.

27. Smith, *History,* 2:191–94; Lawrence Henry Gipson, *The British Empire Before the American Revolution,* 15 vols. (New York, 1939–70), 6:133–34, 176–80.

28. Instructions to Sir Charles Hardy as governor of the province of New York, Apr. 3, 1755, PRO/TNA, CO 5/1128, Instruction no. 84 (quote); Hardy to Morris, Apr. 16, 1756, *Colonial Records of Pennsylvania,* 16 vols. (Harrisburg, 1851–53), 7:101, 103.

29. Hardy to Board of Trade, July 10, 1757, *Docs. Col. NY,* 7:271 (quote); [Archibald

Kennedy], *Observations on the Importance of the Northern Colonies Under Proper Regulations* (New York, 1750), 7–23; Charles M. Andrews, *The Colonial Period of American History,* 4 vols. (New Haven, 1964), 4:202–5; Frank Wesley Pitman, *The Development of the British West Indies, 1700–1763* (New Haven, 1917), 311.

30. Alex. Colden to Harison, Oct. 24, 1756, Jan. 24, 1756, Harison Papers (quotes); Smith, *History,* 2:203–4; Hardy to Board of Trade, May 10, 1756, *Docs. Col. NY,* 7:81–82; James A. Henretta, *"Salutary Neglect": Colonial Administration Under the Duke of Newcastle* (Princeton, 1972), 319–47; Stanley Nider Katz, *Newcastle's New York: Anglo-American Politics, 1732–1753* (Cambridge, Mass., 1968), 242–44.

31. Cunningham to Greg, May 10, 1756, Greg & Cunningham to Yzendoorn, June 14, 1756, Greg & Cunningham to Yzendoorn, June 4, 1756, *Letterbook of G&C* (1756–57), 110, 142, 133 (quotes).

32. Hardy to Board of Trade, July 10, 1757, *Docs. Col. NY,* 7:272 (quote); Phil. Cuyler to Corn. Cuyler, June 30, 1756, Cuyler Letter Book (quote); Hardy to Board of Trade, July 15, 1757, BL, Add. MSS 32,890, fols. 507–10.

33. Cunningham to Greg, June 15, 1756, Greg & Cunningham to Hope, June 14, 1756, Cunningham to Jos. Chew, July 7, 1756, *Letterbook of G&C* (1756–57), 143, 138, 168 (quotes).

34. Wharton to Waddell, June 2, 1756, Thomas Wharton Letterbook, 1756–57, Wharton and Willing papers, 1669–1887, HSP (quote); Johnson, "Fair Traders," 133–40.

35. *PG,* Sept. 16, 1756 (quote); Greg & Cunningham to Mierop, Sept. 13, 1756, *Letterbook of G&C* (1756–57), 202 (quote).

36. *NYGWPB,* Dec. 6, 1756 (quote).

37. Greg & Cunningham to Hope, July 26, 1756, Cunningham to Greg, Sept. 12, 1756, *Letterbook of G&C* (1756–57), 186, 204 (quotes).

38. Cunningham to Greg, Oct. 11 and Nov. 12, 1756, *Letterbook of G&C* (1756–57), 212, 238 (quotes).

39. Hardy to Morris, Apr. 16 and May 5, 1756, *Colonial Records of Pennsylvania,* 7:101, 122–25; Hardy to Board of Trade, May 10, 1756, *Docs. Col. NY,* 7:81–82; *Col. Laws of NY,* 3:1121–22; Copy of all the Proceedings Had and the State of the Viva Voce Evidence Taken Before the Commissioners of Trade and Plantations in the Year 1750 Relating to the Trade Carried on by the British Northern Colonies with the Foreign Sugar Colonies, PRO/TNA, CO 5/38 [transcription in LC], 1–44; Johnson, "Fair Traders," 126–28.

40. Instructions to Sir Charles Hardy as governor of the province of New York, Apr. 3, 1755, PRO/TNA, CO 5/1128, Instruction no. 84 (quote); George Chalmers, comp., *Opinions of Eminent Lawyers on Various Points of English Jurisprudence, Chiefly Concerning the Colonies, Fisheries and Commerce of Great Britain* (Burlington, Vt., 1858), 626 (quote).

41. *Col. Laws of NY,* 3:1050–51 (quote on p. 1050); *NY Assembly Journal,* 2:438.

42. *Col. Laws of NY,* 3:1050–51 (quote on p. 1051); Johnson, "Fair Traders," 128–40. William Walton, Sr., a member of the New York General Assembly, played a leading role in crafting the language of the February 1755 statute (*NY Assembly Journal,* 2:437).

43. Morris to DeLancey, Mar. 4, 1755, in *Pennsylvania Archives,* 1st series, ed. Samuel Hazard, 12 vols. (Philadelphia, 1852–56), 2:261–62 (quotes).

44. *Col. Laws of NY,* 3:1121–24 (quote on p. 1122); *NY Assembly Journal,* 2:452.

45. *Col. Laws of NY,* 3:1121–24; *NYM,* Apr. 5 and 12, 1756; Hardy to Morris, Apr. 16 and May 9, 1756, *Colonial Records of Pennsylvania,* 7:101, 123–24; Richard Pares, *War and Trade in the West Indies, 1739–1763* (Oxford, 1936), 326–43, 375–90.

46. *NYM,* Apr. 12, 1756 (quote).

47. Hardy to Board of Trade, June 19, 1756, *Docs. Col. NY,* 7:117 (quote); Hardy to Board of Trade, May 10, Oct. 13, 1756, *Docs. Col. NY,* 7:81–82, 163–64; *Documents Relating to the Colonial History of the State of New Jersey,* ed. Frederick W. Ricord, 10 vols. (Trenton, 1892), 17:23, 55–58; Johnson, "Fair Traders," 135–42.

CHAPTER THREE. Frenchified Bottoms

1. Examination of John Abeel, May 20, 1756, Examination of John Maerschalk, May 21, 1756, Examination of Gilbert Shirer, May 22, 1756, NY/DOR, PL 1754–1837 K443; *Cal. Hist. MSS.,* 653.

2. Ibid.; Examination of Peter Stoutenburgh, May 29, 1756, NY/DOR, PL 1754–1837 K443 [hereafter "Exam. of Peter Stoutenburgh"]; *NYM,* May 17 and 24, 1756; Naval Office Shipping Lists for New York, 1713–65, PRO/TNA, CO 5/1228, fols. 30–33.

3. Exam. of Peter Stoutenburgh; *NYM,* May 17 and 24, 1756; The King v. Samuel Stilwell, [n.d.], NY/DOR, PL 1754–1837 K443.

4. *Daily Advertiser* (London), May 19, 1756 (quote).

5. Ibid. (quote); *LM* (May 1756): 247 (quote).

6. *GM* (May 1756): 261, (July 1756): 360, (Aug. 1756): 411, (Sept. 1756): 452.

7. Jonathan R. Dull, *The French Navy and the Seven Years' War* (Lincoln, Neb., 2005), 50–55; N. A. M. Rodger, *The Command of the Ocean: A Naval History of Britain, 1649–1815* (New York, 2005), 263–67; Lawrence Henry Gipson, *The British Empire Before the American Revolution,* 15 vols. (New York, 1939–70), 6:398–417.

8. *Daily Advertiser* (London), June 25, 1756 (quote); *GM* (June 1756): 296–97, (July 1756): 360–61, (Aug. 1756): 411, (Sept. 1756): 452; *NYM,* Sept. 20, 1756; *PG,* Sept. 9, 1756.

9. *BEP,* Sept. 13, 1756 (quote); *Cork Evening Post,* May 26, 1760; *NYM,* July 26, 1756; HMS *Nightingale,* logbook, June 27 and 28, 1756, PRO/TNA, ADM 51/3921.

10. *BEP,* July 19 and Aug. 2, 1756 (quotes).

11. Cuyler to Vanderheyden, Sept. 23, 1756, Cuyler Letter Book (quote); *BNL,* Feb. 25, 1757; James G. Lydon, *Pirates, Privateers, and Profits* (Upper Saddle River, N.J., 1970), 158; Virginia D. Harrington, *The New York Merchant on the Eve of the American Revolution* (New York, 1935), 303–8.

12. *NYM,* Nov. 28, 1757 (quote); *NYM,* Sept. 20, 1756.

13. *BEP,* Sept. 13, 1756 (quote); *NYM,* Nov. 22, 1756, and May 2, 1757 (quotes); *Antigua Gazette,* quoted in *NYM,* Aug. 8, 1757.

14. *NYM,* May 16, 1757 (quote); *NYGWPB,* Jan. 17, 1757; *NYM,* Dec. 20, 1756.

15. *NYM,* May 23, 1757 (quote).

16. *NYM,* Apr. 11, 1757 (quote); Richard Pares, *War and Trade in the West Indies, 1739–1763* (Oxford, 1936), 359–62.

17. *NYM,* May 23, 1757 (quote); Greg & Cunningham to Hope, Oct. 13, 1756, *Letterbook of G&C* (1756–57), 219, 220–21n; Dull, *French Navy,* 60–61, 84; Kenneth J. Banks, *Chasing Empire Across the Sea: Communications and the State in the French Atlantic, 1713–1763* (Montreal, 2002), 170; Pares, *War and Trade,* 360–64.

18. *NYM,* Dec. 27, 1756 (quote); Examination of Andries Zeegard, Apr. 24, 1759, PRO/TNA, HCA 45/1 [ship *De Pieter*]; Answer and claim of Jacob Spin, Dec. 18, 1758, PRO/TNA, HCA 45/1 [ship *Dolphin*]; Examination of David Mushart, Dec. 19, 1758, PRO/TNA, HCA 45/3 [ship *Sea Post*]; Examinations of Gerrit Rieverts and Christopher Rector, Feb. 6, 1759, PRO/TNA, HCA 45/5 [ship *Resolute*].

19. Ledgers of Imports and Exports of Ireland, PRO/TNA, CUST 15; L. M. Cullen, *An Economic History of Ireland Since 1660* (London, 1972), 11–13, 21, 26–29, 41–42, 50–58; Thomas M. Truxes, *Irish-American Trade, 1660–1783* (Cambridge, 1988), 260–81; Jean Agnew, *Belfast Merchant Families in the Seventeenth Century* (Dublin, 1996), 50, 105–11.

20. Truxes, *Irish-American Trade,* 260–61.

21. Ibid.

22. *LM* (May 1756): 237 (quote).

23. "The King Against the Betsey of Dublin," Sept. 6, 1760, PRO/TNA, SP 42/42 (1), fols. 234–37 (quotes on fols. 234, 235, and 237); Clark to Lords Justices . . . of Ireland, Apr. 5, 1757, PRO/TNA, CO 388/47.

24. "Report of the Judge of the Admiralty Court in Ireland upon the Case of the Ship *Helena,*" Mar. 9, 1759, Public Record Office of Northern Ireland, Belfast, T1060/5, fols. 5–10 (quote on fols. 5–6); *LEP,* July 24, 1756; Ferrell to Peisly, Jan. 26 and 28, 1758, cited in Frank Wesley Pitman, *The Development of the British West Indies, 1700–1763* (New Haven, 1917), 331n; Hardy to Board of Trade, June 19, 1756, *Docs. Col. NY,* 7:117.

25. Hardy to Board of Trade, June 19, 1756, *Docs. Col. NY,* 7:117 (quote).

26. DeLancey to Board of Trade, Mar. 18, 1755, *Docs. Col. NY,* 6:941; Morris to DeLancey, Mar. 4 and Sept. 1, 1755, in *Pennsylvania Archives,* 1st series, ed. Samuel Hazard, 12 vols. (Philadelphia, 1852–56), 2:261–62, 398; Morris to Assembly, [June] 1755, in *Pennsylvania Archives,* 4th series, ed. George Edward Reed, 12 vols. (Harrisburg, 1900–1902), 2:416–17; *BEP,* July 26, 1756; *CG,* June 28, 1755; *NYM,* May 24, 1756; "Thoughts as to the Supply of the French Troops in America [1757]," Peter Force Papers, MS in LC; *Col. Laws of NY,* 3:1050–51, 1121–24, 4:96; Lawrence Henry Gipson, *The Coming of the Revolution, 1763–1775* (New York, 1954), 29.

27. *LEP,* July 24, 1756 (quote); Thos. Allen to Sam. Allen, July 27, 1755, Nath. Allen to Thos. Allen, Aug. 24, 1755, Thos. Allen to Nath. Allen, Aug. 31 and Dec. 6, 1755, Allen Collection; Derby to Mesury, Jan. 24, 1756, PRO/TNA, CO 5/1068, fol. 37; Hardy to Board of Trade, May 10, 1756, *Docs. Col. NY,* 7:81–82.

28. Thos. Allen to Nath. Allen, Dec. 6, 1755, Allen Collection (quote).

29. "Thoughts as to the Supply of the French Troops" (quote); Hough, *Reports,* 176 (quote); *LEP,* July 24, 1756; Thos. Allen to Sam. Allen, Sept. 2, 1755, Allen Collection; Pitman, *Development,* 310–14.

30. David Macpherson, *Annals of Commerce, Manufactures, Fisheries, and Navigation, with Brief Notices of the Arts and Sciences Connected with Them,* 4 vols. (London, 1805), 3:161 (quote); Richard Gardiner, *An Account of the Expedition to the West Indies Against Martinico* (London, 1762), 88.

31. *Journal of a Lady of Quality,* ed. Evangeline Walker Andrews and Charles McLean Andrews (New Haven, 1921), 137 (quote).

32. Ibid., 136 (quote); Thos. Allen to Sam. Allen, Sept. 2, 1755, Allen Collection (quote).

33. Goelet to Allen, Dec. 24, 1755, Allen to Jos. Chew, Mar. 10, 1757, Allen Collection; *CG,* July 29, 1758; Ossian Lang, *History of Freemasonry in the State of New York* (New York, 1922), 12, 25–26.

34. David Watts, *The West Indies: Patterns of Development, Culture, and Environmental Change Since 1492* (New York, 1987), 287; Cornelis Ch. Goslinga, *The Dutch in the Caribbean and in the Guianas, 1680–1791* (Assen/Maastricht, The Netherlands, 1985), 127–55, 189–230.

35. Sam. Wells to Fran. Wells, May 12, 1757, PRO/TNA, CO 5/1068, fols. 27, 37 (quote on fol. 27); Saltonstall to Thos. Allen, Oct. 6, 1755, Thos. Allen to Jos. Chew, Mar. 10, 1757, Allen Collection.

36. Greg & Cunningham to Hathorn, July 11, 1756, *Letterbook of G&C* (1756–57), 174 (quote); *CG,* July 29, 1758; Kenneth Scott, ed., *The Voyages and Travels of Francis Goelet, 1746–1758* (New York, 1970), [10].

37. Wim Klooster, *Illicit Riches: Dutch Trade in the Caribbean, 1648–1795* (Leiden, 1998), 59–172; Wim Klooster, "Curaçao and the Caribbean Transit Trade," in *Riches from Atlantic Commerce: Dutch Transatlantic Trade and Shipping, 1585–1817,* ed. Johannes Postma and Victor Enthoven (Leiden, 2003), 203–18; Goslinga, *Dutch in the Caribbean,* 78–83; Cotes to Clevland, July 19, 1759, PRO/TNA, ADM 1/235.

38. Pamphleteer, quoted in Goslinga, *Dutch in the Caribbean,* 95; Harrington, *New York Merchant,* 192; Klooster, *Illicit Riches,* 100; Coun. Mins., 406; Naval Office Shipping Lists for New York, 1713–65, PRO/TNA, CO 5/1228, fol. 36; Riché to Gouverneur, Mar. 21, 1759, Riché Letter Books.

39. *NYM,* Nov. 15, 1756 (quote).

40. *NYM,* Mar. 7, 1757 (quote).

41. Malachy Postlethwayt, *The Universal Dictionary of Trade and Commerce,* 2 vols. (London, 1751–55), 1:872 (quote); Deposition of Charles Ross, Mar. 21, 1761, and Deposition of John Jacob Seevalt, Mar. 23, 1761, PRO/TNA, HCA 45/3 [ship *St. Croix*]; The Respondent's Case, PRO/TNA, HCA 45/5 [ship *The Adventure*]; Claim of James McLaughlin, Feb. 26, 1761, BL, Add. MSS 36,215, fol. 178; Anon. to Blakes, Dec. 18, 1758, PRO/TNA, ADM 1/235; Jefferys, *West-Indian Atlas,* 27; Pares, *War and Trade,* 425–26, 456; Orla Power, "Beyond Kinship: A Study of the Eighteenth-Century Irish Community at Saint Croix, Danish West Indies," *Irish Migration Studies in Latin America* 5:3 (November 2007): 207–14, www.irlandeses.org/imsla0711.htm, and Power, The 'Quadripartite' Concerns of St. Croix, 1751–1757: An Irish Catholic Plantation in the Danish West Indies," in *The Irish in the Atlantic World,* ed. David T. Gleeson (Columbia S.C., forthcoming in 2009).

42. G. G. Beekman to Kortright & Lawrence, Apr. 14, 1756, *Beekman Papers,* 1:278 (quote); Philip L. White, *The Beekmans of New York in Politics and Commerce, 1647–1877* (New York, 1956), 213–14; *Abstracts of Wills,* 8:304. For Cornelius Kortright's dealings in sugar, coffee, and cotton at Christiansted, Saint Croix (including shipments to New York), see National Archives and Records Administration, College Park, Maryland, Record Group 55, Entry 465 (Records of the Weighmaster in Christiansted, 1748—78, vols. 9 [June 1, 1759], 11 [June 16–19, July 23, 27, and 31, 1761], 12 [April 1, 1762], 13 [June 10 and 30, 1763]). Thanks to Orla Power for bringing my attention to this source.

43. *NYM,* Dec. 6, 1756 (quote).

44. Thomas M. Truxes, "Transnational Trade in the Wartime North Atlantic: The Voyage of the Snow *Recovery,*" *Business History Review* 79 (winter 2005): 751–80.

45. Walton & Co. and Greg & Cunningham to Castle, Mar. 18, 1760, BL, Add. MSS 36,213, fol. 63 (quote).

46. Ibid. (quote); Truxes, "Transnational Trade," 764–65.

47. Truxes, "Transnational Trade," 768

48. Richard Pares, *Colonial Blockade and Neutral Rights, 1739–1763* (Oxford, 1938), 245; "Case on Behalf of the Respondent," BL, Add. MSS 36,209, fols. 15–16; Le Mesle to Le Mesle, Nov. 18, 1757, and De Vallemont to Le Mesle, Jan. 31, 1758, BL, Add. MSS 36,209,

fol. 204; Examinations of Andries Zeegard and Laurens Mandall, Apr. 24, 1759; PRO/TNA, HCA 45/1 [ship *De Pieter*]; Kavanagh, Belloc and Co. to Boutieller, Aug. 8, 1757, PRO/TNA, HCA 45/2 [ship *Maria Johanna*]; Depositions of Abraham Wibe, Jan. 17 and 18, 1758, and Mar. 16 and 17, 1758, PRO/TNA, HCA 45/2 [ship *Maria Johanna*]; Examination of William Vankall, Nov. 27, 1758, PRO/TNA, HCA 45/2 [ship *Juffrouw Johanna*]; Sir William Burrell, *Reports of Cases Determined by the High Court of Admiralty* (London, 1885), 208–11.

49. Pares, *Colonial Blockade*, 171–75, 279–85.

50. Mitchell to Frederick II, Aug. 22, 1755, quoted in Pares, *Colonial Blockade*, 243; Pares, *Colonial Blockade*, 242–55.

51. *LM* (May 1756): 237 (quotes); Pares, *Colonial Blockade*, 172–80, 202–24.

52. *GM* (Oct. 1756): 460 (quote).

53. Alice Clare Carter, *The Dutch Republic in Europe in the Seven Years' War* (London, 1971), 50–68.

54. Nicolas Magens, *An Essay on Insurances*, 2 vols. (London, 1755), 1:435 (quote); *GM* (Sept. 1758): 401–3.

55. Pares, *Colonial Blockade*, 180–204; Anon. to Blakes, Dec. 18, 1758, PRO/TNA, ADM 1/235.

56. Lord Hardwick, quoted in Pares, *Colonial Blockade*, 197.

57. Hardy to Board of Trade, June 19, 1756, *Docs. Col. NY*, 7:117 (quote); Hardy to Board of Trade, Oct. 13, 1756, *Docs. Col. NY*, 7:163–64 (quote on p. 163).

58. Coun. Mins., 122; The King v. Samuel Stilwell, [n.d.], NY/DOR, PL 1754–1837 K443; *Col. Laws of NY*, 3:1121–24; Julius Goebel, Jr., and T. Raymond Naughton, *Law Enforcement in Colonial New York: A Study in Criminal Procedure, 1664–1776* (New York, 1944), 241.

59. *NYM*, May 24, 1756 (quote).

60. The King v. Samuel Stilwell, [n.d.] (quote); Court Min. Book (1754–57), 307, 319 (quote on p. 307); William Smith, Jr., *The History of the Province of New-York*, ed. Michael Kammen, 2 vols. (Cambridge, Mass., 1972), 2:246–47.

61. Court Min. Book (1754–57), 305, 314, 317, 319, 336 (quote on p. 319); Memorial of Samuel Stilwell, Jan. 10, 1757, NY/DOR, PL 1754–1837 K443; Colden to Harison, June 22, 1756, Harison Papers; *NYGWPB*, Sept. 27, 1756; Coun. Mins., 143–44; Edward Coke, *The Third Part of the Institutes of the Laws of England, Concerning High Treason, and Other Pleas of the Crown, and Criminal Causes*, 5th ed. (London, 1671), 2.

62. Memorial of Samuel Stilwell, Jan. 10, 1757, NY/DOR, PL 1754–1837 K443 (quotes); Court Min. Book (1754–57), 348 (quote); Goebel and Naughton, *Law Enforcement*, 241.

63. Pares, *War and Trade*, 356–59, 403–19, 467–68; Thomas C. Barrow, *Trade and Empire: The British Customs Service in Colonial America, 1660–1775* (Cambridge, Mass., 1967), 160–61; Hardy to Board of Trade, June 19, 1756, *Docs. Col. NY*, 7:81–82, 117.

64. Fox to Hardy, Aug. 14, 1756, PRO/TNA, WO 34/30, fol. 9 (quote).

65. Board of Trade to Governors in America, Oct. 9, 1756, *Docs. Col. NY*, 7:162 (quote); *NYG*, Dec. 20, 1756 (quote); Coun. Mins., 152–53; Board of Trade, *Journal*, 10:265, 300; *NYG*, Jan. 3, 1757; George Louis Beer, *British Colonial Policy, 1754–1765* (New York, 1907), 81.

66. *The Journals of Hugh Gaine, Printer*, ed. Paul Leicester Ford, 2 vols. (New York, 1911), 2:5 (quote); Benjamin Franklin, *The Autobiography of Benjamin Franklin*, ed. Leonard W. Labaree et al. (New Haven, 1964), 253 (quote); Loudoun to the governors of New York,

New Jersey, Pennsylvania, Maryland, Virginia, Connecticut, Rhode Island, Massachusetts, Mar 2, 1757, Loudoun Papers, LO 2959; Fleming to Belcher, May 22, 1757, Loudoun Papers; *Cal. Coun. Mins.*, 432.

67. Board of Trade, *Journal,* 10:285 (quotes); *Journals of the House of Commons* (Nov. 8, 1547, to May 19, 1796), 51 vols. (London, 1803), 27:653, 658, 661, 669, 671, 675–76, 683, 705, 708.

68. Alex. Colden to Cad. Colden, July 12, 1757, *Colden Papers,* 5:157 (quote); 30 George II, c. 9, i, iv (British) (quote in sec. iv); *Cal. Coun. Mins.* 434; *NYGWPB*, July 11, 1757.

69. *NYGWPB,* July 11, 1757; Beer, *British Colonial Policy,* 83–85.

70. "Sentence of Judge of the Vice-Admiralty of New-York, Given 31st March 1757," PRO/TNA, HCA 45/1 [schooner *La Virgin del Rosario yel Sancto Christo de Buen Viage*]; Decision of Judge Morris, May 24, 1758, PRO/TNA, HCA 45/2 [ship *Maria Johanna*]; Minute Book, 1753–1757, NY Vice-Adm. Recs., 246–82; Hough, *Reports,* 88–100; Lydon, *Pirates,* 155–60.

71. Pares, *War and Trade,* 375–93.

72. *Oxford DNB,* 25:203–5; *CG,* Aug. 21, 1756; Smith, *History,* 2:198–99, 216; Hardy to Board of Trade, Aug. 2, 1756, *Docs. Col. NY,* 7:122.

73. Smith, *History,* 2:214–28; Mary Lou Lustig, *Privilege and Prerogative: New York's Provincial Elite, 1710–1776* (Madison, N.J., 1995), 99–102; Gipson, *British Empire,* 6:144.

74. Coun. Mins., 171–73; DeLancey to Board of Trade, June 3, 1757, PRO/TNA, CO 5/1068, fol. 5; Smith, *History,* 2:214.

75. HMS *Nightingale,* logbook, June 3, 1757, PRO/TNA, ADM 51/3922 (quote); Smith, *History,* 2:214; HMS *Sutherland,* logbook, June 3 and 4, 1757, PRO/TNA, ADM 51/952.

76. Loudoun to Falkingham, Apr. 8, 1757, Loudoun to Holbourne, May 28, 1757, Hardy to Holbourne, May 28, 1757, Loudoun to Pitt, May 30, 1757, Loudoun Papers; June 4 to 19, 1757, John Campbell's Memorandum Book (HM 1717), Loudoun Papers.

77. Hardy to Board of Trade, June 14, 1757, PRO/TNA, CO 5/1068, fols. 20–21.

CHAPTER FOUR. Mountmen

1. HMS *Sutherland,* logbook, June 4–20, 1757, PRO/TNA, ADM 51/952; HMS *Vulture,* logbook, May 28, 1757, PRO/TNA, ADM 51/1025; Examinations of John Boutin and John Mourphy, June 9, 1757, PRO/TNA, CO 5/1068, fols. 22–23; Statement of Martin Garland, May 30, 1757, PRO/TNA, ADM 1/481 [transcription in LC], pp. 57–59 (hereafter cited as "State. of M. Garland"); Deposition of Martin Garland, May 31, 1757, PRO/TNA, CO 5/1068, fol. 18 (hereafter cited as "Dep. of M. Garland"); Hardy to Board of Trade, June 14, 1757, PRO/TNA, CO 5/1068, fols. 20–21.

2. Dep. of M. Garland (quotes); State. of M. Garland; Samuel Hazard, *Santo Domingo, Past and Present; With a Glance at Hayti* (New York, 1873), 391–93.

3. *BEP,* June 6, 1757 (quote); Dep. of M. Garland.

4. Loudoun to Cumberland, June 22, 1757, *Military Affairs,* 376 (quote); Hardy to Board of Trade, June 14, 1757, PRO/TNA, CO 5/1068, fols. 20–21.

5. 30 George II, c. 9, iv (British) (quote); Robinson to [Treasury], Mar. 18, 1760, PRO/TNA, T 1/403, fol. 94 (quote).

6. "Exports. Coastways," fols. 303–10.

7. *NYG,* Jan. 11 and 18 and Feb. 8, 1762; *NYM,* Oct. 23 and Dec. 18, 1758, Jan. 22, Feb. 26, Mar. 5, May 7, 21, and 28, and Sept. 24, 1759, July 20, Aug. 10 and 24, Sept. 7, 14, and 28,

Oct. 26, and Nov. 2, 1761, Feb. 1 and 15, and Mar. 1, 1762; Deposition of Waddell Cunningham, Dec. 20, 1760, PRO/TNA, CO 5/20, fols. 151–52; Thomas M. Truxes, "Transnational Trade in the Wartime North Atlantic: The Voyage of the Snow *Recovery*," *Business History Review* 79 (winter 2005): 751–80.

8. "State of the Case, Touching the North American Trade to Monte Christo," PRO/TNA, WO 34/102, fols. 152–53; "Reply to 'The State of the Case, Touching the North American Trade to Monte Christo,'" PRO/TNA, WO 34/102, fols. 154–55.

9. Van Horne et al. to Ward, Sept. 26, 1759, PRO/TNA, HCA 45/3 [snow *London*] (quote).

10. Robinson to [Treasury], Mar. 18, 1760, PRO/TNA, T 1/403, fol. 94 (quote); "Imports. Coastways," fols. 310, 313–15; Mercer to Greg & Cunningham, Nov. 6, 1760, BL, Add. MSS 36,213, fol. 64.

11. BL, Add. MSS 36,214, fols. 16–27 [brig *Sea Flower*]. Other owners included Benjamin Blagge, James Fairly, Thomas Gelston, John Jones, Thomas Jones, Samuel Judah, Hayman Levy, and John Williams (Claim of Thomas Gelston, Nov. 20, 1761, BL, Add. MSS 36,214, fol. 18).

12. *NLS*, Feb. 2, 1759 (quote); Andrew Burnaby, *Travels Through the Middle Settlements in North-America in the Years 1759 and 1760. With Observations Upon the State of the Colonies* (London, 1775), 66.

13. This is a conservative estimate. In May 1762, fifty-four New York City merchants publicly acknowledged participation in the Monte Cristi trade. This group did not include some of the city's most active participants: Waddell Cunningham, James Depeyster, George Folliot, Samuel Stilwell, James Thompson, Jacob Van Zandt, and Thomas White (Chalmers: NY, vol. 3, fol. 22).

14. DeLancey to Lords of Trade, June 3, 1757, PRO/TNA, CO 5/1068, fol. 6; DeLancey to Lords of Trade, July 30, 1757, *Docs. Col. NY*, 7:273; *Cal. Coun. Mins.*, 434; DeLancey to Amherst, Aug. 24, 1759, PRO/TNA, WO 34/29, fol. 173.

15. Richard Pares, *War and Trade in the West Indies, 1739–1763* (Oxford, 1936), 309, 345–46, 364, 395, 402–4, 407, 414, 426; L. M. Cullen, "Merchant Communities Overseas, the Navigation Acts and Irish and Scottish Responses," *Comparative Aspects of Scottish and Irish Economic and Social History, 1600–1900*, ed. L. M. Cullen and T. C. Smout (Edinburgh, 1977), 165–74.

16. *NY Marriages*, 139; Gregory Palmer, *Biographical Sketches of Loyalists of the American Revolution* (Westport, Conn., 1984), 281; *NYM*, Nov. 20, 1758; Cad. Colden to Collinson, Oct. 1755, *Colden Papers*, 5:38.

17. *NYM*, Apr. 23, 1753 (quote); *NYM*, Oct. 10, 1757; *Abstracts of Wills*, 7:227–28; Walton Genealogy [n.d.], Walton Family Papers, NYHS; *NY Marriages*, 445; Examination of John Hall, March 1760, PRO/TNA, HCA 45/3 [ship *Nancy*]; Truxes, "Transnational Trade," 755, 758–59.

18. For George Folliot and Jane Harison (1758), Thomas Lynch and Catharine Groasbeek (1759), John Torrans and Elizabeth Blanche Smith (c. 1757); Hugh Wallace and Sally Low (1760), and Thomas White and Ann Hinson (1760) see *NY Marriages*, 241, 456, *Historical Memoirs of William Smith . . .*, ed. William H. W. Sabine, 2 vols. (New York, 1956), 2:xxv, and Virginia D. Harrington, *The New York Merchant on the Eve of the American Revolution* (New York, 1935), 16.

19. "Claim of Capt. [Nicholas] Horton," June 6, 1760, BL, Add. MSS 36,211, fol. 275; Clearance from the Port of New York, Nov. 6, 1759, BL, Add. MSS 36,211, fol. 279.

20. *NYG,* Dec. 10, 1759 (quote); Deposition of Nicholas Horton, May 8, 1760, BL, Add. MSS 36,211, fol. 273; Jefferys, *West-Indian Atlas,* 23–24; *NM,* Apr. 17, 1759; *NYGWPB,* Apr. 9, 1759; *NYM,* Apr. 30, 1759.

21. Holmes, "Memorial 2nd," fols. 156–63 (quote on fol. 158); Hinxman to Holmes, Apr. 13, 1761, PRO/TNA, ADM 1/236, fol. 214 (quote); Saul B. Cohen, ed., *The Columbia Gazetteer of the World* (New York, 1998), 2033; Hazard, *Santo Domingo,* 352; Otto Schoenrich, *Santo Domingo: A Country with a Future* (New York, 1918), 100–101; Samuel Eliot Morison, *Admiral of the Ocean Sea: A Life of Christopher Columbus,* 2 vols. (Boston, 1942), 1:395.

22. Schoenrich, *Santo Domingo,* 116–31.

23. Ibid., 100–103, 273; Hazard, *Santo Domingo,* 351–56.

24. Holmes, "Memorial 2nd," fol. 156 (quote); Examination of Nathaniel Davis, June 1, 1759, PRO/TNA, SP 42/41 (2), fols. 459–60.

25. Holmes, "Memorial 2nd," fols. 156–57 (quote on fol. 156); *A Plan of Monte-Christe Bay with the Seven Brothers on the North Coast of St. Domingo* (London, 1779); Truxes, "Transnational Trade," 768–70.

26. "Certificate from the Spanish Commander at Monte Cristi," Nov. 10, 1760, BL, Add. MSS 36,213, fol. 52 (quote).

27. Holmes, "Memorial 2nd," fols. 156–63, (quote on fol. 158); Schoenrich, *Santo Domingo,* 272; *Columbia Gazetteer,* 2033.

28. Holmes, "Memorial 2nd," fol. 156 (quote); Claim of Thomas Gelston, Nov. 20, 1761, BL, Add. MSS 36,214, fol. 18 [brig *Sea Flower*] (quote); Tuder to Witter, Oct. 20, 1759, Thomas Witter Papers, 1738–1806, NYHS; BL, Add. MSS 36,211, fols. 272–79 [brig *Charming Polly*].

29. For a sampling, see entries for February and April 1759 in Logbook of the Privateer *Duke of Cumberland,* 1758–60, Naval History Society Collection, MS in NYHS; Grant to Champlin, Apr. 20, 1760, *Commerce of Rhode Island,* 1:82; Greg & Cunningham to Nichols, Nov. 7, 1759, BL, Add. MSS 36,211, fol. 247; John Hinxman, "An Account of the Ships and Vessels Spoken with in Monte Cristi," Mar. 10 to 23, 1761, PRO/TNA, ADM 1/236, fols. 225–28; HMS *Defiance,* logbook, Aug. 31 to Oct. 18, 1761, PRO/TNA, ADM 51/226.

30. Holmes, "Memorial 2nd," fols. 156–63; Hinxman to Holmes, Apr. 13, 1761, PRO/TNA, ADM 1/236, fol. 214.

31. Robinson to [Treasury], Mar. 18, 1760, PRO/TNA, T 1/403, fol. 95 (quote); Representation of the Board of Trade to His Majesty, Aug. 31, 1759, PRO/TNA, T 1/396, fol. 66 (quote).

32. Affidavit of Samuel Little, Sept. 22, 1760, BL, Add. MSS 36,212, fol. 154 (quote); Mercer to Greg & Cunningham, Nov. 6, 1760, BL, Add. MSS 36,213, fol. 64.

33. William Kelly & Co. to Horton, Nov. 30, 1759, BL, Add. MSS 36,211, fol. 274 (quotes); Examination of Matthew Douglas, May 9, 1760, BL, Add. MSS 36,211, fol. 276 (quote); G. G. Beekman to Sears, Oct. 17, 1760, *Beekman Papers,* 1:347; Examination of Joseph Lawrence, Jan. 27, 1761, BL, Add. MSS 36,213, fol. 61; *NY Marriages,* 260.

34. Holmes, "Memorial 2nd," fol. 159 (quote); Mercer to Poaug, Apr. 14, 1761, BL, Add. MSS 36,213, fol. 140.

35. Cotes to Clevland, Feb. 28, 1759, PRO/TNA, ADM 1/235 (quote); Holmes, "Memorial 2nd," fol. 159; Deposition of John Knowland, May 9, 1760, BL, Add. MSS 36,211, fol. 273.

36. Examination of Nicholas Horton, May 8, 1760, BL, Add. MSS 36,211, fol. 278

(quote); Cotes to Clevland, Feb. 28, 1759, PRO/TNA, ADM 1/235 (quote); Plan of Coast of Hispaniola Between Cape François and Monte Cristi, 1761, PRO/TNA, MPG/1/598 (quote); Examination of James Grougan, May 24, 1760, BL, Add. MSS 36,211, fol. 246.

37. Carnegy to Baillie, Nov. 18, 1759, PRO/TNA, HCA 45/3 [snow *London*] (quote); Holmes, "Memorial 2nd," fols. 159–60; Hinxman to Holmes, Apr. 13, 1761, PRO/TNA, ADM 1/236, fol. 214; Deposition of Balthazar Kipp, Dec. 12, 1760, PRO/TNA, CO 5/20, fol. 70; Deposition of William Taggart, Apr. 21, 1760, PRO/TNA, CO 23/7, fols. 5–6.

38. Thos. Riché to John Riché, Aug. 22, 1759, Riché Letter Books (quote).

39. Cotes to Clevland, Feb. 28, 1759, PRO/TNA, ADM 1/235 (quote); HMS *Viper*, logbook, Jan. 30 to Feb. 12, 1759, PRO/TNA, ADM 51/4002.

40. Cotes to Clevland, June 4, 1759, PRO/TNA, ADM 1/235 (quotes).

41. Ibid. (quote) ; Hugh White & Co. to McLaughlin, Oct. 1, 1760, PRO/TNA, ADM 1/236, fol. 188 (quote); BL, Add. MSS 36,215, fols. 176–85 [ship *Ravenes*].

42. Cotes to Clevland, June 4, 1759, PRO/TNA, ADM 1/235 (quote).

43. Logbook of the Privateer *Duke of Cumberland*, Feb. 5 to 18 and Mar. 24 to Apr. 11, 1759; Hough, *Reports*, 94–100, 131–36, 148–52.

44. Examination of William Nichols, July 3, 1760, BL, Add. MSS 36,211, fol. 247 (quote); *PG*, July 19, 1759 (quote); Pares, *War and Trade*, 454–55.

45. *PG*, July 19, 1759 (quote).

46. Walton & Co. and Greg & Cunningham to Castle, July 29, 1760, BL, Add. MSS 36,213, fol. 62 (quote); "The Case of the Captor and Respondent," BL, Add. MSS 36,213, fols. 56–57 (quotes).

47. "The Case of the Captor and Respondent," BL, Add. MSS 36,213, fol. 56 (quotes).

48. Deposition of William Callow, Dec. 11, 1760, Deposition of Martin Harford, Dec. 2, 1760, Deposition of Simon Stevenson, Dec. 11, 1760, Depositions of Andrew Caldwell, n.d., and Dec. 22, 1760, PRO/TNA, HCA 45/3 [schooner *Gideon*].

49. Turner to Symmers, Dec. 1, 1760, BL, Add. MSS 36,213, fol. 65 (quotes).

50. "Certificate of the Governor of Monte Christi," Mar. 15, 1760, BL, Add. MSS 36,211, fol. 275; Gill and Amiel to Langlois, Mar. 10, 1760, BL, Add. MSS 36,211, fol. 279.

51. Cotes to Clevland, Feb. 14, 1760, PRO/TNA, ADM 1/235 (quote).

CHAPTER FIVE. Flag-Trucers

1. *NYM*, Apr. 16, 1759; Robinson to [Treasury], Mar. 18, 1760, PRO/TNA, T 1/403, fol. 94; DeLancey to Amherst, Aug. 24, 1759, DeLancey to Amherst, Sept. 10, 1759, PRO/TNA, WO 34/29, fols. 173, 193.

2. *NYM*, May 23, 1757 (quote); Thomas Jefferys et al., *The Natural and Civil History of the French Dominions in North and South America* (London, 1759), 65, 68–69.

3. Jefferys, *West-Indian Atlas*, 24.

4. Ibid. (quote); *NYM*, Apr. 23, 1759; *BPB*, Aug. 20, 1759; *NLS*, Sept. 7, 1759.

5. Thos. Allen to Eliz. Allen, Dec. 8, 1761, Allen Collection (quote); James E. McClellan III, *Colonialism and Science: St. Domingue in the Old Regime* (Baltimore, 1992), 75–107; Samuel Hazard, *Santo Domingo, Past and Present; With a Glance at Hayti* (New York, 1873), 402–3.

6. "Exports. Coastways," fol. 305; "Imports. Coastways," fol. 312.

7. *NYG*, Sept. 24, 1759 (quote); Coun. Mins., 295.

8. *NYG*, Sept. 24, 1759 (quote).

9. Francis Von A. Cabeen, "The Society of the Sons of Saint Tammany of Philadelphia [part 2]," *Pennsylvania Magazine of History and Biography* 26 (1902): 11 (quote); DeLancey to Amherst, Sept. 24, 1759, DeLancey to Amherst, Oct. 22, 1759, PRO/TNA, WO 34/29, fols. 205, 237; Coun. Mins., 295; Court Min. Book (1756–61), 152, 154, 158, 165.

10. Richard Pares, *War and Trade in the West Indies, 1739–1763* (Oxford, 1936), 446–55.

11. Cuyler to Richards & Coddington, Jan. 14, 1760, Cuyler Letter Book. This estimate of the composition of trade is based on the aggregate weight of evidence.

12. Pares, *War and Trade,* 388; for contending viewpoints, see *A State of the Trade Carried on with the French on the Island of Hispaniola, by the Merchants in North America, Under Colour of Flags of Truce* (New York, 1760) and Holmes, "Memorial 1st."

13. Robinson to [Treasury], Mar. 18, 1760, PRO/TNA, T 1/403, fol. 94 (quote).

14. Deposition of Obadiah Hunt (on the claimant's interrogatories), n.d., BL, Add. MSS 36,213, fol. 216 (quote); *Cal. Coun. Mins.,* 440, 444–45; Flag of truce commission, New York, Mar. 10, 1760, BL, Add. MSS 36,213, fol. 217.

15. "Case on Behalf of the Appellants," BL, Add. MSS 36,213, fol. 212 (quote); BL, Add. MSS 36,213, fols. 212–21 [brig *General Amherst*].

16. Flag of truce commission, New York, Mar. 10, 1760, BL, Add. MSS 36,213, fol. 217 (quote); Clearance from the Port of New York, Mar. 8, 1760, BL, Add. MSS 36,213, fols. 216, 217; *NYG,* Mar. 10, 1760.

17. Examination of William Atkinson, June 23, 1760, PRO/TNA, HCA 45/5 [brig *Achilles*]; Examination of Obadiah Hunt, June 23, 1760, BL, Add. MSS 36,213, fol. 214; "Case on Behalf of the Appellants," BL, Add. MSS 36,213, fol. 212.

18. Deposition of Obadiah Hunt (on the captor's interrogatories), n.d., BL, Add. MSS 36,213, fol. 215 (quote); Examination of Alexander Page, June 23, 1760, BL, Add. MSS 36,213, fol. 215.

19. Robinson to [Treasury], Mar. 18, 1760, PRO/TNA, T 1/403, fol. 94 (quote); Deposition of Obadiah Hunt (on the captor's interrogatories), n.d., BL, Add. MSS 36,213, fol. 215.

20. Examination of Robert Elder, June 23, 1760, BL, Add. MSS 36,213, fols. 214–15 (quote on fol. 215); Examination of Alexander Page, June 23, 1760, BL, Add. MSS 36,213, fols. 215; Deposition of Obadiah Hunt (on the claimant's interrogatories), n.d., BL, Add. MSS 36,213, fol. 216; Examination of William Atkinson, June 23, 1760, PRO/TNA, HCA 45/5 [brig *Achilles*]; Thomas Jefferys, *An Authentic Plan of the Town and Harbour of Cape Francois in the Isle of St. Domingo* (London, 1759).

21. Cuyler to Rowe, Feb. 21, 1760, Cuyler Letter Book (quote).

22. Hopkins to Pitt, Dec. 20, 1760, *Correspondence of William Pitt When Secretary of State with the Colonial Governors and Military and Naval Commissioners in America,* ed. Gertrude Selwyn Kimball, 2 vols. (New York, 1906), 2:373–78.

23. Cuyler to Tweedy, Sept. 14, 1759, Cuyler Letter Book (quote); "Exports. Coastways," fols. 303–10.

24. Examination of Thomas Rodman, Jan. 22, 1760, PRO/TNA, HCA 45/3 [ship *Brawler*]; "Imports. Coastways," fols. 311–16; Beekman to Bowler, Feb. 14, 1760, *Beekman Papers,* 1:352–54; Lister to Champlin, Feb. 2, 1760, *Commerce of Rhode Island,* 1:79–80; Cuyler to Richards & Coddington, Nov. 27, 1759, Cuyler Letter Book.

25. Cuyler to Tweedy, Mar. 11, 1760, Cuyler Letter Book (quote); Cuyler to Tweedy, Aug. 29, 1759, Cuyler Letter Book; Examination of Ferdinando Bowd, Mar. 24, 1760, BL, Add. MSS 36,213, fols. 37–38.

26. Penn to Pitt, 12 Sept. 1759, PRO/TNA, CO 5/19 (1), fol. 134 (quote); Nicholas B. Wainwright, "Governor William Denny in Pennsylvania," *Pennsylvania Magazine of History and Biography* 81 (1957): 193–94; Register of Flags of Truce (April 28 to September 28, 1759), RG-21, Records of the Proprietary Government; Provincial Council; Misc. Papers, no. 228, Pennsylvania State Archives, Harrisburg.

27. *Oxford DNB*, 15:839–40 (quote on p. 839); Wainwright, "Denny," 170–98.

28. Hamilton to Pitt, Nov. 1, 1760, *Correspondence of William Pitt*, 2:351–52 (quotes).

29. Examination of John Hall, Mar. 29, 1760, PRO/TNA, HCA 45/3 [ship *Nancy*] (quote); Flag of truce commission, Philadelphia, Oct. 9, 1759, PRO/TNA, HCA 45/3 [ship *Nancy*] (quote); *PG*, Dec. 16, 1756, and Oct. 27, 1757; PJ, Jan. 14, 1762; Examination of Bartholomew Rooke, March 1760, PRO/TNA, HCA 45/3 [ship *Nancy*]. See also the case of the snow *Greyhound* of New York, owned by Francis Lewis and Nicholas Bogert (PRO/TNA, HCA 45/3 [snow *Greyhound*]).

30. Examination of Bartholomew Rooke, March 1760 (on behalf of the captors), PRO/TNA, HCA 45/3 [ship *Nancy*] (quote); Cuyler to Wanton, Sept. 14, 1759, Cuyler to Tweedy, Oct. 8, 1759, Cuyler Letter Book; Riché to Van Zandt, Sept. 23, 1759, Riché Letter Books.

31. Examination of Ferdinando Bowd, Mar. 24, 1760, BL, Add. MSS 36,213, fols. 37–38; Examination of François Laine, Feb. 15, 1760, BL, Add. MSS 36,213, fols. 38, 41; Examination of Simon Oquan, Feb. 15 and Mar. 28, BL, Add. MSS 36,213, fols. 38, 41.

32. Riché to Van Zandt, Apr. 2, 1759, Riché Letter Books (quote).

33. Examination of John Long, Mar. 20, 1760, PRO/TNA, HCA 45/3 [ship *Molly*]; Riché to Lewis & Co., May 21, 1759, Riché Letter Books; Affidavit of Francis Lewis, n.d., in "[List of] the Papers Produced and Read at the Hearing of This Cause," PRO/TNA, HCA 45/3 [snow *Greyhound*]; PRO/TNA, ADM 7/299, fols. 1–6; Examination of Thomas Moore, June 24, 1760, BL, Add. MSS 36,213, fol. 210.

34. Examination of Thomas Moore, June 24, 1760, BL, Add. MSS 36,213, fol. 210; Examination of Alexander Page, June 23, 1760, BL, Add. MSS 36,213, fol. 215; "Case Against the Brig *John and William*," PRO/TNA, ADM 7/299; Examination of John Walker, June 23, 1760, PRO/TNA, HCA 45/5 [brig *Achilles*]; Sir William Burrell, *Reports of Cases Determined by the High Court of Admiralty* (London, 1885), 193; HMS *Zephyr*, logbook, June 10, 1760, PRO/TNA, ADM 51/1098.

35. *CG*, Nov. 25, 1758; *NLS*, Sept. 29, 1758; Suckling to Cotes, Sept. 9, 1758, PRO/TNA, ADM 1/235; Merchants of New Providence to Shirley, Oct. 18, 1761, PRO/TNA, CO 23/7, fols. 52–56; Pares, *War and Trade*, 454–55.

36. Cotes to Clevland, May 26, 1758, PRO/TNA, ADM 1/235 (quote); *NLS*, Jan. 5 and Feb. 23, 1759; *PG*, Feb. 8 and Mar. 1, 1759; Pinfold to Thomas, Apr. 29, 1759, Pinfold Letter Book, 1756–66, MS in LC.

37. Cotes to Clevland, Feb. 28, 1759, PRO/TNA, ADM 1/235.

38. Fred Anderson, *Crucible of War: The Seven Years' War and the Fate of Empire in British North America, 1754–1766* (New York, 2001), 297–316; Frank McLynn, *1759: The Year Britain Became Master of the World* (New York, 2004), 99–105.

39. Marshall Smelser, *The Campaign for the Sugar Islands, 1759: A Study of Amphibious Warfare* (Chapel Hill, N.C., 1955), 28–126.

40. Ibid.

41. Ibid.

42. Richard Gardiner, *An Account of the Expedition to the West Indies Against Martinico* (London, 1762), 46; Smelser, *Campaign for the Sugar Islands*, 170.

43. Smelser, *Campaign for the Sugar Islands,* 120–43.

44. Ibid., 143–45; Anderson, *Crucible of War,* 315.

45. Moore to Cotes, June 17, 1759, PRO/TNA, ADM 1/235 (quote); Smelser, *Campaign for the Sugar Islands,* 145–47.

46. Anderson, *Crucible of War,* 344–68; McLynn, *1759,* 138–39, 153.

47. *PG,* July 5, 1759 (quote); William Laird Clowes, *The Royal Navy: A History from the Earliest Times to the Present,* 7 vols. (London, 1897–1903), 3:203–10.

48. Robert Beatson, *Naval and Military Memoirs of Great Britain from 1727 to 1783,* 6 vols. (London, 1804), 2:311–12 (quote).

49. HMS *Cerberus,* logbook, July 21 to Aug. 6, 1759, PRO/TNA, ADM 51/180 (quote on Aug. 3); Cotes to Clevland, Aug. 1 and 28, 1759, PRO/TNA, ADM 1/235 (quote on Aug. 28).

50. HMS *Cerberus,* logbook, July 30 and Aug. 6 to 12, 1759, PRO/TNA, ADM 51/180 (quote on Aug. 7); Cotes to Clevland, Aug. 28, 1759, PRO/TNA, ADM 1/235.

51. Cotes to Clevland, Aug. 28, 1759, PRO/TNA, ADM 1/235 (quote); *NLS,* Aug. 3, 1759 (quote); HMS *Cerberus,* logbook, July 30, 1759, PRO/TNA, ADM 51/180; "Cargo of the Cartel Snow Hercules . . . Taken by HMS Cerberus, Captain Webber, as She Was Going into Port Louis on Hispaniola," PRO/TNA, T 1/389, fol. 72; Miller to Pavageau & Rousseau, June 25, 1759, PRO/TNA, ADM 1/235.

52. *NLS,* Aug. 3, 1759 (quote).

53. *BEP,* Oct. 29, 1759 (quote); Cotes to Clevland, Nov. 1, 1759, PRO/TNA, ADM 1/235 (quote); *NYG,* Nov. 5, 1759; *PG,* Nov. 8, 1759.

54. Cotes to Clevland, Aug. 28 and Dec. 9, 1759, PRO/TNA, ADM 1/235 (quotes).

55. Cotes to Clevland, Dec. 9, 1759, PRO/TNA, ADM 1/235.

56. HMS *Hampshire,* logbook, Nov. 20, 1759, to Feb. 5, 1760, PRO/TNA, ADM 51/426 (quote on Jan. 21, 1760).

57. HMS *Hampshire,* logbook, Jan. 6, 1760, to Feb. 5, 1760, PRO/TNA, ADM 51/426 (quote on Jan. 6).

58. HMS *Trent,* logbook, Jan. 5 to 19, 1760, ADM 51/3994; "English Vessels Seized by HMS *Trent* and Brought into Port Royal, Jamaica," Jan. 24, 1760, PRO/TNA, ADM 1/235; James Oldham, *English Common Law in the Age of Mansfield* (Chapel Hill, N.C., 2004), 321.

59. Cotes to Clevland, Feb. 14, 1760. PRO/TNA, ADM 1/235; Examination of John Hall, Mar. 29, 1760, PRO/TNA, HCA 45/3 [ship *Nancy*].

60. Monro to Willing & Morris, Mar. 2, 1760, PRO/TNA, ADM 1/235 (quote); Examination of Thomas Tunstall, Feb. 15, 1760, PRO/TNA, HCA 45/3 [ship *Nancy*].

61. Examination of Peleg Rogers, Feb. 11, 1760, PRO/TNA, HCA 45/3 [ship *Nancy*] (quote); Examination of Bartholomew Rooke, Apr. 2, 1760, PRO/TNA, HCA 45/3 [ship *Nancy*] (quote).

62. Examination of Peleg Rogers, Feb. 11, 1760, PRO/TNA, HCA 45/3 [ship *Nancy*] (quotes).

63. HMS *Lively,* logbook, Feb. 1, 1760, PRO/TNA, ADM 51/545; HMS *Cerberus,* logbook, Feb. 1, 1760, PRO/TNA, ADM 51/180.

64. Examination of Bartholomew Rooke, Apr. 2, 1760, PRO/TNA, HCA 45/3 [ship *Nancy*] (quote); Examination of Peleg Rogers, Feb. 11, 1760, PRO/TNA, HCA 45/3 [ship *Nancy*] (quote); HMS *Lively,* logbook, Feb. 2 and 3, 1760, PRO/TNA, ADM 51/545 (quote on Feb. 2); HMS *Cerberus,* logbook, Feb. 2 and 3, 1760, PRO/TNA, ADM 51/180 (quote on Feb. 3).

65. HMS *Lively*, logbook, Feb. 8 to 11, 1760, PRO/TNA, ADM 51/545; *BEP*, Apr. 21, 1760;*Boston Weekly News Letter*, May 22, 1760.

66. *NYG*, July 21, 1760; Examination of Thomas Rodman, Jan. 22, 1760, PRO/TNA, HCA 45/3 [ship *Brawler*].

67. Estimate of captured French sugar stored at Port Royal, Jamaica, and French sugar aboard British ships in the ports of Hispaniola [1760], PRO/TNA, ADM 1/235 (quote); Cotes to Clevland, Mar. 22, 1760, and "Lists of English Ships and Vessels Taken" [March 1760], PRO/TNA, ADM 1/235 (quote); Lister to Champlin, Feb. 2, 1760, *Commerce of Rhode Island*, 1:79–80; *NHG*, July 11, 1760.

68. G. G. Beekman to Wm. Beekman, June 14, 1760, *Beekman Papers*, 1:358 (quote); G. G. Beekman to Townsend, July 14, 1760, *Beekman Papers*, 1:363 (quote).

CHAPTER SIX. Mixed Messages

1. Spencer to "the Printer," May 20, 1760, PRO/TNA, CO 5/60, fol. 165 (quotes).

2. Julius Goebel, Jr., and T. Raymond Naughton, *Law Enforcement in Colonial New York: A Study in Criminal Procedure, 1664–1776* (New York, 1944), 283n227 (quote).

3. Spencer to "the Printer," May 20, 1760, PRO/TNA, CO 5/60, fol. 165 (quote).

4. *NYG*, May 19, 1760 (quote).

5. *NYG*, Oct. 6, 1760 (quote).

6. *NYGWPB*, Sept. 27, 1756 (quote); *NYM*, May 24, 1756.

7. *Col. Laws of NY*, 3:1050 (quote).

8. *NLS*, June 13, 1760 (quote); *NYG*, May 19, 1760 (quote).

9. *LM* (May 1756): 237; 30 George II, c. 9 (British).

10. *NYG*, Sept. 1, 1760 (quote); Watts to Barré, Feb. 28, 1762, *Watts Letter Book*, 27 (quote); Robinson to [Treasury], Mar. 18, 1760, PRO/TNA, T 1/403, fols. 94–95.

11. "State of the Case, Touching the North American Trade to Monte Christo," PRO/TNA, WO 34/102, fol. 152 (quote); "Observations on the Trade Which Is Now Carrying On by the English to Monto Christi, a Spanish Settlement on Hispaniola," BL, Add. MSS 36,211, fols. 256–57.

12. "State of the Case, Touching the North American Trade to Monte Christo," PRO/TNA, WO 34/102, fol. 152 (quote).

13. "Reply to 'The State of the Case, Touching the North American Trade to Monte Christo,'" PRO/TNA, WO 34/102, fol. 154 (quote).

14. Ibid. (quote).

15. Ibid. (quote).

16. *A State of the Trade Carried on with the French on the Island of Hispaniola, by the Merchants in North America, Under Colour of Flags of Truce* (New York, 1760), 6 (quote).

17. Ibid., 6–11 (quote on p. 6).

18. Ibid., 3–15 (quotes on pp. 12–13, 4).

19. Watts to Barré, Feb. 28, 1762, *Watts Letter Book*, 27 (quote).

20. Gilliland to Shaw, Feb. 10, 1760, Nathaniel and Thomas Shaw Papers, Sterling Memorial Library, Yale University, New Haven, Connecticut.

21. *NYG*, Jan. 7, 1760 (quote).

22. Gilliland to Shaw, Jan. 19, 1760, Shaw Papers (quote).

23. For lawsuits initiated by George Spencer in the New York court of vice-admiralty and the New York Supreme Court of Judicature, see John Tabor Kempe, "Notes on Mr. Alsop's bills," n.d. [c. Feb.–May 1761], Kempe Papers.

24. Spencer to Monckton, Aug. 2, 1763, Chalmers: NY, vol. 4, fol. 3 (quotes).

25. Ibid. (quote); Spencer to Kempe, Aug. 23, 1765, Kempe Papers; Goebel and Naughton, *Law Enforcement in Colonial New York,* 283n227; Spencer to "the Printer," May 20, 1760, PRO/TNA, CO 5/60, fol. 165; Report of William Smith, Dec. 24, 1760, PRO/TNA, CO 5/20, fol. 37; John Tabor Kempe, "Notes on Mr. Alsop's Bills," n.d. [c. Feb.–May 1761], Kempe Papers.

26. Alsop to Kempe, June 10, 1760, and Feb. 18, 19, and 21, 1761, Kempe to Alsop, Feb. 19 and 26 and May 2, 1761, Kempe Papers.

27. Spencer to Monckton, Aug. 2, 1763, Chalmers: NY, vol. 4, fol. 3 (quote); Spencer to "the Printer," May 20, 1760, PRO/TNA, CO 5/60, fol. 165 (quote); Report of William Smith, Dec. 24, 1760, PRO/TNA, CO 5/20, fol. 37. For violations of the Flour Act, George Spencer brought prosecutions in the New York Supreme Court of Judicature against Theophilact Bache, Robert Dale, James Depeyster, Elias Desbrosses, Judah Hays, John Milligan, Lawrence Reade, and David Van Horne (Spencer to Monckton, Aug. 2, 1763, Chalmers: NY, vol. 4, fols. 3–5).

28. *NYG,* Aug. 4, 1760 (quote).

29. Ibid. (quote).

30. Ibid. (quotes); William Smith, Jr., *The History of the Province of New-York,* ed. Michael Kammen, 2 vols. (Cambridge, Mass., 1972), 2:244.

31. *NYM,* Aug. 4, 1760 (quote).

32. Coun. Mins., 316; *Cal. Coun. Mins.,* 448; *Oxford DNB,* 12:495–96.

33. Admiralty Board to Pitt, Aug. 24, 1759, PRO/TNA, SP 42/41 (2), fol. 455 (quote); Board of Trade to the King, Aug. 31, 1759, PRO/TNA, T 1/396, fols. 65–70.

34. Pitt to Governors in North America and the West Indies, Aug. 23, 1760, *Correspondence of William Pitt When Secretary of State with the Colonial Governors and Military and Naval Commissioners in America,* ed. Gertrude Selwyn Kimball, 2 vols. (New York, 1906), 2:320–21 (quotes); Cotes to Clevland, June 4, 1759, and Moore to Clevland, Oct. 3, 1759, PRO/TNA, SP 42/41 (2), fols. 457–58, 561–62; Admiralty Board to Pitt, Feb. 12, 1760, PRO/TNA, SP 42/42 (1), fols. 9, 45–47.

35. Boone to Pitt, Oct. 24, 1760, Fauquier to Pitt, Oct. 28, 1760, Hamilton to Pitt, Nov. 1, 1760, Bernard to Pitt, Nov. 8, 1760, *Correspondence of William Pitt,* 2:344, 350, 355, 358 (quotes).

36. Hopkins to Pitt, Dec. 20, 1760, *Correspondence of William Pitt,* 2:373–78 (quotes on pp. 374, 376–77).

37. Cad. Colden to Pitt, Oct. 27, 1760, PRO/TNA, CO 5/19 (2), fols. 289–90 (quotes).

38. Spencer to Bute, Mar. 29, 1763, BL, Add. MSS 38,200, fol. 281; "Spencer v. Welch & Langley [Tingley] (1760)," Ordinary Marine Cases, 1746–74, Box A, NY Vice-Adm. Recs.; Hough, *Reports,* 181–83.

39. Spencer to Amherst, Nov. 29, 1760, PRO/TNA, CO 5/60, fol. 168 (quote); "Judgment upon the Plea to the Jurisdiction," in "Spencer v. Richardson," Customs Cases, 1757–75, Box 10, NY Vice-Adm. Recs. (quote); Minute Book, 1758–74, NY Vice-Adm. Recs., 143; 30 George II, c. 9, i, iv (British).

40. Spencer to Amherst, Nov. 29, 1760, PRO/TNA, CO 5/60, fol. 168 (quotes).

41. Smith, *History,* 2:252 (quote); Bradley to Amherst, Dec. 5, 1760, PRO/TNA, WO 34/30, fols. 287–89 (quote on fol. 287); Amherst to Cad. Colden, Dec. 6, 1760, PRO/TNA, WO 34/30, fol. 293 (quote); Petition of Augustus Bradley, Nov. 17, 1760, Kempe Papers.

42. *Cal. Coun. Mins.*, 451 (quote); Minutes of the New York Council, Dec. 8 and 24, 1760, PRO/TNA, CO 5/20, fols. 32–33, 37–40 (quote on fol. 32).

43. Bradley to Amherst, Dec. 5, 1760, PRO/TNA, WO 34/30, fols. 287–89 (quote on fol. 289); Examination of Augustus Bradley, Dec. 9, 1760, PRO/TNA, CO 5/20, fols. 42–44 (quotes on fols. 43–44, 42); Bradley to Amherst, Dec. 5, 1760 (quote on fol. 288).

44. Minutes of the New York Council, Dec. 11, 1760, PRO/TNA, CO 5/20, fols. 33–34; Deposition of John Stevenson, Dec. 9, 1760, Deposition of John Meuls, Dec. 9, 1760, Deposition of Philip Livingston, Dec. 9, 1760, Deposition of Allen Popham, Dec. 9, 1760, Deposition of William Coventry, Dec. 10, 1760, Deposition of John Cruger, Dec 11, 1760, PRO/TNA, CO 5/20, fols. 46, 48, 50, 52, 54, 56; *Cal. Coun. Mins.*, 451.

45. Deposition of William Coventry, Dec. 10, 1760, PRO/TNA, CO 5/20, fol. 54 (quote); Deposition of Allen Popham, Dec. 9, 1760, PRO/TNA, CO 5/20, fol. 52 (quote); Deposition of John Stevenson, Dec. 9, 1760, PRO/TNA, CO 5/20, fol. 46.

46. Deposition of John Cruger, Dec. 11, 1760, PRO/TNA, CO 5/20, fol. 56 (quote).

47. Bradley to Kempe, Dec. 10 and 11, 1760, Kempe Papers (quotes).

48. Spencer to Pitt, Dec. 14, 1760, PRO/TNA, CO 5/60, fol. 161.

49. Deposition of George Spencer, Dec. 12, 1760, PRO/TNA, CO 5/20, fol. 68 (quotes).

50. Deposition of Balthazar Kipp, Dec. 12, 1760, PRO/TNA, CO 5/20, fol. 70 (quotes); "Minutes of [New York] Council," Dec. 12, 1760, PRO/TNA, CO 5/20, fols., 34–35.

51. Spencer to Pitt, Dec. 14, 1760, PRO/TNA, CO 5/60, fol. 161 (quote).

52. Ibid. (quote).

53. Deposition of Waddell Cunningham, Dec. 20, 1760, PRO/TNA, CO 5/20, fols. 151–52; Riché to Lewis, May 21 and 31, June 14 and 16, and July 19, 1759, Riché Letter Books; Affidavit of Francis Lewis, n.d., in "[List of] the Papers Produced and Read at the Hearing of This Cause," PRO/TNA, HCA 45/3 [snow *Greyhound*]; Extracts from Customs House Books, Nov. 10, 1761, to Feb. 13, 1762, *Colden Papers,* 6:210–11; New York Merchants to Cad. Colden, May 29, 1762, Chalmers: NY, vol. 3, fol. 22.

54. Deposition of Francis Lewis, Dec. 23, 1760, PRO/TNA, CO 5/20, fol. 78 (quote).

55. Deposition of George Harison, Dec. 23, 1760, PRO/TNA, CO 5/20, fol. 82 (quotes).

56. Spencer to Holdernesse, Apr. 1, 1756, BL, Eg. 3490, fols. 198–200 (quotes on fols. 198 and 200).

57. Spencer to Wallace, June 23, 1756, BL, Eg. 3490, fol. 206 (quotes).

58. Spencer to Wallace, June 24, 1756, BL, Eg. 3490, fol. 211 (quote).

59. Deposition of George Harison, Dec. 23, 1760, PRO/TNA, CO 5/20, fol. 82 (quote).

60. Bradley to Cad. Colden, n.d., PRO/TNA, CO 5/60, fol. 178 (quote).

61. Ibid. (quote; "The answer verbal that my letters were all impertinent and that he would not answer them, A.B.").

62. Report of William Smith, Dec. 24, 1760, PRO/TNA, CO 5/20, fols. 37–40 (quotes on fols. 37, 40).

63. Cad. Colden to Pitt, Dec. 27, 1760, PRO/TNA, CO 5/20, fols. 23–24 (quotes on fol. 23).

64. *BEP,* Dec. 29, 1760 (quote); *BPB,* Dec. 29, 1760 (quote); HMS *Fowey,* logbook, Dec. 27, 1760, PRO/TNA, ADM 51/3845.

CHAPTER SEVEN. Business as Usual

1. *NHG*, Jan. 9, 1761 (quote); Cad. Colden to Board of Trade, Jan. 10, 1761, *Docs. Col. NY*, 7:453.

2. *PJWA*, Jan. 22, 1761 (quote); *BPB*, Jan. 19, 1761; *NYG*, Jan. 12, 1761; *PG*, Jan. 22, 1761.

3. HMS *Fowey*, logbook, Jan. 16 and 17, 1761, PRO/TNA, ADM 51/3845 (quote on Jan. 17); Coun. Mins., 350–54.

4. *NYG*, Jan. 19, 1761 (quote); HMS *Fowey*, logbook, Jan. 17, 1761, PRO/TNA, ADM 51/3845.

5. *NYM*, Jan. 26, 1761 (quote); "Proclamation of Accession of King George III by New York Council and Leading Citizens," Jan. 17, 1761, *Colden Papers*, 6:6–9.

6. *NYM*, Jan. 26, 1761 (quote); *NYG*, Jan. 19, 1761 (quote); Coun. Mins., 354; *Journal of Jeffery Amherst*, 264.

7. *PG*, Jan. 22, 1761 (quote); *NYM*, Jan. 26, 1761.

8. William Smith, Jr., *The History of the Province of New-York*, ed. Michael Kammen, 2 vols. (Cambridge, Mass., 1972), 2:252 (quote); Thomas M. Truxes, "Transnational Trade in the Wartime North Atlantic: The Voyage of the Snow *Recovery*," *Business History Review* 79 (winter 2005): 777.

9. *Cork Evening Post*, July 7, 1760 (quote); *NYG*, May 12, 1760 (quote); William Laird Clowes, *The Royal Navy: A History from the Earliest Times to the Present*, 7 vols. (London, 1897–1903), 3:224; Kelly to Thompson, Oct. 5, 1761, Duane Papers, MS in NYHS; *Boston Weekly News Letter*, May 22 and July 17, 1760; *Cork Evening Post*, June 9 and Sept. 11, 1760; *NHG*, July 11, 1760.

10. Cotes to Clevland, Aug. 28 and Dec. 9 1759, and Feb. 14 and Mar. 22, 1760, PRO/TNA, ADM 1/235; Cuyler to Richards & Coddington, Mar. 25, 1760, Cuyler Letter Book.

11. *NHG*, July 11, 1760 (quote); PRO/TNA, HCA 45/3 [ship *Nancy*]; Moore to Galloway & Co., May 21 and June 10, 1760, Samuel and John Galloway Papers, 1739–1812, NYPL; Richard Pares, *War and Trade in the West Indies, 1739–1763* (Oxford, 1936), 455.

12. Richard Pares, *Colonial Blockade and Neutral Rights, 1739–1763* (Oxford, 1938), 88–89 (quote on p. 89); Pares, *War and Trade*, 416–18; 29 George II, c. 34 (British); 30 George II, c. 9 (British).

13. Ben. Chew to Galloway & Co., June 24, 1760, Galloway Papers (quote); Pares, *Colonial Blockade*, 85.

14. Holmes, "Memorial 2nd," fol. 156 (quote); Holmes to Clevland, July 23, 1760, PRO/TNA, ADM 1/236, fol. 48 (quote).

15. Holmes to Clevland, July 23, 1760, PRO/TNA, ADM 1/236, fol. 49 (quote).

16. *Boston Weekly News Letter*, Oct. 30, 1760 (quote); Holmes to Clevland, Nov. 11, 1760, PRO/TNA, ADM 1/236, fols. 84–87 (quote on fol. 86); HMS *Hussar*, logbook, July 15 to Sept. 30 and Oct. 17 to Dec. 16, 1760, PRO/TNA, ADM 51/4223.

17. Jos. Gale, Jr., to Jos. Gale, Sr., Dec. 2, 1760, BL, Add. MSS 36,213, fol. 63 (quote); Derby to Brome, Dec. 10, 1760, Richard Derby's Letterbook, no. 3 (May 23, 1760, to April 24, 1772), Phillips Library, Peabody Essex Museum, Salem, Massachusetts (quote); Forrest to Clevland, Dec. 20, 1761, PRO/TNA, ADM 1/1787 [Forrest].

18. Mercer to Walton & Co. and Greg & Cunningham, Nov. 6, 1760, BL, Add. MSS 36,213, fol. 64 (quote).

19. "The Case of the Captor and Respondent," BL, Add. MSS 36,213, fols. 56–57; *Letterbook of G&C* (1756–57), 87–88.

20. HMS *Hussar,* logbook, Dec. 3 to Dec. 11, 1760, PRO/TNA, ADM 51/4223 (quotes on Dec. 11, Dec. 6).

21. Ibid., Oct. 17 and 24, Nov. 1, 11, 12, and 24, Dec. 7 and 11, 1760 (quote on Dec. 11).

22. Ibid., Dec. 14 and 15, 1760 (quote on Dec. 14).

23. Ibid., Dec. 15 and 16, 1760 (quote on Dec. 15).

24. Examination of Robert Castle, Dec. 16, 1760, and Jan. 27, 1761, BL, Add. MSS 36,213, fols. 60–61 (quotes); PRO/TNA, HCA 42/92 [snow *Recovery*], fol. 4; "Some Merchants and Others of Kingston to Rear Admiral Holmes," July 11, 1761, PRO/TNA, ADM 1/236, fol. 281; Virginia D. Harrington, *The New York Merchant on the Eve of the American Revolution* (New York, 1935), 13, 39.

25. PRO/TNA, HCA 42/92 [snow *Recovery*], fols. 1–3 (quotes on fols. 2, 3); "The Case of the Captor and Respondent," BL, Add. MSS 36,213, fols. 56–57.

26. PRO/TNA, HCA 42/92 [snow *Recovery*], fols. 4–7 (quotes on fols. 7, 5); Pares, *War and Trade,* 460.

27. "The Appellant's Case," BL, Add. MSS 36,213, fol. 52 (quote); PRO/TNA, HCA 42/92 [snow *Recovery*], fols. 8–37.

28. PRO/TNA, HCA 42/92 [snow *Recovery*], fols. 37–38 (quotes).

29. Lister to Champlin, Feb. 2, 1760, *Commerce of Rhode Island,* 1:80 (quote); Duncan to Bowler and Champlin, Feb. 14, 1760, *Commerce of Rhode Island,* 1:86 (quote).

30. HMS *Port Royal,* logbook, Mar. 11, 1761, PRO/TNA, ADM 51/717 (quote); Holmes to Clevland, Mar. 18, 1761, PRO/TNA, ADM 1/236, fols. 203–6; Hinxman to Holmes, Apr. 13, 1761, PRO/TNA, ADM 1/236, fol. 214; Deposition of Thomas Murray, June 6, 1761, BL, Add. MSS 36,213, fol. 143; John Hinxman, "An Account of the Ships and Vessels Spoken with in Monte Christi," Mar. 10 to 23, 1761, PRO/TNA, ADM 1/236, fols. 225–28. For the sloop *Little David,* see *Colden Papers,* 6:210; for the snow *Kingston,* see BL, Add. MSS 36,213, fols. 136–43.

31. *NYM,* July 7, 1755, Apr. 12, 1756, Jan. 7 1760; "Imports. Coastways," fols. 315–16; Mercer to Greg & Cunningham, Nov. 6, 1760, Mercer to Waddell, Nov. 21, 1760, BL, Add. MSS 36,213, fol. 64; Holmes, "Memorial 2nd," fol. 160.

32. *NYM,* Jan. 7, 1760 (quote); "Imports. Coastways," fols. 315–16.

33. Mercer to Greg & Cunningham, Nov. 6, 1760, BL, Add. MSS 36,213, fol. 64 (quote).

34.Condemnation of the Brig *Polly* of New York in the Nova Scotia Court of Vice-Admiralty, June 29, 1761, PRO/TNA, ADM 1/482 (2), fols. 188–91 (quotes on fols. 188, 189).

35. Ibid. (quotes on fol. 189).

36. *BPB,* Apr. 13, 1761 (quote); Merchants of New Providence to Shirley, Oct. 18, 1760, PRO/TNA, CO 23/7, fol. 52 (quote); Examination of Samuel Henshaw, Mar. 16, 1761, PRO/TNA, HCA 45/5 [ship *Catherine*].

37. Clark to Dromgoole, May 20, 1761, Daniel Clark, Invoices and Letters, 1760–1762, HSP (quote); *Cal. Hist. MSS.,* 721–22.

38. *NYG,* May 18 and July 27, 1761 (quotes); Examination of John Walker, June 23, 1760, PRO/TNA, HCA 45/5 [brig *Achilles*]; *Abstracts of Wills,* 7:227–28; Kelly to Thompson, Oct. 5, 1761, Duane Papers.

39. Cad. Colden to Amherst, June 8, 1761, *Colden Letter Books,* 1:90 (quote); Amherst to Cad. Colden, June 11, 1761, *Colden Papers,* 6:38–39 (quote).

40. *Cal. Coun. Mins.,* 453 (quote); Amherst to Cad. Colden, Aug. 2, 1761, *Colden*

Papers, 6:62 (quote); Cad. Colden to Fitch, Aug. 10, 1761, *Colden Letter Books,* 1:102–3 (quote); Amherst to Cad. Colden, Aug. 9, 1761, PRO/TNA, WO 34/30, fol. 345; Coun. Mins., 380–81.

41. Amherst to Cad. Colden, Aug. 2, 1761, *Colden Papers,* 6:62 (quote); Cad. Colden to Fitch, Aug. 10, 1761, *Colden Letter Books,* 1:102–3 (quote); Amherst to Cad. Colden, Aug. 16, 1761, *Colden Papers,* 6:67 (quote).

42. *CG,* Apr. 11, 1761 (quote).

43. *NYGWPB,* Sept. 24, 1761 (quote).

44. Ibid. (quote); Sir William Burrell, *Reports of Cases Determined by the High Court of Admiralty* (London, 1885), 225.

45. Holmes to Clevland, Mar. 18, 1761, PRO/TNA, ADM 1/236, fol. 204 (quote); *NYG,* July 20, 1761 (quote); HMS *Pembroke,* logbook, Sept. 12, 1761, PRO/TNA, ADM 51/686 (quote); *NYG,* July 20, 1761 (quote); Pares, *War and Trade,* 269–71. For naval activity off Monte Cristi in the late summer and autumn of 1761, see HMS *Pembroke,* logbook, Aug. 13 to Sept. 13, 1761, PRO/TNA, ADM 51/686, and HMS *Portmahon,* logbook, Sept. 2 to Oct. 29, 1761, PRO/TNA, ADM 51/715; for activity off Cape François, see HMS *Centaur,* logbook, Sept. 13 to Oct 30, 1761, PRO/TNA, ADM 51/171.

46. *NYGWPB,* Oct. 15, 1761 (quotes).

47. Ibid. (quotes).

48. Bourdieu to Lewis, Dec. 16, 1761, PRO/TNA, SP 42/42, fol. 514 (quote); *CG,* Apr. 17, 1762 (quote); *Kent's Directory* (London, 1761), 18; [Mortimer's] *The Universal Director* (London, 1763), [part 3], 15.

49. *CG,* Apr. 17, 1762 (quote); Pares, *War and Trade,* 463–64.

50. Forrest to Clevland, Dec. 20, 1761, PRO/TNA, ADM 1/1787 [Forrest] (quote); HMS *Centaur,* logbook, Nov. 23, 1761, PRO/TNA, ADM 51/171 (quote); David Syrett and R. L. DiNardo, *The Commissioned Sea Officers of the Royal Navy, 1660–1815* (Aldershot, Hants., 1994), 225.

51. Thos. Allen to Mumford, Dec. 13, 1761, Allen Collection (quote); Forrest to Clevland, Dec. 20, 1761, PRO/TNA, ADM 1/1787.

52. Forrest to Clevland, Dec. 20, 1761, PRO/TNA, ADM 1/1787 (quotes).

53. Spencer to Monckton, Aug. 2, 1763, Chalmers: NY, vol. 4, fol. 5 (quote); Spencer to Cad. Colden, Nov. 25 and 26 and Dec. 16, 1761, *Colden Papers,* 6:89–99.

54. Holmes, "Memorial 2nd," fol. 160 (quote); Spencer to Monckton, Aug. 2, 1763, Chalmers: NY, vol. 4, fols. 3–5; "Extract from the Custom House Books of New York," Nov. 10, 1761, to Feb. 13, 1762, *Colden Papers,* 6:210.

55. Prat to Board of Trade, May 24, 1761, PRO/TNA, CO 5/1070, fols. 158–59 (quotes); *Cal. Coun. Mins.,* 454; Smith, *History,* 2:253–58, 262–66, 270–71; Stephen C. Steacy, "Cadwallader Colden: Statesman and Savant of Colonial New York" (Ph.D. diss., University of Kansas, 1987), 184–97; Mary Lou Lustig, *Privilege and Prerogative: New York's Provincial Elite, 1710–1776* (Madison, N.J, 1995), 109; Milton M. Klein, "Prelude to Revolution in New York: Jury Trials and Judicial Tenure," *WMQ* 17:4 (October 1960): 448–51.

56. Spencer to Monckton, Aug. 2, 1763, Chalmers: NY, vol. 4, fol. 5 (quote).

57. Clerk of Benjamin Franklin to Strahan, June 14, 1762, *The Papers of Benjamin Franklin,* ed. Leonard W. Labaree et al., 39 vols. to date (New Haven, 1959–), 10:105 (quote).

CHAPTER EIGHT. Crackdown

1. Alex. Colden to Harison, June 22, 1756, Harison Papers; Amherst to Cad. Colden, June 11 and 26 and Aug. 16, 1761, and Apr. 24, 1762, *Colden Papers,* 6:38–39, 59, 66–67, 155; Cad. Colden to Amherst, Apr. 8 and 17, 1762, PRO/TNA, WO 34/29, fols. 479, 455; Amherst to Monckton, May 13, 1762, PRO/TNA, WO 34/30, fol. 485; Amherst to Hamilton, May 16, 1762, PRO/TNA, WO 34/32, fol. 195; Amherst to Cad. Colden, Apr. 16, 1762, Lory to Rieux, Feb. 6 and 22 and Mar. 11, 1762, Amherst to Hamilton, May 1, 1762, PRO/TNA, CO 5/62, fols. 104, 155, 173–74; Amherst to Monckton, Sept. 4, 1762, Chalmers: NY, vol. 3, fol. 51; "List of French Subjects to Be Examined," May 2, 1762, PRO/TNA, WO 34/102, fol. 164; "[List of] Papers Belonging to the French King's Subjects," May 4, 1762, PRO/TNA, WO 34/102, fols. 101–2; "Extract of a Letter from New England to Gidney [Gedney] Clarke, Esqr., Collector of His Majesty's Customs at Barbados, dated 3d. May 1762," PRO/TNA, ADM 1/237, fol. 93; "Jean Baptiste La Ville (1762)," Case Papers, 1757–1775, Box 2, NY Vice-Adm. Recs.

2. Kempe to Jury, Apr. 21, 1763, Cunningham-White Trial (quote); Anon. to Clark, May 3, 1762, PRO/TNA, ADM 1/237, fol. 93 (quote).

3. Anon. to Clark, May 3, 1762, PRO/TNA, ADM 1/237, fol. 93 (quote).

4. Cad. Colden to Amherst, Apr. 17, 1762, PRO/TNA, WO 34/29, fol. 455 (quote); *NYGWPB,* Oct. 29, 1761; *Colden Papers,* 6:149–54, 210–11; Amherst to Cad. Colden, Apr. 16, 1762, PRO/TNA, CO 5/62, fol. 104.

5. HMS *Enterprise,* logbook, Jan. 6 to Jan. 25, 1762, PRO/TNA, ADM 51/313 (quote on Jan. 25); *Siege and Capture,* 9–18.

6. HMS *Enterprise,* logbook, Jan. 26 to Feb. 26, 1762, PRO/TNA, ADM 51/313 (quotes on Feb. 5, Feb. 26); *NYM,* Apr. 5, 1762 (quote).

7. *NYM,* Apr. 5, 1762 (quote).

8. HMS *Enterprise,* logbook, Mar. 1 to Mar. 31, Apr. 1, 1762, PRO/TNA, ADM 51/313.

9. Lawrence Henry Gipson, *The British Empire Before the American Revolution,* 15 vols. (New York, 1939–70), 8:228–54; Jean O. McLachlan, "The Uneasy Neutrality: A Study of Anglo-Spanish Disputes over Spanish Ships Prized, 1756–1759," *Cambridge Historical Journal* 6 (1938–40): 55–76.

10. Dessande to De Martineu, Jan. 16, 1762, in "Extracts of Several Letters [Taken] Out of a French Prize," Council Minutes, Saint Iago de la Vega, Jamaica, Jan. 24, 1762, PRO/TNA, ADM 1/1788 (quote); Forrest to Anson, Jan. 28, 1762, PRO/TNA, ADM 1/1788 (quote).

11. Forrest to Clevland, Jan. 28, 1762, PRO/TNA, ADM 1/1788.

12. *CG,* Apr. 17, 1762 (quote); Affidavit of Jas. O'Bryan, Apr. 3, 1762, Lyttelton Papers, 1761–62, William L. Clements Library, University of Michigan (quote).

13. Lesley to Forrest, Feb. 12, 1762, PRO/TNA, ADM 1/1788 (quote).

14. *NYG,* Apr. 5, 1762 (quote); The Answer and Claim of James Kirkwood, Aug. 26, 1762, "Sea Horse (1762)," Case Papers, 1757–75, Box 4, [fols. 1–8], NY Vice-Adm. Recs. (quote on fol. 5); *NHG,* Apr. 16, 1762; *NYG,* Apr. 19 and May 3, 1762; Forrest to Clevland, Dec. 20, 1762, Deposition of William Turner, Jan. 26, 1762, PRO/TNA, ADM 1/1788; Hough, *Reports,* 206–7; Richard Pares, *War and Trade in the West Indies, 1739–1763* (Oxford, 1936), 461–65.

15. Gilliland to Bryan, Apr. 1762, Bryan Papers, 1756–1859, HSP (quote).

16. Cunningham to Monckton, n.d., Chalmers: NY, vol. 2, fol. 61 (quote); *NYM,* Apr. 12, 1762; Interrogation of Richard Mercer, Mar. 13, 1764, "New York (1764)," Case Papers, 1757–75, Box 9, NY Vice-Adm. Recs.

17. HMS *Enterprise,* logbook, Mar. 28 to Apr. 3, 1762, PRO/TNA, ADM 51/313; Coun. Mins., 439

18. Amherst to Gage, Apr. 2, 1762, Amherst Papers, vol. 6 (quote).

19. Egremont to Amherst, Jan. 13, 1762, *Siege and Capture,* xiv, 9–12; Amherst to Clevland, Apr. 6, 1762, PRO/TNA, WO 34/74, fol. 185; William Laird Clowes, *The Royal Navy: A History from the Earliest Times to the Present,* 7 vols. (London, 1897–1903), 3:246; N. A. M. Rodger, *The Command of the Ocean: A Naval History of Britain, 1649–1815* (New York, 2005), 285.

20. Egremont to Amherst, Jan. 13, 1762, *Siege and Capture,* 10–11 (quotes).

21. Amherst to Gage, Apr. 2, 1762, Amherst Papers, vol. 6 (quote); *NHG,* Apr. 16, 1762 (quote); Gipson, *British Empire,* 8:261–62; Egremont to Amherst, Jan. 13, 1762, *Siege and Capture,* 10–11.

22. Amherst to Randolph, Apr. 1762, PRO/TNA, WO 34/102, fol. 131.

23. Amherst to Cad. Colden, Apr. 15, 1762 (1), PRO/TNA, WO 34/30, fol. 377; Cad. Colden to Amherst, Apr. 15, 1762, PRO/TNA, WO 34/29, fol. 451; Amherst to Cad. Colden, Apr. 15, 1762 (2), PRO/TNA, WO 34/30, fol. 379; Coun. Mins., 442–43.

24. HMS *Enterprise,* logbook, Apr. 13, 1762, PRO/TNA, ADM 51/313; Deposition of George Moore, Apr. 22, 1762, *Colden Papers,* 6:149–51 [hereafter cited as "Dep. of Geo. Moore"]; W. E. May, *The Boats of Men of War* (London, 2003), 91–99; Amherst to Cad. Colden, Apr. 16, 1762, PRO/TNA, CO 5/62, fol. 104; Jonathan R. Dull, *The French Navy and the Seven Years' War* (Lincoln, Neb., 2005), 224–25; Rodger, *Command of the Ocean,* 284.

25. Amherst to Cad. Colden, Apr. 16, 1762, PRO/TNA, CO 5/62 fol. 104 (quote).

26. Ibid. (quote); Spencer to Amherst, Nov. 29, 1760, PRO/TNA, CO 5/60, fol. 168.

27. Jas. Thompson to Cath. Thompson, Mar. 16, 1762, PRO/TNA, WO 34/102, fol. 134 (quote).

28. Ibid. (quote); Jas. Thompson to Cath. Thompson, Apr. 6, 1762, PRO/TNA, ADM 1/237, fol. 95.

29. Jas. Thompson to Cath. Thompson, Apr. 6, 1762, PRO/TNA, WO 34/102, fol. 95 (quote); Jas. Thompson to Dishington, Apr. 6, 1762, PRO/TNA, ADM 1/237, fol. 94 (quote); Jas. Thompson to Jos. Chew, Apr. 6, 1762, PRO/TNA, ADM 1/237, fol. 95.

30. Jas. Thompson to Dishington, Apr. 6, 1762, PRO/TNA, ADM 1/237, fol. 94 (quote).

31. Ibid. (quote); Jas. Thompson to Cath. Thompson, Apr. 6, 1762, PRO/TNA, ADM 1/237, fol. 95 (quote).

32. *NYG,* Apr. 19, 1762 (quote).

33. Cad. Colden to Amherst, Apr. 15, 1762, PRO/TNA, WO 34/29, fol. 451 (quote); Coun. Mins., 442–43.

34. Cad. Colden to Amherst, Apr. 17, 1762, PRO/TNA, WO 34/29, fol. 455.

35. Ibid. (quote); DeLancey to Amherst, Nov. 5, 1759, PRO/TNA, WO 34/29, fol. 243; Hamilton to Amherst, Apr. 19, 1762, PRO/TNA, WO 34/33, fol. 305 (quote).

36. *NYG,* Apr. 19, 1762 (quote).

37. Dep. of Geo. Moore, 149 (quote); Cad. Colden to Amherst, Apr. 17, 1762, PRO/TNA, WO 34/29, fol. 455; Amherst to Cad. Colden, Apr. 18, 1762 [9 at night], *Colden*

Papers, 6:144; Cad. Colden to Amherst, Apr. 20, 1762, PRO/TNA, WO 34/29, fol. 459; Amherst to Cad. Colden, Apr. 20, 1762, PRO/TNA, WO 34/30, fol. 395; Kempe to Cad. Colden, Apr. 20, 1762 ["1/4 past 4 o'Clock"], 6:147–48.

38. Dep. of Geo. Moore, 150 (quote); Deposition of James Cole, Apr. 22, 1762, *Colden Papers,* 6:154 (quote); Dep. of Geo. Moore, 150 (quote).

39. Dep. of Geo. Moore, 151 (quote); Amherst to Cad. Colden, Apr. 16, 1762, PRO/ TNA, CO 5/62, fol. 104; Cad. Colden to Amherst, Apr. 24, 1762, PRO/TNA, WO 34/29, fol. 463.

40. Kempe to Cad. Colden, Apr. 18, 1762 [5:00 P.M.], *Colden Papers,* 6:143 (quote); Kempe to Cad. Colden, Apr. 18, 1762 [7:00 P.M.], PRO/TNA, WO 34/30, fol. 389 (quote); "Schedule of Papers," May 12, 1762, PRO/TNA, WO 34/74, fols. 229–35; Hamilton to Amherst, Apr. 19, 1762, PRO/TNA, WO 34/33, fol. 305; Amherst to Fitch, May 5, 1762, PRO/ TNA, CO 5/62, fol. 107.

41. Cad. Colden to Amherst, Apr. 23, 1762, PRO/TNA, WO 34/29, fol. 461 (quote).

42. *CG,* May 1, 1762 (quote); Esther Singleton, *Social New York Under the Georges, 1714–1776* (New York, 1902), 171–256, 301–7.

43. "Order for the Arrest of Frenchmen in the City of New York as Prisoners of War," Apr. 20, 1762, *Colden Papers,* 6:148 (quote); Amherst to Hamilton, May 1, 1762, PRO/ TNA, CO 5/62, fols. 173–74; Amherst to Williams, May 2, 1762, PRO/TNA, WO 34/102, fol. 163; Cad. Colden to Amherst, May 2, 1762, PRO/TNA, WO 34/29, fol. 477; Cad. Colden to Roberts, May 2, 1762, PRO/TNA, WO 34/29, fol. 475; Amherst to Cad. Colden, May 3, 1762, PRO/TNA, WO 34/30, fol. 403; Cad. Colden to Amherst, May 3, 1762, PRO/TNA, WO 34/29, fol. 479.

44. "List of French Subjects to Be Examined," May 2, 1762, PRO/TNA, WO 34/102, fol. 164 (quote); "Jean Baptiste La Ville (1762)," Case Papers, 1757–75, Box 2, NY Vice-Adm. Recs.

45. "[List of] Papers Belonging to the French King's Subjects," May 4, 1762, PRO/ TNA, WO 34/102, fol. 101 (quote); Amherst to Cad. Colden, May 4, 1762 [11:00 P.M.], PRO/TNA, WO 34/30, fol. 407; Cad. Colden to Amherst, May 5, 1762, PRO/ TNA, WO 34/29, fol. 485; "[List of] Papers Belonging to the French King's Subjects," May 4, 1762, PRO/TNA, WO 34/102, fols. 101–2.

46. "[List of] Papers Belonging to the French King's Subjects," May 4, 1762, PRO/ TNA, WO 34/102, fols. 101–2 (quotes); Dargout to Gouverneur de Kneticutt, Dargout to Gouverneur de la Nouvelle Yorck, Dargout to Gouverneur de la Caroline, Feb. 1, 1762, PRO/TNA, WO 34/102, fols. 113, 115, 116.

47. Cad. Colden to Monckton, Mar. 30, 1762, *Colden Letter Books,* 1:184 (quote); Cad. Colden to Amherst, May 2, 1762, PRO/TNA, WO 34/29, fol. 477 (quote); Cad. Colden to Monckton, Mar. 30, 1762, (quote); *NYM,* May 24, 1762 (quote); Cad. Colden to Amherst, May 2, 1762 (quote); Cad. Colden to Johnson, May 3, 1762, *Colden Letter Books,* 1:198.

48. Amherst to Cad. Colden, May 6, 1762, *Colden Papers,* 6:161–62 (quote on p. 161); Examination of William Dobbs, May 18, 1762, "Susannah and Anne (1762)," Case Papers, 1757–75, Box 4, NY Vice-Adm. Recs. (quote).

49. Deposition of William Williams, May 18, 1762, "Johnson (1762)," Case Papers, 1757–75, Box 2, NY Vice-Adm. Recs. (quote in 14th interrogatory); Deposition of William Williams, May 14, 1762, PRO/TNA, WO 34/102, fols. 177–79.

50. Libel of John Houlton, Commander of HMS *Enterprise,* n.d., "Industry (1762)," Case Papers, 1757–75, Box 2, NY Vice-Adm. Recs. (quote); Amherst to Cad. Colden, May

6, 1762, *Colden Papers,* 6:163 (quote); Deposition of William Paulding, May 18, 1762, "Susannah and Anne (1762)," Case Papers, 1757–75, Box 4, NY Vice-Adm. Recs.; Deposition of William Dobbs, May 14, 1762, PRO/TNA, WO 34/102, fols. 170–71; Deposition of Thomas Smith, May 14, 1762, PRO/TNA, WO 34/102, fol. 167; Deposition of John Barne, May 19, 1762, "York Castle (1762)," Case Papers, 1757–75, Box 5, NY Vice-Adm. Recs.

51. Amherst to Cad. Colden, May 6, 1762, *Colden Papers,* 6:163 (quote); Cad. Colden to Amherst, May 9, 1762 (9:00 P.M.), *Colden Letter Books,* 1:202 (quote).

52. Amherst to Cad. Colden, May 10, 1762, PRO/TNA, WO 34/30, fol. 423 (quote).

53. Cad. Colden to Board of Trade, May 11, 1762, *Docs. Col. NY,* 7:499 (quote); *Cal. Coun. Mins.*, 458; Amherst to Cad. Colden, May 8, 1762, *Colden Papers,* 6:166–67; Cad. Colden to Amherst, May 8, 1762, *Colden Letter Books,* 1:200–201; Cad. Colden to Amherst, May 13, 1762, PRO/TNA, WO 34/29, fol. 501; Amherst to Cad. Colden, May 13, 1762, PRO/TNA, WO 34/30, fol. 425.

54. Kempe to Cad. Colden, May 12, 1762, *Colden Papers,* 6:171–73 (quote on p. 171).

55. Depositions of William Williams (master), and John Martin and Harry Henry Crowder (mariners) of the snow *Johnson* of New York; Depositions of Thomas Smith (master), Philip Smith (mate), and John Barney (mariner) of the brig *York Castle* of New York; Depositions of William Dobbs (master), William Paulding (mate), and Samuel Garraway (mariner) of the sloop *Susannah and Anne* of New York; Depositions of Theunis Thew (master) and Jas. Bell and Phil. Caswell (mariners) of sloop *Industry* of New York, May 14 and 15, 1762, PRO/TNA, WO 34/102, fols. 167–81.

56. Hamilton to Amherst, Apr. 19, 1762, PRO/TNA, WO 34/33, fol. 305; Amherst to Hamilton, Apr. 22 and 23 and May 7 and 16, 1762, PRO/TNA, WO 34/32, fols. 185, 187, 193, 195; Amherst to Fitch, May 5, 1762, PRO/TNA, CO 5/62, fol. 107; Fitch to Amherst, May 10, 1762, PRO/TNA, WO 34/28, fol. 82; Amherst to Fitch, May 20, 1762, PRO/TNA, WO 34/28, fol. 178; "Proclamation" [of Gov. Thomas Fitch of Connecticut], May 19, 1762, *CG,* May 29, 1762.

57. *NYG,* May 24, 1762; Cad. Colden to Amherst, May 22, 1762, PRO/TNA, WO 34/29, fol. 507; Amherst to Cad. Colden, May 22 and 24, 1762, PRO/TNA, WO 34/30, fols. 431, 435.

58. Rieux and Comte to Cad. Colden, May 25, 1762, *Colden Papers,* 6:181 (quote); Rieux and Comte to Cad. Colden (received) May 22, 1762, *Colden Papers,* 6:180 (quote).

59. Watts to Erving, May 30, 1762, *Watts Letter Book,* 60 (quote); "List of Persons Trading to the Enemy from the Port of New York and of Their Cargoes," n.d. [c. May 1762], Kempe Papers (quote); Minute Book, 1758–74, NY Vice-Adm. Recs., 233–35; Josiah Hardy to Amherst, May 28, 1762, PRO/TNA, WO 34/31, fol. 193; Daniel J. Hulsebosch, *Constituting Empire: New York and the Transformation of Constitutionalism in the Atlantic World, 1664–1830* (Chapel Hill, N.C., 2005), 120–21. The others facing criminal charges were merchants, countinghouse clerks, and mariners, including James Bell, William Dobbs, John Fox, John Keating, Thomas Livingston, John Martin, George Moore, William Paulding, Philip Smith, Thomas Smith, Theunis Thew, William Williams, and Hamilton Young ("List of Persons Trading to the Enemy from the Port of New York and of Their Cargoes," n.d. [c. May 1762], Kempe Papers; "Note of Recognizances").

60. HMS *Intrepid,* logbook, May 28, 1762, PRO/TNA, ADM 51/474 (quote); Amherst to Hamilton, May 27, 1762, PRO/TNA, WO 34/32, fol. 197 (quote).

61. New York Merchants to Cad. Colden, May 29, 1762, Chalmers: NY, vol. 3, fol. 22 (quotes).

62. Cad. Colden to Board of Trade, June 12, 1762, *Colden Letter Books,* 1:213 (quote).

63. Ibid. (quote); Cad. Colden to Egremont, June 12, 1762, *Colden Letter Books,* 1:214 (quote).

CHAPTER NINE. The Trial

1. *CG,* July 10, 1762 (quote); HMS *Enterprise,* logbook, PRO/TNA, July 1, 1762, ADM 51/313; *Siege and Capture,* xiv, xxxii, 13–15, 110.

2. *BNL,* Oct. 1, 1762 (quote).

3. "Note of Recognizances" (quote).

4. Ibid.; Bail for the snow *Johnson*'s captain, William Williams, was fixed at £4,000 (New York currency); that for Hamilton Young, a junior partner at Greg and Cunningham, at £2,000, and that for John Martin, a sailor aboard the snow *Johnson,* at £500. For the thirteen men associated with other offending vessels, Judge Horsmanden set bail at £2,000 each for eleven and at £1,000 each for two ("Note of Recognizances").

5. Deposition of Waddell Cunningham, Dec. 20, 1760, PRO/TNA, CO 5/20, fols. 151–52; "The King v. Waddell Cunningham," July Term, 1762, Kempe Papers, Lawsuits (g–l); BL, Add. MSS 36,212, fols. 153–59 [ship *General Johnston*]; Add. MSS 36,213, fols. 52–65 [snow *Recovery*]; Add. MSS 36,213, fols. 136–43 [snow *Kingston*]; Add. MSS 36,215, fols. 176–85 [ship *Ravenes*].

6. Charles M. Andrews, *The Colonial Period of American History,* 4 vols. (New Haven, 1964), 4:222–71.

7. Minute Book, 1758–74, NY Vice-Adm. Recs., 233; "Johnson (1762)," Case Papers, 1757–75, Box 2, NY Vice-Adm. Recs.

8. Minute Book, 1758–74, NY Vice-Adm. Recs., 235 (quotes); *NYG,* May 31, 1762.

9. "Note of Recognizances" (quote); Amherst to Monckton, Sept. 4, 1762, Chalmers: NY, vol. 3, fol. 51 (quote).

10. Amherst to Ward, Aug. 30, 1762, PRO/TNA, WO 34/24, fol. 173 (quote).

11. Monckton to Board of Trade, Aug. 11, 1762, PRO/TNA, CO 5/1070, fol. 149 (quote); *CG,* June 19, 1762; *NYG,* July 5, 1762; *Cal. Coun. Mins.*, 458; William Berrian, *An Historical Sketch of Trinity Church, New-York* (New York, 1847), 357; Harison to Archbishop of Canterbury, July 5, 1762, Lambeth Palace Library, London, MSS 1123.III.263.

12. Smith to Archbishop of Canterbury, Sept. 27, 1762, Lambeth Palace Library, London, MSS 1123.III.273 (quote).

13. *Rivington's New-York Gazetteer,* Apr. 22, 1773 (quote); Razer to West, May 1754, BL, Add. MSS 34,728, fols. 21–22; Cad. Colden to Collinson, Oct. 1755, Alex. Colden to Cad. Colden, May 18, 1756, *Colden Papers,* 5:38, 80; Thomas C. Barrow, *Trade and Empire: The British Customs Service in Colonial America, 1660–1775* (Cambridge, Mass., 1967), 134–59.

14. "Draft of Information for Trading with the King's Enemies, The King v. Waddell Cunningham and Thomas White," October Term 1762, Kempe Papers, Lawsuits (g–l) (quote). The text of the Crown's complaint against Hamilton Young, Waddell Cunningham's clerk at Greg and Cunningham, is not extant. Language much like that in the charge against Cunningham and White was used against John Keating and William Kennedy, owners of the sloop *Susannah and Anne,* the only other case on the court's docket for the October 1762 term related to New York's trade with the enemy ("Draft of Information for Trading with the King's Enemies, The King v. John Keating and William Kennedy," October Term 1762, Kempe Papers, Lawsuits [g–l]).

15. Cunningham to Monckton, Oct. 23, 1762, Chalmers: NY, vol. 2, fol. 61 (quote).

16. Coun. Mins., 451.

17. Kempe to Monckton, Nov. 3, 1762, Chalmers: NY, vol. 2, fol. 28 (quote).

18. Ibid. (quote); 30 George II, c. 9, i (British). For an example of a provisions bond as required under the Flour Act, see Chalmers: NY, vol. 2, fol. 27.

19. Kempe to Monckton, Nov. 3, 1762, Chalmers: NY, vol. 2, fol. 28 (quote).

20. Ibid.; Kempe to Cad. Colden, Nov. 14, 1763, Chalmers: NY, vol. 2, fol. 34.

21. "1763. The King of England (Plaintiff) vs. Waddell Cunningham, et al. (Defendant), Illegal Correspondence with the King's Enemies. Notes on the Trial," Benjamin Salzer Mayor's Court Papers, Rare Book and Manuscripts Library, Columbia University, New York [hereafter cited as King v. Cunningham and White: Notes on Trial].

22. Gilliland to Bryan, Apr. 1762, Bryan Papers, 1756–1859, HSP (quote); Kempe to Jury, Apr. 21, 1763, Cunningham-White Trial (quote); King v. Cunningham and White: Notes on Trial.

23. *Cal. Coun. Mins.*, 460–61 (quote on p. 460); Coun. Mins., 474; *NYM*, Jan. 24, 1763.

24. Court Min. Book (1762–64), 127, 136 (quote on p. 127); HMS *Intrepid*, logbook, Apr. 19, 1763, PRO/TNA, ADM 51/474.

25. Court Min. Book (1762–64), 136, 137 (quotes); HMS *Intrepid*, logbook, Apr. 21, 1763, PRO/TNA, ADM 51/474. The jury consisted of Abraham Van Gelder (foreman); Joseph Brazier, William DePeyster, Jr., George Elsworth, John Ernest, Jacob Kipp, Nicholas Low, Joseph Marschalck, William Pears, Mathew Rogers, Samuel Sacket, and John Taylor (Court Min. Book [1762–64], 138).

26. Kempe to Jury, Apr. 21, 1763, Cunningham-White Trial (quotes).

27. Kempe to Jury, Apr. 21, 1763, Cunningham-White Trial (quotes). Kempe's claim contradicts the 1756 finding of the attorney general for England and Wales, William Murray (later Baron Mansfield and Lord Chief Justice of the King's Bench), who "reported that a search extending as far as the reign of Edward I had failed to discover a single prosecution [for trading with the enemy] at common law" (Ludwell H. Johnson III, "The Business of War: Trading with the Enemy in English and Early American Law," *Proceedings of the American Philosophical Society* 118:5 [Oct. 15, 1974]: 461).

28. 25 Edward III, Stat. 5, c. 2 (quote); Kempe to Jury, Apr. 21, 1763, Cunningham-White Trial (quote); Edward Coke, *The Third Part of the Institutes of the Laws of England, Concerning High Treason, and Other Pleas of the Crown, and Criminal Causes*, 5th ed. (London, 1671), 2; Notes of Authorities, The King v. Waddell Cunningham and Other Merchants, n.d., Kempe Papers, Lawsuits (g–l); Johnson, "Business of War," 459; Richard Pares, *War and Trade in the West Indies, 1739–1763* (Oxford, 1936), 419.

29. Kempe to Jury, Apr. 21, 1763, Cunningham-White Trial (quote); 3 & 4 Anne, c. 13 (English); G. N. Clark, "War Trade and Trade War, 1701–1713," *Economic History Review* 1:2 (January 1928): 267–78; Pares, *War and Trade*, 419–20. Kempe is exaggerating this point. During the reign of Queen Anne, the ministry had "shown on more than one occasion that it was willing to waive a strict prohibition of trade with the enemy where British interests were peculiarly concerned" (Douglas Coombs, "Dr. Davenant and the Debate on Franco-Dutch Trade," *Economic History Review* 10:1 [1957]: 96).

30. Kempe to Jury, Apr. 21, 1763, Cunningham-White Trial (quote).

31. Ibid. (quote).

32. Kempe to Monckton, Nov. 3, 1762, Chalmers: NY, vol. 2, fol. 28 (quote); Kempe to Jury, Apr. 21, 1763, Cunningham-White Trial (quote).

33. Kempe to Jury, Apr. 21, 1763, Cunningham-White Trial (quotes); Kempe to Monckton, Nov. 3, 1762, Chalmers: NY, vol. 2, fol. 28. According to court records, the snow *Johnson* departed New York City carrying "290 barrels of flour, 28 firkins of butter, 32 kegs of pickled salmon, 2 barrels of fish oil, 30 boxes of spermaceti candles, 60 hogsheads of coals, 20 barrels of pitch, and a large quantity of oak plank, a large quantity of pine plank, 2 kegs of manna, four casks containing woolen and linen cloths, and diverse other commodities and necessaries" (Cunningham-White Trial).

34. Deposition of William Williams, May 14, 1762, PRO/TNA, WO 34/102, fols. 177–79 [hereafter cited as "Dep. of Wm. Williams"] (quotes on fol. 177); Kempe to Jury, Apr. 21, 1763, Cunningham-White Trial.

35. Affidavit of Jas. O'Bryan, Apr. 3, 1762, Lyttelton Papers, 1761–62, William L. Clements Library, University of Michigan (quotes); Dep. of Wm. Williams; Kempe to Jury, Apr. 21, 1763, Cunningham-White Trial; Thomas Jefferys, *An Authentic Plan of the Town and Harbour of Cape Francois in the Isle of St. Domingo* (London, 1759).

36. R.R. to Bache, Feb. 18, 1762, PRO/TNA, WO 34/102, fol. 159 (quote); Ringgold to Galloway, Jan. 7, 1762, Samuel and John Galloway Papers, 1739–1812, NYPL (quote); R.R. to Bache, Feb. 18, 1762, PRO/TNA, WO 34/102, fol. 160 (quote); Thos. Allen to Eliz. Allen, Dec. 8, 1761, Allen Collection.

37. Kempe to Jury, Apr. 21, 1763, Cunningham-White Trial (quote); Dep. of Wm. Williams (quotes on fol. 178); Depositions of Harry Henry Crowder and John Martin, May 14, 1762, PRO/TNA, WO 34/102, fols. 180–81 [hereafter cited as "Deps. of Crowder and Martin"]; Cunningham to Monckton, June 16, 1763, Chalmers: NY, vol. 2, fol. 74.

38. *NLS,* May 14, 1762 (quote); Kempe to Jury, Apr. 21, 1763, Cunningham-White Trial (quote); Dep. of Wm. Williams (quote on fol. 179); Rodney to Forrest, Mar. 23, 1762, and "Intelligence Concerning a Squadron of French Ships Reported by Capt. John Lindsay of HMS *Trent,*" Apr. 2, 1762, Lyttelton Papers; Deposition of Theunis Thew, May 14, 1762, PRO/TNA, WO 34/102, fol. 174; William Laird Clowes, *The Royal Navy: A History from the Earliest Times to the Present,* 7 vols. (London, 1897–1903), 3:244–45; *Siege and Capture,* xvi–xviii.

39. Kempe to Jury, Apr. 21, 1763, Cunningham-White Trial (quote); *NYGWPB,* Apr. 22, 1762 (quote); Deps. of Crowder and Martin; Dep. of Wm. Williams; Libel of Dennis McGillicuddy Against the Snow *Johnson,* May 3, 1762, "Johnson (1762)," Case Papers, 1757–75, Box 2, NY Vice-Adm. Recs.; *CG,* May 1, 1762; James G. Lydon, *Pirates, Privateers, and Profits* (Upper Saddle River, N.J., 1970), 217.

40. Deps. of Crowder and Martin (quotes on fol. 181); Dep. of Wm. Williams (quote on fols. 178–79).

41. Kempe to Jury, Apr. 21, 1763, Cunningham-White Trial (quote); HMS *Bonetta,* logbook, PRO/TNA, Apr. 6, 1762, ADM 51/3791 (quotes); Kempe to Jury, Apr. 21, 1763, Cunningham-White Trial (quote); Lan. Holmes to Shirley, Mar. 26, 1762, Lan. Holmes to Pocock, May 20, 1762, PRO/TNA, ADM 1/237, fols. 46–49; *Siege and Capture,* 42; Deps. of Crowder and Martin.

42. Deps. of Crowder and Martin (quote on fol. 181); Kempe to Jury, Apr. 21, 1763, Cunningham-White Trial (quotes); Dep. of Wm. Williams.

43. Kempe to Jury, Apr. 21, 1763, Cunningham-White Trial (quotes); Deps. of Crowder and Martin (quotes on fol. 181).

44. Kempe to Jury, Apr. 21, 1763, Cunningham-White Trial (quote); Dep. of Wm. Williams (quote on fol. 179); John and Mildred Teal, *The Sargasso Sea* (Boston, [1975]), 3–12.

45. Interrogations of William Williams and Harry Henry Crowder, May 18, 1762, "Johnson (1762)," Case Papers, 1757–75, Box 2, NY Vice-Adm. Recs.; HMS *Enterprise,* logbook, Apr. 9 to 29, 1762, PRO/TNA, ADM 51/313; The King v. Gorardus Van Solen and Thomas Livingston, NY/DOR, MS. 1754–1837 K967.

46. John Tabor Kempe's Notes on Interested Witnesses, Cunningham-White Trial (quotes); King v. Cunningham and White: Notes on Trial; Court Min. Book (1762–64), 138; Subpoena of Archibald Kennedy, The King v. Waddell Cunningham and Thomas White, Jan. 22, 1763, NY/DOR, P-196-K3.

47. King v. Cunningham and White: Notes on Trial (quotes).

48. John Tabor Kempe's Notes on Interested Witnesses, Cunningham-White Trial; King v. Cunningham and White: Notes on Trial; Court Min. Book (1762–64), 138; Affidavit of Waddell Cunningham, Oct. 23, 1762, Chalmers: NY, vol. 2, fol. 63.

49. Kempe to Jury, Apr. 21, 1763, Cunningham-White Trial (quote); King v. Cunningham and White: Notes on Trial.

50. Kempe to Jury, Apr. 21, 1763, Cunningham-White Trial (quote).

51. Julius Goebel, Jr., and T. Raymond Naughton, *Law Enforcement in Colonial New York: A Study in Criminal Procedure, 1664–1776* (New York, 1944), 669 (quote); Court Min. Book (1762–64), 139.

52. Court Min. Book (1762–64), 139 (quote); Report of John Tabor Kempe on the Memorial of Waddell Cunningham, Dec. 15, 1763, NY/DOR, PL 1754–1837 K451, 1 (quotes).

53. Court Min. Book (1762–64), 149–50 (quote on p. 150); King v. Cunningham and White: Notes on Trial. The fine of £1,568 was based on penalties set out in the Flour Act of 1757. According to the charge, the snow *Johnson* carried 1,160 bushels of flour (times 20*s.* per bushel = £1,160), 1,960 pounds of butter (times 12*d.* per pound = £98) and 6,200 pounds of pickled salmon (times 12*d.* per pound = £310) (30 George II, c. 9, i [British]).

54. Report of John Tabor Kempe on the Memorial of Waddell Cunningham, Dec. 15, 1763, NY/DOR, PL 1754–1837 K451, 9 (quote).

CHAPTER TEN. Fruits of Victory

1. Andrew Burnaby, *Travels Through the Middle Settlements in North-America in the Years 1759 and 1760. With Observations Upon the State of the Colonies,* 2nd ed. (London, 1775), 114 (quote).

2. Fred Anderson, *Crucible of War: The Seven Years' War and the Fate of Empire in British North America, 1754–1766* (New York, 2001), 407–9, 490; William S. Sachs, "The Business Outlook in the Northern Colonies, 1750–1775" (Ph.D. diss., Columbia University, 1957), 107–8, 113–31; Virginia D. Harrington, *The New York Merchant on the Eve of the American Revolution* (New York, 1935), 316–24; *CG,* Nov. 28, 1761.

3. Sachs, "Business Outlook," 113–31; Loudoun to Cumberland, June 22, 1757, *Military Affairs,* 376.

4. *CG,* Apr. 2, 1763 (quote).

5. *Boston News-Letter, and New-England Chronicle,* Dec. 15, 1763 (quote); Gary B. Nash, "Urban Wealth and Poverty in Pre-Revolutionary America," *Journal of Interdisciplinary History* 6:4 (spring 1976): 578–79; Marc Egnal, *A Mighty Empire: The Origins of the American Revolution* (Ithaca, N.Y., 1988), 130–32.

6. 3 George III, c. 22 (British) (quote).

7. Ibid.; *Journals of the House of Commons* (Nov. 8, 1547, to May 19, 1796), 51 vols. (London, 1803), 29:630, 633, 665; Neil R. Stout, *The Royal Navy in America, 1760–1775: A Study of Enforcement of British Colonial Policy in the Era of the American Revolution* (Annapolis, Md., 1973), 27–28; Sachs, "Business Outlook," 127–69; Nash, "Urban Wealth and Poverty," 575–79; Egnal, *Mighty Empire*, 126–33; Erwin C. Surrency, "The Lawyer and the Revolution," *American Journal of Legal History* 8:2 (April 1964), 126; *Cal. Coun. Mins.*, 462.

8. James A. Henretta, *"Salutary Neglect": Colonial Administration Under the Duke of Newcastle* (Princeton, 1972), ix, 344; Basil Williams, *The Whig Supremacy, 1714–1760* (Oxford, 1962), 191–93; Thomas C. Barrow, *Trade and Empire: The British Customs Service in Colonial America, 1660–1775* (Cambridge, Mass., 1967), 116, 130.

9. Barrow, *Trade and Empire*, 172–85 ("England's war debt stood at £137,000,000 in January 1763. The interest on borrowed money was nearly £5,000,000 a year. The national yearly budget was only £8,000,000" [177]).

10. Knowles to Admiralty, Apr. 6, 1748, PRO/TNA, ADM 1/234, fols. 94–98 (quotes on fols. 96, 97); Richard Pares, *War and Trade in the West Indies, 1739–1763* (Oxford 1936), 356–59, 426–33, 468n; Barrow, *Trade and Empire*, 160–61.

11. Hardy to Board of Trade, May 10, June 19, Aug. 2 and 22, 1756, *Docs. Col. NY*, 7:81–82, 117, 122, 125; Board of Trade to Hardy, July 26, 1756, *Docs. Col. NY*, 7:120–21; Board of Trade, *Journal*, 10:256, 297; *Journals of the House of Commons*, 27:653, 658, 661, 669, 671, 675–76, 683, 705, 708; George Louis Beer, *British Colonial Policy, 1754–1765* (New York, 1907), 79–85.

12. HMS *Sutherland*, logbook, July 9, 1757, PRO/TNA, ADM 51/952 (quote); DeLancey to Board of Trade, July 30, 1757, *Docs. Col. NY*, 7:273 (quote); DeLancey to Board of Trade, June 3, 1757, *Docs. Col. NY*, 7:225; Hardy to Board of Trade, July 10, 1757, *Docs. Col. NY*, 7:271–72; Hardy to Board of Trade, July 15, 1757, BL, Add. MSS 32,890, fols. 507–10; *Cal. Coun. Mins.*, 434.

13. Board of Trade, *Journal*, 10:336–37 (minutes of Nov. 3, 1757); DeLancey to Board of Trade, June 3, 1757, PRO/TNA, CO 5/1068, fols. 5–6; Hardy to Board of Trade, June 14, 1757, PRO/TNA, CO 5/1068, fols. 20–21; Hardy to Board of Trade, July 10, 1757, *Docs. Col. NY*, 7:271–72; Hardy to Board of Trade, July 15, 1757, BL, Add. MSS 32,890, fols. 507–10; Pownall to Wood, Feb. 24, 1759, PRO/TNA, T 1/392, fol. 35; Wood to West, Mar. 6, 1759, PRO/TNA, T 1/392, fol. 34; Customs Board to Board of Trade, May 10, 1759, PRO/TNA, T 1/392, fols. 38–39; "Papers Respecting Illicit Trade," [May 10, 1759], PRO/TNA, T 1/392, fols. 45–46; Thomas C. Barrow, "Background to the Grenville Program, 1757–1763," *WMQ* 22:1 (January 1965): 98–101.

14. Customs Board to Board of Trade, May 10, 1759, PRO/TNA, T 1/392, fols. 38–39 (quote on fol. 38); Board of Trade to the King, Aug. 31, 1759, PRO/TNA, T 1/396, fol. 66; Cotes to Clevland, Feb. 28, July 19, Aug. 28, and Nov. 1, 1759, PRO/TNA, ADM 1/235; Admiralty Board to Pitt, Aug. 24, 1759, Cotes to Clevland, June 4, 1759, PRO/TNA, SP 42/41, fols. 455–58; Barrow, "Background," 99–101; Barrow, *Trade and Empire*, 165.

15. Board of Trade to King in Council, Aug. 31, 1759, PRO/TNA, T 1/396, fols. 66–70.

16. Barrow, *Trade and Empire*, 161–68, 172–77; Holmes, "Memorial 1st"; Holmes, "Memorial 2nd"; Amherst to Monckton, May 13, 1762, PRO/TNA, WO 34/30, fol. 485; *Oxford DNB*, 23:724.

17. Spencer to Bute, Mar. 29, 1763, BL, Add. MSS 38,200, fol. 281 (quote); *Oxford DNB*, 53:174–76; Spencer to Treasury Board, June 30, 1763, PRO/TNA, T 1/426, fol. 171.

18. Spencer to Treasury Board, June 30, 1763, PRO/TNA, T 1/426, fol. 171 (quote).

19. Spencer to Grenville, July 4, 1763, BL, Add. MSS 38,201, fol. 14 (quote).

20. Egremont to Cad. Colden, July 9, 1763, *Colden Papers,* 6:222–25 (quotes on pp. 224, 223). During the Seven Years' War, the office of secretary of state for the Southern Department was held by Henry Fox (Nov. 14, 1755, to Nov. 13, 1756), William Pitt (Dec. 4, 1756, to Apr. 6, 1757), Robert Darcy, fourth earl of Holdernesse (Apr. 6 to June 27, 1757), William Pitt (June 27, 1757, to Oct. 5, 1761), and Charles Wyndham, second earl of Egremont (Oct. 9, 1761, to Aug. 21, 1763).

21. *NYGWPB,* July 21, 1763 (quote); *NYG,* July 25, 1763 (quote); *NYG,* July 18, 1763; *NYM,* July 25, 1763; Sachs, "Business Outlook," 129–31; Egnal, *Mighty Empire,* 126–32.

22. *NYGWPB,* July 21, 1763 (quote); Anderson, *Crucible of War,* 505–6.

23. Deposition of Francis Moon, Aug. 24, 1762, Chalmers: NY, vol. 2, fol. 52; Jauncey to Monckton, Mar. 9, 1763, Chalmers: NY, vol. 4, fol. 69; Wright to Monckton, [June 1763], Chalmers: NY, vol. 4, fol. 96; Cunningham to Monckton, June 16, 1763, Chalmers: NY, vol. 4, fol. 74; Court Min. Book (1762–64), 91, 211–12, 217, 230, 249, 257–59; Julius Goebel, Jr., and T. Raymond Naughton, *Law Enforcement in Colonial New York: A Study in Criminal Procedure, 1664–1776* (New York, 1944), 281–83; Milton M. Klein, "The Rise of the New York Bar: The Legal Career of William Livingston," *WMQ* 15:3 (1958): 348–49.

24. *NYGWPB,* Oct. 13, 1763 (quote); *NYGWPB,* Aug. 25 1763 (quote).

25. Torrans, Greg, and Poaug to Forsey, July 6, 1763, reprinted in *NYGWPB,* Aug. 25, 1763 (quote).

26. *NYGWPB,* Aug. 25, 1763 (quote); *NYGWPB,* Oct. 13, 1763.

27. *NYGWPB,* Aug. 25, 1763 (quote).

28. Ibid. (quote).

29. *NYGWPB,* Oct. 13, 1763 (quote).

30. *NYG,* Aug. 1, 1763 (quote); HMS *Dublin,* logbook, July 29, 1763, PRO/TNA, ADM 51/278; Anderson, *Crucible of War,* 543–45.

31. *NYM,* Aug. 15, 1763 (quote); *NYG,* Aug. 15, 1763 (quote).

32. *NYG,* Aug. 29, 1763 (quote); *NYG,* Sept. 12, 1763 (quote).

33. Stout, *Royal Navy in America,* 39–42; *NYG,* Oct. 10, 1763; Lawrence A. Harper, *The English Navigation Laws: A Seventeenth-Century Experiment in Social Engineering* (New York, 1939), 3–74.

34. *NYG,* Sept. 26, 1763 (quote).

35. *NYG,* Sept. 19, 1763 (quote); *NYG,* Aug. 8 and 15, and Sept. 12, 1763.

36. *BPB,* Oct. 31, 1763 (quote); *NYG,* Oct. 17, 1763; HMS *Sardoine,* logbook, Oct. 11, 1763, PRO/TNA, ADM 51/859; *Coventry,* logbook, Oct. 15, 1763, PRO/TNA, ADM 51/213.

37. *BPB,* Oct. 31, 1763 (quote); Colville to Admiralty, Oct. 25, 1763, PRO/TNA, ADM 1/482 [transcription in LC], 457 (quote); Stout, *Royal Navy in America,* 27–28.

38. Court Min. Book (1762–64), 276–77 (quote).

39. Examination of William Dobbs, May 18, 1762, "Susannah and Anne (1762)," Case Papers, 1757–75, Box 4, NY Vice-Adm. Recs. (quote in 9th interrogatory); Court Min. Book (1762–64), 273 (quote); Depositions of William Dobbs, William Paulding, and Samuel Garraway, May 14, 1762, PRO/TNA, WO 34/102, fols. 170–73. In addition to the remaining defendants associated with the snow *Johnson* (Capt. William Williams and Hamilton Young, a clerk at Greg and Cunningham), the following faced charges in the New York Supreme Court of Judicature for the wartime involvement with the French of three New York ships: John Keating and William Kennedy, owners of the sloop *Susannah*

and Anne (William Dobbs, master); Abraham Lott, Thomas Lynch, and Jacob Van Zandt, owners of the sloop *Industry* (Theunis Thew, master); and Thomas Livingston and Godardus Van Solingen, owners of the brig *York Castle* (Thomas Smith, master). Van Zandt was also charged in relation to a 1760 voyage of his snow *Hester* (William Dobbs, master) ("Note of Recognizances").

40. Depositions of William Dobbs, William Paulding, and Samuel Garraway, May 14, 1762, PRO/TNA, WO 34/102, fols. 170–73; Court Min. Book (1762–64), 273.

41. Court Min. Book (1762–64), 273, 274 (quotes).

42. The King v. George Harison, Waddell Cunningham, William Kelly, Thomas Lynch, and Philip Branson, NY/DOR, PL 1754–1837 K930; Coun. Mins., 300–301; Spencer to Customs Board, Mar. 27, 1765, Custom House Papers, Philadelphia, 1704–89, III (Nov. 1764–Sept. 1765), HSP; Riché to Van Zandt, Apr. 2, 1759, Riché Letter Books.

43. Amherst to Cad. Colden, May 6, 1762, *Colden Papers,* 6:161–62 (quote on p. 162); Deposition of Theunis Thew, May 14, 1762, PRO/TNA, WO 34/102, fol. 174 (quote).

44. Heads of a Dialogue Between John Temple, Esq., . . . and John Tabor Kempe, Oct. 21, 1763, Chalmers: NY, vol. 2, fol. 36; Court Min. Book (1762–64), 273–74, 289–90; Kempe to Cad. Colden, Nov. 14, 1763, Chalmers: NY, vol. 2, fol. 34.

45. Kempe to Cad. Colden, Nov. 14, 1763, Chalmers: NY, vol. 2, fol. 34 (quote).

46. Ibid. (quote).

47. Court Min. Book (1762–64), 286, 289–90; Deposition of Thomas Lynch, Oct. 25, 1763, Kempe Papers; Goebel and Naughton, *Law Enforcement in Colonial New York,* 243.

48. Heads of a Dialogue Between John Temple, Esq., . . . and John Tabor Kempe, Oct. 21, 1763, Chalmers: NY, vol. 2, fols. 36–41 (quotes on fol. 36); Kempe to Cad. Colden, Nov. 14, 1763, Chalmers: NY, vol. 2, fol. 34.

49. *NM,* Nov. 7, 1763 (quote); The King v. Gorardus Van Solen and Thos. Livingston, NY/DOR, MS. 1754–1837 K967; Kempe to Cad. Colden, May 12, 1762, *Colden Papers,* 6:171–73.

50. *NYG,* Nov. 21, 1763 (quote); Gage to Egremont, Nov. 17, 1763, *Gage Correspondence,* 1:1–2 (quote on p. 1); Kempe to Monckton, Oct. 21, 1763, Chalmers: NY, vol. 2, fol. 33; John Richard Alden, *General Gage in America* (Baton Rouge, 1948), 61–62; Anderson, *Crucible of War,* 552–53; *Journal of Jeffery Amherst,* 325; I. N. Phelps Stokes, *The Iconography of Manhattan Island, 1498–1909,* 6 vols. (New York, 1915–28), 4:738.

51. *NYG,* July 4, 1763 (quote); Kempe to Amherst, Dec. 10, 1763, PRO/TNA, WO 34/102, fol. 150; *NYG,* June 27, 1763.

52. Order of the Lieutenant-Governor and Council Regarding the Memorial of Waddell Cunningham, Dec. 2, 1763, NY/DOR, PL 1754–1837 K451 (quote); Coun. Mins., 500; *Cal. Coun. Mins.,* 462.

53. Report of John Tabor Kempe on the Memorial of Waddell Cunningham, Dec. 15, 1763, NY/DOR, PL 1754–1837 K451, fols. 1–12 (quotes on fols. 1, 2, 8, 11).

54. Brown to Colville, Dec. 12, 1763, PRO/TNA, ADM 1/482 [transcription in LC], 542, 543 (quotes); Herbert A. Johnson and David Syrett, "Some Nice Sharp Quillets of the Customs Law: The *New York* Affair, 1763–1767," *WMQ* 25:3 (July 1968): 432–51; Stout, *Royal Navy in America,* 46. On July 12, 1763, Captain Alexander Claxon and the snow *New York* had cleared New York customs for Jamaica with a cargo of coal, lumber, staves, and shingles (Naval Office Shipping Lists for New York, 1713–65, PRO/TNA, CO 5/1228, fol. 70). For documentation of the snow *New York* episode, see "New York (1764)," Case Papers, 1757–75, Box 9, NY Vice-Adm. Recs.

55. Brown to Colville, Dec. 12, 1763, PRO/TNA, ADM 1/482 [transcription in LC], 543 (quote).

56. Ibid. (quote); Stout, *Royal Navy in America,* 47–48.

57. Brown to Colville, Dec. 12, 1763, PRO/TNA, ADM 1/482 [transcription in LC], 543 (quote); Report of John Tabor Kempe on the Memorial of Waddell Cunningham, Dec. 15, 1763, NY/DOR, PL 1754–1837 K451, fol. 11.

58. Apthorp to Brown, Dec. 10, 1763, PRO/TNA, ADM 1/482 [transcription in LC], 525–26.

59. Cad. Colden to Board of Trade, Dec. 7, 1763, *Colden Letter Books,* 1:258 (quote).

60. Stout, *Royal Navy in America,* 47–50; Minute Book, 1758–74, NY Vice-Adm. Recs., 288–90, 292, 295, 298–302.

61. Brown to Colville, Dec. 12, 1763, PRO/TNA, ADM 1/482 [transcription in LC], 544 (quote).

62. Stout, *Royal Navy in America,* 47–48.

63. Colville to Admiralty, Jan. 22, 1764, PRO/TNA, ADM 1/482 [transcription in LC], 523 (quote); 3 George III, c. 22 (British).

64. "Note of Recognizances" (quote); Court Min. Book (1762–64), 360; HMS *Sardoine,* logbook, Jan. 28, 1764, PRO/TNA, ADM 51/859; HMS *Coventry,* logbook, Oct. 26, 1764, PRO/TNA, ADM 51/213; Naval Office Shipping Lists for New York, 1713–65, PRO/TNA, CO 5/1228, fol. 93.

65. Court Min. Book (1762–64), 360 (quote).

66. King Against Waddell Cunningham, [Dec. 1763], NY/DOR, PL 1754–1837 K1051 (quote); Report of John Tabor Kempe on the Memorial of Waddell Cunningham, Dec. 15, 1763, NY/DOR, PL 1754–1837 K451, fol. 1 (quote); Kempe to Monckton, Dec. 13, 1764, Chalmers: NY, vol. 2, fol. 35 (quote); Hawker to Colville, Dec. 12, 1763, PRO/TNA, ADM 1/482 [transcription in LC], 538 (quote).

Epilogue

1. Spencer to Jenkinson, Feb. 11, 1764, BL, Add. MSS 38,202, fol. 92 (quote). The presentation here is based on the author's conjecture that George Spencer hand delivered this letter. John Rocque, *A Plan of the City of London, the Borough of Southwark, and the Contiguous Buildings* (London, 1755); Allen S. Johnson, "The Passage of the Sugar Act," *WMQ* 16:4 (October 1959): 512–13; Thomas C. Barrow, *Trade and Empire: The British Customs Service in Colonial America, 1660–1775* (Cambridge, Mass., 1967), 181–82.

2. Spencer to Jenkinson, Feb. 11, 1764, BL, Add. MSS 38,202, fol. 92 (quote).

3. Ibid. (quote).

4. Spencer to Bute, Mar. 29, 1763, BL, Add. MSS 38,200, fol. 281; Spencer to Treasury Board, May 7, 1763, PRO/TNA, T 1/423, fols. 271–72; Spencer to Treasury Board, June 30, 1763, PRO/TNA, T 1/426, fol. 171; Spencer to Grenville, July 4, 1763, BL, Add. MSS 38,201, fol. 14; Spencer to Monckton, Aug. 2, 1763, Chalmers: NY, vol. 4, fols. 3–5; Spencer to Jenkinson, Sept. 10, 1763, PRO/TNA, T 1/423, fols. 273–74; Spencer to Jenkinson, Feb. 11, 1764, BL, Add. MSS 38,202, fol. 92.

5. Egremont to Board of Trade, May 5, 1763, quoted in Johnson, "Passage of the Sugar Act," 509; 4 George III, c. 15 (British) (quote); Johnson, "Passage of the Sugar Act," 512–14; Lawrence Henry Gipson, *The British Empire Before the American Revolution,* 15 vols. (New York, 1939–70), 10:223–27

6. 4 George III, c. 15 (British) (quote).

7. Philip Lawson, *George Grenville: A Political Life* (Oxford, 1984), 198–99; Fred Anderson, *Crucible of War: The Seven Years' War and the Fate of Empire in British North America, 1754–1766* (New York, 2001), 581–87.

8. Smith to Monckton, Apr. 13, 1764, Chalmers: NY, vol., 4, fol. 13 (quote).

9. *NYM,* Aug. 27, 1764 (quote); Edwin G. Burrows and Mike Wallace, *Gotham: A History of New York City to 1898* (New York, 1999), 195–98.

10. Court Min. Book (1764–66), 68–69; Court Min. Book (1762–64), 358–59. For the trial and its significance, see Thomas E. Carney and Susan Kolb, "The Legacy of Forsey v. Cunningham: Safeguarding the Integrity of the Right to Trial by Jury," *Historian* 69:4 (winter 2007): 667–87.

11. *Providence Gazette, and Country Journal,* Dec. 15, 1764 (quote); HMS *Coventry,* logbook, Oct. 18 to 25, 1764, PRO/TNA, ADM 51/213; Greg, Cunningham & Co. to Waddell Cunningham, Oct. 9, 1764, Letterbook of G&C (1764–65), 10–12; *Providence Gazette, and Country Journal,* July 14, 1764; *The Report of an Action of Assault, Battery and Wounding, Tried in the Supreme Court of Judicature for the Province of New-York, in the Term of October 1764, Between Thomas Forsey, Plantiff, and Waddel Cunningham, Defendant* (New York, 1764), 1–2; Court Min. Book (1764–66), 69.

12. HMS *Coventry,* logbook, Oct. 26, 1764, PRO/TNA, ADM 51/213 (quote); Court Min. Book (1764–66), 70 (quotes).

13. Greg, Cunningham & Co. to Cunningham, Oct. 26, 1764, Letterbook of G&C (1764–65), 36 (quote); *Providence Gazette, and Country Journal,* Dec. 15, 1764 (quote); Herbert A. Johnson, "George Harison's Protest," *New York History* 50:1 (January 1969): 65–67, 76–82; Milton M. Klein, "Prelude to Revolution in New York: Jury Trials and Judicial Tenure," *WMQ* 17:4 (October 1960): 454.

14. Greg, Cunningham & Co. to Cunningham, Oct. 27, 1764, Letterbook of G&C (1764–65), 41 (quotes); Johnson, "George Harison's Protest," 65–67, 76–82.

15. Cad. Colden to Collinson, Oct. 1755, *Colden Papers,* 5:38 (quote); Johnson, "George Harison's Protest," 65–67, 76–82 ("Crucial to the constitutional issue in the case was an alteration in the gubernatorial instructions issued to Sir Danvers Osborne in 1753. At that time the clerks in the Board of Trade forwarded to the Privy Council an instruction that was slightly different from the previous one governing appeals to the New York Governor and Council. The earlier phraseology had been to permit 'appeals by writ of error,' whereas the 1753 instruction deleted the last four words. Quite possibly the change was a clerical error, but once committed, it was perpetuated in all subsequent instructions" [62–63]).

16. Klein, "Prelude to Revolution," 444–60.

17. R. R. Waddell to Cunningham, Apr. 12, 1765, Letterbook of G&C (1764–65), 281–82 (quote); Johnson, "George Harison's Protest," 67–73; Klein, "Prelude to Revolution," 455–60.

18. *NYG,* May 13, 1765 (quote); Klein, "Prelude to Revolution," 455–56.

19. *NYG,* May 14, 1764 (quote); *BPB,* July 22, 1765 (quote); 5 George III, c. 12 (British); John L. Bullion, *A Great and Necessary Measure: George Grenville and the Genesis of the Stamp Act, 1763–1765* (Columbia, Mo., 1982), 136–63; Edmund S. Morgan and Helen M. Morgan, *The Stamp Act Crisis: Prologue to Revolution* (Williamsburg, Va., 1995), 70–74; *NYG,* Apr. 29 and June 3, 1765; *NYM,* May 6, 1765.

20. McEvers to Trecothick, Aug. 26, 1765, quoted in Morgan and Morgan, *Stamp Act*

Crisis, 158; Morgan and Morgan, *Stamp Act Crisis,* 129–32; Examination of John Long, Mar. 20, 1760, PRO/TNA, HCA 45/3 [ship *Molly*].

21. Spencer to Kempe, Aug. 23, 1765, Kempe Papers (quoted); Kempe to Alsop, May 2, 1761, Kempe Papers.

22. Spencer to Kempe, Aug. 23, 1765, Kempe Papers (quote).

23. Spencer to Customs Board, Mar. 27, 1765, Custom House Papers, Philadelphia, vol. 3 (Nov. 1764–Sept. 1765), HSP (quote).

24. Ibid. (quote).

25. Spencer to Kempe, Aug. 23, 1765, Kempe Papers (quote); Spencer to Customs Board, Mar. 27, 1765, Custom House Papers, Philadelphia, vol. 3 (Nov. 1764–Sept. 1765), HSP (quote).

26. Gage to Halifax, Aug. 10, 1765, Gage to Conway, Sept. 23, 1765, *Gage Correspondence,* 1:64, 68; Cad. Colden to Board of Trade, Dec. 6, 1765, *Colden Letter Books,* 2:68–78; Jesse Lemisch, *Jack Tar vs. John Bull: The Role of New York's Seamen in Precipitating the Revolution* (New York, 1997), 73–104; Burrows and Wallace, *Gotham,* 198–99.

27. *NYM,* Sept. 16, 1765 (quote).

28. Watts to Monckton, Oct. 12, 1765, *Watts Letter Book,* 393 (quote); Klein, "Prelude to Revolution," 461; *NM,* Nov. 7, 1763.

29. Burrows and Wallace, *Gotham,* 198; C. A. Weslager, *The Stamp Act Congress, with an Exact Copy of the Complete Journal* (Newark, Del., 1976), 80–83, 87, 107–12; New York Merchants to Cad. Colden, May 29, 1762, Chalmers: NY, vol. 3, fol. 22; Examination of John Long, Mar. 20, 1760, PRO/TNA, HCA 45/3 [ship *Molly*]; Hugh White & Co. to McLaughlin, Oct. 1, 1760, PRO/TNA, ADM 1/236, fol. 188; "Case Against the Brig *John and William,*" PRO/TNA, ADM 7/299.

30. New York Merchants to Cad. Colden, May 29, 1762, Chalmers: NY, vol. 3, fol. 22 (quote).

31. Weslager, *Stamp Act Congress,* 204; HMS *Garland,* logbook, Oct. 22 and 23, 1765, PRO/TNA, ADM 51/386; HMS *Coventry,* logbook, Oct. 23, 1765, PRO/TNA, ADM 51/213; *Montresor Journals,* 336.

32. Henry B. Dawson, *The Sons of Liberty in New York* (New York, 1859), 82 (quote); Burrows and Wallace, *Gotham,* 198–99 (quote); F. L. Engelman, "Cadwallader Colden and the New York Stamp Act Riots," *WMQ* 10:4 (October 1953), 568–70.

33. Weslager, *Stamp Act Congress,* 128–46, 157–62, 181–218 (quote on p. 201).

34. *NYGWPB* (*The General Advertiser for the New-York Thursday's Gazette*), Oct. 31, 1765 (quote); *NYM,* Nov. 7, 1765 (quote); Gage to Conway, Dec. 21, 1765, *Gage Correspondence,* 1:79 (quote); *NHG,* Nov. 22, 1765.

35. *Montresor Journals,* 336 (quote); Gage to Conway, Dec. 21, 1765, *Gage Correspondence,* 1:79 (quote).

36. *NHG,* Nov. 22, 1765 (quote); Gage to Halifax, Aug. 10, 1765, *Gage Correspondence,* 1:64; Gage to Cad. Colden, Aug. 31, 1765, Alex. Colden to Cad. Colden, Sept. 1765, Montresor to Cad. Colden, Sept. 6, 1765, *Colden Papers,* 7:57–58, 72–74.

37. Cad. Colden to Conway, Oct. 26, 1765, *Colden Letter Books,* 2:47–50; *NYM,* Oct. 28, 1765.

38. *Montresor Journals,* 336 (quote); *NHG,* Nov. 22, 1765 (quote); Engelman, "Colden and the Stamp Act Riots," 571–72.

39. *NHG,* Nov. 22, 1765 (quote); *Montresor Journals,* 336–37; Carther to [Anon.], Nov. 2, 1765, Mercantile Library Association, *New York City During the American Revolution:*

Being a Collection of Original Papers (New York, 1861), 44–45; Engelman, "Colden and the Stamp Act Riots," 571–72.

40. *NHG,* Nov. 22, 1765 (quote).

41. "New York" to Cad. Colden, Nov. 1, 1765, *Colden Papers,* 7:85 (quote).

42. *Montresor Journals,* 337–38 (quotes); *NHG,* Nov. 22, 1765; "Engineers' report on means of strengthening Fort George," Nov. 2, 1765, *Colden Papers,* 7:87–88.

43. *Montresor Journals,* 338 (quote); "To the Freeholders and Inhabitants of the City of New York," Nov. 6, 1765, *Colden Papers,* 7:91.

44. *Montresor Journals,* 339 (quote); *NHG,* Nov. 22, 1765 (quote).

45. *NYM,* Nov. 18, 1765 (quote).

46. *Montresor Journals,* 339 (quote); *NYM,* Nov. 18, 1765 (quote); HMS *Coventry,* logbook, Nov. 14 and 15, 1765, PRO/TNA, ADM 51/213.

47. *Cal. Coun. Mins.,* 515 (quote); *Montresor Journals,* 339; Johnson, "Harison's Protest," 74–75.

48. Burrows and Wallace, *Gotham,* 191–222.

49. Spencer to Treasury Board, London, Jan. 8, 1766, PRO/TNA, T 1/445, fols. 459–60 (quotes). The presentation here is based on the author's conjecture that George Spencer hand delivered this letter. On Bohea tea, Spencer proposed a tax of 12*d.* per pound ("4000 chests of Bohea tea to be annually exported, each chest containing 300 lbs. is 1200000 lbs., and if a duty of 12*d.* per lb. be laid upon it on exportation, that quantity only will amount to £60,000,,0,,0") and a tax of 2*s.* 6*d.* per pound on green tea ("2000 chests of green tea annually exported, each chest containing 300 lbs., is 600000 lbs., and if a duty be also laid upon it on exportation of 2/6 per lb., which is nearly in proportion to the price of Bohea, it will amount to £75,000,,0,,0") (fol. 460).

Conclusion

1. Jack S. Levy and Katherine Barbieri, "Trading with the Enemy During Wartime: Theoretical Explanations and Historical Evidence," a paper prepared for delivery at the 2000 annual meeting of the American Political Science Association (Washington, D.C., 2000), 2 (quote); Katherine Barbieri and Jack S. Levy, "Sleeping with the Enemy: The Impact of War on Trade," *Journal of Peace Research* 36:4 (July 1999): 465.

2. Robinson to [Treasury], Mar. 18, 1760, PRO/TNA, T 1/403, fol. 94 (quote).

3. Kempe to Jury, Apr. 21, 1763, Cunningham-White Trial (quote).

4. *A State of the Trade Carried on with the French on the Island of Hispaniola, by the Merchants in North America, Under Colour of Flags of Truce* (New York, 1760), 6–12.

5. C. A. Weslager, *The Stamp Act Congress, with an Exact Copy of the Complete Journal* (Newark, Del., 1976), 201 (quote); R. B. McDowell, *Irish Public Opinion, 1750–1800* (London, 1944), 9–50.

6. Holmes to Clevland, Aug. 22, 1760, PRO/TNA, ADM 1/236, fols. 62–67.

7. Robinson to [Treasury], Mar. 18, 1760, PRO/TNA, T 1/403, fol. 95 (quote).

8. John J. McCusker and Russell R. Menard, *The Economy of British America, 1607–1789* (Chapel Hill, N.C., 1985), 48–50.

9. Smith to the Secretary, May 1, 1767, *Historical Collections,* 2:416 (quote); *New-York Journal,* Apr. 16, 1767; Frederick Lewis Weis, "The Colonial Clergy of the Middle Colonies: New York, New Jersey, and Pennsylvania, 1628–1776," *Proceedings of the American Antiquarian Society,* 66 (1957): 318; PRO/TNA, PROB/11/1118/IR387.

10. *Rivington's New-York Gazetteer,* Apr. 22, 1773 (quote); Ossian Lang, *History of Freemasonry in the State of New York* (New York, 1923), 35, 37–38, 42–43, 49–50.

11. *BNL,* Dec. 18, 1797 (quote); *Letterbook of G&C* (1756–57), 52–56; *Oxford DNB,* 14:699–701.

12. *Dictionary of Canadian Biography,* 13 vols. (Toronto, 1966–94), 4:149 (quote).

13. *NYGWM,* Oct. 17, 1774 (quote); *New-York Journal,* Nov. 18, 1773 (quote); *NYGWM,* Nov. 22, 1773 (quote); *Abstracts of Wills,* 7:80; *NYM,* Mar. 4, 1765; Will of William Kelly, PRO/TNA, PROB/11/1000/IR205; *NYGWM,* Sept. 19, 1774.

14. *Oxford DNB,* 12:496; *ANB,* 5:199.

15. A. Francis Steuart, ed., *The Last Journals of Horace Walpole During the Reign of George III, from 1771–1783,* 2 vols. (London, 1910), 1:432–33 (quote on p. 433); *Oxford DNB,* 1:950, 38:599; Lawrence Shaw Mayo, *Jeffery Amherst: A Biography* (London, 1916), 277–80, 289.

16. Will of George Folliot, PRO/TNA, PROB/11/1514/IR559 (quote); *NYGGA,* July 31, 1799 (quote); NYPL, American Loyalists Collection, 1777–90, Loyalists' Petitions, 45:495–555; *Col. Recs. of NY Chamber* [part 2], 132; Joseph F. Meany, "Merchant and Redcoat: The Papers of John Gordon Macomb, July 1757 to June 1760" (Ph.D. diss., Fordham University, 1990), 378–79n, 499; Alexander C. Flick, *Loyalism in New York During the American Revolution* (New York, 1901), 213.

17. (New York) *Royal Gazette,* Aug. 8, 1781 (quote); *Connecticut Gazette, and the Universal Intelligencer,* July 14, 1779; *NYGWM,* June 15, 1778; *Abstracts of Wills,* 10:133–34; Kenneth Scott, ed., *Rivington's New York Newspaper: Excerpts from a Loyalist Press, 1773–1783,* New-York Historical Society, *Collections,* vol. 84 (New York, 1973), 268; Sanna Feirstein, *Naming New York: Manhattan Places and How They Got Their Names* (New York, 2001), 34.

18. Will of John Tabor Kempe, PRO/TNA, PROB/11/1223/IR835; Catherine Snell Crary, "The American Dream: John Tabor Kempe's Rise from Poverty to Riches," *WMQ* 14:2 (April 1957): 176–95; Catherine S. Crary, ed., *The Price of Loyalty: Tory Writings from the Revolutionary Era* (New York, 1973), 437–40, 438n.

19. Edward P. Alexander, *A Revolutionary Conservative: James Duane of New York* (New York, 1966), 93–214.

20. *ANB,* 13:571–73 and 13:771–72.

21. *Col. Recs. of NY Chamber* [part 2], 55–68, 170 (quote on p. 68); *Abstracts of Wills,* 7:178–81, 11:116–17; Walton Genealogy [n.d.], Walton Family Papers, NYHS; *Col. Recs. of NY Chamber* [part 2], 55–68, 170–71.

22. NYPL, American Loyalists Collection, 1777–90, Loyalists' Petitions, 41:523–36 (quotes on pp. 523, 526–27); James T. Austin, *The Life of Elbridge Gerry,* 2 vols. (Boston, 1828–29), 1:502 (quote); R. J. Dickson, *Ulster Emigration to Colonial America, 1718–1775* (London, 1966), 242–78; (New York) *Daily Advertiser,* Jan. 14, 1786; George Athan Billias, *Elbridge Gerry: Founding Father and Republican Statesman* (New York, 1976), 147.

Index